Eating Disorders in Childhood and Adolescence

Third Edition

**Edited by Bryan Lask and
Rachel Bryant-Waugh**

Routledge
Taylor & Francis Group

LONDON AND NEW YORK

First Edition published 1993 by Psychology Press, entitled *Childhood Onset Anorexia Nervosa and Related Eating Disorders*

Second Edition published 2000 by Psychology Press, entitled *Anorexia Nervosa and Related Eating Disorders in Childhood and Adolescence*

Third Edition published 2007 by Routledge
27 Church Road, Hove, East Sussex, BN3 2FA

Simultaneously published in the USA and Canada
by Routledge
270 Madison Avenue, New York, NY 10016

Routledge is an imprint of the Taylor & Francis Group, an informa business

Typeset in Times by RefineCatch Limited, Bungay, Suffolk
Printed and bound in Great Britain by
TJ International Ltd, Padstow, Cornwall

British Library Cataloguing in Publication Data
A catalogue record for this book is available from the British Library

Library of Congress Cataloging in Publication Data
  Eating disorders in childhood and adolescence / edited by Bryan Lask and Rachel Bryant-Waugh. — 3rd ed.
     p. : cm.
  Rev. ed. of: Anorexia nervosa and related eating disorders in childhood and adolescence. c2000.
  Includes bibliographical references and indexes.
  ISBN: 978–0–415–39457–4 (hbk)
  ISBN: 978–0–415–42589–6 (pbk)
  1. Eating disorders in children. 2. Eating disorders in adolescence. 3. Anorexia nervosa. I. Lask, Bryan. II. Bryant-Waugh, Rachel. III. Anorexia nervosa and related eating disorders in childhood and adolescence.
     [DNLM: 1. Eating Disorders. 2. Adolescent. 3. Anorexia Nervosa. 4. Child. WS 115 E145 2007]
RJ506.E18A565 2007
618.92′8526—dc22
                                    2006033378

ISBN: 978–0–415–39457–4 (hbk)
ISBN: 978–0–415–42589–6 (pbk)

Eating Disorders in Childhood and Adolescence

In the third edition of this accessible and comprehensive book, Bryan Lask and Rachel Bryant-Waugh build on the research and expertise of the previous two editions. First published in 1993, this was the earliest book of its kind to explore eating disorders in people under 15, a population that is very distinct from those in their late teens and adulthood.

The contributors' experience and knowledge have increased greatly in the past 15 years. This fully revised edition offers a distillation of current information in the younger population, and contains brand new chapters on areas of research and practice such as:

- eating disorders and the brain
- nutrition and refeeding
- motivational approaches

Eating Disorders in Childhood and Adolescence offers the reader knowledge, perception and understanding of this fascinating but challenging patient group. It has both a clinical and research focus and will be an essential text for a wide range of professionals, as well as being readable for parents of children suffering from eating disorders.

Bryan Lask trained at the University of London and was a consultant in child and adolescent psychiatry at Great Ormond Street Hospital for Children for 25 years. There, with Rachel Bryant-Waugh, he initiated the first early onset eating disorders programme in the UK. Subsequently he has written 8 books and over 150 papers. Currently he directs the early onset eating disorders research programme at St. George's University of London, is medical adviser to the Huntercombe Hospitals, UK, and visiting professor and research director at the regional eating disorders service in Oslo, Norway.

Rachel Bryant-Waugh is Consultant Clinical Psychologist and Joint Head of the Feeding and Eating Disorders Service at Great Ormond Street Hospital, London, and Honorary Senior Lecturer at the Institute of Child Health, University of London. She trained in London and obtained a PhD at the University of Sussex investigating children with eating disorders. She has specialised in this area for over 20 years, has taught and published widely and is an internationally respected expert.

Contents

PART III
Assessment and treatment   97

Figures

Tables

Acknowledgements

We are indebted to so many of our colleagues, past and present, in the UK and abroad, far too many to mention in person, who have not contributed directly to this book. Nonetheless, their ideas, creativity, support, encouragement, enthusiasm and hard work are reflected throughout.

The Medical Research Council, the Health Foundation, the Garfield Weston Foundation, the Child Growth Foundation, and the Gordon Carlton Memorial Fund have all contributed generously to our research programme. Without their support, much of our research could not have been carried out.

Contributors

Rachel Bryant-Waugh is Consultant Clinical Psychologist and Joint Head of the Feeding and Eating Disorders Service at Great Ormond Street Hospital, London, and Honorary Senior Lecturer at the Institute of Child Health, University of London.

Deborah Christie is a Consultant Clinical Psychologist, Honorary Senior Lecturer and Head of service for paediatric and adolescent psychology at University College Hospital. She has published on her clinical work with young people with cancer, Tourette's syndrome and eating disorders. She currently works with young people who are searching for ways to live with chronic illness including diabetes, obesity, arthritis, chronic fatigue and chronic pain syndromes.

Morag Close was Principal Physiotherapist to the Huntercombe Hospital Group, UK, until her recent retirement. She has specialised in the treatment of eating disorders for many years.

Jo Davenport is the mother of three daughters, the youngest of whom was admitted to an adolescent eating disorders unit aged 14. Jo is divorced and works with her partner managing his farm office.

Francess Doherty is a Specialist Registrar in Child and Adolescent Psychiatry currently working in the Young People's Centre, Chester. Prior to this she spent a year working in Cheshire and Merseyside Eating Disorder's Service for adolescents.

Ian Frampton trained in Clinical Psychology at Exeter University and was post-doctoral Fellow in Developmental Neuropsychology at the Institute of Psychiatry where he worked with children with neurodevelopmental disorders. He is currently Consultant in Paediatric Psychology in Cornwall and Honorary Fellow in the Centre for Clinical Neuropsychology Research at the University of Exeter. He is a visiting Research Consultant to the Regional Eating Disorders Research Team at Ulleval University Hospital, Oslo, Norway.

Josie Geller is an Associate Professor in the Department of Psychiatry at the

University of British Columbia and the Director of Research in the Eating Disorders Program at St. Paul's Hospital. Over the past five years, her clinical and research interests have focused on applications of readiness and motivation models to the assessment and treatment of eating disorders, and she has expanded her work to other populations, including HIV and substance use.

Simon Gowers is Professor of Adolescent Psychiatry at the University of Liverpool and leads the Cheshire and Merseyside Eating Disorder's Service for adolescents. He chaired the NICE guideline development group which produced guidance on the management of eating disorders in 2004 and has published research into many aspects of the background to eating disorders and their treatment.

Tara Haggiag was born and raised in London. She studied art history and history at Goldsmith's University. On a trip to South East Asia Tara discovered a variety of multicolored handwoven fabrics that inspired her to start her clothing line named Azada (www.azadacouture.com). Tara currently lives with her husband in Rome, Italy.

Melissa Hart is a Statewide Coordinator for Eating Disorders and Dietetics, CAMHSNET, Conjoint Lecturer, University of Newcastle. Melissa has many years' experience working as a clinical dietitian both in Australia and overseas. More recently, Melissa has worked as Area Coordinator of Eating Disorders, Statewide nutrition consultant and senior mental health dietitian. Melissa has a special interest in nutritional management in mental health and clinical research.

Peter Honig is a family therapist currently working at the Phoenix Centre (Adolescent Eating Disorders Service, Cambridge) and at the Tavistock Clinic, London. He has taught and published widely on the subject of family involvement in the treatment of anorexia nervosa, and has a special interest in issues of consent and collaborative approaches. He has been a member of a number of professional guideline development groups including the National Institute of Health and Clinical Excellence, UK.

Anna Hutchinson is a clinical psychologist working at Great Ormond Street Hospital for Children. For the past five years she has also been a member of the Early Onset Eating Disorders Research Team based at St George's Hospital, London. As part of this team she developed an ongoing interest in the neuropsychology of eating disorders. Her recent work has focused on the relationship between visuospatial functioning and body image disturbance in anorexia nervosa.

Debra K. Katzman is an Associate Professor of Pediatrics, Head of the Division of Adolescent Medicine, Department of Pediatrics and University of Toronto, Medical Director of the Eating Disorders Program at the Hospital for Sick Children and Senior Associate Scientist at the

Research Institute at the Hospital for Sick Children. The focus of Dr Katzman's research program has been the physiological and developmental issues in children and adolescent with eating disorders.

Bryan Lask is Emeritus Professor of Child and Adolescent Psychiatry at St. George's University of London, Medical Adviser and Research Director, The Huntercombe Hospitals Group, UK, and Visiting Professor and Research Director at the Regional Eating Disorder Service (RASP), Oslo, Norway.

Jeanne Magagna is Head of Psychotherapy Services at Great Ormond Street Hospital in London where she works on the Eating Disorder Team. She is also a Consultant Psychotherapist at Ellern Mede Centre for Eating Disorders and at Family Futures Adoption and Fostering Consortium. In Italy she is Joint Coordinator of Centro Studi Martha Harris Child Psychotherapy Training and she works fortnightly by video link teaching infant observation to the International Psychoanalytic Institute in the USA.

Dasha Nicholls is Consultant Child and Adolescent Psychiatrist and Head of the Feeding and Eating Disorders Service at Great Ormond Street Hospital. Her clinical and research interests are in childhood onset eating disorders; their clinical characteristics, their basis in terms of biological, familial and psychological contributions, and their continuities/discontinuities with both earlier and later feeding and eating problems. She has published and lectured widely in this area.

Kenneth Nunn is Professor of Child and Adolescent Psychiatry at the University of Newcastle, Australia and Emeritus Consultant at the Children's Hospital, Westmead, Sydney. He specialises in neuropsychiatry of childhood and treats children and young people with acute and severe disorders requiring emergency and intensive care. He is especially interested in ways of helping families and patients to reduce their experience of guilt and failure in the face of eating disorder. He did a PhD on 'The Measurement of Personal Hopefulness' and has recently published on the neurobiological underpinnings of hopefulness as an overarching theory of change.

Leora Pinhas is a child and adolescent psychiatrist and the psychiatric director of the Eating Disorder Program at the Hospital for Sick Children in Toronto, Canada. She is an assistant professor in the Department of Psychiatry at the University of Toronto. She is currently completing a PhD in epidemiology at the University of Toronto.

Suja Srikameswaran is the Professional Practice Leader, Psychology, for Providence Health Care and the Outpatient Psychologist for the Eating Disorders Program at St. Paul's Hospital in Vancouver, British Columbia. She is a Clinical Assistant Professor in the Department of Psychiatry at the University of British Columbia (UBC) and an Adjunct Professor in the Department of Psychology at UBC. Dr Srikameswaran is a member of the Eating Disorders Program's research team.

Cathleen M. Steinegger graduated from the University Of Nebraska College Of Medicine. She completed a pediatric residency and an Adolescent Medicine fellowship at Cincinnati Children's Hospital Medical Center as well as obtaining a master's degree in nutrition science. She is currently Assistant Professor of Paediatrics at the University of Toronto and staff physician in the Division of Adolescent Medicine at The Hospital for Sick Children in Toronto, where she treats adolescents with eating disorders.

Anne Stewart is a Consultant Adolescent Psychiatrist at the Warneford Hospital, Oxford and Honorary Senior Lecturer, University of Oxford. She is actively involved in assessment, treatment and consultation regarding a range of adolescent eating disorders. Her clinical and research interests include ethical and legal issues in the treatment of eating disorders, cognitive behavioural approaches with young people with eating disorders and prevention of eating disorders

Jacinta Tan is an Ethics of Mental Health Researcher at The Ethox Centre, University of Oxford and a Consultant Child and Adolescent Psychiatrist. The focus of her research is examining the issues and dilemmas surrounding treatment decision making, particularly treatment refusal and the use of compulsory treatment, which are relevant to patients, parents and health care professionals in the management of anorexia nervosa.

Anna Tate is currently the Head Teacher of Ellern Mede School at the Ellern Mede Centre for Eating Disorders, London. She is passionate about the establishment of education as a relevant and integral part of multidisciplinary teamwork and at the same time providing an educational service that consistently achieves high standards of teaching and learning. She has developed a keen interest in eating disorders, pervasive refusal syndrome and chronic fatigue syndrome.

Beth Watkins completed her PhD on childhood onset eating disturbance at the University of Reading, UK. She has spent 11 years in the field of child and adolescent eating disorders research, initially at Great Ormond Street Hospital and latterly as a Research Fellow at St George's, University of London.

Preface

In the prologue to the first edition of this book we raised the question of why there should be yet another book on eating disorders. We justified the first edition on the basis that it was the first book to deal with early onset eating disorders, i.e. eating disorders occurring in people below the age of 15. This is a distinct population, quite different in many ways from those who develop eating disorders in their late teens or adult life. Obviously some of the issues are similar, but many are different. In various important respects the aetiology, clinical presentation, phenomenology and treatment all differ. Further there is a wider range of eating disorders in the younger age group. The second edition was written at the end of the twentieth century, when eating disorders, including those of early onset, had become a major public health issue. Referral rates had continued to increase and the need for more and improved services was manifested by the expansion in specialist services for this population.

Our own experience and knowledge have been greatly enhanced by the passage of time, concerted research endeavours, advances in understanding of aetiology and the development of innovative treatments. We believe that the time is ripe for this third edition in which we offer a distillation of current information about eating disorders in this younger population. The contributors to this book are all people at the forefront of work with this fascinating but challenging patient group. Between us we have tried to convey our knowledge, perception and understanding of these problems, and to share our clinical experience of assessment and treatment. The chapters in this third edition are completely new or have been thoroughly revised and updated.

Part 1 of the book opens with a contribution from Ken Nunn which considers the concept of sensitivity, so central to those with eating disorders. With his own empathic sensitivity he conveys the pain, the shame, the fear, the self-loathing, the isolation and the many other emotions that engulf those with anorexia nervosa. But he moves on to show how sensitivity can be utilized to enhance the recovery process. Chapter 2 offers the child's perspective written by Tara Haggiag, now a young adult but many years ago a patient of ours. She vividly describes her childhood experience of anorexia nervosa, her torment and suffering. Tara clearly demonstrates that anorexia nervosa is only superficially about weight, and far more about inner distress. Chapter 3, by Jo Davenport, the mother of a teenager who had anorexia nervosa, provides the parent's perspective. She conveys only too vividly the bewilderment and torment of seeing her daughter so ill, the frustrations of negotiating the medical system, the loneliness and anxiety and the ups and downs of the difficult and lengthy process of treatment. Her account of her daughter's ultimate recovery provides hope for all concerned

Part 2 deals with the clinical presentation, both physical and psychological, of early onset eating disorders, starting with an overview, then chapters on aetiology and outcome. Part 3 is determinedly practical and devoted to clinical issues. The first three chapters provide an outline of assessment, the role of the brain in eating disorders and an overview of treatment. Succeeding chapters deal with motivational approaches, nutrition and refeeding, family approaches, cognitive-behavioural therapy, psychodynamic psychotherapy, physiotherapy and exercise, schooling, and legal and ethical issues. Finally there is an appendix detailing all the available assessment instruments.

Here are a few technical points:

1   We have made frequent use of case illustrations, but for obvious reasons we have changed the children's names to preserve their anonymity.
2   For ease of reading, and because far more girls than boys experience eating disorders, we have referred to the children as girls unless we are specifically discussing boys.
3   The age group represented in this book ranges from about 7 to 16. There is no totally satisfactory term to cover this group. In consequence we have used various terms such as 'children', 'young person', and when appropriate 'adolescent'. It seems difficult to get it right and we hope that we will be forgiven if we have appeared condescending or inappropriate in our terminology.

We hope that readers will find what follows of interest and value. Although we do not expect agreement with all we say, we trust that we have conveyed some of the fascination and challenge we have experienced in working with these children and their families.

Bryan Lask and Rachel Bryant-Waugh
November 2006

Part I
Perspectives

1 The sensitivities that heal and the sensitivities that hinder

Kenneth Nunn

The pain of shame and self-loathing

If you have ever been embarrassed about people seeing you naked; if you have ever felt uncomfortable about being overweight; if you have ever wished you looked different in some way or other; if you have ever experienced pain at the way others viewed you and your body; if you have ever felt your life was not really yours to control – then you may have some capacity to empathise with children and young people who suffer from anorexia nervosa.

The pain they live with day after day is the deep conviction that they are ugly, loathsome, bloated and distended. To be sure, in some this is mild and creates background noise only in their emotional life. But in malignant anorexia nervosa it is an intense, unrelenting, tortured self-concern that renders life unliveable without the most intensive support from those around. For these, starvation is extreme, self-injury is common and death is never far away with casualties at around 5 per cent per decade of the illness. Seriously delayed growth, brain blood-flow shutdown, osteoporosis (sometimes permanently damaged bones), infertility and unstable heart rhythms are commonplace. Many of these complications are normally only encountered in the Third World or the very elderly. The sort of medications that are usually only needed to settle the overwhelming distress of psychosis are increasingly required to quell the distress and psychiatric complications of anorexia nervosa that are unresponsive to any other intervention.

The eating disorder that is more than an eating disorder

Anorexia nervosa is a disorder associated with difficulties of eating, together with weight and shape concerns. But it is much more. It is an illness that can cripple a young girl's ability to get through to the world around her about how she feels. She may be 'locked in' emotionally. It is also an illness that prevents young girls from understanding how those they love feel about them – others are 'locked out' emotionally. It is above all else an illness of communication between the world inside themselves and the world outside – an illness of emotional communication in which they have difficulties expressing and receiving what matters most – their own feelings and the feelings of others.

They have no shortage of feelings, no poverty of emotion and no emptiness of real intentions or motivation. However, feelings are segregated from words, emotions remain all too often disconnected from the tears and choreography of their facial movement. An expressionless, seemingly unconcerned face may mask a tumult within. The usual desires, thoughts and driving forces in young people are utterly captured and held hostage by weight and shape. Like the delusions and hallucinations of a person trapped in the completely dominating world of psychosis, the world of anorexia nervosa is a prison tightly bound by walls of distress at every turn. In the same way, parents may be deeply concerned and this concern may not register or may be misunderstood by children with anorexia nervosa. Parents may be perplexed, bewildered and overwhelmed as to what is happening within their child; sensitive to their distress but at a loss to understand the source of the distress. It is to the sensitivities that may fuel this distress or heal this distress that I want to turn.

A needed pain

The first time I saw a child with hereditary insensitivity to pain, like probably thousands of new medical graduates before me, I was struck by the need for pain. The little two-year old boy had already injured himself many times and there was a danger he would lose some of his toes and fingers through his injuries before he was ready to go to school. Of course, I knew that leprosy affected sensation in feet and hands and that specific nerve damage might lead to particular insensitivities, but it never occurred to me that a child might grow up largely without pain because of a rare condition and that this inability to feel pain might make the child continuously vulnerable. In the same way, the young person with anorexia nervosa may be entirely unaware of the disease that is destroying them and even of the threat this poses to parents as they are traumatised by their child's condition. This inability to personally register anorexia nervosa is one of the most perplexing aspects of the illness and increasingly appears to be medically (brain based) rather than psychologically based. It is this inability to see 'the enemy', that makes 'the enemy' all that more dangerous. The insatiable demand from within about weight, weight loss, shape, the amount and type of food eaten, is so absorbing and overriding of all other concerns that even concerns from loved ones about survival retreat to the background.

A futile pain

At the other extreme of experience, throughout my medical career, in both general and child psychiatry, I have been involved in the treatment of pain, especially chronic pain – the long-term pain that remains unresponsive to the many forms of pain relief that have been so successful in acute medicine. Here the pain may have gone on for months or years. The pain no longer signals acute tissue damage or threat of tissue damage but has become a problem in its own right. Sometimes it signals troubles in the life of the person, past or present. But even where this is so, the pain is yet another burden. Of course, like all my psychiatric and psychological colleagues, I will search out the possibilities that the pain is 'serving a function', 'fulfilling a meaning' hitherto unseen and of which everyone has been unaware. The reality is, however, that for many of those with longer term pain no cause is found, no meaning made and pain is just pain, quietly, inexorably grinding down its owner who searches for any relief we might offer. Sometimes the immediacy of pain obscures its own origins. We are asked to help these patients cope with pain, even when we cannot make sense of the pain, to provide support in the struggle with pain, even when we cannot eliminate the struggle, and to provide what comforts we can, even when the fundamental comfort of relief from pain in not forthcoming.

Responding sensitively to a futile pain

Strangely, anorexia nervosa is a bewildering mixture of insensitivity and sensitivity, a lack of awareness of their underlying condition that renders them vulnerable and a distress with their shape and weight that is overwhelming. Young people with anorexia nervosa can be exquisitely sensitive to an increase in weight or calorie intake and completely unaware that anything is wrong with them. Parents can be utterly overwhelmed with the distress of their child but also unaware of the medical disaster that has crept upon them by stealth.

How can we know to which distress we should respond in these young girls and their families and which distress we should see as a 'futile pain' which only distracts us from what is threatening? How can we help? How can we build treatment around their sensitivities and insensitivities so that it is likely to work more effectively? How can we understand this condition so that parents will feel confident to trust us and not find themselves 'fighting against us' and us, 'against them'? What are the sorts of sensitivities, 'the pains', from which they suffer? We may become so concerned about what this pain and distress mean that we forget that sometimes no meaning can be found, or the meanings that are found, are elaborate, ill-fitting interpretations that say more about what we are thinking, and where we are coming from than about the young person with anorexia nervosa. There is a relief that comes from acknowledging that we do not understand but we do care, that we cannot make sense of what is happening but we are not judging, and that we do not have the answer, but we will continue to be available to provide smaller answers to particular difficulties.

The varieties of sensitivity

Most children with anorexia nervosa love their pets – dogs, cats, goldfish and more recently electronic pets and babies. They are deeply distressed if anything untoward happens to them. They feed them regularly. They do not injure them but nurture them lovingly, tenderly and sometimes tenaciously. I have sometimes asked these young people what they would think if someone starved their kitten to death and injured their tiny paws and ankles. They are distressed at even the thought. Then I have said that this is how it feels for us when we see them starving themselves as so many do when overwhelmed with the inescapable distress of anorexia. Of course, there are no clever words that can cure anorexia nervosa anymore than there are clever words to cure cancer. Treatment is a slow, hard slog with a host of obstacles on the road to recovery. But some of the girls remember these words and try to be just a little kinder to themselves as a result.

To see how 'this might happen to me' or to those we love, to somehow appreciate it even if we are not really aware of what the person is going through, is called *identification* in the jargon of psychiatry. It means we feel for ourselves and those we love when we see their distress – we identify with their distress. There is nothing wrong with this. It is the beginning of feeling for others but should not be confused with the feeling for others that is called sympathy or empathy. Identification is the distress that people communicate when first we tell them our bad news. Many people at funerals want to be reassured and comforted by the bereaved loved ones because they become distressed that 'it might have been them' or someone 'close to them'. When we have shared bad news with others this is also the reason why many people tell us the worst story they have recently heard, of which our story reminded them. We of course do not need to hear or want to hear their worst story.

To see someone else suffering, to feel for them and with them in their distress and to register their pain is *sympathy*. It is to become aware that they are in pain and to want to relieve it. Sympathy is what we often feel when watching starving children on television and we want to relieve their starvation and distress. We feel for them even though we are clear that we will not starve and will not be in their position.

To see someone else suffering and to feel the pain as they feel it, at least in part, is *empathy*. To experience the discomfort that they are feeling in their situation, the pain in their troubles, and to wince with the embarrassment and heartache they must endure, is to understand in a different way, not merely to identify or sympathise. All of us have been children and distressed as children at some time. When we see children we can feel for them and with them.

Who owns these feelings?

There is a deeper, more difficult to put into words variety of this feeling, which often is an experience very close to empathy. It is the confusion between our own feelings and the feelings of those who are suffering. When we spend time with others, feel close to others, have things in common with others, care for others, especially when they are young and vulnerable, we may confuse our feelings, our thoughts and even our predicaments with theirs. Well-trained clinicians learn to use these confusions in ownership of feelings creatively to help those for whom they care. But they can complicate our care and before we know where we are we can find ourselves caring for our own needs, our own problems and our own predicaments. We are taking the problems of others as our own and acting as if their problems were no longer theirs but ours. In short, we are no longer helping troubled young people and their families. We have become troubled ourselves.

The normal tangle of feelings between children and parents

Well, all of this may sound very complicated and pathological but there is a particular type of confusion of ownership of feelings between parents and children, which is very common, very normal and very powerful. Our children may not want to talk with us about their feelings because they are worried. We might be worried but we may be reluctant to talk to our children about our feelings because we do not want to worry them. We as a family might become so worried for each other that we cannot say that we are worried for each other for fear of worrying each other. When we see each other saying 'we are all fine', we cannot feel reassurance or comfort. We are not reassured. We are not comforted. I know that I am worried but cannot talk about it. I become worried that they are not talking about their worries. Each person becomes more and more worried to the point that no one is talking. There is a danger that each person in the family may come to the conclusion that the unmentionable problem must be much bigger and more worrying because no one is discussing what is happening.

This tendency to worry about our loved ones' worries is based upon parents caring for their young children and not wanting to worry them; children caring for their parents and not wanting to worry them. It is also based on the belief as a parent that 'I feel what my child is going through'. It is based upon the understanding of children of what they believe their parent is going through. The problem is that sometimes we as parents get it wrong about our children and sometimes our children get it wrong about us as parents. Sometimes those who are close miss the very obvious things that strangers can see and become convinced of problems that are our own, not our children's. It is only with time and experiences, both good and bad, that we as parents and children can disentangle our feelings from each other. So when I talk about sensitivities it does not make sense to talk about individuals alone. We all find ourselves aware and unaware, sensitive and insensitive, to the supports and threats, nurture and pain of loved ones around us.

Young people with a problem being superficial or a superficial explanation for the problem?

In anorexia nervosa some people find it easy to identify with these children and young people. On the other hand, more than a few become convinced that this is a self-induced, boutique disorder, in indulged upper middle class girls who are saturated with a materialistic and narcissistic culture that causes women to compete in a senseless rivalry of bodily perfection. Dealing with children and young people themselves moves us beyond this to an appreciation and sympathy that they are victims of an illness that is clearly not self-induced at all and not always middle class; they are often far from indulged or saturated with materialistic lifestyles. They are not simply vain or trying to attract boys. In fact, it would often be a real sign of progress if they were well enough even to contemplate how other people, especially young men, felt about them. They are usually so distressed and self-loathing about themselves that they are unable to consider how others might feel about them. When we see how sensitive they are to the imperfections of their own bodies we can begin to sympathise with these girls.

An emotional malignancy

Anorexia nervosa is not a trivial side effect of an over-indulged western society. It is a malignant disease of children with parents usually trying to do more than could be expected of any parent – damned if they do and damned if they don't. Some parents will sit on their hands for far too long while their daughter loses weight, not wishing to overreact, minimising the gravity of her weight loss, ignoring what is 'attention seeking' and hoping that 'she will grow out of it'. Others do become obsessed with food and preparing whatever she might eat in the hope of coaxing her back to food and normal eating. Still others, especially fathers, become angry and even violent, feeling helpless and useless in the face of their daughter's decline. When we are desperate, we do not look as normal, sensible, balanced and open to suggestion as others. If obtaining help has been difficult, if some have been thoughtless or misunderstanding toward us and if miscommunication within the medical system has led to a sense of loss of control and threat to our children, our composure is not as complete as it might be were it someone else's daughter. When assessing parents with ill children the first question of the assessing clinician must be 'how much of the presenting picture is due to a worried parent of a troubled child?'

Of course we require experience to answer this question accurately and helpfully. However, it remains a good rule of thumb: *when in doubt, parents are best seen as normal, caring parents who are worried about their daughter.*

The sensitivity and insensitivity that saves life

When dehydration sets in because drinking is restricted, we must be sensitive to vital signs and much less sensitive to pleas of distress about shape and weight. A young girl can semi-starve for years, almost unnoticed; but just a few days of not drinking and the body will deteriorate quickly. Changes to vital chemicals within the blood – potassium, sodium and phosphate – alter the basic message systems that keep the body's systems working and the energy production that keeps each cell alive. If life is in danger, there is no kindness in listening to a distress, which will soon die along with the child who owns it. If life is in danger it is kind to replace fluids, though unwanted, restore chemical deficiencies, though unnoticed, and refeed, though food is rejected with an outpouring of distress. There is a time to be insensitive to distress in order to save life; there is a time to be cruel to be kind.

The sensitivity and insensitivity that threatens

I once attended an international meeting in London on eating disorders at which an open debate was held on the value of nasogastric tube feeding in anorexia nervosa. The debate was vigorous and the discussion slowly settled on the Dutch position which at that time was that there should be no coercive feeding of those with eating disorders with complete respect for the ill individual's wishes. The Dutch position contrasted with the British and Australian positions. Members from these countries took a strong stand on refeeding when survival is threatened and permanent damage from prolonged starvation is imminent. Of course there were professionals from each national group who did not agree with their fellow nationals' point of view. The audience sentiment was definitely swinging strongly towards the Dutch position with a concern amongst professionals and consumers alike that individual rights should not be overridden. Then someone asked the obvious question: 'What happens when the young person repeatedly and determinedly chooses not to eat or be fed?' The principal Dutch discussant then said that after much consultation and discussion euthanasia is considered, describing a 25 year old who had opted for and was given euthanasia the previous year. Silence moved across the audience with a sense of consternation. The consensus of the meeting changed dramatically.

What each society, clinician and family decide to be sensitive to and insensitive to opens up new issues with new concerns. Increasingly, anorexia nervosa is seen to be a life-threatening mental illness which is often long term but also treatable. Like other mental illnesses, anorexia nervosa requires laws for the provision of protection and treatment, even when the person who is ill does not recognise the need for treatment. We do need to be sensitive to young people's rights to freedom, but there are other rights that compete with those of personal liberty: the right to be cared for when ill; the right to be protected from harm when judgement is impaired; the right to have a future when the present threatens to take it away. Families and loved ones also have rights that compete with individual rights: the right to prevent their children from suffering where possible; the right to protect those they love who can no longer protect themselves; the right to provide needed care and to obtain expert help for loved ones. 'It's my life and I can do with it what I want' may make sense in an academic argument about individual liberty, but against the background of the solidarity of suffering that occurs in most normal families and relationships it smacks of being superficial, insensitive and naive. Perhaps more, it indicates an impaired judgement as to the personal consequences of choosing not to eat.

Tough minds and tender hearts

Where does this leave us? Thomas Jefferson once said that what we often need in this world is a tough mind and a tender heart. We cannot afford to be weak in our appraisal of danger to those we love and for whom we care, nor can we afford to fail to respond with compassion. Physicians and surgeons in former centuries knew this all too well. Surgery without anaesthesia was agonisingly painful but so was the relentless progress of gangrene. The choices were stark and sometimes the treatment offered only a little more benefit than the illness. In the case of anorexia nervosa, we can offer much better alternatives than our forbears could and than the Dutch solution of preserving individual liberty now does. There is pain, there is distress and there are hard decisions to be made that do not always fit with the wishes of the person in pain. Why is it so hard to find those with clear thinking and compassion? Perhaps those who are more tough minded find it hard to sustain compassion. Perhaps those who are tenderhearted have difficulty making tough decisions.

A time to hurt

There is a time to be hurtful, to allow distress, to save a life and to prevent long-term harm. There is a time to be aware of the exquisite sensitivity of these young women to their own bodies and the opinions of others. We cannot ignore fears and distress rooted in shape and weight. But we can become aware of the deeper problems: the problem of being unable to express and receive, accurately, emotional signals from others; the problem of a crippling sensitivity in girls who can nevertheless fail to see their own illness.

To be blind or partially sighted to the world around is a terrible disability. To be emotionally blind to what is going on in those around is often even more crippling than the loss of vision in blindness. The emotional blindness in those who are suffering with anorexia nervosa sits side by side with an anguish in the families that cannot be put into words. When we see the illness that these girls and young women cannot see; when we appreciate the damage that is being done that they cannot feel; when we are sensitive to the heartache of their families that they barely perceive, we are compelled to act on their behalf.

A time to heal

Healing begins as we understand the condition afflicting these girls and their families. It is not yet the healing of cure but of acceptance. However, throughout the world there is a slow recognition that anorexia is not a given of existence which must forever be with us. The sky is blue. The grass is green. But anorexia nervosa is not immortal any more than smallpox or poliomyelitis. It is time to systematically, tenaciously and strategically seek a cure, just as our colleagues in oncology seek a cure to the malignancies they face. We must confront the reality of what we cannot do at this point in time but we must also begin to slowly but surely challenge that reality. There is much that we can do today that even a decade ago we could not have achieved. There is much more we could do if all those who suffer and have loved ones who suffer combined forces with clinicians to 'crack' this malignancy of mind and body. There is so much more suffering that could be relieved by the simple recognition of the community as a whole that those who suffer with anorexia nervosa should be accorded the same dignity as those who suffer with other malignancies. The dream of healing anorexia nervosa will only be realised at a very substantial cost; the cost of us as a community becoming aware of the pain of those who suffer from anorexia nervosa, the anguish of those who care for these young people and our responsibility to relieve their suffering and anguish.

This chapter is based on a paper originally published in K. P. Nunn (2004). Sensitivity and Anorexia Nervosa. *The Clinician*, 3, 4–8.

2   The broken jigsaw

A child's perspective

Tara Haggiag

Recently my sister, Alexandra, visited a friend with anorexia nervosa in hospital. Hearing about my sister's university acceptance, Laura, her friend, suddenly grimaced. Her face contorted into a sarcastic smile and she laughed mockingly. Laura's natural disposition had always been friendly and open and her jealous behaviour was a surprise. At that moment my sister experienced an uncannily clear flashback. She was transported back to our local hospital where I was being treated for anorexia nervosa 12 years ago. I was 9 years old, she was 7. Alexandra remembered calling out, 'Tara, I love you!' but the door slammed shut in her face as I shouted, 'Go away! I hate you!' During the time I had anorexia nervosa Alexandra was completely shut out of my life. Resentful, I felt that somehow my parents' love had been transferred from myself to her.

My sister's sad memory filled my eyes with tears. I could only say, 'I am so sorry. Can you ever forgive me? I feel so badly for the way I acted towards you while I was anorexic.' I realise there is no going back. My own memory of what occurred over those years is like the broken pieces of a jigsaw puzzle that never quite fit. There are chunks of memory which have been amputated from my mind, censored because they were too painful. Nevertheless, certain things remain crystal clear, never to be forgotten.

At 5 years old I began to suffer from compulsive behaviour. This meant that I would take my socks on and off up to four or five times before I was satisfied. When walking along the pavement it was imperative that I avoided the cracks. This obsession with ordinary habits meant that I was late for everything and often my parents would leave me behind as a punishment. This early disorder was a signal that something was wrong. Psychiatrists advised my mother to ignore my 'negative behaviour' and reward 'good behaviour'. As a result I felt rejected and loved only for the 'good' me.

When I was 8 we visited my grandfather in Tuscany and a chance remark deeply affected me. I shall never forget sitting on the grass and looking out at the glistening ocean as I experienced the last few moments of childhood innocence. My grandfather strolled past with my father and remarked, 'Tara is a cute little girl, but when she loses her puppy fat she will be really beautiful.' Presumably my grandfather meant well, but he was unaware of the power his poisonous words were to have. I was sensitive and remember desperately wanting to be perfect in every way.

Before reaching my ninth birthday I had begun dieting. Along with a drastic reduction in my food intake were some rather unusual habits. I started drinking from a baby bottle and using a baby knife and fork. I found clothes from my early childhood in the attic and began wearing them. This baby syndrome was a desire to be a loveable baby again, like my brother who was a year old and loved by everyone. I was the eldest child and felt that somehow I was also the bad child. With my younger sister and brother to take care of, it was difficult for my mother to divide her time equally between us. The younger children required much of her attention and, not fully understanding the situation, I began to feel increasingly left out.

In school during lunch a child in my class tormented me. 'Every bite of food you eat is making you fatter,' he teased. Dieting fads filtered all the way down to the playground. Parents who slimmed passed a 'thin is best' message to their children, encouraged by the media. It is no coincidence that I obtained the starring role in my school play in the midst of my weight loss. The more I suffered from anorexia nervosa the more determined I became to be the best.

Sensitive to the dynamics between my parents, I felt protective towards my mother and tried to prevent my parents from arguing. Refusing food was a way of gaining control over my life. It seemed to distance me from family pressure and made me feel independent. I ate alone, making myself small portions of food in the kitchen, sometimes substituted by a handful of sunflower seeds or a piece of fruit. When anyone mentioned my unusual eating patterns I retaliated with hostility. As time went on my weight fell rapidly and the situation became out of control. Not knowing who to ask for help my mother took me to our local GP. He informed her that it was simply a phase that I would grow out of.

Next we visited a nutritionist who lectured me on the fat and protein content of foods. This encouraged my obsession and increased my growing list of 'bad foods' to eliminate from my diet. I began to keep a diary of the few foods I ate, from half a Ryvita to a bite of apple, and counted each calorie. The diary kept a record of my weight each morning. The goal was to continue losing weight each day. If I maintained my weight, that was acceptable; if I lost weight I was satisfied and relieved. But if I put on even a fraction of a kilo, I was miserable and would restrict myself even more the next day. The result was that I ended up eating just three pieces of fruit a day.

I remember my father chasing me up the stairs of our family house in a rage. I knew how to push all his red buttons at once and he was not always able to restrain himself. On these occasions he seemed to lose his adult mind and become an 8-year-old child like me. Household articles would fly around as we bulldozed through the house leaving behind broken objects and a stream of tears and misery while my mother tried to mend all the shattered pieces.

'She's just a little girl!' my mother cried as we scrambled past. 'She needs discipline and authority, she must know who the real boss is in this family!' my father yelled back. One time, on being chased upstairs for a spanking, my head accidentally hit the corner of the bedside table. As the blood poured from the wound all I can remember feeling was relief. My father and I clashed because we shared a very similar temperament. We were both stubborn and opinionated.

My rage forced him to confront his own rage, so frightening he struggled to keep it locked away. In my relationship with my father I never felt I had the space to be angry without attracting negative attention. This in turn led me to feel insecure and unloveable. I continued unconsciously to provoke him, waiting impatiently for the day when he would love me unconditionally for the real me, however bad I was. My mother reacted very differently when faced with my resentment. She closed up emotionally, seemingly detached and uninvolved. In moments when I felt I needed her most I would come up against what seemed like a blank wall. During this time I wrote a short poem describing the isolation I felt:

I feel as though I'm in a box with a lid shut as tightly as can be, open and shut, open and shut, but the lid never opens for me.

My mother was angry at my father for putting his work first. He often stayed late hours at his office while we all waited for him and dinner became cold. My father never had what could be called a family upbringing. By the age of 3 his parents had divorced and by 10 he was packed off to boarding school in a foreign country. He had no model of fatherhood to follow.

Anorexia nervosa was a downhill struggle. I was convinced that the thinner I was, the more loveable I would be to the rest of the world. Fashion spreads filled the walls of my bedroom and the emaciated figure of the average fashion model became the god I worshipped. The films *Flashdance* and *Footloose* starring skinny women had an effect on my attitude towards food. The protagonist in *Flashdance* lives on Diet Coke and cigarettes while spending the rest of her time dancing and working out. I made a silent vow to myself that I would become like her. The stick-thin fashion models I saw daily in magazines and on the television increased my determination. I insisted that I was eating – it just happened to be when no one was around. When the school doctor weighed me I stole some kilogram weights and hid them in my pocket.

My first experience of being treated for anorexia in our local hospital haunts my mind. I was diagnosed as the bad child because the good child ate what her parents fed her. The bad child refused. The treatment was similarly black and white. The hospital was unaccustomed to dealing with anorexic children and it seems that my case was part of an experimental treatment. I shall never forget a particular family therapy session. Chicken flew across the room as my parents were directed by the head psychiatrist to grab hold of me and force-feed me. Above us a video camera recorded the entire scene as other professionals stood watching the episode through a one-way screen. It was the epitome of humiliation for a family that was already falling apart.

My parents felt labelled as the bad parents whose sin could only be absolved through keeping a tighter rein over their unruly daughter. The mistake made by this psychiatric team was damaging. My father's quick temper was encouraged in a continued attempt to 'control Tara'. It was like fighting fire with fire, and as a result of this therapy I became even more angry and frightened. I ran, kicked and screamed around all doctors and figures of authority. I tried to escape from the confinement of the hospital and from my parents whenever the chance arose. What I needed to know was the reality: that my parents truly loved me and were on my side doing everything they could to ensure my survival. Instead, the power struggle continued.

The therapy that I was subjected to, with its isolation chamber and brutal system of punishment and reward, is something that continues to scar me to this day. I was left alone in an empty room with everything I owned confiscated. The only time I saw the nurses was during meals. Even my mother was not allowed to visit me. She wept alone in the hallway while I sat numbly by myself in bed. I continue to wonder how this treatment was ever meant to give me the will to live? The notion that I was the black sheep, a devil child that had to be fixed in order to be loved, continues to haunt me.

My worst memory comes back to me like a nightmare. I am being grabbed by three nurses and a doctor. They pull me forcefully into a white room where my clothes are stripped off and I am covered by a blue cloth. Then I am held down as a gastric tube is pushed up my nostril and into my stomach. The pain is nauseating. This punishment is not for refusing to eat, but for not finishing my food within a time limit. The tube was never used on me at Great Ormond Street Hospital. On the rare occasions that it was imperative for others it was never used forcefully or as a 'punishment'. In between admissions to the local hospital, on a winter ski holiday with my family, I described my inner struggles:

> I came out of hospital half a year ago. Now I'm at the end of a snowy Swiss holiday. Nothing is going right for me. I'm sad all the time. Me and the family are just not getting on at all. I feel really bad because I stole some money off my parents! My walkman has run out of batteries and Dad refused to buy me new batteries! I really need them badly. I need a little more LOVE from my parents. Pop and break dancing music can't do all of the trick. I need some love. REAL LOVE. Help me someone.

I believe that love is the key word in the recovery from anorexia nervosa. Inside I loathed myself and not eating was a way of expressing my inner feeling of unworthiness. The outer anger that I expressed came as a result of the inner torment that rattled daily within my mind. I did not know how to love myself and did not believe that anyone could possibly love me the way I was. More than anything I needed to be hugged and reassured by my parents that they loved me, but I didn't know how to ask and the distance between us simply continued to grow. The stolen money was an attempt to steal back the parental love I felt deprived of. Feelings of rejection turned into isolation. My anger turned inward against myself and ate me up:

> As I'm skiing down the slopes I hear strange voices. And then thoughts run past my mind. I'm scared . . . What should I do? Do I really want to live anymore? Well not with therapy! I'm scared of eating again. Help me Help me Help me.

Secretly, I wanted to please my parents and make them happy. But my inner voice of negativity always seemed to win me over and eventually I felt powerless, only able to express myself accurately through writing. There was a huge gap between my inner feelings and the negative outer expressions that continued to show themselves. I was bad and my efforts to be good and loveable always failed:

> The world seems to be closing in behind me. Like when you see a beautiful flower open and give you joy just to smell and look at it. And then you realise its leaves are going brown and it is going to close and die soon. Well I expect that is how it is for me and my mum and dad. I am the bud or flower or whatever and they have to watch me going backwards.

I wished my mother would take me in her arms and hold me, telling me over and over how much she loved me. Sometimes she exclaimed, 'I don't understand why you feel so unloved.' Malnourishment had shattered my nerves and my reactions were unpredictable. In reality I was by no means the easiest child to love. Yet underneath was just a frightened little girl needing reassurance. My worst enemy was myself and my own unconscious; a negative voice that constantly affirmed my unworthiness. It is something I struggle with to this day.

The local hospital seemed convinced that if my parents could learn to force-feed me and if the hospital could ensure my weight gain then everything else would work itself out. Anorexia nervosa is not that simple. At Great Ormond Street Hospital, where I was transferred after many months of unsuccessful treatment, they understood that my neurosis had to be treated at its roots. This had less to do with food and more to do with family relations. By this advanced stage in our crisis positive rebuilding was crucial to enable the family to find the hope and strength to recover.

The way forward only emerged when I entered Great Ormond Street. I went into long-term treatment and lived there for ten months. My parents came in for meals and family therapy. Great Ormond Street insisted that the family eat meals together. During these meals my parents practised working as a team. This was a major change from previous meals, which were filled with arguments and anxiety. They learned how to listen and communicate when there was tension. Weekends were spent at home where the skills we had learnt during the week were practised. Because I was a child my parents were able to keep me at Great Ormond Street and in retrospect that was incredibly lucky.

The goal treatment was particularly effective. If I behaved and ate properly I would achieve my goal in the form of a special treat. Outings involved anything from visiting the zoo to challenging the chutes at the Richmond waterslides. These activities were not only essential as an incentive to get better, but they also revived my enthusiasm for living. Another aspect of Great Ormond Street essential to my recovery was the love and support I felt from members of staff. No one was on a power trip to exercise their authority over the children. In contrast my personal helpers showed true compassion that seemed miles away from the sterile theories tried and tested on me at the local hospital.

From the beginning of my hospitalisation I had individual therapy sessions. I drew pictures from a box filled with crayons and pens. For a long time I simply drew but said nothing. It took a while before I trusted my therapist enough to speak. Sometimes I felt frustrated by the long lapses of silence. I often wished that we could have a real conversation together not based on theory. Apart from gaining intuition about my anorexia, I needed to get away from dwelling on negativity and concentrate on the positive aspects of my life. Therapy became a constant and stable part of my life and continued throughout the four years later spent at boarding school. I came home from boarding school every weekend to have therapy. By the time I was in boarding school I had learnt the skill of articulation and therefore spoke frequently. The time spent in therapy was an important back-up in times of anxiety and stress inevitably encountered at school.

Luckily the environment at boarding school was a positive experience. Inherent was a structured life within a caring community. At age 11, one year after being discharged from Great Ormond Street, my ability to express myself had developed. This can be seen in a letter written to my parents from boarding school:

17.2.88

Dear Mom and Dad,

I don't know how to explain myself in words, but letters are something else. I feel badly because I feel I do everything wrong sometimes and I don't know what to do about it. Sometimes I feel as though I embarrass or upset you, but why I do not know. I want so much for you to understand me but sometimes I think you cannot. That's why I would like to spend more time with you so that you can understand the way I think. I'm sorry if I've caused you any inconveniences. I hope you don't think I'm just a stupid spoilt brat. I'm sorry if you think this letter is stupid. I love you both more than words can say. If I don't live up to your standards please let me know.

Love Tara.

p.s. Please don't be angry with me whatever the reason I'm sorry.

Today I rarely think about the time I spent overcoming anorexia. Yet situations do occur that shock me into the realisation that the mindset of anorexia is like a contagious drug. It captures its innocent victims early on in a neurosis that continues to spread rapidly. Seemingly innocent Barbie, for instance, can have a traumatising effect on a young child. I thought little of the impact Barbie had on me until recently something happened while babysitting Amy, a 5-year-old girl, which brought it all back. Amy was playing in the bathtub with seven Barbies. Suddenly she shot up out of the water, 'Look at my tummy!' she yelled, pointing to her child-shaped stomach. 'It's not at all like Barbie's! Her waist goes in and mine sticks out . . . that means I'm fat!' I empathised with her and felt sad.

In September 1996, Nicki Pope, the medical correspondent of the *Daily Express*, published an article called 'Sindy the Slim Sinner'. The subtitle read 'Waif-like doll blamed for causing anorexia in girls as young as nine'. This immediately caught my eye as it was the precise age I became anorexic. In her article, Pope relates Sindy to models like Jodie Kidd and suggests that such extreme thinness contributes to the rise of anorexia in young girls: 'Supermodels such as Jodie Kidd, Kate Moss and Trish Goff have been blamed for spreading the cult of ultra-thinness. But now experts say Sindy and her arch rival Barbie also play a key role in reinforcing the body-image message.' The article explains how Sindy's once doll-like figure in the early 1960s has been transformed to become 'pointedly thin.'

So, what does cause anorexia nervosa in children? It seems to me that there is a variety of contributing factors: parental relations, school pressures including academic expectations and relationships with other children, media images which are often absorbed unconsciously, and an extremely negative self-image. As an anorexic child I struggled daily with intense feelings of negativity that seemed to confirm my unworthiness. In my mind I was not valuable enough to be fed properly. From personal experience I believe that one of the greatest needs during anorexia is reassurance and the continual confirmation that the sufferer is loveable and worthy.

Skilled treatment at Great Ormond Street enabled my family and me to gain the communication skills and confidence to relate positively towards each other again. Slowly the relationship with my parents improved. On difficult days, when feeling imperfect, I try to remember that buried within is a little girl who still needs support to live each day without punishing herself. It takes strength to love oneself. Luckily I was supported by my parents and the staff at Great Ormond Street in my time of need, which is why I am here today. Recently a family friend asked; 'How did you ever recover from anorexia?' I replied without hesitation, 'It was through love.'

3   A parent's perspective

Jo Davenport

Five years ago, my 14-year-old daughter was officially diagnosed with anorexia nervosa and obsessive compulsive disorder (OCD). It had been preceded by a frightening year of overwhelming uncertainty, frustration and despair and I have since endured five years as a parent battling against the devastating grip these illnesses have held over my daughter's life.

Before my daughter developed anorexia nervosa, my limited interpretation of the illness was of an individual whose refusal to eat was exemplified by a 'skeleton frame' and in some way the illness revolved around unhappiness and control. I naively concluded that anyone immediately involved in that person's well-being must have either been very unperceptive to allow the situation to become so out of control or they simply must not have cared. It was all so obvious until it happened to our family.

The history is that I am divorced, have three daughters, an absentee father of my children and a partner for whom I work as a farm secretary. My youngest daughter was admitted to an inpatient eating disorder unit aged 14. Maintaining a secure environment where my children could thrive has always been one of my priorities. Despite the changing dynamics of our family, our home had always been a happy one.

It is very hard to write with one clear perspective in mind as my aspirations and expectations have changed throughout the duration of the illness. As I have gained in experience and knowledge of anorexia as a powerful and manipulative disease, my perspective as a parent has grown and changed enormously – I expect it will continue to be so. To write generally of a parent's perspective is also extremely difficult. It goes without saying that as each family is different so is every child within that family. Therefore my contribution towards this book will simply consist of experiences I encountered and views I gained as a parent whilst learning my way around my daughter's unanticipated illness.

I can now look back on the last five years with a certain amount of understanding of the enormous and sometimes seemingly insuperable hurdles we had to cross once my daughter was diagnosed as having anorexia. Although there is no clear finishing post I am tremendously proud of my daughter and all that she has achieved as she continues to struggle with her battle to take complete control of her anorexia. Today, my perspective remains tainted by this struggle but because of her determination I am always optimistic that my perspective could change.

As a parent my predicament has been in coming to terms with the enormity and complexity of the illness, accepting there is no hard and fast path to recovery, learning how best to 'support' my daughter and coping with the enormous demands that anorexia has made on my family and friends.

As with any illness, early diagnosis is an advantage but I was in blissful ignorance of the warning signs. My usually delightful 14-year-old daughter quietly withdrew from family activities and demonstrated a new interest in healthy eating products, but I simply justified her uncharacteristic behaviour as normal adolescent traits. There was no obvious tangible problem to tackle and so two or three months passed without too much concern. However, the atmosphere at home began to change, new tensions developed, rows began to erupt especially during meal preparation and I began to sense that a storm was brewing.

I was concerned and asked family and friends if they too had noticed anything which could explain my daughter's rather unreasonable behaviour. Generally the view was that I was fussing. They thought she was merely being a sulky adolescent and I should ignore the attention that my daughter was obviously seeking. 'I'm fine,' she assured me when I shared my concerns with her. I wasn't so sure. I felt something was bothering her and in hindsight probably protected and defended her rather than choosing to tackle the issues which she was clearly avoiding. The quiet deterioration continued. Her busy social life began to lapse; instead she became immersed in her schoolbooks and her participation in every sporting activity the school offered increased. There was no doubt that her endless deliberations in the supermarket were beginning to make an impression and she was losing weight. However, her interest in anything to do with food, be it recipe books, cookery demonstrations on television or the pleasure she experienced preparing meals for the rest of the family, neatly disguised her personal anguish.

After about four months my daughter quietly mentioned in passing that she hadn't had a period for a while and I was hugely relieved when she finally agreed to visit a general practioner. Her last encounter with our GP had been over three years ago when obsessive compulsive disorder was diagnosed, but because she had apparently managed to completely overcome the 'rituals' which had plagued her I hadn't considered that it might have any relevance to the problems she was now encountering. Her water consumption was enormous and she looked drained, tired and thin. My naive diagnosis was diabetes but I had never considered pregnancy, which the GP suggested. A urine test ruled out both and so we returned home none the wiser. We had missed any chance to nip in the bud whatever was coming.

On reflection, during the following months it can only be said that I lost control of my youngest daughter. I suppose I am extraordinarily fortunate in that I had never really had to be a heavy-handed disciplinarian as far as the children's behaviour was concerned. My two older daughters had gone through adolescence with reasonable ease but it was becoming increasingly apparent that my third daughter was not going to be quite so simple. Although on the whole she was polite, helpful and extremely studious, it was also very obvious that she was not her usual self and especially unreasonably demanding as far as food was concerned. I was apprehensive that should I challenge her attitude she would withdraw even more and eat even less. My family and friends became increasingly frustrated and angry with her new demands. In turn I became increasingly angry and frustrated that they would not consider that something was going terribly wrong. The familiarity of our relaxed and happy home began to be eroded. As her weight dropped at a horrendous rate, so too did all the characteristics of my daughter which had given and shown such pleasure in the past. Anorexia nervosa finally made itself cruelly obvious as our unwelcome houseguest.

Having a label for the illness did nothing to prevent us from sinking further. The GP advised 'alternative medicine' which was quickly dismissed by my daughter. I arranged weekly appointments for her with a counsellor who specialised in OCD and eating disorders, but the slide only continued. A pile of books grew on the kitchen table offering guidance to families and sufferers. The sufferer refused to look at them and was infuriated when any relevant passages were pointed out to her. I searched for explanations and solutions. My interpretation of the primary role of a parent caring for a child suffering from anorexia was 'support', but what did that mean? I had always supported the children but this was new territory. Was I meant to be a prop, a disciplinarian or simply to encourage as I always had before? I read the suggested new meal plans with disbelief. I tried patience, persuasion, encouragement, bribery and sometimes, in exasperation, anger. But nothing could entice my daughter to increase or even maintain her minimal intake of daily food. It was the most terrifying and bewildering time to be a parent. What had gone so horrendously wrong in my daughter's life that she could put herself through such hell?

One of the most agonising aspects of the decline was my discovery that we lived within 20 miles of a National Health Service specialist adolescent eating disorders unit. Its existence was never mentioned by any of the services that we had sought and perhaps because of its association with mental health it carried a stigma which I was reluctant to accept. We were desperate when I eventually asked our GP for a referral to the unit. It had taken eight months to arrive exhausted, petrified and ashamed with an emaciated child at the professional's table. How could any parent feel a bigger failure?

From this early stage and throughout the trials ahead, coming to terms with the fact that my daughter was suffering from what many perceive as a 'mental illness' was one of the hardest aspects of anorexia that I, my family and friends had to tolerate. When faced with solving such suffering that appeared to be self-inflicted, a whole host of reactions are experienced – denial, fear, guilt, pity, anger, and above all the incessant questioning of how this came to be. All of these reactions tempered my attitude towards my daughter's illness. I had to remember that just as I did not want this situation to exist, neither did my daughter, but she had no mental control over it.

Our first 'assessment' meeting with the professionals left me with a confusion of emotions. It was not a sympathetic or reassuring afternoon. We were introduced to a team of experts who, it was explained, would be assessing the interviews through a one-way window. Our family history and the dynamics within the family came under close scrutiny. We gave a factual account of events leading up to our appointment. I left with the feeling that all my inadequacies had been exposed and an enormous apprehension that perhaps I had been judged as a poor parent. On the other hand, I had no doubt that finally we had found the help we so desperately needed. Surely if I gave all my energies to the care of my daughter, the professionals would see that I was not in fact a poor parent and combined with their professional expertise my daughter would begin to recover. It took a further four months to realise that this was not going to be the case.

To begin with my daughter attended weekly appointments at the unit. I stopped working and removed her from school (much to her aggravation) but still we failed even to stabilise her declining health. I could not begin to explain to family and friends just how out of control we were and to save explanation, embarrassment and argument I decided to change our living arrangements. The antagonism had reached such a level between my middle daughter and her younger sister that I had suggested she stay with friends during the summer university vacation to avoid further disruption. I asked my partner to stay away so that I could spend every minute of every waking hour monitoring meals and exercise.

The professionals had always offered the facility of a 'safety net' should we fail at home. To my relief, my daughter was admitted to day patient status seven days a week including all meals. This route cruelly exposed the fact that I became unable to manage the simple requirement of getting my daughter to bed and back to the unit for breakfast in the mornings. The more her daily calories increased, the more she excessively exercised, or more specifically jumped to the point of apparent insanity. Vomiting developed and OCD had returned with a vengeance. The weekly weighing sessions at the unit provided a solid indicator that we were not making any progress. It was obvious that my daughter had chosen to resist the programme set by the unit. However, she continually beseeched me, most often in letters, 'not to give up on her' and expose the horrific extent of her jumping and my failure to impose any control during her mornings and evenings at home. She assured me that with my help she was indeed making progress and most of all reiterated how much she relied on my love and support.

A sick child is every parent's nightmare. My child was desperately ill and obviously not responding to treatment and I had no idea what I should do to help her. I was terrified that if I insisted she be admitted full time against her will she would withdraw totally. The professionals had consistently advised me that because of the added complication of OCD my daughter might find it particularly difficult to return home after a full admission because of its association with her fears and rituals. The combination of these factors inhibited me from admitting the full extent of desolation at home. I hated anorexia: I hated it for the destruction of my daughter; I hated it for destroying my happy family; and I hated it because I couldn't find anyone who understood. This was my period of private hell, isolation and eventual acceptance that the 'anorexic' minx was a far more sinister creature than I had ever envisaged. While my single aim had been to 'support' my daughter I had in fact became totally manipulated by the beast.

So my daughter and I battled on through tears, confusion and exhaustion. Eventually the professionals set such a tight and measured programme of combined goals, expectations and assessment of improvement that we were finally left with no alternative but to ask for full-time inpatient admission. I did not break my daughter's trust. It was a defining moment when we both accepted we had hit the rock-bottom depths of our own mental and physical torment.

On admission the unit immediately put my daughter on bed rest; one-to-one, 24-hour nursing supervision – for her this was the most terrifying and agonising trial yet. I received suicidal letters and phone calls beseeching me to take her home. Even if it meant enduring total rejection, I recognised that I could not provide the answer for her any more. The 'anorexic mentality' was way beyond my comprehension but I was beginning to realise that I needed to become an activist in the battle my daughter was going to face. In the fraught weeks that followed she finally succumbed to taking the medication she had ardently resisted. Qualified, confident, emotionally detached professionals imposed a discipline on my daughter that I could never have achieved and gradually she began to regain some control of her actions.

I never doubted the care and expertise which the team of experts offered. Whilst my daughter received intensive treatment, including cognitive and motivational enhancement therapy, our family was given the opportunity to attend weekly appointments with the family therapist and monthly 'review' meetings with the entire team of staff directly involved. We practised family meals under the supervision and care of staff and the unit also offered the facility to meet other parents at a 'parent support' group which met every two weeks.

Throughout the duration of the admission, I participated in the parent support group. Initially I was reluctant to attend these meetings, fearing that I would find myself in a room full of alarming parents who would undoubtedly provide the explanation for their child's anorexia. My anxieties were quickly dispelled when I realised that the people in the group were no different from me. I was amongst parents who loved their children and experienced the same doubts, fears, bewilderment and failings before these children were finally admitted to the care of a specialist adolescent eating disorder unit. During these meetings I had the opportunity to listen to parents who were pleased with their child's progress, others who were experiencing their child's second or third admission, parents who were preparing for their child's discharge and parents whose child had been discharged. Finally I found an environment where I met kindred spirits and for the first time had the benefit of receiving first-hand information about so many of the problems.

Both my older daughters had been tremendously supportive in contributing to as many of the different meetings as they could manage in their already busy schedule. During the early meetings with the family therapist it had become apparent that they were both going to have different approaches. My eldest daughter had a more gentle and sympathetic attitude while my middle daughter was taking a more confrontational and demanding stance towards her sister. It was an effective combination of attitudes. Throughout the following years the patience and understanding of my eldest daughter has been invaluable to me and in times of difficulty the plain talking of her middle sister has often been the sufferer's first port of call.

My partner had been very supportive to me throughout my daughter's admission. Before we met he had suffered a nervous breakdown and as a consequence felt he could identity with many of the agonies my daughter was encountering. Unfortunately our first appointment with the family therapist upset him and he could not be persuaded to participate in any further meetings with the professionals. The role of the family therapist was further hampered by the rift between my ex-husband and me. Although I had made every attempt to inform him of our daughter's declining health, he had made no contact with her until the professionals invited him to attend a review meeting. Without doubt we fitted into the category of a dysfunctional family. As much as I wished I could create the perfect surroundings for my daughter's recovery, it was not going to be possible to resolve our embedded problems during weekly or monthly appointments with the professionals. Our meetings with the family therapist went on to expose the 'protective wall' that I had unconsciously built around my daughter and me, leaving everyone else revolving on the outside.

Most of all I dreaded the review meetings. Although I had the utmost respect for the psychiatrist, as each month went by my apparent failings only seemed to magnify and my confidence to diminish. Perhaps it was not until my daughter's condition began to stabilise that I was able to take a more rational approach to these meetings. My two older children remained tremendously loyal but they were frustrated by my reluctance to admit to the professionals the full extent of the turmoil at home. I too longed for an opportunity to give an honest account of the nightmare we were experiencing but was afraid of the consequences of publicly betraying my daughter's trust. However, at the point of my daughter's full admission all the cards were laid on the table; it was only then that I dropped my defences and felt more able to participate at these meetings.

In hindsight it took me a long time to understand the 'collaborative' approach which the unit advocated between themselves, parents and patients.

I am not sure whether I failed to recognise this from the beginning of my daughter's admission because I was too distressed or because it was not clearly explained by the professionals. It is such a fragile triangle between the professionals, patient and parents and in order for it to succeed all parties must work together on an equal footing. I feel the professionals must remember that parents are at their most vulnerable by the time of their child's admission. What they see every day leaves parents traumatised. As a parent this was perhaps the harshest sentence I received from the professionals: '[the mother] is so overwhelmed or so manipulated by her daughter that she is unable to function as a parent and needs decisions made for her.' Perhaps if the professionals had explained and shared more of their knowledge and expertise in layman's terms, I would have felt more confident to share my experiences and better informed as to how I should reach my decisions.

With all responsibilities for my daughter's declining health removed, I came to understand that I needed to be stronger in the 'support' I was offering her. However, I wanted to maintain an optimistic approach. In spite of everything that had happened during the last year nothing could take away the life that I knew she had enjoyed before the onset of anorexia, most notably family, friendships and school. While the professionals held complete responsibility for every aspect of her care, all I could do was reassure her that we were constantly there for her and remind and encourage her towards the life she had lost. Her greatest friend made an enormous contribution towards this goal, making frequent visits to the unit.

With the support of the staff at the unit I overcame the terrifying prospect of preparing a sandwich for my daughter and eating a meal with her. However, my initial euphoria began to fade when I gradually realised that I was being manoeuvred into making one or two alterations to the rigid meal plan set by the unit. I allowed 'treats' – raisins instead of apples – only to be found in pockets days later; an extra glass of water here and there. Experience revealed the grim reality that once a precedent had been set there was no going back to the rule book. In many ways we were back at the starting point. I could see that I had made mistakes and resolved that I would maintain my strong and optimistic approach but I would not to let myself fall into the same traps again.

Miraculously, under the expertise offered by the professionals, my daughter slowly began to change and to follow the programme. In the security of the unit we began the process of building up a new trust and confidence in each other. The relentless rituals which had terrified me even more than the starvation were considerably less apparent. For the first time in months my daughter sat peacefully for half an hour talking to me. Gradually she began to accept my new-found consistency. Only two months before I had resigned myself to the bleakness of the situation, but now I was walking into the unit with a new optimism that perhaps my daughter had joined the 'positive' camp of some her fellow patients.

With the family therapists' invaluable assistance we discussed our apprehensions and formulated a detailed plan which we needed to maintain when my daughter returned home. Against all the odds, the first visit home was a huge success – my daughter walked into the house and smiled. In all the days of her illness, this was the monumental one for me – my daughter could come home. I will forever be indebted to the help we received in making that day possible.

The concluding weeks at the unit passed with frightening speed. What had seemed impossible became possible. My daughter set her sights on returning to school and to mainstream life. The target weight which had seemed so unattainable came closer and closer. While I was of course delighted that my daughter was making such an improvement, I also became increasingly apprehensive that soon we were going to lose the sanctuary of the unit for the normality of everyday life when in reality life was still far from normal.

Fortunately, we did have the one enormous advantage of location which entitled my daughter to continue to receive outpatient treatment under the care of familiar professionals. It was with a tremendous mixture of emotions that we drove away from the unit. I had no doubt that without the vast expertise, patience and support offered by the team of professionals we would never have begun to find a basis from which to begin to tackle my daughter's illness. There had been some hostile times when the intensity of anorexia held its most terrifying grip. However, my respect and trust of the professionals had continued to grow as they skilfully negotiated their way through her endless maze of objections. I just hoped that I had learnt a sufficient amount to maintain and build on the fragile equilibrium they had established.

By the time of discharge my daughter had returned to school three days a week and was spending weekends at home. The frequent visits of her friend to the unit had provided an invaluable bridge between days at the unit and her return to school. We had a rigid routine at home which we were managing. However, on the day of her discharge I was under no illusions as to the extent of the obstacles that lay ahead. I began to acknowledge the enormity of conflicting views that anorexia imposed. Although my daughter was being discharged from hospital looking much better, we could not say how much better she looked. She hated the inference that she was seeking attention but inevitably she was going to need considerable time and attention to help her maintain control. What I thought to be relaxing she construed as lazy and most obviously while I was delighted that the skeletal frame which had distressed me for so long was less apparent, she hated her reflection in the mirror.

It became obvious very quickly after her discharge that although my daughter had every intention of overcoming her anorexia, it was going to be a tremendous battle for her. If we altered our routines or schedules in any way she lost weight. Without the continued support of the unit following her discharge, I doubt we would have been able to avoid another admission. Had I been in full-time employment or had younger siblings with their own demands, it would have been impossible to give my daughter the time and attention she received.

The route we chose has asked a vast amount of our family and friends. I had no specific targets other than doing everything I could to ensure that I was providing an environment which enabled my daughter to strive for the goals she set herself while maintaining her weight. During her first months at home my days revolved around my daughter's routine. I measured and ate breakfast with her. Rather than having her catch the school bus I took her to school and met her for lunch. I collected her from school, sat with her while she ate her afternoon snack, joined her for a 20-minute walk, prepared her supper, talked to her during and after supper, hoped she would close her schoolbooks and relax, and then chatted with her while she prepared for bed. The weekends were similar except that I needed to find some activity that filled in the hours that school provided during the week. As a parent had confessed after her daughter's discharge 'it's like having a baby again'. The timetable was demanding, but not as emotionally draining as being the parent of a very vulnerable child endeavouring to claw her way back into everyday life. Spontaneity was a thing of the past and our lives pivoted on my daughter's progress or lack of it. I could not imagine how we were ever going to find a path which would enable her to break away from the frustratingly restrictive routines that maintained her stability.

I became less involved with the professionals as my daughter had decided that she did not see any further reason to continue our appointments with the family therapist. Meetings with the staff nurse who helped her with motivational enhancement therapy gradually progressed from weekly to monthly appointments, but apart from changes in meal plan which reflected weight gain or loss I really had very little idea of their conversations concerning my daughter's state of mind. However, I did receive useful suggestions about ways in which I could encourage my daughter to expand her curriculum. Appointments with the psychiatrist, however, were often the key factor in persuading her to regain the weight that she was sometimes unable to maintain.

Sometimes her progress was so slow or so trivial it could almost have gone unnoticed, other times it was difficult to keep up with her, but most challenging were the prolonged periods of waiting to see which way she was going to go. While she struggled to achieve more independence my role varied from either encouraging her to take on more responsibility or taking back control when it was apparent that she was failing. As simple as it sounds, it was gruelling trying to achieve the correct balance between the two. Although we became increasingly adept at discussing her anxieties and formulating plans, we were walking on eggshells. It was not until we had experienced the frightening cycle of peaks and troughs that it became apparent that my daughter had in many ways taken more steps forward than back.

Most noticeably during the three years under outpatient care, my daughter made excellent progress at embracing life. She showed tremendous courage in taking some risks in her attempts to move forward. Gradually routines were altered which enabled her to become more independent and resume the more typical existence of a teenager. However, neither the professionals nor I could help with her distorted view of body image and the fear and discomfort about weight gain prevailed. As she approached 18 and her final discharge from the unit, it was obvious that there were still many anorexic features which had yet to be resolved. While I was tremendously apprehensive, my daughter was confident that she was sufficiently in control of her anorexia to manage without the continued support of the professionals.

It would be unrealistic to pretend our lives were in any way normal during those years. As a parent it was impossible to get away from the loneliness and anxiety which accompanied anorexia. Although friends tried to be supportive and interested, they really could not understand the difficulties that I encountered. While my daughter experienced her own personal torment of the questions anorexia asked, I found it tremendously frustrating trying to explain the demons she was fighting or to justify my aspirations on her behalf. In times of relapse questions arose as to why she was being so unreasonable. Surely she had seen the error of her ways? Or alternatively she was so consumed by a mental illness that it was ridiculous to pretend she could in any way pursue the life she longed for. It was only when I met with parents with similar problems that I could unload my fears and anxieties without feeling judged or incompetent. Who else but the parent of an anorexic would begin to understand the severity of eruption after a careless purchase of tinned tuna in oil rather than brine?

It is almost ironic that the hardest part is 'letting go'. Just as my daughter cannot quite take the risk of letting go of her anorexia, I have found it incredibly difficult to let go of her. In hindsight, from the earliest stages of my daughter's illness I have protected the principal bond of our mother–daughter relationship: love and trust. As far I was concerned, if my daughter and I continued to have a trusting relationship I felt I stood a better chance of helping her gain control and beat the mental afflictions which plagued her. There have been long periods when the rigours of anorexia have consumed our family, inevitably resentment has occurred and those closest to us might argue that I should have broken the trust and been more challenging towards my daughter. My approach throughout has been largely influenced by my terror of anorexia and the nightmare scenario of both my daughter and myself once again losing control to its tentacles. As a result I have probably taken a very regimented and protective role in supporting my daughter to maintain her own control and to protect me from the guilt that should everything go wrong again it would not be because I had failed her. I know that I have changed from being an easygoing, relaxed individual to an organised, punctual woman consumed with anxiety. My role as a mother to an anorexic daughter has been a completely different one to the mother my older daughters know and it would be perfectly fair for them to suggest that their younger sister has been 'spoilt'. Perhaps in many ways she has, but it has been incredibly difficult trying to find a way to improve her confidence and self-esteem without giving her considerably more time and financial benefits than either of my older daughters received.

On a positive note, if I can give myself credit for anything, I have always held a deep belief that my daughter would in the end find a way through her anorexia and have encouraged her wholeheartedly to experience life and realise her ambitions. Education has been an obvious factor to incorporate into my daughter's objectives. Bullying had not been a problem but academic fulfilment provided a vital incentive for her motivation. While I wished she could set herself standards which were not overly demanding, I felt my doubt would only reflect her own lack of confidence and so I supported her aspirations. One teacher in particular made an exceptional contribution to my daughter's well-being. He visited her several times while she was in the unit and provided invaluable understanding when she returned to school.

The stigma of mental illness and the statistics and explanation for the onset of anorexia have not provided an easy platform for a positive approach. As a caring parent it is exasperating to cope with the stereotypical thinking that accompanies anorexia in everyday life. A throwaway comment said it all: 'I'm sorry to hear your daughter has anorexia, I always thought you were such a happy family.' We were a happy family but somewhere something completely unintended went horribly wrong. Once it had happened, striving to regain a normal life when the restrictions of anorexia have tried in every way to prohibit its existence has been draining. Even during the six years that I have encountered anorexia, I feel that some of the myths surrounding it have been dispelled. Occasionally I return to the unit and share conversations with families whose children are receiving treatment and I am stunned by how much more aware they are of the psychological issues and accompanying problems that anorexia brings than I was during my daughter's admission. But as parents are most likely to bear the longevity of their child's anorexia, it can only be advantageous if they are as well equipped as possible to manage the problems ahead.

It is intimidating to be writing a parent's perspective in a professional text. I have attempted not to dwell on aspects that are undoubtedly significant to our family but which would not be relevant to other families. Personally I have had to come to terms with the possibility that perhaps my daughter's anorexia stemmed from our divorce and her difficulties accepting my partner. The aftermath is that after four years the contact between the children and their father has slightly improved, my partner has continued to be tremendously supportive and a great friendship still exists between the three sisters. However, the eternal question of why did this happen remains unanswered. My daughter, perhaps to save recrimination, would say it was genetic rather than environmental and I would obviously prefer to agree with her. The media are an easy target for blame, but as a family image had not played an overly significant part in our lives. However, media influence was detrimental during her battle for recovery. The 'perfectionist' drive is the hardest characteristic to manage. While it provides the motivation, its demands are gruelling and enormously stressful.

My perspective today is of course delight that my daughter has come through so much and realised so many of her aspirations. She may not have achieved a full recovery, but when we both look back it is hard to believe the progress she has made. After a gap year she has completed her first year at university and is excited about her future. Although anxieties with body image and weight gain continue to play heavily on her mind, she has succeeded in finding the control necessary for a life beyond anorexia. Her path has not been eased by her reluctance to admit socially to the problems she has experienced and still in many ways faces today. While she continues to strive for independence I am aware that the relationship between us is unusually close, but I can only hope that as her confidence increases and her life expands she will become less reliant on my support and I will not need the reassurance that she is coping.

Without the contribution of the professionals I doubt my daughter would have succeeded in so many ways to overcome her anorexia. Her friends have been exceptional in their patience and understanding and have played an enormous part in providing the support and encouragement she needed while returning to everyday life. Thankfully our home life has recovered and although my daughter continues to prepare her meals separately we can once again all sit together and laugh around the kitchen table. My concerns most obviously are over the long-term damage that her body has endured. She too shares these anxieties but has not yet been able to make the extra effort to rectify the problems. While I always hope that she will get there I have finally accepted that the choice is hers.

Part II

Context and course of early onset eating disorders

4 Overview of the eating disorders

Rachel Bryant-Waugh and Bryan Lask

Introduction

The eating disorders anorexia nervosa (AN), bulimia nervosa (BN) and related presentations most commonly affect adolescent girls and young adult women. Women between the ages of 15 and 35 represent the majority of those presenting with and receiving treatment for eating disorders. Yet eating disorders are also known to occur in men and boys (e.g. Bryant-Waugh, 1994; Fichter and Daser, 1987; Vandereycken and Van den Broucke, 1984), older women (e.g. Gowers and Crisp, 1990), and prepubertal children of both sexes (e.g. Fosson, Knibbs, Bryant-Waugh, and Lask, 1987; Gowers, Crisp, Joughin, and Bhat, 1991; Jacobs and Isaacs, 1986). In general there seems to be little disagreement that men and older women present with 'true' eating disorders, that is, that they fulfil existing accepted diagnostic criteria for AN or BN such as those of *ICD–10* (World Health Organisation, 1992) or those of *DSM-IV* (American Psychiatric Association, 1994). The clinical picture in these individuals is very similar to that seen in the main female population.

The situation regarding children has been less clear, with ongoing debate and confusion around a range of aspects of eating disorder presentations and other clinically significant eating disturbances seen in this age group (Rosen, 2003). This confusion has arisen for a number of reasons. First, there is a continuum of eating and feeding difficulties that can occur from birth onwards. Infant feeding problems and subsequent weaning difficulties are relatively common. The food faddiness or very selective eating patterns of preschool children are also relatively common, and in the majority of cases not a particular cause for concern. Some very young children will of course present with more serious problems which may be having an adverse effect on their growth and development. Some infants and young children suffering from complex medical problems may not have been able to learn to feed normally and may present with significant difficulties. Such children will need to be monitored closely, and may require skilled interventions to address their feeding difficulties.

On the whole though, feeding problems occurring in preschool children are commonplace and the majority are appropriate to the child's stage of development, involving experimentation with new tastes and textures as well as testing out the impact of actions on carer behaviour. Such normal mild to moderate feeding difficulties tend to pass as the child matures and are correctly regarded as 'phases' that in the majority of cases the child will outgrow. One difficulty here is that when such eating problems persist or develop in older children, they may still be regarded as a phase to be grown out of, or as awkward or stubborn behaviour. The main difference is that such feeding and eating problems are not developmentally normal in these older children. In addition, in many cases the child's cognitive development is by then much more sophisticated and eating problems will be much more likely to be related to underlying psychological issues.

Second, there has been much confusion and inconsistency in the literature about the nature of eating difficulties in children and the terminology used to describe them (see e.g. Chatoor and Surles, 2004). Some believe that the eating disorders commonly associated with young women simply do not occur in children. Our own clinical experience suggests that the youngest patients with true AN are around 8 years of age. Yet diagnostic criteria that require the presence of amenorrhoea for a diagnosis of AN present problems in premenarcheal girls and have been excluded by some for consideration, as by definition they cannot fulfil an integral part of the diagnosis. In contrast to this exclusion of children is the use of the term 'infantile anorexia nervosa' (e.g. Chatoor, Egan, Getson, Menvielle, and O'Donnell, 1987) to describe a specific form of infant feeding difficulties and/or failure to thrive. Infants clearly cannot fulfil the more usually accepted diagnostic criteria for AN (*ICD–10* and *DSM-IV*) as they do not have the required cognitive capacities. In our view the use of the term infantile anorexia nervosa is rather unhelpful as it implies some developmental continuity for which there is at present no convincing evidence.

Other children may present with one of a range of problems described further in this chapter, and there remains a lack of consensus and clarity as to whether these are age-related precursors of the formal eating disorders or something else entirely. For example, some clinicians might describe childhood presentations not meeting full criteria for AN as eating disorder not otherwise specified (EDNOS) while others might consider them a different type of disorder entirely (e.g. a primary phobic disorder characterised by food avoidance). It is most likely that we are seeing a mixture of different types of clinically significant presentations, some which may be related to formal eating disorders and some are not. There is much scope for further work in this area to achieve greater clarity around the classification of childhood onset eating disorders.

Third, there are real difficulties related to the assessment of specific eating disorder psychopathology and the basis for other forms of clinical eating disturbances occurring in children. This is in part related to the general lack of psychometrically sound, standardised instruments appropriate for age and presentation, and in part related to the cognitive competencies of children (the Appendix provides an overview of currently available measures). This has meant that much of the published work on the subject has been based on clinical case reports. These have described children from the age of 8 upwards (e.g. Fosson et al., 1987; Gowers et al., 1991; Higgs, Goodyer, and Birch, 1989; Jacobs and Isaacs, 1986). Whereas many of the children included in these case series have received formal diagnoses of an eating disorder, it has been difficult to demonstrate this on the basis of objective, reliable assessment because the necessary tools simply have not been available.

There has been much media interest in the occurrence of eating disorders in children over recent years. This interest has unfortunately helped to promote two myths. The first is that we are currently seeing some sort of 'epidemic' and the second is that eating disorders in children are a new phenomenon, with eating disorder sufferers becoming ever younger. Neither is true. The first point is dealt with in more detail in Chapter 5. Although it does seem true that there is a general increase in weight sensitivity and even dieting behaviour in children, these do not necessarily lead on to full eating disorders, which remain relatively rare in the childhood population. It may well be that attempts to manipulate weight in childhood lead to a greater risk of developing an eating disorder later, but the rates of children with AN presenting under the age of 12 appear relatively stable (although again there are significant difficulties getting good epidemiological data).

The second myth can be easily dispelled by looking at some of the historical literature. Two of the earliest authors who are attributed as describing cases of AN in children were Collins (1894) and Marshall (1895). Collins wrote a case history of a 7-year-old girl who was emaciated and refusing food. Further details of the case history suggest that this was not simply related to physical illness, but that there was a psychological component to the girl's food avoidance. Marshall wrote about what he termed 'anorexia nervosa' in an 11-year-old girl, who eventually died from starvation. Since this time there have been many other reports in the literature. In the earlier publications, these were mostly individual case studies, but later case series began to be described. It is evident that in the eyes of the authors of such papers, for the most part child and adolescent mental health practitioners, the young age of the patient has never excluded a possible diagnosis of AN.

It is difficult to be certain that a similar concept of AN has been held throughout the period it has been described in the literature, and in fact it is likely that this is not the case. After all, the diagnostic criteria we are using at the start of the twenty-first century remain in a constant state of revision. Criteria included under the term 'anorexia nervosa' in the past differ from current criteria. The case series described a few decades ago by Warren (1968) seems likely to include children who would not now fulfil diagnostic criteria for AN, but instead presented with food fads, food refusal, or other more commonly occurring childhood eating difficulties. The fact remains, however, that children have for a very long time been known to suffer from alterations in eating patterns, which are recognised to have a psychological component and can lead to very serious physical complications. This situation is by no means new, and not a twentieth or twenty-first century phenomenon.

It is really only over the last two or three decades that children with eating disorders have come to be regarded as a subgroup of interest. The literature on all aspects of eating disorders specifically relating to this younger population remains small in relation to that relating to older adolescents and adults, yet continues to grow. This chapter aims to describe the different types of eating disorder and eating disturbance occurring in children aged 14 and under. We use the terms 'early onset' and 'childhood onset' to refer to eating disorders occurring in children between the ages of 7 and 14 years.

Eating disorders and eating disturbance occurring in childhood

We have worked in child and adolescent mental health clinics specifically providing a service for children and their families where undereating, food restriction, low weight and/or avoidance of weight gain are primary features, and found that a significant number of children aged 8 to 14 at referral are likely to have AN and related presentations. The majority of children with AN are girls, although a smaller but steady number of boys also present with formally diagnosable AN. The remainder of those who attend such clinics have a range of different types of eating disorder or eating disturbance. Many of the children we see demonstrate behaviours related to the avoidance of normal food intake, and most have no organic cause for their eating difficulties. The types of problem most commonly seen in this context in this age range, where restriction of normal intake and/or avoidance or failure of normal weight gain are key, are the following:

- AN (and atypical or subclinical forms)
- BN (and atypical or subclinical forms)
- food avoidance emotional disorder (FAED)
- selective eating
- restrictive eating
- food refusal
- specific fear or phobia leading to avoidance of eating (includes functional dysphagia)
- pervasive refusal sydrome
- appetite loss secondary to depression.

The interrelationship between these different types of eating disturbance is as previously stated not always clear, and there are certainly areas of overlap between them. They will be described in more detail in the following sections. It should be noted that there is a further set of types of eating disturbance not in the above list, and not further discussed here. These include presentations such as binge eating disorder, compulsive overeating, overeating associated with organic disease and pica (the deliberate ingestion of non-food substances). In addition, feeding disorder of infancy and early childhood and other feeding difficulties encountered in preschool children are also not covered here. The interested reader is referred to other volumes and publications regarding presentations not covered in this chapter (e.g. Cooper and Stein, 2006; Decaluwé, Braet, and Fairburn, 2003; Marcus and Kalarchian, 2003).

The diagnosis of eating disorders in children

The diagnosis of an eating disorder in children remains in many cases problematic. Diagnostic criteria are in a constant state of revision, and at the time of writing those of *ICD–10* (WHO, 1992) and *DSM-IV* (American Psychiatric Association, 1994) are in most common use. Using the *ICD–10* system the following eating disorder diagnoses are possible:

* anorexia nervosa (F50.0)
* atypical anorexia nervosa (F50.1)
* bulimia nervosa (F50.2)
* atypical bulimia nervosa (F50.3)
* overeating associated with other psychological disturbances (F50.4)
* vomiting associated with other psychological disturbances (F50.5)
* other eating disorders (F50.8)
* eating disorder, unspecified (F50.9).

The *DSM-IV* eating disorder diagnoses are:

* 307.1 anorexia nervosa

  – restricting type
  – binge eating/purging type

* 307.51 bulimia nervosa

  – purging type
  – non-purging type

* 307.50 eating disorder not otherwise specified (EDNOS).

If we consider the different types of clinically significant eating disturbance already mentioned, it is evident that the terms used to describe these presentations do not always neatly translate into diagnostic labels. For the purposes of research it is essential strictly to apply formal, accepted diagnostic criteria, and to be explicit about which diagnostic system is being used. If this is not done, the value of the results of the research may be limited as it will be difficult to make comparisons with findings from other studies. For example, comparing results of outcome studies is only possible if the selection of individuals included in the different studies has been based on similar criteria for inclusion. However, for clinical purposes, it may be less essential to apply strict diagnostic criteria as, for a large group of children with eating difficulties, this will not be a particularly meaningful exercise as they simply do not fit (Nicholls, Chater, and Lask, 2000). The clinician works with presenting symptoms and difficulties in an attempt to alleviate the situation and it can be argued that in this respect it is in many cases relatively immaterial which diagnostic label is attached to the child's problem.

We know that around half of all adults attending eating disorder clinics will receive a diagnosis of EDNOS (Fairburn and Harrison, 2003; Turner and Bryant-Waugh, 2004), and that within this group a number of distinct subgroups can be identified (e.g. those with binge eating disorder; those not quite meeting diagnostic criteria for AN; and those not quite meeting diagnostic criteria for BN). If we were to use EDNOS for all types of clinically significant eating disturbance seen in children, the heterogeneity of the group would be so great that it would mean nothing. It seems on balance more sensible to reserve EDNOS for children who present with the core cognitive features of AN and BN, but who may not meet full diagnostic criteria for these. Presentations such as selective eating and food avoidance emotional disorder (see below) are clearly different, and should in our view not be included under the EDNOS umbrella. At present there are no satisfactory widely accepted diagnostic terms for such presentations. In the meantime, we suggest that the continued use of descriptive terms remains clinically worthwhile. The sections below describe in a little more detail the various types of disturbances commonly encountered.

Anorexia nervosa

AN is characterised by determined attempts to lose weight or avoid weight gain. This can be achieved through avoiding or otherwise restricting normal food intake, self-induced vomiting, laxative abuse, excessive exercising, or more usually a combination of one or more of these. Weight and/or body mass index (BMI) drop to a level well below that necessary to allow the child to continue to grow and develop. Because children should be growing, failure to gain weight can be regarded as equivalent to weight loss in adults. Weight loss is a matter of considerable concern in childhood, and is particularly worrying in prepubertal children who have relatively low total body fat levels. As well as dietary restriction leading to weight loss, restriction of fluid intake is not uncommon in young AN patients. In a relatively early paper Irwin (1981) highlighted this 'refusal to maintain hydration' which can rapidly lead to a state of dangerous dehydration.

Children with AN have characteristic thoughts about weight and/or shape, often believing they are fat when they are underweight, or displaying a pronounced fear of becoming overweight, which directly influence their eating behaviour and attempts to manage their weight. They tend to have a tremendous sense of dissatisfaction regarding their bodily appearance, which can initially become worse as treatment progresses and weight increases. Many children with AN suffer from a preoccupation with their weight, shape, food, and/or eating, to the extent that their concentration can be significantly impaired. They may be experts at calorie counting and are acutely aware of the calorie content of every mouthful they eat.

Such children provide a range of reasons for refusing food. The most common, in our experience, is a fear of fatness, but they may also give feelings of fullness, nausea, abdominal pain, appetite loss and difficulty in swallowing as reasons (Fosson et al., 1987). In order to fulfil a diagnosis of AN though, there must be some evidence of specific concerns around weight, shape or body composition.

In terms of weight reduction/avoidance of weight gain strategies used by children, aside from restriction of food intake, the most common by far are excessive exercising and self-induced vomiting. Laxative abuse is less common. Excessive exercising may have developed out of an increase in activity levels that has initially been encouraged. Daily exercise workouts, excessive swimming, jogging, or other routines, can become time-consuming features of the child's life. Exercising may be done in secret, often at night. Vomiting is a strategy used by many children, to such an extent that it is often prudent to assume that a child who is not gaining weight once treatment has started must be vomiting. Laxative abuse is probably less common in younger individuals due to limitations in access. However, laxative abuse does occur and potential electrolyte imbalances and mineral deficiencies need to be monitored.

In our experience, children may develop AN from around the age of 8 onwards. The clinical presentation of AN in childhood is very similar to that in adulthood (with the obvious exception of absence of menstruation in premenarcheal patients). The only slight exception to this is perhaps the fact that, in most boys with AN, shape appears to be much more of an issue than weight. These boys are more concerned to avoid becoming fat, unfit or unhealthy, and may not be so much set on losing weight as on preventing the development of a flabby shape. The end result is however very similar, with the avoidance of foods regarded as being fattening or unhealthy, usually excessive exercising, and subsequent significant weight loss.

There continues to be debate around which of the clinical features of AN should be included as prerequisites for diagnosis (see e.g. Hebebrand, Casper, Treasure, and Schweiger, 2004), and which represent commonly occurring characteristics that may or may not be present. The finer detail of the physical, behavioural, cognitive and emotional aspects of the disorder are likely to differ between individuals, indicating that different children will require different priorities in treatment. In addition, the AN will be associated with an accompanying depression in a significant number of children (see also the later subsection on appetite loss secondary to depression). In some cases, it may be associated with clear obsessive-compulsive symptomatology, and may come and go in intensity in an inverse relationship with the obsessive compulsive disorder. It has been shown that, in particular, boys with AN present with relatively high levels of obsessive-compulsive features (Shafran, Bryant-Waugh, Lask, and Arscott, 1995).

Bulimia nervosa

Bulimia nervosa is an eating disorder characterised by episodes of overeating in which the person experiences a sense of loss of control, with accompanying attempts to avoid weight gain by self-induced vomiting, laxative abuse, diuretic abuse, dietary restriction, or excessive exercise. Weight and shape concern are core features, as in the case of AN, and are manifested by attempts to control weight and minimise the weight gain that might normally result from overeating. Self-induced vomiting is the most common method used to avoid weight gain in young patients with BN. BN is often accompanied by other forms of self-harm such as wrist scratching, burning the skin with lighted cigarettes, alcohol and drug abuse, overdosing, and other risk-taking behaviour. None of these additional features are essential to making the diagnosis as their presence is very variable between individuals.

BN appears to be rare in childhood and early adolescence, with very few below the age of 14 presenting for treatment. It is of interest to note, however, that many bulimic women, who typically only present for treatment after many years of having the disorder, often report that their bulimia started in early adolescence. In our own experience, we have seen only very small numbers of children aged 13 and under who have received a full diagnosis of BN. Of those whom we have seen, and one was only 7 years old, none has manifested the more dramatic forms of self-harming seen in older patients. However, as they go through adolescence they do seem to develop a tendency to participate in risk-taking behaviour.

Food avoidance emotional disorder

Food avoidance emotional disorder (FAED) is a term that was first used by Higgs and colleagues to describe a group of children who have a primary emotional disorder where food avoidance is a prominent feature (Higgs et al., 1989). These authors originally described a group of children who did not fully meet diagnostic criteria for AN, but who did present with weight loss and food avoidance. They suggested that FAED may be an intermediate condition between AN and childhood emotional disorder (with no eating disorder), that is, a partial syndrome of AN with an overall more favourable prognosis. The characteristics of FAED were originally set out as follows (Higgs et al., 1989):

- a disorder of the emotions in which food avoidance is a prominent symptom in the presenting complaint
- a history of food avoidance or difficulty (e.g. food fads or restrictions)

- a failure to meet the criteria for AN
- the absence of organic brain disease, psychosis, illicit drug abuse, or prescribed drug related side effects.

Our experience of children who fall into the FAED category is that they are often extremely unwell physically, with very low weight and growth impairment. They do not necessarily have a less serious or milder form of eating disorder than those with AN, although there is considerable variability within both groups in terms of prognosis and outcome. It is clear that children with FAED do not have the same preoccupation with weight and shape, nor do they have a distorted view of their own weight or shape. They do have mood disturbance, combined with weight loss and determined food avoidance. The mood disturbance tends to take the form of mild depression or more generalised anxiety, which is difficult to diagnose in its own right. Interestingly many of these children come from families who experience a significant level of non-specific illness, aches, pains and health-related impairment. Often such children will have missed the odd day of school here and there throughout their school career. It is interesting to speculate whether such children learn to express difficulty with emotions physically through family modelling and reinforcement. There is no evidence for this but there is no doubt that it is extremely difficult for these children to eat normally.

Although organic brain disease is an exclusion criterion, we have noted that some children with FAED do have other physical illnesses or disorders. These children seem to develop food avoidance as part of their emotional response to physical ill health and in such cases the food avoidance is not a direct symptom of the child's illness.

Selective eating

This term is used to describe children who limit their food intake to a very narrow range of preferred foods (see e.g. Nicholls, Christie, Randall, and Lask, 2001). Typically they may only eat five or six different foods, often being particular about brands or where the food is bought. The diet is usually high in carbohydrates, often including bread, chips, or biscuits. A typical example might be a child who will eat only one particular brand of baked beans, white sliced bread from a certain supermarket, cheese and onion crisps, and chocolate biscuits, again of a particular make. Drinks will also be selected, but many children will include milk, or a milk-based drink. Attempts to widen the repertoire of food are usually met with extreme resistance and distress, sometimes accompanied by gagging and retching.

Children with this form of extremely selective eating behaviour are often of appropriate weight and height for their age. In other words, their growth does not seem to be adversely affected by their eating habits. We see more boys than girls with this type of eating pattern. Parental requests for help and advice are usually precipitated by the impact that the selective eating patterns have on social functioning, and by increasing parental concern given the advancing age of the child. Some parents are worried that their child may not be getting the nutrients they need for good health, and worry about vitamin and mineral intake. In most instances, parents have been able to manage the child's extreme fussiness around food largely by making sure they have access to preferred foods. However, as the child becomes older and engages in more social activities with peers, the eating may present more of a problem. Typical events precipitating help seeking include an inability to take part in social events such as birthday parties or sleepovers, impending school trips, or planned change of school. In the majority of cases, selective eaters are seen because of social rather than physical concerns, although there are strong behaviour and management issues as well.

These children are clearly distinguishable from those with AN and BN as they do not share a preoccupation with weight and/or shape or a distorted perception of their own body size. Their weight is usually within normal limits and they tend to have a relatively longstanding history of selective food intake. They also differ from children with FAED as they do not have a problem consuming normal amounts of calories as long as they come from their preferred range of foods. They generally do not present with a prominent fear of gagging or choking (see functional dysphagia, discussed later), although they may do so if forced to eat foods outside their repertoire. In the majority of cases selective eating problems tend eventually to resolve. We get many referrals of children below the age of 10 who are selective eaters, but otherwise growing and developing normally and in good general health. Invariably they are not at all motivated to change their eating behaviour.

Our usual approach to such situations is to recommend some physical monitoring over the coming years to check the child is going through puberty normally, to recommend keeping options open for involvement with food (e.g. cooking), and to let us know when they feel ready to work on making changes. As they grow older, peer group influence becomes stronger and the need to conform in adolescence will often result in a relaxation of the limits placed on dietary intake. Some will, however, persist in accepting only a very narrow range of foods, becoming adult selective eaters. As a rule of thumb, as long as the eating habits are not having an adverse effect on social, physical and emotional development, they should not form a focus for concern.

Restrictive eating

Restrictive eaters are those children who seem never to have eaten very large amounts, and who on the whole do not express a particular interest in or enjoyment of food. There is no evidence of mood disturbance and on the whole restrictive eaters are fine as long as they are not forced to eat more than is their natural inclination. Physically, they tend to be small and light, but within the normal range of variation. Again, as long as growth proceeds steadily along a constant centile, there is usually not cause for real concern. Restrictive eaters will accept a normal range of types of food, but simply do not eat very much. They seem to have very small appetites.

These children may run into difficulties as they approach puberty with its additional energy requirements. Height and weight centiles should be monitored, and it may be necessary to encourage the child to take some particularly energy-rich sources of food to ensure sufficient intake over this period. These children do not present with body image distortion or preoccupation with weight or shape. Their eating pattern tends to be normal and they do not actively avoid food, or attempt to lose weight. They may present with weight loss around the time of puberty, but are usually willing to accept energy supplements or dietary advice to ensure continued growth.

Food refusal

Food refusal is a common phenomenon in younger children, and one which often causes much anxiety and distress. Preschool children quickly learn the effects of refusing food and some will use this as a strategy to get other things. In older children, food refusal can persist and is clearly distinguishable from the eating disorders and other types of eating disturbance. Food refusers tend to be less consistent in their avoidance of food. They will typically eat favourite foods without any problem at all, or will reserve the refusal for one or two particular people, or particular situations. Examples here include children who refuse to eat at school but eat normally at home, or the child of separated parents whose eating behaviour is resistant and problematic during the week when with the mother, but completely problem free when with the father at weekends. Such children are not preoccupied with weight and shape and tend not to have weight problems. As with most types of eating disturbance in childhood, there is some unhappiness or worry that is underlying the child's food refusal. Once this has been identified and worked upon, hopefully the refusal will lessen. Whereas food refusal is developmentally normal in toddlers, it is not in older children and usually represents a difficulty in the direct expression of existing concerns or uncertainties. In many cases it will not represent a serious threat to the child's general health and well-being, but it can interfere with the quality of relationships with the child.

Specific fear/phobia leading to avoidance of eating (includes functional dysphagia)

Children with functional dysphagia and other specific phobias (e.g. fear of vomiting, fear of going to the toilet) also display a marked avoidance of food, often of a certain type or texture. The characteristic feature of children with functional dysphagia is a fear of swallowing, or choking, which makes them anxious and resistant to eating normally. There is in many cases a clear precipitant in the form of an aversive event that has resulted in the fear of swallowing or choking. Examples might include: traumatic gastrointestinal investigations; a choking incident on a piece of food; or experience of abuse, which becomes associated with particular types or textures of food. Other children have had food poisoning and felt they lost control completely, or a bout of diarrhoea and vomiting where they may have vomited or soiled themselves in public, which has led to a fear of eating. Children with such fears and those with functional dysphagia do not have the weight and shape concerns of AN and BN. They can, however, present at extremely low weights and will experience real fear at the prospect of eating normally.

Pervasive refusal syndrome

The term 'pervasive refusal' was first used in 1991 to describe a small group of children who presented with a potentially life-threatening condition manifested by a profound and pervasive refusal to eat, drink, walk, talk, or care for themselves in any way over a period of several months (Lask, Britten, Kroll, Magagna, and Tranter, 1991). The authors of this paper noted that children with this particular combination of symptoms and presenting features do not fit any existing diagnostic category, and suggested that the condition may be understood as an extreme form of post traumatic stress disorder (PTSD). Since this first paper, others have been published (Lask, 2004; McGowan and Green, 1998; Nunn and Thompson, 1996; Thompson and Nunn, 1997), describing the condition, presenting case histories and offering a model for understanding the development and clinical phenomena of pervasive refusal syndrome (PRS). Thompson and Nunn (1997: 163) conclude that the 'term PRS remains a descriptive label for a group of children who present with a constellation of clinical features which is distinct from other related disorders'.

Children with PRS present as underweight and often dehydrated, adamantly refusing food and drink. In this way their presentation may be confused with that of a child with acute AN. However, a diagnosis of AN would be inappropriate because, first, the child tends not to be communicating sufficiently to ascertain whether the cognitive criteria for AN are fulfilled, and, second, the refusal extends across all areas of social and personal functioning, which is not the case in AN.

PRS is a rare but potentially life-threatening disorder that invariably requires hospital admission. Treatment is rarely straightforward and often distressing for all concerned. It may be lengthy and intensive, but children can recover. It has been suggested that there may be a relationship between the length of illness prior to presentation and the degree of improvement while in treatment and the time taken to recover (Thompson and Nunn, 1997). The differential roles of trauma, personality traits and somatising tendencies need further investigation, and the syndrome itself requires further study before any more definite statements can be made.

Appetite loss secondary to depression

Appetite loss secondary to depression is of course not an eating disorder in itself but a well-recognised symptom of clinical depression. Many depressed adults suffer from poor appetite and can lose quite substantial amounts of weight. For a number of reasons children with true 'anorexia' (that is, appetite loss, not AN) may be referred for treatment of an eating disorder. If there is a history of poor eating and weight loss, combined with a change in mood and behaviour, an eating disorder may be suspected. It is important to distinguish between a primary depressive disorder and a primary eating disorder, as the treatment required differs considerably. It is usually not difficult to tell the difference as the central features of AN, such as determined food avoidance, body image distortion and preoccupation with body weight and shape, are absent in depressed children. Some of the other features, including social withdrawal, may however be very similar.

There is undoubtedly a common association of childhood onset AN with depression. Over half of our own clinical population have been found to be moderately to severely depressed (Cooper, Watkins, Bryant-Waugh, and Lask, 2002; Fosson et al., 1987). There is an extensive literature relating to the relationship between affective and eating disorders, with much debate around the nature of this relationship. Most of this literature pertains to the situation in older adolescents and adults, and it may not be appropriate to extrapolate findings and conclusions in relation to a younger population. DiNicola, Roberts, and Oke (1989) have cautioned that in children the relationship between eating and mood disorder is more complex than in an older population, and suggest that the two types of disorder are even more likely to be intertwined.

Summary points

This chapter gives an overview of the main types of eating disturbance occurring in children aged 8 to 14 years. The group of children with AN and related presentations is predominantly female, though a constant number of boys are seen. Children who present with disorders other than AN show a more even gender balance across this group as a whole, although there are some differences between the different types of eating disturbance in relation to the relative numbers of boys and girls.

Working definitions of the types of eating disorder and eating disturbance described in this chapter are as follows:

1   *Anorexia nervosa*

   - determined weight loss (e.g. through food avoidance, self-induced vomiting, excessive exercising, abuse of laxatives)
   - abnormal cognitions regarding weight and/or shape
   - morbid preoccupation with weight and/or shape, food and/or eating.

2   *Bulimia nervosa*

- recurrent binges and purges and/or food restriction
- sense of lack of control
- abnormal cognitions regarding weight and/or shape.

3   *Food avoidance emotional disorder*

- food avoidance
- weight loss
- mood disturbance
- no abnormal cognitions regarding weight and/or shape
- no preoccupations regarding weight and/or shape
- no organic brain disease, psychosis, illicit drug use or prescribed drug related side effects.

4   *Selective eating*

- narrow range of foods (for at least two years)
- unwillingness to try new foods
- no abnormal cognitions regarding weight and/or shape
- no morbid preoccupations regarding weight and/or shape
- weight may be low, normal, or high.

5   *Restrictive eating*

- smaller than usual amounts for age eaten
- diet is normal in terms of nutritional content, but not in amount
- no abnormal cognitions regarding weight and/or shape
- no morbid preoccupations regarding weight and/or shape
- weight and height tend to be low.

6   *Food refusal*

- tends to be episodic, intermittent, or situational
- no abnormal cognitions regarding weight and/or shape
- no morbid preoccupations with weight and/or shape.

7   *Functional dysphagia and other phobic conditions*

- food avoidance
- specific fear underlying food avoidance, e.g. fear of swallowing, choking, vomiting
- no abnormal cognition regarding weight and/or shape
- no morbid preoccupation with weight and/or shape.

8   *Pervasive refusal syndrome*

- profound refusal to eat, drink, walk, talk, or self-care
- determined resistance to efforts to help.

References

American Psychiatric Association. (APA, 1994). *Diagnostic and statistical manual of mental disorders* (4th ed.). Washington, DC: American Psychiatric Association.

Bryant-Waugh, R. (1994). Anorexia nervosa in boys. In B. Dolan and I. Gitzinger (Eds.), *Why women?: Gender issues and eating disorders*. London: Athlone Press.

Chatoor, I., Egan, J., Getson, P., Menvielle, E., and O'Donnell, R. (1987). Mother–infant interactions in infantile anorexia nervosa. *Journal of the American Academy of Child and Adolescent Psychiatry*, *27*, 535–540.

Chatoor, I., and Surles, J. (2004). Eating disorders in mid-childhood. *Primary Psychiatry*, *11* (4), 34–39.

Collins, W. (1894). Anorexia nervosa. *The Lancet*, *I*, 202–203.

Cooper, P., Watkins, B., Bryant-Waugh, R., and Lask, B. (2002). The nosological status of early onset anorexia nervosa. *Psychological Medicine*, *32*, 873–880.

Cooper, P., and Stein, A. (2006). *Childhood feeding problems and adolescent eating disorders*. London: Routledge.

Decaluwé, V., Braet, C., and Fairburn, C. (2003). Binge eating in obese children and adolescents. *International Journal of Eating Disorders*, *33*, 78–84.

DiNicola, V., Roberts, N., and Oke, L. (1989). Eating and mood disorders in young children. *Psychiatric Clinics of North America*, *12*, 873–893.

Fairburn, C.G., and Harrison, P.J. (2003). Eating disorders. *The Lancet*, *361*, 407–416.

Fichter, M.M., and Daser, C. (1987). Symptomatology, psychosexual development and gender identity in 42 anorexic males. *Psychological Medicine*, *17*, 409–418.

Fosson, A., Knibbs, J., Bryant-Waugh, R., and Lask, B. (1987). Early onset anorexia nervosa. *Archives of Disease in Childhood*, *621*, 114–118.

Gowers, S., and Crisp, A. (1990). Anorexia nervosa in an eighty year old woman. *British Journal of Psychiatry*, *157*, 754–757.

Gowers, S., Crisp, A., Joughin, N., and Bhat, N. (1991). Premenarcheal anorexia nervosa. *Journal of Child Psychology and Psychiatry*, *32*, 515–524.

Hebebrand, J., Casper, R., Treasure, J., and Schweiger, U. (2004). The need to revise the diagnostic criteria for anorexia nervosa. *Journal of Neural Transmission*, *111*, 827–840.

Higgs, J., Goodyer, I., and Birch, J. (1989). Anorexia nervosa and food avoidance emotional disorder. *Archives of Disease in Childhood*, *64*, 346–351.

Irwin, M. (1981). Diagnosis of anorexia nervosa in children and the validity of DSM III. *American Journal of Psychiatry*, *138*, 1382–1383.

Jacobs, B., and Isaacs, S. (1986). Pre-pubertal anorexia nervosa: A retrospective controlled study. *Journal of Child Psychology and Psychiatry*, *27*, 237–250.

Lask, B. (2004). Pervasive refusal syndrome. *Advances in Psychiatric Treatment*, *10*, 153–159.

Lask, B., Britten, C., Kroll, L., Magagna, J., and Tranter, M. (1991). Children with pervasive refusal. *Archives of Disease in Childhood*, *66*, 866–869.

Marcus, M., and Kalarchian, M. (2003). Binge eating in children and adolescents. *International Journal of Eating Disorders*, *34*, S47–S57.

Marshall, C. (1895). Fatal case in a girl of 11 years. *The Lancet*, *I*, 817.

McGowan, R., and Green, J. (1998). Pervasive refusal syndrome: A less severe variant with defined aetiology. *Clinical Child Psychology and Psychiatry*, *3* (4), 583–589.

Nicholls, D., Chater, R., and Lask, B. (2000). Children into DSM don't go: A comparison of classification systems of eating disorders for children. *International Journal of Eating Disorders, 28* (3), 317–324.

Nicholls, D., Christie, D., Randall, L., and Lask, B. (2001). Selective eating: Symptom, disorder or normal variant. *Clinical Child Psychology and Psychiatry, 6* (2), 257–270.

Nunn, K.P., and Thompson, S.L. (1996). The pervasive refusal syndrome: Learned helplessness and hopelessness. *Clinical Child Psychology and Psychiatry, 1*, 121–132.

Rosen, D. (2003). Eating disorders in children and young adolescents: Etiology, classification, clinical features, and treatment. *Adolescent Medicine, 14*, 49–59.

Shafran, R., Bryant-Waugh, R., Lask, B., and Arscott, K. (1995). Obsessive-compulsive symptoms in children with eating disorders: A preliminary investigation. *Eating Disorders: The Journal of Treatment and Prevention, 3*, 304–310.

Thompson, S.L., and Nunn, K.P. (1997). The pervasive refusal syndrome: The RAHC experience. *Clinical Child Psychology and Psychiatry, 2*, 145–165.

Turner, H.M., and Bryant-Waugh, R. (2004). Eating Disorder Not Otherwise Specified (EDNOS): Profiles of those who present at a community eating disorder service. *European Eating Disorders Review, 12*, 18–26.

Vandereycken, W., and Van den Broucke, S. (1984). Anorexia nervosa in males: A comparative study of 107 cases reported in the literature. *Acta Psychiatrica Scandinavica, 70*, 447–454.

Warren, W. (1968). A study of anorexia nervosa in young girls. *Journal of Child Psychology and Psychiatry, 9*, 27–40.

World Health Organisation (WHO, 1992). *The ICD–10 classification of mental and behavioural disorders: Clinical descriptions and diagnostic guidelines*. Geneva: WHO.

5 Aetiology

Dasha Nicholls

Introduction

'What caused my daughter's eating disorder?' or even 'Did I cause it?' are questions that parents often ask health professionals. The question is likely to produce unsatisfactory answers on two counts: first, no single factor is likely to have caused a disorder so insidious and complex in nature; second, unlike some illnesses, recognising the cause(s) does not necessarily suggest a solution. For example, if an episode of weight-related teasing is identified as the trigger for anorexia nervosa (AN), addressing the bullying will not in itself address the AN. For this reason it is usual to think of aetiology in terms of predisposing (or risk) factors, precipitating factors (or triggers), and perpetuating (or maintaining) factors. This chapter will focus on our current understanding of the predisposing and precipitating factors. Our current treatments, however, are largely aimed at perpetuating factors, since these are often easier to influence than those that might be understood as causal.

Other ways of understanding aetiological factors include considering factors specific to the child (individual factors), immediate family factors (systemic) and factors in the wider sociocultural system. Alternatively we talk about biological, psychological and sociocultural factors in aetiology. The latter has been chosen here as an approach to outlining the predisposing and precipitating factors displayed in eating disorders. It is important to recognise that there may be overlap between biological, psychological and social factors. For example, there is a very close relationship between temperament/personality and neurodevelopmental profile, although the latter may be thought of as more biologically and genetically determined.

Understanding of the aetiology of AN has been subject to definite 'fashions' over the century or so since its description (Schmidt, 2003). At the time of writing there has been an increased interest in the biological aspects, thanks largely to exciting advances in the fields of neuroscience, particularly neuroimaging, and molecular genetics. It has even been suggested that the plausibility of sociocultural theories has held back scientific progress in seeking aetiological factors, in particular the genetic and neurobiological basis that can account for such serious illnesses (Bulik, 2004). The tide is turning, however, and better understanding of the necessary preconditions or bio-logical substrate on which psychological and social risk factors impact is now beginning to help us delineate who is and who is not at risk. Ultimately this will start to explain why, within one family, one member but not another can be affected.

This chapter focuses on the aetiology of AN, bulimia nervosa (BN) and related eating disorders, for the simple reason that no research has yet been undertaken on the other childhood eating problems described elsewhere in this book. We hope that this will not always be the case.

Understanding causality

Aetiology is defined as the assignment of a cause, an origin, or a reason for something, particularly a disease or disorder. In complex multifactorial dis-orders, however, the reason is often a number of factors coming together. Some of these factors may be *correlates*, i.e. there is a statistically significant chance of their being associated with eating disorders. An example might be the association between eating disorders and depression. If correlates clearly precede the onset of the illness, they are known as *risk factors*. Risk factors can be changing or influenced by intervention (*variable risk factors*, e.g. age, medication), or non-changing (*fixed markers*, e.g. race, gender). If manipulat-ing a risk factor can be shown to change the outcome or influence onset of the disorder, then it is known as a *causal risk factor*. This differentiates it from *variable markers* which cannot be manipulated. Risk factors can therefore only be identified by longitudinal studies, in order to establish cause and effect, and causal risk factors can only be identified through trials of inter-vention, to demonstrate the effect of changing the risk factor. This scientific approach to understanding causality has become dominant in the past few decades. Consequently, pressure has increased on theory-based understand-ings of eating disorders to demonstrate their 'truth' through the development of testable hypotheses.

Over 30 risk factors for eating disorders have been identified thus far, with varying degrees of significance depending on the type of study (i.e. longi-tudinal, retrospective, etc.). Those for which a reasonable degree of evidence exists are listed in Table 5.1. This number of risk factors suggests that they are neither necessary nor sufficient to account for eating disorders on their own. A distinction is made in most studies between risk factors for AN and those for BN. This distinction is somewhat artificial, however, given the overlap between the two disorders in terms of psychopathology and over time. For example, 50 per cent of patients with AN go on to develop BN and about a third of patients with BN have had a previous episode of AN. In addition there is increasing recognition of the large number of patients, around 50 per cent of those presenting to clinical services, who do not fit neatly into either category and who would be diagnosed with eating disorder not otherwise specified (EDNOS: Fairburn and Bohn, 2005). As a result, some researchers have

Table 5.1 Risk factors for anorexia nervosa (AN) and bulimia nervosa (BN) (adapted from Jacobi, Morris, and de Zwann, 2004).

	Age	*AN*	*BN*
Preterm/birth trauma	Birth	✓	
Pregnancy complications/gestational age	Birth	✓	✓
Genetic factors	Birth	✓	✓
Female gender	Birth	✓	✓
Ethnicity	Birth	✓	✓
Infant sleep pattern difficulties	Infancy	✓	
High concern parenting	Infancy	✓	
Feeding/GI problems	Infancy	✓	
Digestive problems/picky eating/eating conflicts	Infancy/childhood	✓	
Childhood obesity	Childhood		✓
Childhood anxiety disorders	Childhood	✓	✓
Sexual abuse/neglect	Childhood	✓	✓
OCPD	Childhood/adolescence	✓	
Pubertal timing	Childhood/adolescence	✓	✓
Sexual abuse/adverse life events	Childhood/adolescence	✓	
Acculturation	Childhood/adolescence	✓	✓
Adolescence	Adolescence	✓	✓
BDD	Adolescence	✓	
High level exercise	Adolescence	✓	
Dieting (bingeing)	Adolescence	✓	✓
OCD	Adolescence	✓	
Perfectionism	Adolescence	✓	
Negative self-evaluation	Adolescence	✓	✓
Adverse family experiences	Adolescence		✓
Weight concerns/negative body image	Adolescence		✓
Parental obesity	Adolescence		✓
Parental substance misuse	Adolescence		✓
Social phobia	Adolescence		✓
Psychiatric morbidity/negative affect	Adolescence		✓
Low interoception	Adolescence		✓
Escape avoidance coping	Adolescence		✓
Low social support	Adolescence		✓
Prodromal symptoms	Adolescence		✓
Parental criticism esp. re weight	Adolescence		✓

chosen to explore the basis for individual behaviours or beliefs (such as self-induced vomiting, low weight or perfectionism) rather than full syndrome diagnoses.

Biological factors

Genetic basis for eating disorders

Eating disorders are not monogenic disorders, and as such we will never discover a 'gene that causes anorexia'. Complex or multifactorial disorders arise where there is thought to be a complex interplay between genetic predisposition or vulnerability and environmental factors. In disentangling these factors it is usual to separate non-shared environmental factors (i.e. experiences specific to the individual) from shared environmental factors (i.e. experiences to which others are exposed too such as media pressure). Family factors, such as parental illness or separation, are considered shared between siblings. This is important in some types of genetic studies in which sibling pairs are examined.

Evidence for the importance of heritance in the development of eating disorders comes from family studies, twin studies and adoption studies. In family studies, the frequency with which a disorder occurs in the families of affected individuals is compared with the risk in families without an affected member. In the largest study of this kind, for the full syndrome of AN, the relative risks were 11.3 and 12.3 in female relatives of subjects with AN and BN, respectively. The relative risks for BN were 4.2 and 4.4 for female relatives of subjects with AN and BN respectively (Strober, Freeman, Lampert, Diamond, and Kaye, 2000). This means that a female relative of someone with a clinical eating disorder is more than four times as likely to have BN and more than eleven times as likely to have AN than someone with no family history of eating disorders. The risk for subclinical eating problems may be even higher (Stein et al., 1999), and there is a large degree of overlap between AN and BN within families, suggesting that at least some of the genetic risk is common to both disorders (Walters and Kendler, 1995) and that there may be a continuum of genetic liability within families (Strober et al., 2000).

In twin studies the frequency of a disorder in identical (monozygotic) twins, who share all their genes, is compared with the frequency in non-identical (dizygotic) twins, who share no more genes than other siblings. This powerful study design assumes that both twins are exposed to similar environmental risk factors (the equivalent environment assumption, EEA), which may not always be the case. This assumption, together with small numbers in many studies, makes for considerable variation in findings, but to date AN has an estimated heritability of 58 to 76 per cent (Holland, Sicotte, and Treasure, 1988; Klump, Kaye, and Strober, 2001) and BN an even wider range from 31 to 83 per cent depending on the study (Bulik, Sullivan, Wade, and Kendler, 2000).

In addition to heritability for full eating disorder syndromes, there is considerable evidence for genetic contributions to individual symptoms, attitudes and behaviours, which together with environmental factors increase risk for the disorders within individuals. For example, binge eating and self-induced vomiting have been shown to have heritabilities ranging from 46 to 70 per cent in twin studies (Sullivan, Bulik, and Kendler, 1998), and personality traits conferring risk, such as perfectionism and interpersonal mistrust, are increased in the relatives of subjects with BN (Lilenfeld et al., 2000). Interestingly, Klump, McGue, and Iacono (2000b) have shown that there are marked differences in heritability for subscale scores of the eating disorder inventory

(EDI) between pre-adolescent girls (mean age 11) and adolescent girls (mean age 17) from a twin study, with the genetic effects being stronger in the adolescent girls. It has been suggested that puberty may activate some aspect of the genetic heritability for eating disorders.

With the latter decades of the twentieth century came the technology necessary to begin identifying specific genes that may be involved in disease processes. Candidate genes are genes suggested from pharmacological, physiological or genetic evidence, and their possible role in the disease process is explored by one of two methods: linkage analysis or association studies. Linkage studies often involve sibling pairs where one or both are affected. In *non-parametric linkage analysis*, marker alleles are identified as occurring more frequently than would be expected by chance in affected siblings, suggesting a link between the allele and the disease. A LOD score, which stands for logarithm of the odds and is based on the logarithm of the likelihood ratios for linkage versus non-linkage, of more than 3.3 is usually taken to suggest significant linkage. In *genome wide linkage studies*, quantitative trait loci (QTL) are chromosomal regions that may contain genes contributing to a quantitative trait which can be identified in sibling pairs with extreme scores of that trait.

A number of genome wide linkage studies have now been published, from the large multisite, international collaborative studies necessary to obtain the necessary sample sizes. So far only modest evidence for linkage on chromosomes 1, 4, 11, 13 and 15 were found when all forms of eating pathology (i.e. AN, BN and EDNOS) were included. However, when repeated on a subgroup with restrictive AN where two family members were affected the evidence for a susceptibility locus on chromosome 1p was much higher (LOD score 3.03; Grice et al., 2002).

For BN, on a sample of 308 families, a double peak was seen on linkage analysis, with the highest LOD score of 2.92 on chromosome 10. Where two family members showed evidence of self-induced vomiting the highest LOD score was 3.39, observed on chromosome 10. These results suggest a susceptibility locus for BN on chromosome 10p (Bulik et al., 2003a). Linkage studies have also identified greater evidence of linkage for traits such as age at menarche and anxiety in relatives of BN subjects than for obsessionality and low BMI in relatives of AN subjects (Bacanu et al., 2005).

For association studies either case controls or family trios are used. In the former, the frequency of a genetic variant of a candidate gene (an allele) is compared in the affected and the control groups. If it is directly involved in the genetic susceptibility to a disease process, the allele will occur more frequently in the cases than controls. Candidate genes that have been studied are generally those associated with monoamine functioning or with weight control and energy balance.

Several studies have looked at serotonin genes, based on evidence of 5HT dysregulation in both AN and BN (Kaye et al., 2005b). A meta-analysis of nine studies examining the 5-HT2a receptor gene found significant associations between AN and the _1438/A allele and AA genotype (Gorwood, Kipman, and Foulon, 2003). Although not all studies have replicated these findings, the quality of the evidence does suggest a role for the 5-HT2a receptor gene in the aetiology of AN. In addition a possible association between AN and ser23 allele of the 5-HT2c receptor gene has been suggested as a result of two studies (Hu et al., 2003; Westberg et al., 2002). Findings for other serotonin-related genes have been less promising.

Candidate genes from other neurotransmitter systems that have been examined include the dopamine and opioid systems, as well as those associated with weight and appetite regulation such as neuropeptide Y and leptin. Here the evidence is not yet strong enough to point to specific genes and studies require duplication. For a summary of these studies see Klump and Gobrogge (2005). Much is still to be uncovered about the mechanism by which these genes exert their influence. For example, the role of the 5-HT2a receptor in AN may be to influence affect regulation (e.g. anxiety, depression) and personality traits (e.g. harm avoidance) that predispose an individual to the development of AN rather than be linked to specific AN psychopathology.

The interplay of biological mechanisms is also a promising area for further research. For example, serotonin receptors are regulated by oestrogen, which in turn is known to be associated with the onset of eating disorders and to weight and appetite regulation. It has been suggested therefore that interactions between serotonin and oestrogens may influence genetic susceptibility to AN, accounting for increased heritability during puberty (Klump and Gobrogge, 2005). The hypotheses are that puberty may activate the genetic influence on AN by:

- activating oestrogen genes, such as the recently discovered ERb receptor genes, that directly influence liability to AN
- increasing levels of estrogens which then influence the transcription of the 5-HT2a receptor gene
- or some combination of the two.

Neurodevelopmental basis

The increased sophistication of neuroimaging techniques paired with detailed neuropsychological testing have improved our ability to target specific areas of brain function in an attempt to understand the neural bases of behaviour, beliefs and ultimately disorder. Eating disorders are no exception, although at the time of writing this is still a relatively new field of research. Structural neuroimaging, such as computed tomography (CT) and magnetic resonance imaging (MRI), have demonstrated ventricular enlargement in the low-weight stages of AN in adults and adolescents (Katzman, Zipursky, Lambe, and Mikulis, 1997; Palazidou, Robinson, and Lishman, 1990). These findings are thought to be attributable to neuronal damage secondary to malnutrition, with some degree of reversibility associated with myelin regeneration (Katzman, Christensen, Young, and Zipursky, 2001). In the majority of these studies, weight gain has been associated with improvement in structural deficits (e.g. Golden et al., 1996; Swayze et al., 1996), although in a more recent study total and regional cerebrospinal fluid (CSF) volumes were significantly decreased in patients with weight normalisation whereas white and gray matter volumes increased (Swayze et al., 2003).

To date, some preliminary evidence suggests that reported cognitive deficits in patients with AN may be associated with structural brain abnormalities (Kerem and Katzman, 2003). However, despite reduction of between 8 per cent (Connan et al., 2006) and 25 per cent (Giordano et al., 2001) in volume of the hippocampus of underweight subjects with AN compared to control women, there appears to be no associated impairment of hippocampus-dependent cognitive function nor a correlation with clinical features of AN, including BMI (Connan et al., 2006). It is unclear to what extent hippocampal atrophy might reflect a cause or an effect of the illness.

More interesting perhaps are the additional insights gained through the use of functional neuroimaging techniques which, as the name suggests, map function not simply structure. To date very few functional imaging studies of brain activity in early-onset AN have been performed (Lask, Gordon, Christie, Frampton, Chowdhury, and Watkins, 2005). Those that have, involved the use of single-photon emission computed tomography (SPECT) measuring regional cerebral blood flow (rCBF), which correlates closely with regional cerebral glucose metabolism. Reduced rCBF therefore reflects hypometabolism, which in turn reflects impaired brain function. Gordon, Lask, Bryant-Waugh, Christie, and Timimi, (1997) found unilateral hypoperfusion predominantly in the temporal lobe of 13 out of 15 patients (87 per cent) with early onset AN. These results have been replicated by the same group, who also found that there was no association between rCBF and cerebral dominance, nutritional status, length of illness, mood, or eating disorder psychopathology (Chowdhury, Gordon, Lask, Watkins, Watt, and Christie, 2003). RCBF was correlated, however, with aspects of neuropsychological functioning, including impaired visuospatial ability, impaired complex visual memory, and enhanced information processing (Lask et al., 2005). The combination of reduced rCBF and impairments of cognitive function independent of nutritional status suggest a systemic rather than a focal abnormality, with the limbic system, important for emotion and appetite regulation, memory, motivation, and perception, being the hypothesised link (Chowdhury et al., 2003).

Studies in adults have produced more conflicting results, with cingulate, frontal, temporal and parietal regions all being implicated in AN (Frank, Bailer, Henry, Wagner, and Kaye, 2004). Emotional and food-related challenges also activate some of these regions, and data suggest disturbances can persist after recovery from AN (Kaye, Bailer, Frank, Wagner, and Henry, 2005a).

Fewer studies have been conducted in BN or binge eating disorder, although disturbances of serotonin metabolism in similar brain regions have been postulated. The full implications from these studies remain obscure, but the future hope is that the brain pathways contributing to the aetiology of eating disorders become clearer, and with them the implications for psychopharmacological and psychotherapeutic approaches to treatment.

Finally in this section, it has been suggested that a small proportion of cases of AN may be triggered by infection, a phenomenon known as pediatric auto-immune neuropsychiatric disorder associated with streptococcus (PANDAS: Sokol, 2000; Sokol, Ward, Tamiya, Kondo, Houston, and Zabriskie, 2002). PANDAS have already been linked to other childhood onset illnesses such as obsessive compulsive disorder (OCD) and tic disorders. Evidence of strepto-coccal infection comes from clinical evaluation, throat cultures and two sero-logical tests: anti-deoxyribonuclease B (anti-DNase B) and anti-streptolysin O (ASO) titers. In addition, the rheumatic fever susceptibility trait marker D8/17 is found more frequently in subjects with AN who have other evidence of streptococcal infection than those with no eating disorder and no PANDAS characteristics (Sokol et al., 2002). The implication is that, in those cases where strong evidence exists for a PANDAS association, antibiotics may be a useful adjunct to treatment. Larger studies are needed to determine whether the association is robust enough for streptococcal infection to be considered a routine part of screening.

Perinatal influences

The importance of perinatal risk factors has been highlighted in a number of studies, the commonest hypothesised risks including hypoxic-induced brain damage and inadequate pre- and postnatal nutrition. Most studies have examined general rather than specific obstetric risk and found an overall increase in obstetric complications in patients with subsequent AN. A few specific associations that have been identified include very preterm birth and cephalohematoma (Cnattingius, Hultman, Dahl, and Sparen, 1999; Lindberg and Hjern, 2003), maternal anaemia, diabetes mellitus and pre-ecamplasia associated with AN, and retarded foetal growth (lower birth weight and length, decreased head circumference) in BN (Favaro, Tenconi, and Santonastaso, 2006). For both AN and BN, the increased risk associated with multiple rather than individual perinatal findings such as hyporeactivity, low birth weight and placental infarctions suggests a 'dose-response' effect (Favaro et al., 2006). The suggested mechanism is one of mild hypoxia affecting hippocampal and cortical brain development.

The role of puberty

The sexual dimorphism of eating disorders is one of their most characteristic and yet complex features. Explanations for the ten-fold increase in risk for females over males exist in the biological, psychological and socio-cultural domains. Puberty has long been recognised as a trigger for the onset of eating disorders, or at least that the risk in females increases most significantly at that time, fuelled by the observation that the ratio of boys to girls is higher in the prepubertal population (Bryant-Waugh and Lask, 1995). Puberty is associated with a greater increase in fat mass in girls than in boys, and with it increases in leptin production, the peripheral hormone that provides feedback to the hypothalamus regulating weight and appetite (Mantzoros, 1999). This leptin-driven enhanced appetite may be one of the factors associated with body dissatisfaction and dieting (O'Dea and Abraham, 1999), particularly in those already predisposed to obesity.

In addition to body weight and shape changes, many brain changes take place during adolescence. Some precede and initiate puberty; others continue for around a decade beyond. Some are directly associated with gonadal hormones and sex differences in brain development during puberty may reflect the different effects of male and female gonadal hormones. Early studies focused on the hypothalamus and other regions directly involved in reproductive function. Recent studies, however, also demonstrate influences on the hippocampus, striatum, cerebellum amygdala and cerebral cortex. Three known oestrogen receptors mediate the effects of gonadal hormones on cholinergic, noradrenergic, serotinergic and dopaminergic neurotransmitter systems. The functions affected include cognitive abilities, aggression, affect regulation, learning and memory. In animal studies an increased response to stress in females becomes evident in early adolescence, a process that is partially mediated by ovarian hormones (Arnsten and Shansky, 2004). In humans, there is also some evidence for pubertal changes in sex-specific responses to stressors with men showing greater HPA reactivity to achievement challenges and women to social rejection (Stroud, Salovey, and Epel, 2002).

A possibility that problems arise because of a mismatch between the emotional reactions and cognitive capacities of the younger adolescent has long interested clinicians, and led to a number of studies exploring the timing of puberty as a risk factor for eating disorders (e.g. Hayward et al., 1997; Killen et al., 1992). The findings are somewhat mixed, and the interpretation of cross-sectional studies potentially misleading. A number of studies have found no association between the timing of puberty and subsequent eating pathology (Stice, Agras, and Hammer, 1999; The McKnight Investigators, 2003), while Striegel-Moore et al. (2001) found early-onset menarche to be a risk factor for the development of body image and dieting concerns, the timing of menarche being largely determined by body weight. Kaltiala-Heino et al. (2001) found that bulimic-type eating pathology among girls was associated with early menarche. Jacobi (2005), reviewing the evidence, considers that puberty can be considered a non-specific fixed marker of AN and BN, but that there is no longitudinal basis for classifying puberty as a risk factor. In one longitudinal study of a student population, early puberty was one predictor of chronic symptomatology (Graber et al., 1994, cited in Jacobi, 2005).

Psychological and behavioural theories

There are a number of psychological theories about the development of eating disorders: some are specific to constructs thought to be important in maintenance of disorder, such as the centrality of control (Fairburn, Shafran, and Cooper, 1999b). Others are thought to be necessary preconditions, such as the temperamental trait of perfectionism (Bulik, Tozzi, Anderson, Mazzeo, Aggen, and Sullivan, 2003b). Those best characterised are temperament, early experience in terms of attachment, psychodynamic theories, low self-esteem, early feeding behaviour, the processing of negative emotional experiences, particularly trauma and threat, and weight and shape concern and the related behaviour of dieting.

In addition there is emerging evidence that specific cognitive profiles, in terms of cognitive flexibility, cognitive inhibition, visuo-spatial construction and memory, may be relevant to aetiology (Holliday, Tchanturia, Landau, Collier, and Treasure, 2005; Tchanturia, Morris, Anderluh, Collier, Nikolaou, and Treasure, 2004b; Tchanturia et al., 2004a). These studies are discussed in more detail in Chapter 8.

Temperament

Temperament is best understood as those innate characteristics unique to children that they bring to their actions, behaviours and relationships. Temperament is often understood as the precursor to personality, although the two constructs are distinct. The term 'personality' is not generally used when referring to children and young adolescents, for the simple reason that the characteristic patterns of behaviour which personality types confer are not yet fully developed. While it is unlikely that temperamental characteristics per se lead to disordered eating, it is argued that in combination with other risk factors, certain temperamental characteristics may increase vulnerability (Martin, Wertheim, Prior, Smart, Sanson, and Oberklaid, 2000). Temperamental traits that have been consistently associated with AN include harm avoidance, low novelty seeking, high persistence and low self-directedness (Fassino, Abbate-Daga, Amianto, Leombruni, Boggio, and Rovera, 2002; Klump et al., 2000a), with subtle temperament and character differences independent of body weight distinguishing subtypes of AN (Klump et al., 2000a). Women with BN showed high novelty seeking in the context of harm avoidance and low self-directedness (Fassino et al., 2002). Some temperamental features are distinct across eating disorder subtypes and could reflect differential vulnerabilities for the development of specific eating disorder symptom clusters.

Attachment

Attachment behaviour is defined as proximity seeking behaviour by a dependent organism (infant or child) when he or she senses discomfort of any sort, including pain, fear, cold or hunger (Glaser, 2000). It is not simply affection, but a biological drive important for survival. Anxious, insecure attachment styles are a consistent finding in the adult eating disorders literature (Ward, Ramsay, Turnbull, Benedettini, and Treasure, 2000), although it is important to remember that attachment is specific to a child, not to a parent. The contributions that both bring to the relationship are important, hence the need to consider the temperament of the child, as well as the parent's own attachment relationships with their parents/carers. In one study, 25 per cent of parents experienced loss of a child through miscarriage or severe obstetric complications in the pregnancy before the child with subsequent AN was born, compared to 7.5 per cent of control parents whose child did not develop AN (Shoebridge and Gowers, 2000). Qualitative data also suggested that the loss or trauma was still resonant for those mothers many years later. In addition, obstetric complications and birth trauma have been shown to be increased three- to four-fold in subjects with AN compared to controls (Cnattingius et al., 1999). It would not be surprising if such experiences led to heightened anxiety in relation to early parenting and impact on the attachment relationship. Against this background the tendency to minimise emotional distress and failure to learn processing of difficult and negative emotions, particularly anger and loss, is a tentative but plausible model that would account for the so called 'alexithymia' (literally 'no words for feelings') frequently described in patients with AN (Corcos et al., 2000).

Psychodynamic theories

It is a short hop from attachment to psychodynamic theory, the prominence of which is declining in terms of our understanding of aetiology, although psychodynamic concepts remain central to routine treatment practice. Disturbed eating in a psychodynamic framework has a number of symbolic meanings, from suppressed rage, omnipotent control of parental figures, fear of intrusion, denial of self and needs, etc. Particularly influential has been the work of Hilde Bruch in the 1970s, who wrote about eating disturbance as a 'solution or camouflage for the problems of living' (Bruch, quoted in Lask, 2000). Bruch's description of the patient with AN is of having failed to develop a sense of herself as independent and entitled to take initiative, rather adopting a compliant stance of the perfect child, with the consequence that she feels controlled and adopts safe predictable routines to determine her behaviour and control her environment. In this model, the difference in a mother's relationship with a girl compared to a boy is thought to account for the gender imbalance in eating disorder presentations; specifically the hypothesis that mothers assume they know a girl's needs, whereas they seek to understand their male children differently. Bruch's concept of the infant who has not learnt to discriminate her inner states and communicate her need to be looked after has been incorporated into the concept of 'infantile anorexia' (Chatoor, Hirsch, Ganiban, Persinger, and Hamburger, 1998), a feeding disorder of early infancy. Infant–mother relationships in this group of infants have been characterised by a lack of reciprocity, conflict and a struggle for control, at which food refusal is central. The relationship, if any, between 'infantile anorexia' and AN is not established.

Early feeding behaviour

Although clinical studies suggest that eating problems tend to emerge during adolescence, there is mounting evidence that eating disturbances are often present in childhood. Stice et al. (1999) found that inhibited eating, secretive eating, overeating and vomiting became increasingly apparent over the early years up to age 5, and in their sample of 216 children were associated with parental weight and shape concern, including maternal body dissatisfaction, internalisation of the thin-ideal, dieting, bulimic symptoms and both maternal and paternal body mass. The only infant characteristics that predicted these later eating disturbances were body mass and feeding behaviour (sucking duration) during the first month of life. Two other longitudinal studies have further explored the relationship between early feeding problems and later eating disorders. The first by Marchi and Cohen (1990) found an association between digestive problems and picky eating and later AN. In the second, Kotler, Cohen, Davies, Pine, and Walsh (2001) found eating conflicts, struggles with food and unpleasant meals (but not picky eating) in early childhood were risk factors for the later development of AN but not BN. The authors conclude that 'a clearer understanding of the mechanisms by which developmental processes influence the maintenance or change in eating attitudes or behaviors over time is an important goal for future research'.

Low self-esteem

Low self-esteem is an established risk factor for the development of BN (Fairburn, Welch, Doll, Davies, and O'Connor, 1997), although it is unclear the extent to which this is directly related to overweight (a risk factor for a proportion but not all with BN) or specific to weight and shape concerns. For example, women high in perfectionism who consider themselves overweight exhibit bulimic symptoms only if they have low self-esteem (Polivy and Herman, 2002). The picture for AN is bit more complex. Whilst many with AN do have low self-esteem, this has not been supported by risk factor studies (Fairburn, Cooper, Doll, and Welch, 1999a). This is especially true of children. Indeed, many children with AN give the impression of being quite confident, and poor self-evaluation really only becomes obvious in the context of perfectionistic standards. It is likely that in some, low self-esteem is specific to the body image (Geller, Johnston, Madsen, Goldner, Remick, and Birmingham, 1998) and social domains, but can be relatively intact and therefore protective in relation to abilities, intelligence, etc. (Geller, Zaitsoff, and Srikameswaran, 2002). Social desirability is a specific area of poor self-evaluation but high importance in prepubertal onset AN (Arnow, Sanders, and Steiner, 1999).

Trauma and threat

The relationship between adverse personal experiences has been widely documented although remains contentious, particularly in relation to childhood sexual abuse and its lack of specificity to eating disorders. Smolak and Murnen (2002) have argued that this is applying more stringent criteria than for other risks factors, many of which are also non-specific. In a meta-analysis of 53 studies, they found a modest relationship between childhood sexual abuse and eating disorders, in the face of considerable methodological variation. Nevertheless, a high prevalence of sexual trauma in clinical eating disorder cases, more in BN than AN (Wonderlich, Brewerton, Jocic, Dansky, and Abbott, 1997), has led to attempts to understand the mechanism by which trauma may result in the psychopathology characteristic of eating disorders. Psychological mechanisms include rejection of sexuality through weight loss and a heightened sense of personal disgust, and a wish to disgust others (Waller and Kennerly, 2003). In recent years a significant body of evidence has developed that patients with BN process threat cognitions differently, threats not related to weight, shape and food. Specifically, patients with BN have an attentional bias towards threats to self-esteem with less attention toward physical threats (McManus, Waller, and Chadwick, 1996), and that the threats may then fail to be adequately processed, but rather avoided (Meyer, Serpell, Waller, Murphy, Treasure, and Leung, 2005) or denied.

In a study of more general adversity precipitating eating disorders, Schmidt, Tiller, Blanchard, Andrews, and Treasure (1997) found that patients with AN and BN did not differ from community controls in terms of the proportion of patients with at least one severe life event or difficulty. However, more AN and BN patients had experienced a major difficulty and this was most commonly in the year before the onset of eating difficulties. These life events usually concerned close relationships with family and friends for both BN and AN, while specific to AN were events related to 'pudicity' (events and difficulties with the potential to evoke sexual shame or disgust, including premature, inappropriate or 'forbidden' sexuality, or sexual situations which posed a moral dilemma for the patient). This is in keeping with clinical experience in younger patients, as well as in the adults to whom the study relates.

Weight and shape concern and dieting

Clinical eating disturbances present at any age, but specific behaviours associated with weight and shape concerns are seen clinically in children as young as 7 years old, with children as young as 6 years expressing fears of becoming fat and body image concerns (Feldman, Feldman, and Goodman, 1988). By the age of 8 to 10 years, 29 per cent of boys and 41 per cent of girls endorse exercise and dieting as methods of weight control (Shapiro, Newcomb, and Loeb, 1997). In addition to gender bias, dieting awareness is linked to negative self-evaluation (Hill and Pallin, 1998). In a review of the development of weight and shape concerns in the aetiology of eating disorders, Gowers and Shore (2001) emphasise the multifactorial contributions to weight and shape concerns, including the risk that parents pass on their concerns to their children. Smolak, Levine, and Schermer (1999) explored the conflicting evidence about the significance of parental weight concerns and comments about weight and found that direct comments, particularly by mothers, were more influential in the development of weight concerns in schoolchildren than modelling. This is especially true if the mother has an eating disorder herself (Agras, Hammer, and McNicholas, 1999). Gowers and Shore (2001) conclude that 'most factors in the aetiology of eating disorders are mediated through weight and shape concern or the need for restraint. It is suggested that it is these cognitions that lead to dieting behaviour and thence to AN and often to BN'. They call for a better understanding of the vulnerability and resilience factors that operate between other aetiological factors and the development of weight concerns. Dieting is well established as a risk factor for the development of BN (Fairburn et al., 1997), particularly in those premorbidly overweight or predisposed to obesity through heritability. Dieting or weight loss precedes binge eating in a large proportion of those who go on to develop BN (Brewerton, Dansky, Kilpatrick, and O'Neil, 2000). In a study by Patton, Selzer, Coffey, Carlin, and Wolfe (1999) 'dieters' had an eighteen-fold increased risk of developing eating disorders (BN or EDNOS) compared to non-dieters. The role of dieting in the onset of AN is less clear (Fairburn et al., 1999a). In a recent study of almost 3000 dieting women, Fairburn, Cooper, Doll, and Davies (2005) found that 3.5 per cent went on to develop an eating disorder over the next two years. Of these, around 70 per cent could be identified by self-report of binge eating, eating in secret, BMI below 19, purging and fear of losing control over eating. The majority developed BN or EDNOS, with only 10 per cent developing full syndrome AN, underlining the more tentative link between AN and dieting.

In terms of high risk groups for weight and shape concern and associated weight control behaviours, perhaps most has been written about athletes and dancers. Ballet dancers, for example, are between 6 and 25 times more likely to develop eating disorders than young women in the general population. Possible factors include heightened genetic vulnerability and environmental pressure, but even amongst dancers some will be at higher risk than others. Thomas, Keel, and Heatherton (2005) suggest that dancers who exhibit high levels of perfectionism and, perhaps consequently, place themselves in highly competitive environments, may exhibit a significantly increased risk for disordered eating in comparison to dancers who are less perfectionistic and/or less competitive.

Sociocultural theories

The sociocultural perspective is perhaps the most well-documented framework used to explain why eating disorders occur, identifying pressure to be thin as a major source of body image disturbance and eating disordered behaviour. A glance at any glossy magazine aimed at women, and increasingly those aimed at men, reveals the preoccupation with physical attractiveness guaranteed and arguably intended to increase body awareness and promote weight control behaviours, particularly dieting. It is clear, however, that the so-called obesogenic environment, with an abundance of cheap, highly calorific foods seen as responsible for the current obesity 'epidemic' in the west at the same time creates a context for body dissatisfaction and dieting that can herald the onset of eating disorder pathology. While the fashion and diet industries are targeted primarily at adults, exposure to idealised body images also occurs at much younger ages, including dolls. One study found that three popular dolls, including 'Florida Barbie', had an equivalent BMI ranging from 11.8 to 13.4 kg/m^2 (Wells and Nicholls, 2001). This and similar studies highlight the severity with which female body shape is deformed in commercial images. Field, Cheung, Wolf, Herzog, Gortmaker, and Colditz (1999) have demonstrated a relationship in pre-adolescent and adolescent girls between unhappiness with their weight and shape and the frequency with which they read fashion magazines.

The effect of media portrayal of body image on a population has been most clearly documented in the study by Becker, Burwell, Gilman, Herzog, and Hamburg (2002) on the island of Fiji, where changes in attitude to body weight and shape were examined following the introduction of television. The study found increases in overall scores on the Eating Attitudes Test and a higher incidence of self-induced vomiting to lose weight following prolonged television exposure, with subjects explicitly linking these thoughts and behaviours with their aesthetic ideals drawn from western television influence.

The extent to which media images impact on normal individuals, or are only selectively misinterpreted by those susceptible to or suffering from eating disorders, is a matter of continued interest. In addition, the thin ideal to which these images aspire is a product of specific cultures. Nevertheless, eating disorders can no longer be thought of as 'culture bound syndromes' however, cases having now been documented across the globe (Nasser, 1997). A key factor is thought to be societies or cultures undergoing socioeconomic transition. Katzman and Lee (1997) have argued that eating disorders may be precipitated by problems with transition, dislocation and oppression that produce solutions in manipulations of weight, diet and food. Postulated mechanisms range from gender politics to economic influences. For example, it has been suggested that the changing commercialism of eastern Europe, coupled with reduced state benefits such as education, health care, and employment, may result in changes to the marketing of beauty (Nasser and Katzman, 2003). The 'new millennium' in sociocultural models of eating disorders has moved beyond western cultures and gender politics to one of worldwide cultural dynamics, cultures in transition and confused identities (Nasser and Katzman, 2003).

Hoek, van Harten, Hermans, Katzman, Matroos, and Susser (2005) found that in the Caribbean island of Curacao the overall incidence of AN was much lower than in the affluent societies of the United States and western Europe. However, within the island population no cases of AN were found in the majority black population, while the incidence among the minority mixed and white population on Curacao was similar to that of the United States and the Netherlands. The authors hypothesise that norms in the black population about body size might serve to protect young women from the increasing emphasis on thinness in the media and other influences in the island culture.

Integrating aetiological models

The challenge for the eating disorders field now goes beyond simply adding to the number of identified risk factors and elucidating their role and specificity. It is to find ways to integrate what we know into casual pathways or models that might explain the emergence of eating disorders in their many guises. It is likely that not one, two or even three models will be sufficient to account for all clinical presentations, since eating disorders are often described of as the 'final common pathway' of a number of possible risk factors. Any good model will be testable and should enable one pathway (phenotype) to be distinguished from another.

One such aetiological model to have emerged over the last few years is the neurodevelopmental model for restrictive AN proposed by Connan, Campbell, Katzman, Lightman, and Treasure (2003). It is the first time that developmental factors have been put together with the greater body of knowledge from animal and adult based research to provide a plausible mechanism for the onset of AN. The hypothesis is that genetic factors and early life experience interact to generate susceptibility to a chronic submissive stress type response and to hypothalamic-pituitary-adrenal (HPA) dysregulation. This vulnerability is then activated by the changes associated with puberty, eliciting aberrant HPA responses in response to stress. The authors propose that in AN there is continued secretion of corticotrophin releasing hormone (CRH) rather than release of other adrenocorticoids such as arginine vasopressin (AVP).

Prolonged CRH secretion in turn leads to loss of nutritional homeostasis, thus compromising the body's natural appetite and energy balance.

The HPA axis is a key modulator of the stress response, and is shaped by early experience, including loss, trauma and attachment. Parenting can positively or negatively modify this stress response, so that with positive early experiences birth trauma need not necessarily lead to heightened stress response, but equally early neglect or deprivation could modulate the HPA response in such as way that chronic hypercortisolaemia results. Early alterations in HPA regulation have been shown to impact, amongst other things, on appetite regulation.

In this model, those vulnerable to AN enter the challenging realms of adolescence with significant impairments in self-awareness and the processing of difficult emotional experiences particularly within interpersonal relationships, and in the biological systems controlling stress responses and appetite. Low self-esteem, disempowerment and temperamental traits such as a tendency to placate and perfectionism may foster a tendency to chronic stress similar to that seen in animal models such as the 'thin sow syndrome', in which female pigs lowest in the social ranking develop anorexia, infertility, overactivity and severe weight loss (Treasure and Owen, 1997).

The chronic stress response seen in AN differs from that seen in depression: in those predisposed to AN, HPA dysregulation leads to persistently elevated CRH, in turn leading to loss of appetite and weight loss in those predisposed to leanness. Once established, the anabolic/catabolic imbalance is subject to factors that maintain the process, such as in the cognitive behavioural model proposed by Fairburn et al. (1999b).

Although limited in its specificity to the restrictive subtype of AN, the model has important implications for treatment in terms of the centrality of attachment relationship, emotional processing skills and self-efficacy in addition to those elements of treatment that address the nutritional and cognitive aspects of the disorder.

Conclusions

Eating disorders are complex in their aetiology, with biological, psychological and social factors all playing important parts in our understanding (see Figure 5.1). The greatest growth in knowledge over the past two decades has been in our understanding of the genetic and neurobiological basis for eating disorders. Although as yet treatment is not based primarily on aetiology, better understanding the aetiology of eating disorders may in future have important implications for specific elements of treatment in vulnerable individuals, and improve our ability to detect and target those most at risk. At this time, whilst our knowledge of correlates and risk factors increases daily, it remains very difficult to demonstrate causality for many of the factors discussed above and consequently further research in this area remains a priority if potentially preventable risks can be identified.

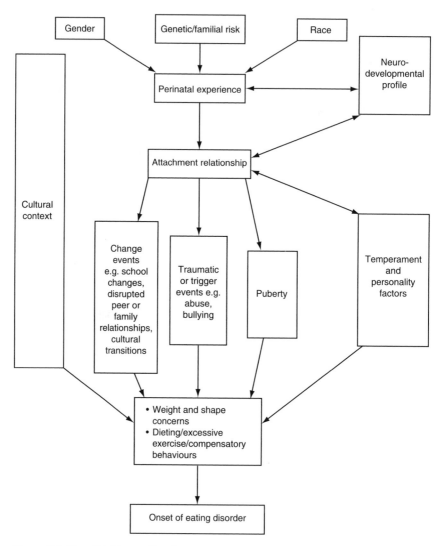

Figure 5.1 Simplified 'causal' pathway.

References

Agras, W. S., Hammer, L., and McNicholas, F. (1999). A prospective study of the influence of eating-disordered mothers on their children. *International Journal of Eating Disorders*, 25, 253–262.

Arnow, B., Sanders, M. J., and Steiner, H. (1999). Premenarcheal versus postmenarcheal anorexia nervosa: A comparative study. *Clinical Child Psychology and Psychiatry*, 4, 403–414.

Arnsten, A. F., and Shansky, R. M. (2004). Adolescence: Vulnerable period for stress-induced prefrontal cortical function? Introduction to part IV. *Annals of the New York Academy of Science, 1021,* 143–147.

Bacanu, S. A., Bulik, C. M., Klump, K. L., Fichter, M. M., Halmi, K. A., Keel, P., et al. (2005). Linkage analysis of anorexia and bulimia nervosa cohorts using selected behavioral phenotypes as quantitative traits or covariates. *American Journal of Medical Genetics. Part B, Neuropsychiatric Genetics, 139,* 61–68.

Becker, A. E., Burwell, R. A., Gilman, S. E., Herzog, D. B., and Hamburg, P. (2002). Eating behaviours and attitudes following prolonged exposure to television among ethnic Fijian adolescent girls. *British Journal of Psychiatry, 180,* 509–514.

Brewerton, T. D., Dansky, B. S., Kilpatrick, D. G., and O'Neil, P. M. (2000). Which comes first in the pathogenesis of bulimia nervosa: Dieting or bingeing? *International Journal of Eating Disorders, 28,* 259–264.

Bryant-Waugh, R., and Lask, B. (1995). Eating disorders in children. *Journal of Child Psychology and Psychiatry, 36,* 191–202.

Bulik, C. M. (2004). Role of genetics in anorexia nervosa, bulimia nervosa and binge eating disorder. In T.D. Brewerton (Ed.), *Clinical handbook of eating disorders: An integrated approach* (pp. 165–182). New York: Marcel Dekker.

Bulik, C. M., Devlin, B., Bacanu, S. A., Thornton, L., Klump, K. L., Fichter, M. M., et al. (2003a). Significant linkage on chromosome 10p in families with bulimia nervosa. *American Journal of Human Genetics, 72,* 200–207.

Bulik, C. M., Sullivan, P. F., Wade, T. D., and Kendler, K. S. (2000). Twin studies of eating disorders: A review. *International Journal of Eating Disorders, 27,* 1–20.

Bulik, C. M., Tozzi, F., Anderson, C., Mazzeo, S. E., Aggen, S., and Sullivan, P. F. (2003b). The relation between eating disorders and components of perfectionism. *American Journal of Psychiatry, 160,* 366–368.

Chatoor, I., Hirsch, R., Ganiban, J., Persinger, M., and Hamburger, E. (1998). Diagnosing infantile anorexia: The observation of mother–infant interactions. *Journal of American Academy of Child and Adolescent Psychiatry, 37,* 959–967.

Chowdhury, U., Gordon, I., Lask, B., Watkins, B., Watt, H., and Christie, D. (2003). Early-onset anorexia nervosa: Is there evidence of limbic system imbalance? *International Journal of Eating Disorders, 33,* 388–396.

Cnattingius, S., Hultman, C. M., Dahl, M., and Sparen, P. (1999). Very preterm birth, birth trauma, and the risk of anorexia nervosa among girls. *Archives of General Psychiatry, 56,* 634–638.

Connan, F., Campbell, I. C., Katzman, M., Lightman, S. L., and Treasure, J. (2003). A neurodevelopmental model for anorexia nervosa. *Physiological Behaviour, 79,* 13–24.

Connan, F., Murphy, F., Connor, S. E., Rich, P., Murphy, T., Bara-Carill, N., et al. (2006). Hippocampal volume and cognitive function in anorexia nervosa. *Psychiatry Research, 146,* 117–125.

Corcos, M., Guilbaud, O., Speranza, M., Paterniti, S., Loas, G., Stephan, P., et al. (2000). Alexithymia and depression in eating disorders. *Psychiatry Research, 93,* 263–266.

Fairburn, C. G., and Bohn, K. (2005). Eating disorder NOS (EDNOS): An example of the troublesome 'not otherwise specified' (NOS) category in DSM-IV. *Behaviour Research and Therapy, 43,* 691–701.

Fairburn, C. G., Cooper, Z., Doll, H. A., and Davies, B. A. (2005). Identifying dieters who will develop an eating disorder: A prospective, population-based study. *American Journal of Psychiatry, 162,* 2249–2255.

Fairburn, C. G., Cooper, Z., Doll, H. A., and Welch, S. L. (1999a). Risk factors for anorexia nervosa: Three integrated case-control comparisons. *Archives of General Psychiatry*, *56*, 468–476.

Fairburn, C. G., Shafran, R., and Cooper, Z. (1999b). A cognitive behavioural theory of anorexia nervosa. *Behaviour Research and Therapy*, *37*, 1–13.

Fairburn, C. G., Welch, S. L., Doll, H. A., Davies, B. A., and O'Connor, M. E. (1997). Risk factors for bulimia nervosa. A community-based case-control study. *Archives of General Psychiatry*, *54*, 509–517.

Fassino, S., Abbate-Daga, G., Amianto, F., Leombruni, P., Boggio, S., and Rovera, G. G. (2002). Temperament and character profile of eating disorders: a controlled study with the Temperament and Character Inventory. *International Journal of Eating Disorders*, *32*, 412–425.

Favaro, A., Tenconi, E., and Santonastaso, P. (2006). Perinatal factors and the risk of developing anorexia nervosa and bulimia nervosa. *Archives of General Psychiatry*, *63*, 82–88.

Feldman, W., Feldman, E., and Goodman, J. T. (1988). Culture versus biology: Children's attitudes toward thinness and fatness. *Pediatrics*, *81*, 190–194.

Field, A. E., Cheung, L., Wolf, A. M., Herzog, D. B., Gortmaker, S. L., and Colditz, G. A. (1999). Exposure to the mass media and weight concerns among girls. *Pediatrics*, *103*, E36.

Frank, G. K., Bailer, U. F., Henry, S., Wagner, A., and Kaye, W. H. (2004). Neuroimaging studies in eating disorders. *CNS Spectrums*, *9*, 539–548.

Geller, J., Johnston, C., Madsen, K., Goldner, E. M., Remick, R. A., and Birmingham, C. L. (1998). Shape- and weight-based self-esteem and the eating disorders. *International Journal of Eating Disorders*, *24*, 285–298.

Geller, J., Zaitsoff, S. L., and Srikameswaran, S. (2002). Beyond shape and weight: Exploring the relationship between nonbody determinants of self-esteem and eating disorder symptoms in adolescent females. *International Journal of Eating Disorders*, *32*, 344–351.

Giordano, G. D., Renzetti, P., Parodi, R. C., Foppiani, L., Zandrino, F., Giordano, G., et al. (2001). Volume measurement with magnetic resonance imaging of hippocampus-amygdala formation in patients with anorexia nervosa. *Journal of Endocrinological Investigation*, *24*, 510–514.

Glaser, D. (2000). Child abuse and neglect and the brain – a review. *Journal of Child Psychology and Psychiatry*, *41*, 97–116.

Golden, N. H., Ashtari, M., Kohn, M. R., Patel, M., Jacobson, M. S., Fletcher, A., et al. (1996). Reversibility of cerebral ventricular enlargement in anorexia nervosa, demonstrated by quantitative magnetic resonance imaging. *Journal of Pediatrics*, *128*, 296–301.

Gordon, I., Lask, B., Bryant-Waugh, R., Christie, D., and Timimi, S. (1997). Childhood-onset anorexia nervosa: Towards identifying a biological substrate. *International Journal of Eating Disorders*, *22*, 159–165.

Gorwood, P., Kipman, A., and Foulon, C. (2003). The human genetics of anorexia nervosa. *European Journal of Pharmacology*, *480*, 163–170.

Gowers, S. G. and Shore, A. (2001). Development of weight and shape concerns in the aetiology of eating disorders. *British Journal of Psychiatry*, *179*, 236–242.

Grice, D. E., Halmi, K. A., Fichter, M. M., Strober, M., Woodside, D. B., Treasure, J., et al. (2002). Evidence for a susceptibility gene for anorexia nervosa on chromosome 1. *American Journal of Human Genetics*, *70*, 787–792.

Hayward, C., Killen, J. D., Wilson, D. M., Hammer, L. D., Litt, I. F., Kraemer, H. C., et al. (1997). Psychiatric risk associated with early puberty in adolescent girls. *Journal of the American Academy of Child and Adolescent Psychiatry*, *36*, 255–262.

Hill, A. J., and Pallin, V. (1998). Dieting awareness and low self-worth: Related issues in 8-year-old girls. *International Journal of Eating Disorders*, *24*, 405–413.

Hoek, H. W., van Harten, P. N., Hermans, K. M., Katzman, M. A., Matroos, G. E., and Susser, E. S. (2005). The incidence of anorexia nervosa on Curacao. *American Journal of Psychiatry*, *162*, 748–752.

Holland, A. J., Sicotte, N., and Treasure, J. (1988). Anorexia nervosa: Evidence for a genetic basis. *Journal of Psychosomatic Research*, *32*, 561–571.

Holliday, J., Tchanturia, K., Landau, S., Collier, D., and Treasure, J. (2005). Is impaired set-shifting an endophenotype of anorexia nervosa? *American Journal of Psychiatry*, *162*, 2269–2275.

Hu, X., Giotakis, O., Li, T., Karwautz, A., Treasure, J., and Collier, D. A. (2003). Association of the 5-HT2c gene with susceptibility and minimum body mass index in anorexia nervosa. *Neuroreport*, *14*, 781–783.

Jacobi, C. (2005). Psychosocial risk factors for eating disorders. In S. Wonderlich, J. Mitchell, M. de Zwann, and H. Steiger (Eds.), *Eating disorders review: Part 1* (pp. 59–86). Abingdon: Radcliffe Publishing.

Jacobi, C., Morris, L., and de Zwann, M. (2004). An overview of risk factors for anorexia nervosa, bulimia nervosa and binge eating disorder. In T. Brewerton (Ed.), *Clinical handbook of eating disorders: An integrated approach* (pp. 117–164). New York: Marcel Dekker.

Kaltiala-Heino, R., Rimpela, M., Rissanen, A., and Rantanen, P. (2001). Early puberty and early sexual activity are associated with bulimic-type eating pathology in middle adolescence. *Journal of Adolescent Health*, *28*, 346–352.

Katzman, D. K., Christensen, B., Young, A. R., and Zipursky, R. B. (2001). Starving the brain: Structural abnormalities and cognitive impairment in adolescents with anorexia nervosa. *Seminars in Clinical Neuropsychiatry*, *6*, 146–152.

Katzman, D. K., Zipursky, R. B., Lambe, E. K., and Mikulis, D. J. (1997). A longitudinal magnetic resonance imaging study of brain changes in adolescents with anorexia nervosa. *Archives of Pediatric and Adolescent Medicine*, *151*, 793–797.

Katzman, M. A., and Lee, S. (1997). Beyond body image: the integration of feminist and transcultural theories in the understanding of self starvation. *International Journal of Eating Disorders*, *22*, 385–394.

Kaye, W. H., Bailer, U. F., Frank, G. K., Wagner, A., and Henry, S. E. (2005a). Brain imaging of serotonin after recovery from anorexia and bulimia nervosa. *Physiology and Behaviour*, *86*, 15–17.

Kaye, W. H., Frank, G. K., Bailer, U. F., Henry, S. E., Meltzer, C. C., Price, J. C., et al. (2005b). Serotonin alterations in anorexia and bulimia nervosa: New insights from imaging studies. *Physiology and Behaviour*, *85*, 73–81.

Kerem, N. C., and Katzman, D. K. (2003). Brain structure and function in adolescents with anorexia nervosa. *Adolescent Medicine*, *14*, 109–118.

Killen, J. D., Hayward, C., Litt, I. F., Hammer, L. D., Wilson, D. M., Miner, B., et al. (1992). Is puberty a risk factor for eating disorders? *American Journal of Disease in Childhood*, *146*, 323–325.

Klump, K. L., Bulik, C. M., Pollice, C., Halmi, K. A., Fichter, M. M., Berrettini, W. H., et al. (2000a). Temperament and character in women with anorexia nervosa. *Journal of Nervous and Mental Disease*, *188*, 559–567.

Klump, K. L., and Gobrogge, K. L. (2005). A review and primer of molecular genetic studies of anorexia nervosa. *International Journal of Eating Disorders, 37 Suppl,* S43–S48.

Klump, K. L., Kaye, W. H., and Strober, M. (2001). The evolving genetic foundations of eating disorders. *Psychiatric Clinics of North America, 24,* 215–225.

Klump, K. L., McGue, M., and Iacono, W. G. (2000b). Age differences in genetic and environmental influences on eating attitudes and behaviors in preadolescent and adolescent female twins. *Journal of Abnormal Psychology, 109,* 239–251.

Kotler, L. A., Cohen, P., Davies, M., Pine, D. S., and Walsh, B. T. (2001). Longitudinal relationships between childhood, adolescent, and adult eating disorders. *Journal of the American Academy of Child and Adolescent Psychiatry, 40,* 1434–1440.

Lask, B. (2000). Aetiology. In B. Lask and R. Bryant-Waugh (Eds.), *Anorexia nervosa and related eating disorders in childhood and adolescence* (2nd ed., pp. 63–80). Hove, UK: Psychology Press.

Lask, B., Gordon, I., Christie, D., Frampton, I., Chowdhury, U., and Watkins, B. (2005). Functional neuroimaging in early-onset anorexia nervosa. *International Journal of Eating Disorders, 37 Suppl,* S49–S51.

Lilenfeld, L. R., Stein, D., Bulik, C. M., Strober, M., Plotnicov, K., Pollice, C., et al. (2000). Personality traits among currently eating disordered, recovered and never ill first-degree female relatives of bulimic and control women. *Psychological Medicine, 30,* 1399–1410.

Lindberg, L., and Hjern, A. (2003). Risk factors for anorexia nervosa: A national cohort study. *International Journal of Eating Disorders, 34,* 397–408.

Mantzoros, C. S. (1999). Leptin and the hypothalamus: Neuroendocrine regulation of food intake. *Molecular Psychiatry, 4,* 8–7.

Marchi, M., and Cohen, P. (1990). Early childhood eating behaviors and adolescent eating disorders. *Journal of the American Academy of Child and Adolescent Psychiatry, 29,* 112–117.

Martin, G. C., Wertheim, E. H., Prior, M., Smart, D., Sanson, A., and Oberklaid, F. (2000). A longitudinal study of the role of childhood temperament in the later development of eating concerns. *International Journal of Eating Disorders, 27,* 150–162.

McManus, F., Waller, G., and Chadwick, P. (1996). Biases in the processing of different forms of threat in bulimic and comparison women. *Journal of Nervous and Mental Disease, 184,* 547–554.

Meyer, C., Serpell, L., Waller, G., Murphy, F., Treasure, J., and Leung, N. (2005). Cognitive avoidance in the strategic processing of ego threats among eating-disordered patients. *International Journal of Eating Disorders, 38,* 30–36.

Nasser, M. (1997). The EAT speaks many languages: Review of the use of the EAT in eating disorders research. *Eating and Weight Disorders, 2,* 174–181.

Nasser, M., and Katzman, M. (2003). Sociocultural theories of eating disorders: An evolution in thought. In J. Treasure, U. Schmidt, and E. van Furth (Eds.), *Handbook of eating disorders* (2nd ed., pp. 139–150). Chichester: John Wiley and Sons.

O'Dea, J. A., and Abraham, S. (1999). Onset of disordered eating attitudes and behaviors in early adolescence: Interplay of pubertal status, gender, weight, and age. *Adolescence, 34,* 671–679.

Palazidou, E., Robinson, P., and Lishman, W. A. (1990). Neuroradiological and neuropsychological assessment in anorexia nervosa. *Psychological Medicine, 20,* 521–527.

Patton, G. C., Selzer, R., Coffey, C., Carlin, J. B., and Wolfe, R. (1999). Onset of adolescent eating disorders: Population based cohort study over 3 years. *British Medical Journal, 318*, 765–768.

Polivy, J., and Herman, C. P. (2002). Causes of eating disorders. *Annual Review of Psychology, 53*, 187–213.

Schmidt, U. (2003). Aetiology of eating disorders in the 21(st) century: New answers to old questions. *European Child and Adolescent Psychiatry, 12, Suppl 1*, 130–137.

Schmidt, U., Tiller, J., Blanchard, M., Andrews, B., and Treasure, J. (1997). Is there a specific trauma precipitating anorexia nervosa? *Psychological Medicine, 27*, 523–530.

Shapiro, S., Newcomb, M., and Loeb, T. B. (1997). Fear of fat, disregulated-restrained eating, and body-esteem: Prevalence and gender differences among eight- to ten-year-old children. *Journal of Clinical Child Psychology, 26*, 358–365.

Shoebridge, P., and Gowers, S. G. (2000). Parental high concern and adolescent-onset anorexia nervosa. A case- control study to investigate direction of causality. *British Journal of Psychiatry, 176*, 132–137.

Smolak, L., Levine, M. P., and Schermer, F. (1999). Parental input and weight concerns among elementary school children. *International Journal of Eating Disorders, 25*, 263–271.

Smolak, L., and Murnen, S. K. (2002). A meta-analytic examination of the relationship between child sexual abuse and eating disorders. *International Journal of Eating Disorders, 31*, 136–150.

Sokol, M. S. (2000). Infection-triggered anorexia nervosa in children: Clinical description of four cases. *Journal of Child and Adolescent Psychopharmacology, 10*, 133–145.

Sokol, M. S., Ward, P. E., Tamiya, H., Kondo, D. G., Houston, D., and Zabriskie, J. B. (2002). D8/17 expression on B lymphocytes in anorexia nervosa. *American Journal of Psychiatry, 159*, 1430–1432.

Stein, D., Lilenfeld, L. R., Plotnicov, K., Pollice, C., Rao, R., Strober, M., et al. (1999). Familial aggregation of eating disorders: Results from a controlled family study of bulimia nervosa. *International Journal of Eating Disorders, 26*, 211–215.

Stice, E., Agras, W. S., and Hammer, L. D. (1999). Risk factors for the emergence of childhood eating disturbances: A five-year prospective study. *International Journal of Eating Disorders, 25*, 375–387.

Striegel-Moore, R. H., McMahon, R. P., Biro, F. M., Schreiber, G., Crawford, P. B., and Voorhees, C. (2001). Exploring the relationship between timing of menarche and eating disorder symptoms in Black and White adolescent girls. *International Journal of Eating Disorders, 30*, 421–433.

Strober, M., Freeman, R., Lampert, C., Diamond, J., and Kaye, W. (2000). Controlled family study of anorexia nervosa and bulimia nervosa: Evidence of shared liability and transmission of partial syndromes. *American Journal of Psychiatry, 157*, 393–401.

Stroud, L. R., Salovey, P., and Epel, E. S. (2002). Sex differences in stress responses: Social rejection versus achievement stress. *Biology and Psychiatry, 52*, 318–327.

Sullivan, P. F., Bulik, C. M., and Kendler, K. S. (1998). Genetic epidemiology of binging and vomiting. *British Journal of Psychiatry, 173*, 75–79.

Swayze, V. W., Andersen, A., Arndt, S., Rajarethinam, R., Fleming, F., Sato, Y., et al. (1996). Reversibility of brain tissue loss in anorexia nervosa assessed with a computerized Talairach 3-D proportional grid. *Psychological Medicine, 26*, 381–390.

Swayze, V. W., Andersen, A. E., Andreasen, N. C., Arndt, S., Sato, Y., and Ziebell, S. (2003). Brain tissue volume segmentation in patients with anorexia nervosa before and after weight normalization. *International Journal of Eating Disorders, 33*, 33–44.

Tchanturia, K., Anderluh, M. B., Morris, R. G., Rabe-Hesketh, S., Collier, D. A., Sanchez, P., et al. (2004a). Cognitive flexibility in anorexia nervosa and bulimia nervosa. *Journal of the International Neuropsychology Society, 10*, 513–520.

Tchanturia, K., Morris, R. G., Anderluh, M. B., Collier, D. A., Nikolaou, V., and Treasure, J. (2004b). Set shifting in anorexia nervosa: an examination before and after weight gain, in full recovery and relationship to childhood and adult OCPD traits. *Journal of Psychiatric Research, 38*, 545–552.

The McKnight Investigators (2003). Risk factors for the onset of eating disorders in adolescent girls: results of the McKnight longitudinal risk factor study. *American Journal of Psychiatry, 160*, 248–254.

Thomas, J. J., Keel, P. K., and Heatherton, T. F. (2005). Disordered eating attitudes and behaviors in ballet students: Examination of environmental and individual risk factors. *International Journal of Eating Disorders, 38*, 263–268.

Treasure, J., and Owen, J. B. (1997). Intriguing links between animal behavior and anorexia nervosa. *International Journal of Eating Disorders, 21*, 307–311.

Waller, G., and Kennerly, H. (2003). Cognitive-behavioural treatments. In J. Treasure, U. Schmidt, and E. van Furth (Eds.), *Handbook of eating disorders* (2nd ed., pp. 233–252). Chichester: John Wiley and Sons.

Walters, E. E., and Kendler, K. S. (1995). Anorexia nervosa and anorexic-like syndromes in a population-based female twin sample. *American Journal of Psychiatry, 152*, 64–71.

Ward, A., Ramsay, R., Turnbull, S., Benedettini, M., and Treasure, J. (2000). Attachment patterns in eating disorders: Past in the present. *International Journal of Eating Disorders, 28*, 370–376.

Wells, J. C., and Nicholls, D. (2001). The relationship between body size and body composition in women of different nutritional status. *European Eating Disorders Review, 9*, 416–442.

Westberg, L., Bah, J., Råstam, M., Gillberg, C., Wentz, E., Melke, J., et al. (2002). Association between a polymorphism of the 5-HT2C receptor and weight loss in teenage girls. *Neuropsychopharmacology, 26*, 789–793.

Wonderlich, S. A., Brewerton, T. D., Jocic, Z., Dansky, B. S., and Abbott, D. W. (1997). Relationship of childhood sexual abuse and eating disorders. *Journal of the American Academy of Child and Adolescent Psychiatry, 36*, 1107–1115.

6 Outcome and prognosis

Simon Gowers and Francess Doherty

Introduction

The course of an eating disorder is extremely variable and may range from a brief, mild episode leading to full recovery, to an illness with a chronic course lasting many years, sometimes leading to a fatal outcome. In childhood and adolescence this is especially so. Most adults with a long and chronic history will have started off as young people in the early stages of their illness, but without the benefit of hindsight it can be difficult to predict how the condition will develop.

In thinking about outcomes and prognosis there are a number of ways in which young people are different from adults, chiefly because they are at a different developmental stage. In adult-onset anorexia nervosa (AN), recovery generally implies restoration to a premorbid state of physical health, i.e. return of weight and hormonal functioning against a background of completed growth. In pubescent girls, treatment imposed weight gain may precipitate growth and their menarche, with all that implies experientially. A recovering adult might anticipate return to a previous level of social functioning and occupation, whereas a young person's recovery will mean climbing back on to the developmental treadmill. In short, a positive outcome for a child or adolescent will involve a greater degree of facing the uncertainty of a physical and social identity that hasn't been experienced before. In a number of respects this will mean 'growing up', and facing the attendant anxieties which may have played a part in the original development of the condition. A related issue concerns the need to ensure that the 'recovered' child or adolescent doesn't 'stand still'. That is to say a 13 year old restored to a normal weight might be considered recovered *to date*, but their health will decline if they are unable to keep pace with the 'moving goalposts' of physical and social development.

In this chapter we address what is known of the long-term outcome of eating disorders and attempt to clarify the variables which predict outcome in a given case. Despite numerous outcome studies to date, research difficulties abound and there are few areas of certainty. As those with severe eating disorders inevitably attract medical attention, it is difficult to distinguish the natural history of the condition from the outcome of treatment. Ethical issues preclude the use of 'no treatment' control groups in treatment research in this area and whilst waiting list controls can often provide some measure of comparison, these are generally of short duration. We therefore also attempt to identify factors which predict response to treatment. Finally, we review prognostic factors indicating good or poor outcomes.

Making clear statements about outcomes is difficult because of a number of research methodological issues and the consequent shortcomings of many of the treatment trials. For a clinical series (cohort) to provide useful outcome information, it should have the following features:

1   Adequate size.
2   Specified diagnostic criteria.
3   Representativeness: the series should not be selected from the larger eligible population in a way that might distort the outcome findings. Furthermore the size of the total population of subjects under consideration should be specified.
4   Specified follow-up rate: missing data should be accounted for, i.e. it should be specified if they were not traced or refused follow-up: This is particularly crucial in any estimate of mortality.
5   Specified and adequate follow-up period.
6   Outcomes measured using reliable and valid measures.

For a clinical trial reporting outcomes of a particular intervention there ought to be:

1   Recruitment details: e.g. population based or referrals to a specialist centre.
2   A control group or intervention.
3   A fully described intervention (ideally with a manual to assist replication) and a check of adherence to the treatment protocol.
4   Outcome assessment, rated blind to treatment received.
5   Adequate power to detect a difference between groups, if one exists, based on the main outcome measure.
6   Subgroup analysis of those with differential outcome, but only if numbers permit.

Addressing the above poses particular problems in children and adolescents in comparison with adults.

Diagnostic issues

Although both *DSM-IV* and *ICD-10* include detailed criteria for the diagnosis of anorexia nervosa (AN) and bulimia nervosa (BN), many fail to fit these diagnostic categories. Young people with atypical disorders or eating disorders not otherwise specified (EDNOS) make up more than 50 per cent of those presenting to services with clinically significant disorders (Nicholls, Chater, and Lask, 2000).

The diagnosis of AN in particular can be difficult to make in younger cases owing to a degree of overlap with feeding disorders of childhood which may extend into this age range, and atypical disorders such as food avoidance emotional disorder (FAED: Higgs, Goodyer, and Birch 1989). There also appears to be a greater prevalence of symptoms such as obsessive rumination and compulsion which may make for diagnostic uncertainty.

It can be difficult to estimate a child's degree of underweight, particularly when stunting of growth has slowed height (see Chapter 7). In younger subjects, it can also be difficult to elicit psychopathological features. Sometimes this is a developmental issue, the child not having the cognition or communication skills to describe their thoughts and fears. Sometimes the characteristic preoccupation with fatness can be difficult to elicit, either because it does not appear to be present or because the child is scared to reveal their motives for dietary restraint.

Outcome measures

When choosing an outcome measure, it is helpful to consider the following.

Whose perspective is relevant?

A researcher or clinician may not necessarily have the same perspective on outcomes as the young person or their parents, with the former possibly rating clinical measures such as weight gain and hormonal restoration as of major importance, whilst family members may focus on educational or psychosocial adjustment.

What is the important measure?

Combining results from outcome research is hampered by the variable measures used. Many of these may be valid, but care must be exercised in combining results from studies which use different outcomes (Gowers and Bryant-Waugh, 2004). For example, an intervention may predict a good outcome in one area (weight gain) and a poor outcome in another (psychological adjustment).

Many studies report either outcome in one area only (e.g. weight gain or change in self-report scores of abnormal eating cognitions) or a crude outcome such as death.

Recovery

Recovery is an important outcome. Many parents will want to know the likelihood of their son or daughter making a full recovery from a particular intervention, in a specified time. A categorical outcome based on a range of physical and psychosocial variables as used in the Maudsley studies (e.g. Eisler, Dare, Russell, Szmukler, Le Grange, and Dodge, 1997; Eisler, Dare, Hodes, Russell, Dodge, and Le Grange, 2000) may be very helpful. Within this a good outcome of AN implies weight restoration, return of normal hormonal functioning, absence of dieting/purging behaviour and satisfactory psychosocial adjustment. A poor outcome would imply that the subject still fulfilled diagnostic criteria for AN, whether or not there was some improvement, with an intermediate outcome indicating something in between. This would frequently mean weight gain without resumption of menstruation.

Mortality

This is clearly an important outcome and research should distinguish death from an eating disorder, incidental cause, or suicide.

Physical measures

Weight should be expressed with reference to age and height. Endocrine functioning should take into account premorbid pubertal status.

Psychosocial adjustment

This is central to recovery and may well predict weight maintenance or loss after treatment as well as success in, for example, return to education.

Global outcomes

These enable a composite assessment of recovery in a number of domains. Global quantitative measures such as the Eating Disorder Examination, modified for children (Bryant-Waugh, Cooper, Taylor, and Lask 1996) and the Morgan Russell Outcome Assessment Scale (Morgan and Hayward, 1988) enable statistical analysis of change over time.

Outcome

Anorexia nervosa

Outcome can be defined as the long-term result of a pathological process. There has been a recent increase in the outcome literature for AN, including those with adolescent and prepubertal onset. Hsu (1996) outlined the following quality criteria for outcome studies of AN:

- explicitly stated diagnostic criteria
- greater than 25 subjects

- minimum follow-up four years from onset of illness
- failure to trace rate less than 10 per cent
- use of direct interview in greater than 50 per cent
- use of multiple well-defined outcome measures.

Studies following the course of AN in young people often start from the point when they are discharged from treatment, with repeated follow-up assessments, and investigate a range of outcomes – global outcome, change in eating disorder, physical health, mental health, mortality and psychosocial functioning. Some studies have followed young people with AN for up to 24 years.

Global outcome

Global outcome is generally reported as good, intermediate/fair or poor, with good outcome generally equating to full recovery. Steinhausen (2002) systematically reviewed and analysed 119 outcome studies of AN, dividing them into two age groups: those aged less than 17 years at onset and those above 17 years. Overall he found a good outcome in 46.9 per cent, intermediate outcome in 33.5 per cent and a poor outcome in 20.8 per cent, (based on a combined series of 5590 subjects). Outcome was slightly better for normalisation of core symptoms such as menstruation, weight and eating behaviour than good outcome overall. There was a trend towards better outcome in younger patients.

Recent outcome studies following up adolescents with AN confirm this trend, with good outcome between 49 per cent and 75.8 per cent, intermediate outcome between 10.5 per cent and 41 per cent, and poor outcome between 8 per cent and 14 per cent, after ten or more years follow-up (Herpertz-Dahlmann, Müller, Herpertz, Heussen, Hebebrand, and Remschmidt, 2001; Råstam et al., 2003; Saccomani, Savoini, Cirrincione, Vercellino, and Ravera, 1998; Strober, Freeman, and Morrell, 1997).

Bryant-Waugh, Knibbs, Fosson, Kaminski, and Lask (1988) reported on the long-term follow-up of 30 younger children with AN whose initial treatment had been completed more than two years previously. The mean age of onset was 11.7 years and mean length of follow-up was 7.2 years. Outcome measures comprised nutritional state, menstrual function, mental state, psychosexual state and psychosocial adjustment. They reported a good outcome in 62 per cent, an intermediate outcome in 13 per cent and a poor outcome in 25 per cent. Just over a quarter of subjects had required further inpatient treatment. The subjects tended to rate their own progress more favourably than objective measurement.

Rates of recovery usually increase with a longer duration of follow-up. Steinhausen's systematic review found that the number of adolescent onset cases recovering increased from 46 per cent of those followed up for less than four years to 76 per cent of those followed up for longer than ten years.

Nilsson and Hägglöf (2005) meanwhile reported on a series of 68 adolescent females with AN followed up at 8 and 16 years and found that recovery increased from 68 per cent to 85 per cent. Strober et al. (1997) suggested that mean time to recovery ranged between 57 and 79 months and that full recovery was uncommon in the first three years. However, they found that relapse after full recovery was uncommon. It should be noted though that as well as improving outcomes with longer follow-up, most studies have found an increase in reported deaths over time (see below).

Overall, good outcome is achieved in over a half of young people with adolescent onset AN and the literature suggests that further improvements occur with time. Although adolescent onset series report better outcomes than adult onset series, the very young, (particularly prepubertal cases) appear to have poor outcomes (Russell, 1992).

Change in eating disorder

Although many young people with AN make progress over time, a number appear to progress through other eating disorders on the way to recovery. In the long-term follow-up of adolescents diagnosed with AN, between 3 per cent and 6 per cent continue to have AN, between 4 per cent and 9.5 per cent progress to bulimia nervosa (BN) and between 18 per cent and 23 per cent develop EDNOS (Råstam, Gillberg, and Wentz, 2003; Herpertz-Dahlmann et al., 2001; Strober et al., 1997). Råstam et al. (2003) reported that half of their subjects had a lifetime diagnosis of BN. Strober et al. (1997) reported that almost a third of young people with restricting AN developed binge eating during follow-up, though this reduced to none after five years. In their two-year follow-up of 23 young people with AN, Fichter and Quadflieg (1996) found that 30.2 per cent had AN, 21.7 per cent had BN, 47.8 per cent were below any diagnostic threshold and only 18 per cent had no eating disorder.

This recent literature on the progress of adolescent AN to another eating disorder suggests that this is particularly common in the first few years, with further improvements in the longer term. Nilsson and Hägglöf (2005), for example, found that between 8- and 16-year follow-up of 68 subjects showed that rates of AN were steady at 3 per cent, while EDNOS decreased from 24 per cent to 10 per cent and BN reduced from 6 per cent to 1 per cent.

Physical health

Physical outcomes, details of weight and menstrual status are less commonly reported in the literature than global outcomes. Adolescent onset eating disorders may confer a number of physical risks for the future, even if a reasonable degree of recovery is achieved. For example, peak bone mass achieved as a young adult determines bone density and fracture risk later in life. Lucas, Melton, Crowson, and O'Fallon (1999) in a retrospective population-based cohort study found that young women with AN were at increased risk of any fracture later in life. Zipfel, Seibel, Lowe, Beumont, Kasperk, and Herzog (2001) in a prospective study of bone mineral density (BMD) found significantly reduced BMD in chronic binge/purging AN at 3.6 year follow-up, increasing the risk of osteopenia and osteoporosis.

Nilsson and Hägglöf (2005) meanwhile found tooth enamel damage remained after normalisation of eating behaviour. They also reported height increases up to eight years following inpatient treatment of adolescent AN and median BMD increase at both eight and 16 years.

In the longer term, eating disorders may have an impact on those who become pregnant, the literature suggesting that both AN and BN may affect the developing foetus. Kouba, Hällströn, Lindholm and Hirschberg (2005) found that women with previous or active eating disorders gave birth to a higher number of infants with low body weight, small head circumference and microcephaly and they were often small for gestational age. They also found that 22 per cent of women had a relapse of their eating disorder during pregnancy.

Mental health

Young people with AN have been found to have a number of psychiatric difficulties or personality disorders at follow-up. It is important to distinguish between those present at the time of diagnosis, which may influence outcome, from those that may be an outcome of having AN. Steinhausen (2002) found a large proportion of additional psychiatric disorders including anxiety disorders, phobias, affective disorders, substance misuse disorders, obsessive compulsive disorder (OCD) and personality disorders at follow-up.

Herpertz-Dahlmann et al. (2001) reported that at ten-year follow-up a half of their adolescent subjects had an Axis I psychiatric disorder and almost a quarter had a personality disorder. However, long-term recovered subjects were no more likely than controls to have a current psychiatric diagnosis or personality disorder. Råstam et al. (2003) found that almost all young people with AN had a lifetime diagnosis of an affective disorder, but this was present in only 10 per cent at ten-year follow-up. Nilsson and Hägglöf (2005) also found that mental health problems decreased with follow-up of 16 years. However, 15 per cent of subjects considered their mental health to be bad or very bad.

Mortality

The majority of outcome studies on AN report crude mortality rates, though standard mortality rates (SMR – observed mortality divided by expected mortality) are easier to interpret. Mortality in adolescent AN is said to be higher than in other psychiatric disorders, reported as high as 15 per cent in some studies (Herzog, Rathner, and Vandereycken, 1992).

In the series reviewed by Steinhausen (2002) the mean crude mortality rate was reported as 5 per cent. This was lower in adolescent onset AN compared with the adult condition and he concluded more deaths were expected with increasing age at onset and also with length of follow-up. Bryant-Waugh et al. (1988) found two deaths in their series of childhood onset AN. A boy aged 14 died from an unrelated asthma attack and a girl aged 12 died from complications of a ruptured oesophagus. Nilsson and Hägglöf (2005) found one death in their sample of 76 subjects. This death occurred within eight years due to cardiac failure following intravenous nutrition, at the age of 23 years.

Nielsen, Moller-Madsen, Isager, Jorgensen, Pagsberg, and Theander (1998) reviewed ten eating disordered populations and found that the standardised mortality rate was raised in AN, particularly for subjects presenting aged 20 to 29 years, in which it was three times higher than expected. The SMR was 3.1 in childhood onset AN and 3.2 in adolescent onset AN. The highest mortality was in the first year after presentation in females and in the first two years after presentation in males. In females the risk of death was 2 per cent in the first year, with an annual risk of death of 0.59 per cent thereafter. In males the risk of death was 5 per cent in the first two years and then 0 per cent. They found that the length of follow-up had an inverse effect on SMR, but this was significantly increased for at least 15 years after presentation. A lower weight at presentation was associated with higher SMR; overall though, this was not found in children with AN. More deaths were found to be due to suicide and other/unknown causes and fewer due to the eating disorder than previously reported.

Psychosocial functioning

Hsu, Crisp, and Harding (1979) found disturbed family relationships in 40 per cent of patients at follow-up. In the follow-up of 22 subjects over the age of 18 years, Bryant-Waugh et al. (1988) found two subjects were married and both had children. At least four other women were cohabiting. Nilsson and Hägglöf (2005) found 17 per cent of subjects avoided sexual relationships at 16-year follow-up. They also reported a significant difference in sexuality, number of children and social contacts in subjects recovered at 16 years compared to those who still had an eating disorder.

Bulimia nervosa

There are few long-term outcome studies in BN focusing on children and adolescents. Many adults with BN report symptoms starting in adolescence. Outcome studies in the literature are mainly prospective and exclusively of females.

Global outcomes

Steinhausen (1999) reviewed 24 studies of BN, with a total of 1383 patients. The age of onset ranged from 14 years and 4 months to 22 years and 2 months. Full recovery was reported in 47.5 per cent, intermediate outcome in 26 per cent and poor outcome in 26 per cent, after a mean follow-up of 2.5 years.

Quadflieg and Fichter's (2003) literature review found a steady rate of recovery with increasing length of follow-up. Good outcome was observed in 28 per cent to 78 per cent after 6 months to 1 year, 38 per cent to 69 per cent after 1.5 to 2 years, 13 per cent to 77 per cent after 3 to 6 years and 47 per cent to 73 per cent after 9 to 11 years. Between two thirds and three-quarters of women with BN show at least partial recovery after ten-year follow-up. Relapse rates varied considerably between studies. There were lower relapse rates with longer follow-up. Poor outcome was observed in 3 per cent to 67 per cent after 6 months to 1 year, 5 per cent to 50 per cent after 1.5 to 2 years, 19 per cent to 87 per cent after 3 to 6 years and 9 per cent to 30 per cent after 9 to 11 years. One-quarter of women may still have BN after ten-year follow-up.

Change in eating disorder

Progression from BN to AN is much less common than the reverse. Quadflieg and Fichter (2003) reported that there is some evidence to suggest cross-over from BN to EDNOS. However, interpretation is difficult as this finding could reflect partial recovery or the development of subsyndromal disorders.

Physical health

Zipfel et al. (2001) found bone mineral density (BMD) to be within the normal range for recovered and chronic BN at 3.6 year follow-up, suggesting no increased risk of osteopenia or osteoporosis.

Mental health

Patton, Coffey, and Sawyer (2003) found higher rates of depression and alcohol consumption in adolescents with bulimia partial syndrome, suggesting that this condition might be better viewed as a variant of early onset affective disorder.

Mortality

Steinhausen (1999) found an average crude mortality rate of 0.7 per cent, with a range of 0 per cent to 6 per cent. Nielsen et al. (1998) found no firm evidence that SMR was raised in BN. Quadflieg and Fichter (2003) reported that it was difficult to identify a cause of death directly attributable to the specific eating habits of BN.

Psychosocial functioning

Quadflieg and Fichter (2003) found that improvements in social functioning were observed over time, and subjects with a good global outcome showed a better social outcome. Social outcome (based on leisure activity and having confidantes) was reported as good in 52.1 per cent, intermediate in 22.4 per cent and poor in 25.5 per cent, at six-year follow-up. Outcome in terms of sexual adjustment was reported less favourably, with good outcome in 40 per cent, intermediate outcome in 17.6 per cent and poor outcome in 42.4 per cent of subjects, after six-year follow-up.

Eating disorder not otherwise specified (EDNOS)

Eating disorder not otherwise specified (EDNOS) covers a range of eating difficulties not fulfilling criteria for either AN or BN. There is disagreement in the literature as to the progression of this diagnosis to others and there is little on the natural course and outcome. Patton et al. (2003) performed a prospective community-based study, following up 982 female participants over six years. They found that 8.8 per cent reported an eating disorder across the six-year period. Out of 55 subjects with any eating disorder in adolescence, 11 per cent had persisting eating difficulties into young adulthood. They concluded that the lifetime experience of subsyndromal eating disorders are quite high in young women, but in many are self-limiting.

Outcome of treatment

Anorexia nervosa

AN in children and adolescents is a very visible disorder in which weight loss and food avoidance are readily evident to family members, peers and school teachers. It is difficult therefore for the young person to escape detection and attempts to direct them towards treatment. As a result there are no large series of untreated young people from which to ascertain the natural history of the condition. For similar reasons, it is difficult to gauge the impact of treatment; that is the extent to which treatment improves the outcome over and above no treatment. One attempt, however, a medium sized (n = 90) randomised controlled trial (RCT) of three treatments versus no treatment, in a mixed age (14–30) series (Crisp et al., 1991), showed better outcomes for the three treated groups compared to the no treatment group. In this section we will review the main evidence for the effectiveness of different treatments, which are discussed more fully in the relevant treatment chapters.

Physical treatments

FOOD SUPPLEMENTS, NASOGASTRIC AND PARENTERAL FEEDING

Food supplements and dietary alternatives to food are generally given either in cases of severe physical concern or in situations of non-compliance with normal eating. The UK National Institute for Health and Clinical Excellence (NICE) guideline (2004) found that there was limited evidence that nasogastric feeding but not total parenteral nutrition (TPN) produced greater weight gain than standard care. There was little or no evidence of their acceptability to patients or their impact on core eating disorder psychopathology. TPN was associated with high levels of adverse effects. The guideline concluded that feeding against the will of the patient should be a treatment of last resort in AN and that TPN should not be given unless there was evidence of gastrointestinal dysfunction which precluded enteral feeding. One small trial of zinc supplementation to an inpatient treatment regime in subjects aged over 15 suggested that rates of daily weight gain were greater in the zinc supplementation group despite nearly all subjects having zinc levels in the normal range before embarking on treatment (Birmingham, Goldner, and Bakan 1994). However, the NICE guideline concluded there was insufficient evidence to support its use and this finding requires replication.

PHARMACOLOGICAL AGENTS

Randomised controlled trials have examined a range of drugs in low weight AN, though almost exclusively in adults.

Antidepressants   Antidepressants have been used to promote eating and weight gain and also to relieve depressive symptoms when these are present comorbidly. The use of selective serotonin reuptake inhibitor antidepressants (SSRIs) in children and adolescents is difficult to evaluate currently whilst major reservations exist about their use in childhood depression (Whittington et al., 2004).

Three RCTs of SSRIs (two with fluoxetine, Attia, Haiman, Walsh, and Flater, 1998; Kaye et al., 2001; and one with citalopram, Fassino et al., 2002) failed to find advantages of active drug over placebo or no treatment for weight gain, maintenance or eating behaviour, though the citalopram study reported a trend towards a greater improvement in mood symptoms in the group receiving the active drug. A trial of the tricyclic antidepressant amitriptyline meanwhile in 48 early onset cases (mean age 16.6 years) failed to find an advantage relative to placebo (Biederman et al., 1985).

Major tranquillisers/neuroleptic drugs   These are sometimes used to reduce extreme anxiety or because of their noted potential to increase appetite. A systematic review found no convincing evidence of any beneficial effect of these drugs in AN, whilst concerns were expressed about their potential to prolong the electrocardiographic QT interval, which is often already increased in AN (Treasure and Schmidt, 2004). This may add to the risk of severe cardiac complications already conferred by emaciation.

Psychological therapies

Given that the physical manifestations of AN are largely viewed as secondary to the psychological disorder, it would seem logical that those receiving psychological therapies would have better outcomes than those without. In practice the evidence to support psychological therapies is limited. On the basis of a meta-analysis of three studies, however, the NICE guideline concluded that there was limited evidence that a range of psychological treatments with more therapeutic contact was superior to 'treatment as usual' with a lower rate of contact, both in terms of weight gain and proportion of patients recovered (NICE, 2004).

The psychotherapy trials in the literature are notable for their small size and hence lack of power and also the presence of confounding treatments. A number have compared individual treatments to family-based treatments, but most would view it as difficult or inappropriate to deliver a treatment to a young person without providing at least some family intervention alongside. Thus, in one randomised study comparing individual therapy with family therapy, those receiving the individual therapy option also received parental counselling (Robin et al., 1999). Some trials are also difficult to interpret, as a variable number of subjects have received inpatient treatment alongside the therapy under investigation.

Although there have been a few small (adult) trials of cognitive behavioural therapy (CBT), cognitive analytic therapy (CAT), interpersonal therapy (IPT) and focal psychodynamic therapy, in general there is insufficient evidence to conclude advantages of any specialist psychotherapy over another (NICE, 2004).

Despite the clear role of abnormal specific and non-specific abnormal cognitions in AN, there are few studies of individual CBT-based treatments (Gowers, 2006, Gowers and Bryant-Waugh, 2004). The published studies (Channon, De Silva, Hemsley, and Perkins, 1989, Pike, Walsh, Vitousek, Wilson, and Bauer, 2003, Serfaty, 1998) suggest that CBT may be moderately effective but possibly no more so than other therapies. One relatively large RCT (Gowers et al., 2006) found no advantages for a specialist outpatient CBT programme over generic child mental health service treatment (which may have had some CBT elements but generally included more family interventions) at one or two years.

The most impressive findings relate to family therapies in this age group, (Lock and Gowers, in press) but some caution should be used in interpreting the findings. First, the studies tend to be very small. Second, different studies employ a different entry point (i.e. subjects may enter the trial at low weight as in Lock, Agras, Bryson, and Kraemer, 2005; or after inpatient weight restoration as in the Maudsley study, Eisler et al., 1997). Finally, despite the relatively good body of evidence suggesting the benefit of family interventions, uncertainty exists about which families benefit and the optimal style of treatment. Eisler et al. (2000), for example, showed that the outcomes were very poor for conjoint family therapy in the presence of high maternal expressed emotion. It may be that such families do better when the family intervention is delivered as parental guidance, without the child being present.

Multifamily day therapy aims to help family members learn by identifying with members of other families with the same condition, by analogy. It is generally delivered within a day hospital programme, in which up to ten families with an adolescent with anorexia attend a mixture of whole family group discussions, parallel meetings of parents and adolescents and creative activities. Preparation of lunch and communal eating is a central part of the programme. This treatment is at an early stage of evaluation but preliminary findings suggest a high degree of acceptability and promising outcomes, particularly in terms of a reduced need for hospitalisation (Scholtz and Asen, 2001).

Service issues

Medical inpatient admission is necessary and unavoidable in cases of severe physical compromise or where initiation of feeding can not be achieved on an outpatient basis. However, the role of inpatient management in improving recovery from AN as opposed to achieving physical stability is unclear. To date two RCTs (Crisp et al., 1991; Gowers et al., 2006) have failed to show a benefit for inpatient management over outpatient treatment at two-year follow-up, the latter in an adolescent-only series. The TOuCAN trial (Gowers et al., 2006) showed that the one-year outcomes of those who were initially assigned outpatient management but later transferred to inpatient management on clinical grounds were especially poor, this naturalistic outcome replicating a finding from a cohort study in which only 3/21 young people with anorexia treated as inpatients had fully recovered four years later (Gowers, Weetman, Shore, Hossain, and Elvins, 2000).

Increasingly, day programmes are being developed in an effort to reduce costs, but more importantly to avoid potentially negative consequences of inpatient admission. Significant therapeutic factors may include the importance of mobilising resources within the family and the multifamily day unit approach (Scholtz and Asen, 2001) is yielding promising early findings in this regard.

Bulimia nervosa

Bulimia, being easier to hide from parental or medical attention, is a condition that frequently goes untreated for several years before, often in young adulthood, the sufferer seeks help as they realise the condition is interfering with health or social functioning. Anecdotally we know from adult series of bulimia that the mean length of history before presentation is often seven to ten years (Fairburn and Harrison, 2003), suggesting that outcome without treatment has in these cases been poor. What we do not know here is how many young people have made a full recovery without treatment and therefore do not later present to adult services.

Physical treatments

Selective serotonin reuptake inhibitors (SSRIs) have been shown in adults to improve symptoms of bulimia and also mood, though long-term follow-up data are scarce, suggesting possibly that beneficial effects are obtained only while on the drugs. One systematic review found no differences in outcome between antidepressants and CBT (Bacaltchuk and Hay, 2003).

Psychological therapies

There is now quite a substantial body of literature to suggest that a course of cognitive behavioural therapy specifically designed for bulimia (Fairburn, Marcus, and Wilson 1993) reduces bulimic symptoms and improves non-specific symptoms of depression compared to waiting list controls (Hay and Bacaltchuk, 2004). A further RCT (Agras, Walsh, Fairburn, Wilson, and Kraemer, 2000) found CBT was more effective than interpersonal therapy (IPT) in producing abstinence by the end of treatment, but the differences were lost by 8- and 12-month follow-up. To date, however, the treatment evidence base for adolescents with the condition is very limited.

Service issues

All the current evidence-based treatments for BN are delivered on an out-patient basis, with inpatient management being reserved for extreme severity, comorbidity or suicidal risk. The outcome of inpatient management has not been fully evaluated.

Self-help

Manualised CBT-based self-help programmes may help overcome the sensitivities of young people to discussing embarrassing behaviours and enable them to work on their problems in their own time. Pure and 'guided' forms have been tested on adults with early promising results when self-help was combined with fluoxetine (Mitchell et al., 2001). A multicentre internet-based self-help programme is currently under investigation in the UK.

'Transdiagnostic' approaches

Fairburn and Harrison (2003) have argued that existing classification systems are unsatisfactory and that there are more features in common between the eating disorder categories than differences. They therefore propose a 'transdiagnostic' approach to treatment, based on the established CBT for bulimia programme. This is currently being evaluated.

Prognosis

Prognosis is defined as the means to make a forecast or prediction about the probable course and the final outcome of a disease. A number of outcome studies of early onset AN have looked at prognostic predictors, that is, variables present at the onset of the disorder influencing outcome. So far, the literature has been largely conflicting with few consistent findings. Motivation to change and degree of psychological concern with weight and shape may be amongst the most important in predicting outcome.

Anorexia nervosa

Age of onset

An older age of onset (above 20 years) is often reported as having a poorer outcome (Hsu et al., 1979). A number of recent reports have found a better prognosis with younger age of onset (Deter, Schellberg, Köpp, Friederich, and Herzog, 2005; Ratnasuriya, Eisler, Szmukler, and Russell, 1991). However, Strober et al. (1997) found age of onset to have no significant effect and Steinhausen (2002) concluded that findings were ambiguous on the basis of his large systematic review. It may be that the early onset cases comprise two groups with different outcomes linked to their pubertal status (see below).

Gender and socioeconomic status

There is no conclusive evidence that gender has a significant effect on outcome of AN. Neither does socioeconomic status appear to have a significant effect on outcome (Steinhausen, 1999).

Physical status

Outcome for prepubertal onset AN has been reported as poorer than adolescent onset AN. Bryant-Waugh et al. (1998) found a poor prognosis in their study and a young age of onset was positively correlated with low weight at follow-up. The outcome seems to be particularly poor in the group that have premorbid developmental abnormalities (Steinhausen, 1999). Low BMI at presentation is often reported as predicting a poorer outcome (Casper and Jabine, 1996; Gowers and Bryant-Waugh, 2004; Hsu et al., 1979). Steinhausen (2002) found the literature on this to be unclear. Bryant-Waugh et al. (1988) meanwhile found low BMI did not influence prognosis in their early onset AN study.

Eating disorder symptoms

Various symptoms associated with AN have been reported to affect outcome and a shorter duration of symptoms at presentation seems favourable (Hsu et al., 1979; Ratnasuriya et al., 1991; Steinhausen, 2002). However, this finding was not found in the Great Ormond St Hospital early onset series (Bryant-Waugh et al., 1988).

The bulimic subtype, i.e. vomiting, bulimia and purgative abuse, has been consistently found to predict a poor outcome (Gowers and Bryant-Waugh, 2004; Hsu et al. 1979; Steinhausen, 2002). Strober et al. (1997) found binge eating was not a predictor of long-term chronicity. Steinhausen (2002) reported that hyperactivity and dieting were not significant predictors of outcome. However, excessive exercise has been reported to predict a poor outcome (Casper and Jabine, 1996; Strober et al., 1997). Unsurprisingly, chronicity in AN predicts an unfavourable prognosis (Steinhausen, 2002) and good outcome at five years predicts a good long-term outcome (Ratnasuriya et al., 1991).

Life events

Life event research is often hampered by the poor quality of self-report life event questionnaires. However, North, Gowers, and Bryam (1997), using a standardised semi-structured interview, found that a severe negative life event occurring in the year before onset predicted a good outcome two years later, on the hypothesised basis that overcoming the life event reduced the need for the eating disorder as a coping strategy.

Comorbidity

Outcome is often reported as less favourable in the presence of other psychiatric disorders, suicidal behaviour, personality disorder or substance abuse. Comorbid mood disorders are well documented but the relationship between these and outcome is unclear. North and Gowers (1999) found greater improvement in eating disorder symptomatology at two years in adolescents with AN who had comorbid depression at presentation compared to those without comorbidity. However, Bryant-Waugh et al. (1988) found that depressive features during the initial illness in prepubertal AN conferred a poor prognosis. Saccomani at al. (1998) reported that mood and personality disorders predicted a poor outcome and that anxiety disorders had no prognostic value.

Steinhausen (2002) found that 25 per cent of patients with AN had anxiety disorders and 25 per cent had mood disorders at follow-up. He also found that OCD had no effect on outcome. Different personality disorders may affect prognosis. Steinhausen (2002) found that a histrionic personality predicted a favourable outcome, whereas an obsessive-compulsive personality predicted an unfavourable outcome. Saccomani et al. (1998) found that borderline personality disorder showed a tendency towards chronicity and poorer outcome.

Family functioning

Poor childhood social adjustment predicts poor outcome and disturbed relationships with or between parents predicted poor outcome in one study (Hsu et al., 1979). Conversely, a good parent–child relationship appears to be associated with a favourable outcome (Steinhausen, 2002). North et al. (1997) found that poor family functioning (based on the McMaster model) as rated by either a clinician or the young person predicted a poor outcome at one and two years, whilst the parent's assessment of their family's functioning had no predictive power. Bryant-Waugh et al. (1988) found a number of family structures which predicted a poor outcome in prepubertal onset AN: one-parent families, families in which one or both parents had been married before and families with several generations living together.

Bulimia nervosa

There is little on prognostic factors for BN in the literature and NICE (2004) provide no prognostic indicators for adolescents.

Age of onset

It is unclear whether age of onset predicts outcome in BN (Steinhausen, 1999).

Eating disorder symptoms

Although not conclusive, Quadflieg and Fichter (2003) found that a short duration of symptoms at presentation may predict a better outcome. They also found that more severe symptoms at presentation predicted a poorer outcome. A history of AN did not affect outcome per se, though low body weight was considered a negative predictor. Vomiting and laxative abuse are reported to predict a poor outcome (Steinhausen, 1999). Frequency of vomiting seems to be a better predictor than binge frequency (Quadflieg and Fichter, 2003). Steinhausen (1999) reported that frequency of bulimic episodes did not affect outcome.

Comorbidity

Quadflieg and Fichter (2003) found evidence that comorbid Axis I psychiatric diagnoses influenced the outcome of BN contradictory. However, they concluded that certain comorbid personality disorders (i.e. borderline and Cluster B personality disorders) predicted an unfavourable outcome.

Steinhausen (1999) concluded that the presence of substance misuse or obesity did not predict outcome.

Quadflieg and Fichter (2003) reported low self-esteem as a predictor of poor outcome. This seemed particularly influential when combined with high perfectionism and self-perceived overweight. They also suggested that patients with additional impulsive behaviours had a poorer outcome than those without them. Self-harm and alcohol abuse predict a negative outcome (Steinhausen, 1999).

Family functioning

It is unclear whether family features are predictive of outcome in BN. Quadflieg and Fichter (2003) reported ambiguous findings for those with a family history of depression or alcohol abuse. They reported that a stable relationship did not predict outcome, but that an unstable relationship predicted a poor outcome.

Socioeconomic status

There is no conclusive evidence that socioeconomic status has a significant effect on outcome of BN (Quadflieg and Fichter, 2003).

Conclusions

Recent years have shown an increase in understanding of the outcomes of eating disorders treated in a range of services. Most of the outcome data are from adult patients, though increasingly information is emerging from series of children and adolescents, some from meta-analysis of smaller case series. Less is known of the outcomes of the very youngest patients. The outcome of adolescent BN is less well understood than that of AN. The impact of treatment and the relative merits of different approaches is less clear. In particular, psychological therapies have not been tested in adequately powered randomised controlled trials. Prognostic factors suggest that lack of family and social supports and emerging abnormal personality development adversely affect recovery. Further research may help us identify at the earliest stage, which patients may benefit from the most intensive therapies, including hospital admission, so that we can target interventions effectively.

References

Agras, W.S., Walsh, B.T., Fairburn, C.G., Wilson, G.T., and Kraemer, H.C. (2000). A multicenter comparison of cognitive-behavioral therapy and interpersonal psychotherapy for bulimia nervosa. *Archives of General Psychiatry, 57*, 459–466.

Attia, E., Haiman, C., Walsh, B.T., and Flater, S.R. (1998). Does fluoxetine augment the inpatient treatment of anorexia nervosa? *American Journal of Psychiatry, 155*, 548–551.

Bacaltchuk, J., and Hay, P. (2003). Antidepressants versus psychological treatments and their combination for people with bulimia nervosa. *Cochrane Review*, Cochrane Library Issue 1, Oxford.

Biederman, J., Herzog, D.B., Rivinus, T.M., et al. (1985). Amitriptyline in the treatment of anorexia nervosa: A double blind, placebo controlled trial. *Journal of Clinical Psychopharmacology, 5*, 10–16.

Birmingham, C.L., Goldner, E.M., and Bakan, R. (1994). Controlled trial of zinc supplementation in anorexia nervosa. *International Journal of Eating Disorders, 15*, 251–255.

Bryant-Waugh, R., Cooper, P., Taylor, C., and Lask, B. (1996). The use of the eating disorder examination with children: A pilot study. *International Journal of Eating Disorders, 19*, 391–398.

Bryant-Waugh, R., Knibbs, J., Fosson, A., Kaminski, Z., and Lask, B. (1988). Long term follow up of patients with early onset anorexia nervosa. *Archives of Disease in Childhood, 63*, 5–9.

Casper, R.C., and Jabine, L.N. (1996). An eight year follow-up: Outcome of adolescent compared to adult onset anorexia nervosa. *Journal of Youth and Adolescence, 25* (4), 499–517.

Channon, S., De Silva, P., Hemsley, D., and Perkins, R. (1989). A controlled trial of cognitive behavioural and behavioural treatment of anorexia nervosa. *Behaviour Research and Therapy, 27*, 529–535.

Crisp, A.H., Norton, K.W.R., Gowers, S.G., Halek, C., Levett, G., Yeldham, D., et al. (1991). A controlled study of the effect of therapies aimed at adolescent and family psychopathology in anorexia nervosa. *British Journal of Psychiatry, 159*, 325–333.

Deter, H.C., Schellberg, D., Köpp, W., Friederich, H.C., Herzog, W. (2005). Predictability of a favourable outcome in anorexia nervosa. *European Psychiatry, 20* (2), 165–172.

Eisler, I., Dare, C., Hodes, M., Russell, G.F.M., Dodge, E., and Le Grange, D. (2000). Family therapy for adolescent anorexia nervosa: The results of a controlled comparison of two family interventions. *Journal of Child Psychology and Psychiatry, 41*, 727–736.

Eisler, I., Dare, C., Russell, G.F.M., Szmukler, G., Le Grange, D., and Dodge, E. (1997). Family and individual therapy in anorexia nervosa. A 5-year follow-up. *Archives of General Psychiatry, 54*, 1025–1030.

Fairburn, C.G., and Harrison, P.J. (2003). Eating disorders. *The Lancet, 361*, 407–416.

Fairburn, C.G., Marcus, M.D., and Wilson, G.T. (1993). Cognitive-behavioral therapy for binge eating and bulimia nervosa: A comprehensive treatment manual.

In C.G. Fairburn and G.T. Wilson (Eds.), *Binge eating: Nature, assessment and treatment* (pp. 361–404). New York: Guilford Press.

Fassino, S., Leombruni, P., Daga, G., Brustolin, A., Migliaretti, G., Cavallo, F., et al. (2002). Efficacy of citalopram in anorexia nervosa: A pilot study. *European Neuropsychopharmacology, 12*, 453–459.

Fichter, M.M., and Quadflieg, N. (1996). Course and two year outcome in anorexic and bulimic adolescents. *Journal of Youth and Adolescence, 25* (4), 545–563.

Gowers, S.G. (2006). Evidence based research in CBT with adolescent eating disorders. *Child and Adolescent Mental Health, 11* (1), 9–12.

Gowers, S., and Bryant-Waugh, R. (2004). Management of child and adolescent eating disorders: The current evidence base and future directions. *Journal of Child Psychology and Psychiatry, 45* (1), 63–83.

Gowers, S.G., Clark, A., Roberts, C., Shore, A., Edwards, V., Bryan, C., et al. (2006). Two year outcomes of a randomised controlled trial for adolescent anorexia nervosa – (the TOuCAN trial). Abstract presented at AED International Conference, Barcelona.

Gowers, S.G., Weetman, J., Shore, A., Hossain, F., and Elvins, R. (2000). The impact of hospitalisation on the outcome of adolescent anorexia nervosa. *British Journal of Psychiatry, 176*, 138–141.

Hay, P., and Bacaltchuk, J. (2004). Bulimia nervosa. *Clinical Evidence – Mental Health*, 33–46.

Herpertz-Dahlmann, B., Müller, B., Herpertz, S., Heussen, N., Hebebrand, J., and Remschmidt, H. (2001). Prospective 10-year follow-up in adolescent anorexia nervosa – course, outcome, psychiatric morbidity and psychosocial adaptation. *Journal of Child Psychology and Psychiatry, 42* (5), 603–612.

Herzog, W., Rathner, G., and Vandereycken, W. (1992). Long term course of anorexia nervosa. A review of the literature. In W. Herzog, J. Detre, and W. Vandereycken (Eds.), *The course of eating disorders* (pp. 15–29). Berlin: Springer Verlag.

Higgs, J., Goodyer, I.M., and Birch, J. (1989). Anorexia nervosa and food avoidance emotional disorder. *Archives of Disease in Childhood, 64*, 346–351.

Hsu, L.K.G. (1996). Outcome of early onset anorexia nervosa: What do we know? *Journal of Youth and Adolescence, 25* (4), 563–569.

Hsu, L.K., Crisp, A.H., and Harding, B. (1979). Outcome of anorexia nervosa. *The Lancet*, 61–65.

Kaye, W.H., Nagata, T., Weltzin, T.E., Hsu, G., Sokol, M.S., Conaha, C.M., et al. (2001). Double-blind placebo controlled administration of fluoxetine in restricting- and restricting-purging-type anorexia nervosa. *Biological Psychiatry, 49*, 644–652.

Kouba, S., Hällström, T., Lindholm, C., and Hirschberg, A.L. (2005). Pregnancy and neonatal outcomes in women with eating disorders. *Obstetrics and Gynaecology, 105* (2), 255–60.

Lock, J., Agras, W., Bryson, S., and Kraemer, H. (2005). A comparison of short and long term family therapy for adolescent anorexia nervosa. *Journal of the American Academy of Child and Adolescent Psychiatry, 44*, 632–639.

Lock, J., and Gowers, S.G. (in press). Effective interventions for anorexia nervosa in adolescence. *Journal of Mental Health.*

Lucas, A.R., Melton, L.J., Crowson, C.S., and O'Fallon, W.M. (1999). Long-term fracture risk among women with anorexia nervosa: A population based cohort study. *Mayo Clinic Proceedings, 74*, 972–977.

Mitchell, J.E., Fletcher, L., Hanson, K., et al. (2001). The relative efficacy of fluoxetine and manual based self help in the treatment of outpatients with bulimia nervosa. *Journal of Clinical Psychopharmacology*, *21*, 298–304.

Morgan, H.G., and Hayward, A.E. (1988). Clinical assessment of anorexia nervosa. The Morgan-Russell Assessment Schedule. *British Journal of Psychiatry*, *152*, 367–372.

National Institute for Health and Clinical Excellence (NICE, 2004). *Eating disorders: Core interventions in the treatment and management of anorexia nervosa, bulimia nervosa and related eating disorders: A national clinical practice guideline.* London: NICE.

Nicholls, D., Chater, R., and Lask, B. (2000). Children into DSM don't go: A comparison of classification systems for eating disorders in children and early adolescence. *International Journal of Eating Disorders*, *28*, 317–324.

Nielsen, S., Moller-Madsen, S., Isager, T., Jorgensen, J., Pagsberg, K., and Theander, S. (1998) Standardized mortality in eating disorders – a quantitative summary of previously published and new evidence. *Journal of Psychosomatic Research*, *44*, 413–434.

Nilsson, K., and Hägglöf, B. (2005). Long-term follow-up of adolescent anorexia nervosa in Northern Sweden. *European Eating Disorders Review*, *13*, 89–100.

North, C., and Gowers, S. (1999). Anorexia nervosa, psychopathology and outcome. *International Journal of Eating Disorders*, *26*, 386–391.

North, C., Gowers, S., and Bryam, V. (1997). Family functioning and life events in the outcome of adolescent anorexia nervosa. *British Journal of Psychiatry*, *171*, 545–549.

Patton, G.C., Coffey, C., and Sawyer, S.M. (2003). The outcome of adolescent eating disorders: Findings from the Victorian Adolescent Health Cohort Study. *European Child and Adolescent Psychiatry*, *12*, 25–29.

Pike, K.M., Walsh, B.T., Vitousek, K., Wilson, G.T., and Bauer, J. (2003). Cognitive behavioral therapy in the post-hospital treatment of anorexia nervosa. *American Journal of Psychiatry*, *160*, 2046–2049.

Quadflieg, N., and Fichter, M. (2003). The course and outcome of bulimia nervosa. *European Child and Adolescent Psychiatry*, *12*, 99–109.

Råstam, M., Gillberg, C., and Wentz, E. (2003). Outcome of teenage-onset anorexia nervosa in a Swedish community-based sample. *European Child and Adolescent Psychiatry*, *12*, 78–90.

Ratnasuriya, R.H., Eisler, I., Szmukler, G., and Russell, G.F. (1991). Anorexia nervosa: Outcome and prognostic factors after 20 years. *British Journal of Psychiatry*, *158*, 495–502.

Robin, A.L., Siegel, P.T., Moye, A.W., Gilroy, M., Dennis, A.B., and Sikand, A. (1999). A controlled comparison of family versus individual therapy for adolescents with anorexia nervosa. *Journal of the American Academy of Child and Adolescent Psychiatry*, *38*, 1482–1489.

Russell, G.F.M. (1992). Anorexia nervosa of early onset and its impact on puberty. In P. Cooper (Ed.), *Feeding problems and eating disorders in children and adolescents* (pp. 85–112). Chur: Harwood Academic.

Saccomani, L., Savoini, M., Cirrincione, M., Vercellino, F., and Ravera, G. (1998). Long-term outcome of children and adolescents with anorexia nervosa: Study of comorbidity. *Journal of Psychosomatic Research*, *44* (5), 565–571.

Scholtz, M., and Asen, E. (2001). Multiple family therapy with eating disordered adolescents. *European Eating Disorders Review*, *9*, 33–42.

Serfaty, M.A. (1998). Cognitive therapy versus dietary counseling in the out-patient treatment of anorexia nervosa. *European Eating Disorders Review*, *7*, 334–350.

Steinhausen, H.C. (1999). Eating disorders. In H.C. Steinhausen and F. Verhulst (Eds.), *Risks and outcomes in developmental psychopathology* (pp. 210–230). Oxford: Oxford University Press.

Steinhausen, H.C. (2002). The outcome of anorexia nervosa in the twentieth century. *American Journal of Psychiatry*, *159* (8), 1284–1293.

Strober, M., Freeman, R., and Morrell, W. (1997). The long-term course of severe anorexia nervosa in adolescents: Survival analysis of recovery, relapse, and outcome predictors over 10–15 years in a prospective study. *International Journal of Eating Disorders*, *22*, 339–360.

Treasure, J., and Schmidt, U. (2004). Anorexia nervosa. *Clinical Evidence – Mental Health*, 1–12.

Whittington, C., Kendall, T., Fonagy, P., et al. (2004). Selective serotonin reuptake inhibitors in childhood depression – a systematic review of published versus unpublished data. *The Lancet*, *363*, 1341–1345.

Zipfel, S., Seibel, M.J., Lowe, B., Beumont, P.J., Kasperk, C., and Herzog, W. (2001). Osteoporosis in eating disorders: A follow-up study of patients with anorexia and bulimia. *Journal of Clinical Endocrinology and Metabolism*, *86*, 5227–5233.

Part III

Assessment and treatment

7 Clinical assessment and physical complications

Leora Pinhas, Cathleen M. Steinegger and Debra K. Katzman

Introduction

A complete assessment of a child or adolescent with an eating disorder (ED) is both similar to and different from the assessment of other psychological disorders. It does require a complete and careful psychological assessment. This may include a structured, semi-structured or free form interview and self-administered standardised questionnaires. Similarly, it usually includes a family assessment. However, unlike other areas of child and adolescent mental health, an ED assessment requires a nutritional assessment, a thorough medical history and physical examination, and appropriate laboratory tests. The family approach to assessment and treatment is covered in Chapter 12.

While a medically trained professional can in theory perform a complete paediatric ED assessment, the literature recommends that the assessment be performed by an interdisciplinary team (e.g. Golden et al., 2003). This approach is both more efficient and more effective. An interdisciplinary team includes two or more people, each of whom brings a different expertise to the process of assessment. The team may include, but is not limited to, a psychiatrist or psychologist, a pediatrician, a nurse, a dietitian, and social worker. The composition of the interdisciplinary team will vary depending on resource availability and geographic location.

Another important potential difference in an ED assessment is that the child with an ED may not be a willing participant in the process. Most children struggling with medical or mental health issues usually experience distress and understand that it is related to or caused by their disorder. They usually want treatment to relieve their symptoms. Children with EDs may not perceive a problem and may not believe that there is any need to change. Often it is the parents who seek help. Therefore, assessing a child individually without any input from an adult, either the parent or at the very least the referring health-care provider, may result in an inconclusive or misleading assessment. Beginning with a family assessment, or at a minimum having an initial meeting with the child and parents together, is often useful. Some children come to an assessment planning to avoid any discussion around eating. However, they often change their minds once the parents reveal explicitly the child's struggles and voice their concerns.

Preparation for the assessment

Creating a respectful relationship with the child is important to the success of the assessment. This is accomplished by working to develop an alliance with her. An alliance is developed in the initial stages of the assessment and is strengthened, as the process continues, by providing a safe, empathic, non-judgemental environment for the child. The team members providing the assessment should introduce themselves and their roles to both the child and parent. A description of what is to happen during the assessment and how long it will take should also be reviewed.

Confidentiality is particularly important for patients seeking psychological assessments, necessitating a discussion of who will be privy to the information disclosed during the assessment. Families may be less forthcoming if they believe that information may be released, for example, to an insurance company. The ethical and legal definitions of confidentiality will vary depending on the locality. Regardless, a clear discussion of the limits of confidentiality should be reviewed with the child and family at the beginning of the assessment. A child or adolescent who is informed and clear about these limitations has the choice of how much to reveal during the interview. Studies have shown that when adolescents are assured confidentiality they are more willing to disclose sensitive information and more likely to trust their clinician (Klostermann, Slap, and Nebrig, 2005). The literature has also shown that parents respond to education about the issues of confidentiality and recognise the importance of allowing a child the opportunity to speak alone with their clinician (Hutchinson and Stafford, 2005).

For most children, the expectation that their parents will take part in their health-care decision making is developmentally appropriate. Even adolescents who are reluctant to include their parents can be encouraged to involve them in the process. A supportive and accepting interview style can help children realise that they are not alone in their struggles with behaviours and thoughts that were previously experienced as embarrassing or humiliating. They may also realise that they do not have to protect their parents from these symptoms. By the end of the interview, most patients will agree to have a discussion about their eating difficulties with their parents.

It is important to remember that children who present with ED can range from 5 to 18 years old (see Chapter 4). It is therefore important that the interviewer be mindful of the child's age and developmental stage. For younger children, questions should be simple and straightforward. The child should be comfortable with the questions rather than intimidated. Some younger children may not yet have developed the ability to abstract and may answer questions in a concrete way. It is developmentally normal for them to have difficulty understanding the symbolic connections between their ED and their life situation. The older the child, the more complex the interview can be, but it remains important to remember that an older adolescent is not an adult. The frontal and prefrontal cortex of their brains, which are responsible for executive functions, are still developing (Miller, 2005).

The individual interview

The interviewer should approach this part of the assessment with the intention of getting 'the story' of the child's troubles, while following a logical order of questions to ensure that all the important topics are covered. The interview should begin with an open-ended question such as 'Tell me about why you and your family decided to come to the assessment today?' or simply, 'What brought you here today?' Answers can range from 'A car brought me here' to 'My parents dragged me here' to 'I have a problem with not eating and I need help'. How a child answers these first questions reveals much about her attitudes, her motivations and her developmental stage. Once the problem has been identified – even if the patient's perception is simply that her parents have labelled her eating as the problem – the next step is to obtain a complete history of the problem.

History of present illness

In an assessment of a child with symptoms of anorexia nervosa (AN) or bulimia nervosa (BN), it is important to track when and how the child's initial concerns about food, weight and shape arose, and to ascertain when these concerns translated into specific behaviours. The child should be asked to describe the initial stages of the disorder:

- Was she trying to lose weight and why?
- What were her initial attempts at weight control?
- Did this work?
- How did her symptoms progress?
- What came next?
- How much weight did she lose?
- Over what length of time?
- Has she binged and/or purged?
- When and how did this start?
- If she has binged, what is the frequency of bingeing, and what are the amounts and types of food she binges on?
- Are there any triggers that start or stop a binge, either emotional or environmental?
- What are the ways in which she purges?
- Is it through vomiting, or the uses of substances, such as laxatives, diuretics, emetics, insulin or amphetamines?
- How often does this occur and what are the triggers?

- Does she exercise, and if so, what kind of activities does she do, how often, and for how long? The specifics are important. For instance, an adolescent may tell the interviewer that she does 'just a few press-ups'. This requires further exploration as a few press-ups may translate into '500 press-ups a day'.
- Does the child participate in sport or dance training that requires long hours of practice or one that idealises an unrealistic body shape?

For a child with food avoidance emotional disorder, it is important to explore what was happening when the child started to decrease her intake and why this happened. Did she feel full more quickly? Did she lose interest in eating? Usually these children did not plan or want to lose weight, and are often as worried as their parents are about their weight loss (Nicholls, Chater, and Lask, 2000).

Children may describe being selective eaters with a history of pickiness. Others may describe a fear of choking that limits what they can eat. All of these possible symptom clusters need to be considered in the assessment of a child with eating difficulties (Nicholls et al., 2000).

A detailed nutritional history is essential (see Chapter 11). This assessment is ideally suited to the dietitian on the team. However, if a dietitian is not available, the following information should be collected. Having the child describe a typical day of eating and drinking can be informative. Start by asking a child when is the first time she eats or drinks anything after awakening. What does she eat? How much? What does she drink? It is important to ask if the food or drink consumed is sugar or fat free. When is the next time in the course of the day that she eats or drinks? This should continue until a daily schedule of eating has been completed. It is also important to ask about nighttime awakenings to eat, exercise, or purge. Are there any foods that are avoided and why? Does she count calories or fat grams? Does the child have food allergies? It is also important to ask about vegetarianism as EDs are overrepresented in adolescent girls who are vegetarian (Neumark-Sztainer, Story, Resnick, and Blum, 1997). While some families are vegetarian for religious or ethical reasons, children with EDs may become vegetarian as a way to avoid eating. It is important to track when the decision to become vegetarian occurred and if vegetarianism is a shared family value. Some children and adolescents may also use caffeine, diet pills or other appetite suppressants. They may use nutritional supplements or complementary and alternative medicines that they believe will help them to lose weight. These possibilities require exploration. Finally, it is important to understand the child's perceptions about her family's attitudes and behaviours about food, weight loss, and health. What are mealtimes like, do they have family meals, and are they peaceful or conflicted? Who prepares the meals?

The next area of focus should be weight and shape concerns. Not every child who presents with eating difficulties experiences these symptoms and some who do may avoid discussing them. It is therefore important to ask about these concerns in a variety of ways. Some children may admit to classic complaints of feeling fat, or being afraid of gaining weight. Others may express pleasure in their current state, but only reveal their distress when asked to return to a normal weight. Others may be happy to gain weight at first, but may want to stop while still underweight. For some, the issue is less related to weight and more to their shape or level of 'fitness'. A boy may be happy to gain weight as long as he believes it will be muscle and not fat. For some girls, their fears may be less about gaining weight and more about avoiding 'curves' that come with a mature female body and which they perceive to attract unwanted attention. Questions that can be useful in exploring these issues include:

• How do you feel about you body?
• What do you think about your shape or weight?
• Is there anything about your body you would wish to change?
• What weight would you want to be at?

There may be a number of changes that the young person or the family has noticed during the course of development of the ED. The child may be described as having undergone a personality change. It is not unusual for the child or adolescent to become socially isolated. This occurs for a variety of reasons. She may start to avoid social situations that involve food including holiday meals, parties, or even movies. As well, as the malnutrition progresses, the child may not have the energy to socialise, or she may be so obsessed by her eating that she would prefer to be in her room planning and researching how, when and how much to eat, or exercising. A comorbid depression may also contribute to increasing isolation.

Children and adolescents with EDs may also begin to have difficulties at school. They may see their grades drop or complain of having to work harder and longer to maintain their grades. This may be due to a number of factors including being distracted by intrusive and distorted thinking about eating and weight. Patients may also experience cognitive difficulties as a result of the ED (see Chapter 8). A comorbid depression may contribute to difficulties with cognition or attention and concentration (Majer et al., 2004).

Another change may be an increase in mood lability – many patients state that they feel 'moody'. People with EDs may be described as more anxious, irritable, angry, sad, tearful, unpredictable, or rigid. Contributing to these perceptions is the fact that the child with an ED may spend a lot of time planning or controlling when and how she will eat or purge, and any change in schedule that prevents her from following her plan is experienced as catastrophic. The direct effects of starvation also contribute to affect dysregulation, as may other common comorbid diagnoses. Having said that, it is important to remember that during the active state of an ED, particularly if the patient is starved, the effects of the ED itself may mimic other psychiatric disorders, including mood disorders, anxiety disorders and obsessive compulsive disorder (OCD).

Past psychiatric history and comorbid psychiatric history

Up to two-thirds of patients with EDs will have another psychiatric disorder at some point in their lives (see Chapter 4). These can pre-date or co-occur with the development of eating problems. The interviewer should ask in detail about a past psychiatric history. During the review of symptoms, the interviewer should also ask specific questions about the more common comorbid diagnoses such as depression, generalised anxiety, other anxiety disorders, or OCD (Steinhausen, 2002). It is also important to find out if they have been treated in other mental health care programmes and if so information from these sources should be sought. This is also the time to ask if the patient is taking or has taken medication, the name of the medication, at what dose, for how long and if it has had any positive or negative effects. It is also important to rule out other psychiatric diagnoses that may lead to weight loss such as depression that can result in loss of appetite; psychotic disorders that result in delusional ideas such as 'all food has been poisoned by some conspiracy'; or OCD which may result in food avoidance due to worries about contaminants.

When completing an assessment of a child with an ED, it is important to ask about self-harm and suicidality. The interviewer needs to know whether a child has a history of these behaviours or whether they have current ideation. Self-harm is a commonly recognised comorbid diagnosis in EDs, particularly in AN and BN (Ruuska, Kaltiala-Heino, Rantanen, and Koivisto, 2005). It is also important to remember that almost half of the mortality associated with EDs relates to suicide, and that active plans for suicide should be taken seriously (Herzog, Greenwood, and Dorer, 2000).

Family history

Parents are in the best position to provide a complete history of illness in the family. However, it is useful to ask the child if she is aware of any members of her family, no matter how distant, who have been unwell, and if so are they genetically related? It is important to match these questions to the child's age and developmental stage. A child's knowledge about family history can give the clinician important information about how the family operates with regards to sensitive information.

Social history and family relationships

Struggling with an ED may be associated with difficulties in relationships both in the family and with peers. It is important to ask about the child's relationship with her parents and siblings. First, ask the child to describe who is in her family and her relationships with her family members, as well as comment on how the family functions as a whole. Were there stressors in the family that triggered or perpetuate the disorder? Are there family members who are weight conscious or dieting? Some children may have siblings who teased them about their weight or shape. It is important to ask whether there have been any changes in the family – either positive or negative – before or after the development of the ED. For example, have the parents become more frustrated with the child and has this led to conflict? Or has the ED brought the family together in some way?

How has the ED affected the child's friendship network and vice versa? Again, it is important to ask the child about her social history: Does she have close relationships? Does she have a lot of friends? Does the child have a best friend? Children with EDs may have friends with eating problems, or they may start to socialise with others who have disordered eating. Friends may actually compete to see who can be the thinnest or may all purge together. It is important to explore whether these factors play a role in the child or adolescent's story (Paxton, Schutz, Wertheim, and Muir, 1999). Potential stresses such as difficulties at school, academically or with peers, should be investigated. The clinician should ask about bullying or 'teasing' related to weight or other issues as a possible trigger or perpetuating factor (Haines, Neumark-Sztainer, Eisenberg, and Hannan, 2006). The clinician should consider the benefit of communicating with the school, particularly if they have assessed or provided any special mental health or academic supports for the child.

It is important to ask questions about common adolescent behaviours such as smoking, drinking, alcohol, and abuse of street drugs or medications (Stock, Goldberg, Corbett, and Katzman, 2002). A comorbid substance abuse problem can increase the patient's risk of mortality in long-term follow-up (Keel, Dorer, and Eddy, 2003). As well, a sexual history including questions about sexual experience and sexual orientation should be gently covered with all adolescents. Finally the presence of abuse, whether physical, sexual or emotional should be sensitively explored. While abuse does not 'cause' EDs, children with EDs are at least as likely to have histories of abuse as the general population and these may play a role in their illness and their treatment (Wentz, Gillberg, Gillberg, Råstam, and Carina, 2005; Wonderlich, Brewerton, Jocic, Dansky, and Abbott, 1997).

Developmental history

As with most psychological assessments, it is important to complete a developmental history. Depending on the age of the child, these questions may be more appropriate for the parents to address. However, it may be useful to ask the child if she was told about any details of her birth or early development. A developmental history should include a history of the pregnancy and birth history, developmental milestones and delays, and an academic history.

Finally, there should also be an exploration of the child's life outside the ED through the course of the assessment. This may include questions about any religious affiliations, her value system, hobbies and wishes for the future.

Mental status examination

No psychological assessment is complete without a mental status examination. Findings may include an appearance that is cachectic, poor eye contact and speech that is slowed or low in volume. Mood may be sad or alexithymic. Affect may appear tearful, sad, anxious, irritable, enraged or blunted, depending on the child or situation. Thought form may show slowing, ruminations, obsessionality, or, in cases of serious starvation, may be tangential or circumstantial. Thought content may include a constant food focus and/or weight and shape preoccupation. There may be current suicidal or self-harm ideation.

Perception is commonly positive for body image distortion in patients with AN and BN, and children with food avoidance emotional disorder may describe vague abdominal sensations that affect their ability to eat. Cognition may be impaired due to starvation and comorbid psychiatric disorder, although it is generally normal (but see Chapter 8). Disorientation raises the possibility of delirium (possibly secondary to refeeding syndrome). Capacity to consent to treatment should also be assessed as part of the mental status examination. An ED may cloud judgement and, as a result, some children may not believe that they are ill, even in the face of obvious medical facts. Some may feel that death is preferable to gaining any weight. Others may not be able to bring themselves to eat under any circumstances. It is important to understand how much the patient actually understands her illness.

Medical assessment

The clinician has two primary objectives in the medical assessment of the child with a suspected ED. The first is to use the medical history and physical examination to make the diagnosis. Medical conditions in children and adolescents that should be excluded when considering a diagnosis of an ED include inflammatory bowel disease, hyperthyroidism, chronic infections, diabetes and malignancy. Brain tumours may co-occur (O'Brien, Hugo, Stapleton, and Lask, 2001) or be disguised as an ED (de Vile, Lask, and Stanhope, 1995). The second goal of the assessment is to evaluate the child or adolescent for any medical complications that may be a result of the ED.

Medical history

It is important to review the child and adolescent's current and past medical history. The child's family doctor or paediatrician can be helpful in providing information about the child's past medical history. Most importantly, the clinician should explore the onset and description of the current symptoms. Has the child ever had anything like this before? What makes it better/worse? Is there a pre-existing medical condition (e.g. inflammatory bowel diseases, diabetes mellitus) associated with weight loss, abnormal eating, gastrointestinal symptoms or metabolic issues? Have there been any hospitalisations for these symptoms now or in the past? What investigations have previously been done? What medical diagnosis has been given to the child or adolescent to explain these symptoms? Is the child taking any medications including vitamins, mineral supplements or complementary and alternative medicines? If yes, what kind of medication(s), at what dose and for how long? Does she have any allergies? A menstrual history should be elicited from all female children and adolescents. Has the child reached menarche? If so, what was the age of the adolescent's first menstrual period? Is the adolescent's menstrual period regular? What is the length of the adolescent's menstrual cycle? Have the cycles stopped? At what weight and date was the adolescent's last normal menstrual period? It is important to ask the mother about her own age of menarche. This can be useful in predicting the age of menarche in a girl who has not reached menarche. Questions about bone pain or fractures and hormone replacement therapy should also be explored.

Physical examination

A thorough physical examination is an essential component in the assessment of a child or adolescent with a suspected ED. Care should be taken to ensure that the child or adolescent has privacy. The physical examination should be performed with the patient alone unless the patient insists otherwise. A male physician should request that a female be present to accompany any female patient during the physical examination. Many female adolescents prefer having a third party present when the examining doctor is male as this is viewed as a positive supporting role during the physical examination. Physical findings may help confirm the diagnosis and may also reveal signs of the physical consequences of the disorders (Table 7.1). On the other hand, the physical examination may be entirely normal even in the face of a serious disorder.

A thorough physical examination should be performed. Children and adolescents with EDs can often lose a large amount of weight in a very short period of time. Clinicians should assess physical growth using the child's weight and stature and plotting these measurements on the growth charts. A series of accurate weights and measurements of stature are important to assess a child's growth pattern. Parental stature is often helpful if there is a nutritional concern. Patients should be weighed in a hospital gown after voiding. Body mass index (BMI) should be calculated (BMI = weight in kilograms divided by height in meters squared) and plotted on the growth curves. The percentage of ideal body weight (IBW, the average weight of children of the same age, height and gender) can also be determined. Vital

Table 7.1 Potential physical abnormalities.

System	AN	BN
General	■ Weight loss ■ Emaciation ■ Dehydration ■ Hypothermia ■ Short stature/delayed growth ■ Mood changes, irritability ■ Flat affect	■ Weight fluctuations ■ Dehydration ■ Mood changes, irritability
Head, ears, eyes, nose and throat	■ Dry, cracked lips and tongue ■ Breath smells of acetone (ketosis)	■ Dry lips and tongue ■ Dental enamel erosion ■ Dental caries ■ Gingivitis ■ Parotid enlargement ■ Palatal erythema
Cardiac	■ Arrhythmias ■ Hypotension ■ Orthostatic heart rate and blood pressure changes ■ Congestive heart failure ■ Mitral value prolapse ■ Acrocyanosis ■ Cool extremities ■ Delayed capillary refill ■ Oedema	■ Arrhythmias ■ Hypotension ■ Oedema
Abdomen	■ Scaphoid ■ Palpable evidence of constipation	■ Epigastric tenderness
Dermatologic	■ Pallor ■ Acrocyanosis (purple discolouration) ■ Yellow/orange discolouration (carotenaemia) ■ Lanugo hair ■ Thinning scalp hair ■ Dry skin ■ Brittle nails ■ Evidence of self-harm	■ Russell's sign (calluses on dorsum of hand) ■ Periorbital petechiae ■ Evidence of self-harm
Extremities	■ Muscular atrophy	
Neurological	■ Diminished deep tendon reflexes ■ Reduced concentration, memory and thinking ability ■ Peripheral neuropathy	■ Reduced concentration, memory and thinking ability

signs, including oral temperature and orthostatic measurements of the heart rate and blood pressure will help determine if the young person is medically stable. Finally, sexual maturity rating (breast and pubic hair for girls, genital and pubic hair for boys) is a crucial part of the exam as pubertal delay may be a consequence of malnutrition.

Laboratory examination

Laboratory findings in children and adolescents with EDs are often completely normal. However, certain laboratory tests can be helpful in ruling out other medical conditions. Initial laboratory tests might include a complete blood cell count, erythrocyte sedimentation rate, electrolyte measurements, glucose, renal and liver function tests, urinalysis and thyroid-stimulating hormone. Renal function is generally normal except in the case of dehydration when the blood urea nitrogen and creatinine may be elevated. Although protein and albumin are typically normal, liver function tests have been reported to be minimally elevated (Sherman, Leslie, Goldberg, Rybczynski, and St. Louis, 1994). Additional tests to be considered in girls who are amenorrheic include a urine pregnancy test, luteinising and follicle-stimulating hormone, and oestradiol levels. A baseline electrocardiograph is helpful in children and adolescents with bradycardia or electrolyte abnormalities.

Low bone mineral density (BMD) is an early and frequent complication of children and adolescents with AN. Dual-energy X-ray absorptiometry (DEXA) scans are often recommended after six months of amenorrhea in patients with AN and in patients with BN who have a history of AN. Results should be interpreted using the Z-scores which compare the patient's bone density to age and gender matched controls. If the result is abnormal or the adolescent remains amenorrhoeic, it is recommended that the DEXA scan be repeated annually (Golden, 2003). Determination of a child's bone age should be considered if there is growth failure. A child's current height and bone age can be used to predict growth potential and final adult height.

Pelvic ultrasound has been shown to be a safe and reliable method for determining ovarian and uterine maturity in children and adolescent girls with AN (Key, Mason, Allan, and Lask, 2002; Lai, de Bruyn, Lask, Bryant-Waugh, and Hankins, 1994). Children with AN and primary amenorrhoea show the prepubertal appearance of the uterus and ovaries, whereas young people with AN and secondary amenorrhea show marked regression in the size of the uterus and ovaries (Figures 7.1–7.4). In particular, the ovaries become quiescent and show no follicular activity. Successful sonographic examination and evaluation in young girls with AN requires accurate knowledge and assessment of both uterine and ovarian size and morphology, equipment that can produce images of high resolution and experience in the reading and interpreting this examination. Over the past decade, ultrasound has played an increasingly important role in determining when a healthy weight has been achieved (Adams, 1993; Key et al., 2002; Lai et al., 1994).

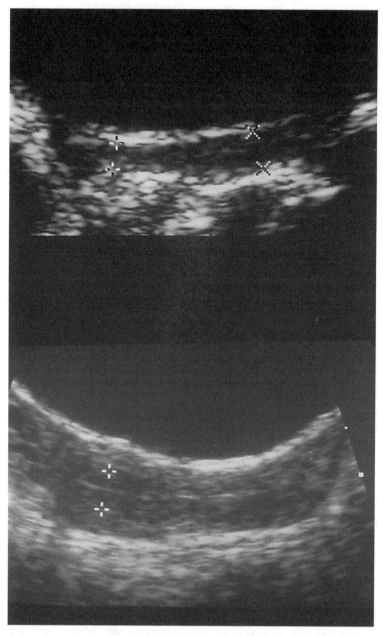

Figure 7.1 Patient aged 13 years with primary amenorrhoea: longitudinal sonogram of the uterus. Top: prepubertal uterus with the cervix thicker than the fundus (marked X). Bottom: one year later, after successful treatment, the uterus now has an adult configuration with a measurable endometrium.

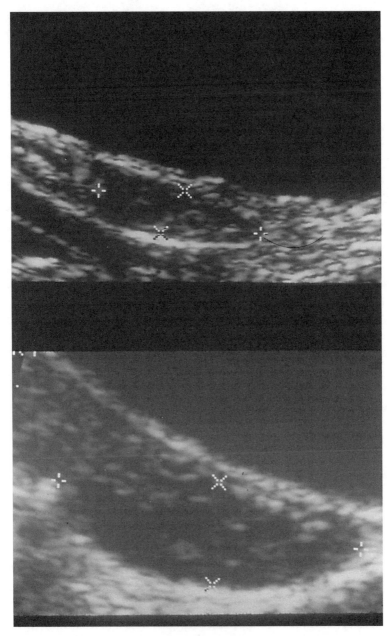

Figure 7.2 Patient aged 13 years with primary amenorrhoea: sonogram of right ovary. Top: small ovary with virtually no follicular activity. Bottom: after one year, and weight gain, a much larger ovary with much more follicular activity seen.

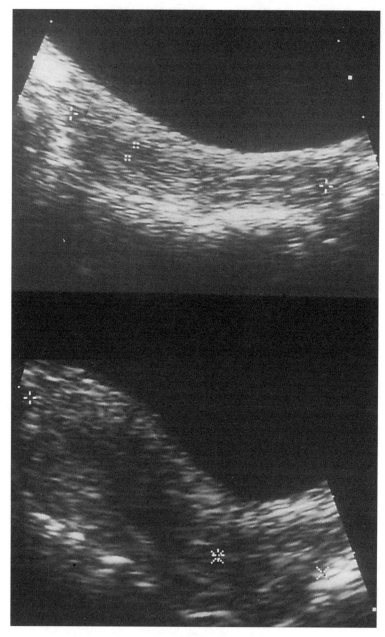

Figure 7.3 Patient aged 13 years with secondary amenorrhoea: longitudinal sonogram of the uterus. Top: small uterus with adult configuration. In patients
with secondary amenorrhoea the uterus never regresses to the prepubertal
appearance. Bottom: after one year with weight gain. The uterus has
grown to a more pronounced adult configuration.

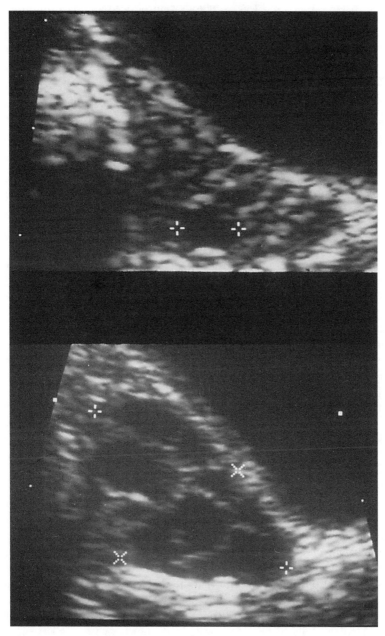

Figure 7.4 Patient aged 13 years with secondary amenorrhoea: sonogram of right ovary. Top: only a single follicle is evident on the ovary (between +), which is also small in volume. Bottom: after one year and weight gain, the ovary now shows a multifollicular appearance, containing more than six follicles of 4 mm in diameter.

Mason, Allan, Hugo, and Lask (2006) have produced an algorithm to assist the clinician in the interpretation of pelvic ultrasound and to determine the next steps

Medical complications

The complications of EDs may be seen in every organ system and are primarily due to weight control practices (e.g. purging) and malnutrition. With early identification and treatment, most complications in children and adolescents are fully reversible.

Metabolic abnormalities and the refeeding syndrome

Recurrent purging may result in serious fluid and electrolyte disturbances. Loss of hydrogen and chloride ions through vomiting may lead to hypochloremic metabolic alkalosis. Abuse of diuretics causes a similar metabolic situation. Bicarbonate loss in diarroea associated with laxative abuse results in hyperchloremic (non-anion gap) metabolic acidosis. Hypokalemia, which occurs in approximately 5 per cent of people with BN (Greenfeld, Mickley, Quinlan, and Roloff, 1995; Wolfe, Metzger, Levine, and Jimerson, 2001) may predispose to cardiac arrhythmias, muscle weakness, or confusion. Potassium chloride supplements and fluids may be necessary to correct these electrolyte abnormalities. Hyponatremia might occur with excessive water intake or the inappropriate secretion of antidiuretic hormone.

Glucose metabolism can be erratic in AN and low blood glucose measurements are not uncommon. Hypoglycaemia is observed secondary to lack of glucose precursors in the diet or low glycogen stores. Rebound hypoglycaemia may occur with refeeding following a hyperinsulinemic response. Bingeing and purging can cause glucose levels to fluctuate widely, which is a particular danger in patients with diabetes mellitus.

Elevated serum cholesterol can be seen in states of prolonged starvation. The proposed aetiologies for this finding include depressed triiodothyronine (T_3) levels affecting cholesterol breakdown, low cholesterol-binding protein levels, and fatty infiltration of the liver causing leakage of intrahepatic cholesterol into the peripheral circulation (Rome and Ammerman, 2003).

Refeeding syndrome refers to severe shifts in fluid and electrolyte levels in children and adolescents with ED that are undergoing nutritional rehabilitation. When the starving patient is given a high glucose meal, insulin release is stimulated which shifts metabolism from catabolic to anabolic. Phosphate moves into the cells to be incorporated into newly synthesised tissues and adenosine triphosphate (ATP: Solomon and Kirby, 1990). The resulting hypophosphatemia may cause cardiovascular, neurologic and haematologic complications. The syndrome can be prevented by slowly refeeding with close cardiac and metabolic monitoring. Supplemental phosphate may be indicated.

Haematologic status

Although the complete blood count is typically normal in children and adolescents with EDs, pancytopenia has been reported (Palla and Litt, 1988). Leukopenia has been observed secondary to increased margination of neutrophils but there does not seem to be an increased risk of infection in children and adolescents with ED. The haemoglobin is typically normal and elevations may suggest dehydration. Anaemia requires further investigation. An iron-deficiency anaemia can be seen in children and adolescents who are vegan. Thrombocytopenia is very rare. The erythrocyte sedimentation rate tends to be low or normal; an elevated value should prompt further investigation for an underlying medical condition. These haematologic abnormalities resolve with nutritional rehabilitation.

Nutritional deficiencies

Overt nutritional deficiencies are rare in patients with EDs. Recently, a role for essential fatty acid deficiency in the pathogenesis and symptomatology of AN has been postulated. In particular, omega-3 polyunsaturated fatty acids (PUFAs) have been found to be deficient in several medical and mental disease states (Ayton, 2004). PUFA deficiencies in AN have been described and the pattern reported is different from that seen with simple essential fatty acid deficiency or chronic malnutrition (Holman et al., 1995). Preliminary studies of PUFA supplementation have yielded promising, but inconclusive results (Ayton, Azaz, and Horrobin, 2004).

Cardiovascular

The cardiac complications of EDs are among the earliest and most dramatic of all the physical effects of the disorders. One-third of deaths in adults with EDs are due to cardiac complications (Isner, Roberts, Heymsfield, and Yager, 1985). Such data does not exist for adolescents.

Electrocardiographic abnormalities are common with AN and are reported in up to 75 per cent of hospitalised adolescent patients (Palla and Litt, 1988). Sinus bradycardia is reported to be present in 35–95 per cent of adolescents with AN (Mont et al., 2003; Olivares, Vazques, Fleta, Moreno, Perez-Gonzalez, and Bueno, 2005; Palla and Litt, 1988) and correlates with disease severity as measured by BMI (Panagiotopoulos et al., 2000). Bradycardia corrects with refeeding and weight gain.

Prolongation of the QTc interval (normal interval < 0.44 seconds) is inconsistently reported in adolescents with AN (Lupoglazoff et al., 2001; Mont et al., 2003; Panagiotopoulos, McCrindle, Hick, and Katzman, 2000; Ulger, Gurses, Ozyurek, Arkan, Levent, and Aydogdu, 2006). Prolonged QTc has been associated with ventricular arrhythmias and sudden death in adults who lost weight rapidly using a liquid protein modified fast (Isner et al., 1985). In studies that report prolonged QTc in adolescents, there does not appear to be a correlation with disease severity and none of these studies report life-threatening arrhythmias. The absence of a prolonged QTc interval should not, however, be taken as a sign of stability.

As with the QTc interval, reports of increased QTc dispersion in adolescents with AN are inconsistent (Panagiotopoulos et al., 2000). When an increase in QTc dispersion has been reported in adolescents with AN, it appeared to correct with refeeding and was not associated with arrhythmias (Mont et al., 2003; Ulger et al., 2006).

Orthostatic heart rate changes (rate increase > 20 bpm on standing) and blood pressure changes (> 10 mmHg) are common in adolescents with EDs and place such teens at risk for syncope. Orthostasis may be due to dehydration, autonomic dysregulation, or atrophy of the peripheral muscles which results in decreased venous return to the heart. Evidence shows that normalisation of orthostatic pulse changes occurs after approximately three weeks of nutritional rehabilitation or when adolescents reach 80 per cent of their IBW (Shamim, Golden, Arden, Filiberto, and Shenker, 2003). Resolution of orthostasis may be used as a one indicator of medical stability.

Echocardiographic changes seen in adolescents with AN include reduced left ventricular mass, reduced cardiac output and mitral valve prolapse. These findings are likely due to heart muscle wasting with malnutrition and improve with refeeding (Mont et al., 2003).

It is important to remember that prescribed medications, illicit drug use, or complementary and alternative medications may have adverse cardiac effects.

Endocrine status

Regular menstruation is an indicator of a normal hypothalamic-pituitary-ovarian axis. Amenorrhoea (absence of three consecutive menstrual periods after the establishment of regular menstruation) is a hallmark of AN. The amenorrhoea of AN is hypothalamic in origin and gonadotropin secretion resembles that of prepubertal females (Stoving, Hangaard, and Hagen, 2001). The aetiology of amenorrhoea in AN is multifactorial and thought to be the result of hypothalamic dysfunction related to weight loss (with low body fat) and exacerbated by excessive exercise, abnormal eating behaviours and stress.

A main aim of weight restoration is the initiation or restoration of regular periods. However, clinicians should be wary of using target weights to achieve this. Weight as a measure is remarkably unreliable and easily open to manipulation. Setting a target weight may reinforce a patient's preoccupation with weight. Furthermore it must be frequently revised as children are in a state of continuous growth and development. One study found that menses returned at approximately 90 per cent of IBW or at least 2.05 kg above the weight at which menses was lost (Golden, Jacobson, Schebendach, Solanto, Hertz, and Shenker, 1997). Serum oestradiol levels of 110 pmol/L (30 pg/mL) were also closely associated with return of menses. In another study, young girls with eating disorders who reached menarche did so when they reached their pre-pubertal growth track (Swenne, 2005). They same group also found that if weight at return of menstruation was expressed in standard deviation scores (SDS), it could be predicted by a linear regression on weight SDS at loss of menstruation (Swenne, 2004). Key et al. (2002) used pelvic ultrasound in adolescent girls with AN to determine the optimal weight-to-height ratio to achieve maturity of the reproductive organs. They found that 88 per cent of the subjects required a weight-to-height ratio of 100 per cent (BMI = 20) to achieve reproductive maturity.

This work suggests that previous target weights had been set too low to ensure reproductive maturity and therefore return of menstruation. Further-more, in contrast, some subjects achieved reproductive maturity at weights below the average range. Also it must be emphasised that the weight at which menstruation returns may not be the final weight required. Children and adolescents are in a state of growth and development and therefore further weight gain may be required for the maintenance of regular ovulatory cycles, the restoration of lean body mass and the continuation of physical health.

Amenorrhoea is an important risk factor for low BMD. Low BMD is an early and frequent complication in children and adolescents with AN. At least 50 per cent of peak bone mass is accrued during adolescence (Theintz et al., 1992). In adolescents with AN, both decreased bone forma-tion and increased bone resorption are responsible for lowering BMD. Poor nutrition, low calcium and vitamin D intake, hypoestrogenemia, low levels of insulin-like growth factor I (IGF-I), increased cortisol levels, low body mass, and exercise all influence bone mineralisation. Whether the loss of BMD is reversible with recovery is unknown. Follow-up studies have found that weight gain (even before the return of menstrual function) increases BMD (Bachrach, Katzman, Litt, Guido, and Marcus, 1991; Hartman, Crisp, Rooney, Rackow, Atkinson, and Patel, 2000; Rigotti, Neer, and Skates, 1991). As such, the most important and effective treatment for low BMD in children and adolescents with AN is weight recovery. Calcium is a major component of bone and vitamin D is crucial in calcium absorption. Although no associ-ation has been found between calcium intake and bone mass in adolescents with AN (Bachrach, Guido, Katzman, Litt, and Marcus, 1990) it is recom-mended that adolescents take 1300 mg/day of calcium and 400 IU/day of vitamin D. To date, there is no evidence that hormone replacement therapy prevents or reduces bone loss in AN (Golden, Lanzkowsky, Schenbendach, Palestro, Jacobson, and Shenker, 2002; Munoz, Morande, Garcia-Centenera, Hervas, Pozo, and Argente, 2002). Such hormonal treatment often causes monthly withdrawal bleeding which may be mistakenly interpreted as a return to health. Although the efficacy and long-term safety of bisphosphonates is currently being explored (Golden et al., 2005), their use in adolescence is absolutely contraindicated because of their potential for teratogenicity as well as because the long term consequences of their use in this age group are unknown.

Adequate nutrition is critical for achieving maximum height potential. Impaired linear growth and possibly permanent short stature may occur as a result of an ED during critical periods of growth. Children and adolescents with AN can present with growth failure or stunting (Nussbaum, Baird, Sonnenblinck, Cowan, and Shenker, 1985; Root and Powers, 1983). The onset of AN in relation to the onset of puberty may also influence linear growth. Adolescents who develop AN in early puberty and before menarche may present with growth retardation compared with those who develop the disorder when they are postmenarcheal. Weight restoration can induce resumption of growth. However, catch-up growth may not be complete and potential adult height may not be reached if skeletal maturation has advanced (Lantzouni, Frank, Golden, and Shenker, 2002; Swenne, 2005).

Growth hormone (GH) levels in adolescents with AN are usually increased, despite low IGF-I levels, suggesting a state of GH resistance (Misra et al., 2003). IGF-I synthesis by the liver is inhibited during states of malnutrition, leading to decreased negative feedback on the hypothalamus. GH action is impaired despite these elevated GH levels. GH secretion in AN probably reflects altered neuroendocrine feedback regulation (Stoving et al., 1999).

'Euthyroid sick syndrome' or 'low T_3 syndrome' characterised by markedly decreased triiodothyronine (T_3), normal or subnormal thyroxine (T_4), and normal thyrotropin (TSH) serum levels, is commonly found in AN (Stoving et al., 2001). Thyroid volume is often markedly reduced. Although commonly thought that the low T3 levels are due to decreased peripheral deiodination of T4 to T3, there is also evidence for hypothalamic-pituitary-thyroid axis dysfunction with poor response of T3 to TSH stimulation (Kiyohara, Tamai, Takaichi, Nakaqawa, and Kumagai, 1989). Thyroid replacement therapy is not indicated and this condition will correct with refeeding.

Hypercortisolemia and abnormalities of the hypothalamic-pituitary-adrenal axis are common in AN. Most patients with AN have an abnormal cortisol suppression during dexamethasone suppression testing (Munoz and Argente, 2002). Cortisol levels rapidly normalise with refeeding and weight gain.

Leptin is an adipocyte-secreted hormone involved in the regulation of food intake and energy expenditure. Additionally, leptin is thought to affect the hypothalamic-pituitary-gonadal axis by signalling sufficient energy stores for puberty and reproduction. Serum leptin levels correlate with fat mass and are low in AN. The mechanisms of action of this hormone are still largely unknown, but many studies demonstrate that its primary target is the hypothalamus (Rogol, 1998). Leptin may be important in mediating the neuroendocrine abnormalities of hypothalamic amenorrhoea. It may also play a role in treatment of bone loss associated with amenorrhoea (Welt et al., 2004). Low leptin levels have been related to increased activity in adolescents with AN (Holtkamp, Herpertz-Dahlmann, and Mika, 2005). Abnormally high levels after refeeding have been associated with relapse (Holtkamp et al., 2005).

Infection

Some recent studies have suggested that AN may be part of the spectrum of the paediatric autoimmune neuropsychiatric disorders associated with streptococcus infection (PANDAS). PANDAS has been described in a subset of children with the sudden onset of OCD and/or tic disorders that occur weeks following a group A B-hemolytic streptococcal infection (GABHS). The hypothesis suggests that antibodies to GABHS may cross-react with neurons in the basal ganglia as part of a post-infectious process, possibly altering emotions and behaviour (Kurlan and Kaplan, 2004; Sokol, 2000). There is no laboratory test that can diagnose PANDAS. At present, the diagnosis of PANDAS is a clinical diagnosis that includes five diagnostic criteria:

- presence of OCD or a tics
- onset between 3 years of age and the beginning of puberty
- abrupt onset or episodic course of symptom severity
- association with GABHS infection (confirmed by culture and/or elevated antistreptococcal titers)
- associated neurological abnormalities (Swedo et al., 1988).

Gastrointestinal

Starvation, bingeing, and vomiting can all have a significant impact on the gastrointestinal system. Starvation may produce slowed gastrointestinal motility and constipation (Benini, Todesco, Dalle Grave, Deiorio, Salandini, and Vantini, 2004; Palla and Litt, 1988). In older adolescents and adults restriction of food intake has also be shown to cause delayed gastric emptying. These gastric symptoms will cause the child and adolescent to complain of early satiety, bloating and constipation, all of which inhibit further oral intake. One of the few studies of the gastrointestinal tract performed in children with EDs (Ravelli, Helps, Devane, Lask, and Milla, 1993) demonstrated that gastric antral electrical dysrhythmias were not a feature of children with AN (age range 11.6 to 15.5). While eight of 14 patients complained of upper gastrointestinal symptoms, this study maintains that there is currently no evidence to support the promotion of gastric emptying with prokinetic drugs in children and young adolescents. Reassurance that symptoms will improve after several weeks of refeeding should be provided (Benini et al., 2004; Waldholtz and Andersen, 1990).

Binge eating has been reported to cause gastric dilation (Barada et al., 2006; De Caprio, Pasanisi, and Contaldo, 2000), gastric rupture, oesophageal rupture, and pancreatitis (Morris, Stephenson, Herring, and Marti, 2004).

Pancreatitis has also been reported and associated with refeeding in AN (Backett, 1985). Vomiting may be elicited by the use of a finger or foreign object (spoon, toothbrush, etc.) to stimulate the gag reflex. In some situations this may progress to the point where mechanical stimulation is not necessary (Palla and Litt, 1988). Frequent vomiting commonly causes oesophagitis and gastro-oesophageal reflux. Antacids, histamine-2 receptor blockers (e.g. ranitidine), or proton pump blockers may be necessary to relieve discomfort associated with acid reflux and oesophagitis.

Effects on the brain

The structural and functional brain abnormalities reported in children and adolescents with ED are discussed in Chapter 8.

Conclusion

By virtue of the complexity of child and adolescent EDs, a comprehensive assessment typically takes longer than most paediatric mental health evaluations. The assessment of a child or adolescent with an ED may occur as a single assessment but commonly requires multiple evaluations over time. Additional interviews with the patient and parents, collecting collateral information from the primary health-care provider, the school system, the caseworker, or the therapist, will help to complete a comprehensive diagnostic assessment for these complex and life-threatening disorders.

References

Adams, J. (1993). 'The role of pelvic ultrasound in the management of paediatric endocrine disorders'. In C.G.D. Brook (Ed.), *Clinical paediatric endocrinology* (pp. 675–691). Oxford: Blackwell.

Ayton, A.K. (2004). Dietary polyunsaturated fatty acids and anorexia nervosa: Is there a link? *Nutritional Neuroscience, 7* (1), 1–12.

Ayton, A.K., Azaz, A., and Horrobin, D.F. (2004). A pilot open case series of ethyl-EPA supplementation in the treatment of anorexia nervosa. *Prostaglandins, Leukotrienes, and Essential Fatty Acids, 71* (4), 205–209.

Bachrach, L.K., Guido, D., Katzman, D., Litt, I.F., and Marcus, R. (1990). Decreased bone density in adolescent girls with anorexia nervosa. *Pediatrics, 86* (3), 440–447.

Bachrach, L., Katzman, D.K., Litt, L., Guido, D., and Marcus, R. (1991). Recovery from osteopenia in adolescent girls with anorexia nervosa. *Journal of Clinical Endocrinology and Metabolism, 72* (3), 602–606.

Backett, S.A. (1985). Acute pancreatitis and gastric dilatation in a patient with anorexia nervosa. *Postgraduate Medical Journal, 61* (711), 39–40.

Barada, K.A., Azar, C.R., Al-Kutoubi, A.O., Harb, R.S., Hazimeh, Y.M., Abbas, J.S., et al. (2006). Massive gastric dilatation after a single binge in an anorectic woman. *International Journal of Eating Disorders, 39* (2), 166–169.

Benini, L., Todesco, T., Dalle Grave, R., Deiorio, F., Salandini, L., and Vantini, I.

(2004). Gastric emptying in patients with restricting and binge/purging subtypes of anorexia nervosa. *American Journal of Gastroenterology, 99* (8), 1448–1454.

De Caprio, C., Pasanisi, F., and Contaldo, F. (2000). Gastrointestinal complications in a patient with eating disorders. *Eating and Weight Disorders, 5* (4), 228–230.

de Vile, C., Lask, B., and Stanhope, R. (1995). Occult intracranial tumours masquerading as anorexia nervosa. *British Medical Journal, 311,* 1359–1360.

Golden, N.H. (2003). Osteopenia and osteoporosis in anorexia nervosa. *Adolescent Medicine: State of the Art Reviews, 14* (1), 97–108.

Golden, N.H., Iglesias, E.A., Jacobson, M.S., Carey, D., Meyer, W., Schebendach, J., et al. (2005). Alendronate for the treatment of osteopenia in anorexia nervosa: A randomized, double-blind, placebo-controlled trial. *Journal of Clinical Endocrinology and Metabolism, 90* (6), 3179–3185.

Golden, N.H., Jacobson, M.S., Schebendach, J., Solanto, M.V., Hertz, S.M., and Shenker, I.R. (1997). Resumption of menses in anorexia nervosa. *Archives of Pediatric and Adolescent Medicine, 151* (1), 16–21.

Golden, N.H., Katzman, D.K, Kreipe, R.E., Stevens, S.L., Sawyer, S.M., Rees, J., et al. (2003). Society For Adolescent Medicine. Eating disorders in adolescents: Position paper of the Society for Adolescent Medicine. *Journal of Adolescent Health, 33,* 496–503.

Golden, N.H., Lanzkowsky, L., Schenbendach, J., Palestro, C.J., Jacobson, M.S., and Shenker, I.R. (2002). The effect of estrogen-progestin treatment on bone mineral density in anorexia nervosa. *Journal of Pediatric and Adolescent Gynecology, 15* (3), 135–143.

Greenfeld, D., Mickley, D., Quinlan, D.M., and Roloff, P. (1995). Hypokalemia in outpatients with eating disorders. *American Journal of Psychiatry, 152* (1), 60–63.

Haines, J., Neumark-Sztainer, D., Eisenberg, M.E., and Hannan, P.J. (2006). Weight teasing and disordered eating behaviors in adolescents: Longitudinal findings from Project EAT (Eating Among Teens). *Pediatrics, 117* (2), 209–215.

Hartman, D., Crisp, A., Rooney, B., Rackow, C., Atkinson, R., and Patel, S. (2000). Bone density of women who have recovered from anorexia nervosa. *International Journal of Eating Disorders, 28* (1), 107–112.

Herzog, D.B., Greenwood, D.N., and Dorer, D.J. (2000). Mortality in eating disorders: A descriptive study. *International Journal of Eating Disorders, 28* (1), 20–26.

Holman, R.T., Adams, C.E., Nelson, R.A., Grater, S.J., Jaskiewicz, J.A., Johnson, S.B., et al. (1995). Patients with anorexia nervosa demonstrate deficiencies of selected essential fatty acids, compensatory changes in nonessential fatty acids and decreased fluidity of plasma lipids. *Journal of Nutrition, 125,* 901–907.

Holtkamp, K., Herpertz-Dahlmann, B., and Mika, C. (2005). Changing parental opinions about teen privacy through education. *Pediatrics, 116* (4), 966–971.

Hutchinson, J.W., and Stafford, E.M. (2005). Changing parental opinions about teen privacy through education. *Pediatrics, 116* (4), 966–971.

Isner, J.M., Roberts, W.C., Heymsfield, S.B., and Yager, J. (1985). Anorexia nervosa and sudden death. *Annals of Internal Medicine, 102* (1), 49–52.

Keel, P.K., Dorer, D.J., and Eddy, K.T. (2003). Predictors of mortality in eating disorders. *Archives of General Psychiatry, 60* (2), 179–183.

Key, A., Mason, H., Allan, R., and Lask, B. (2002). Restoration of ovarian and uterine maturity in adolescents with anorexia nervosa. *International Journal of Eating Disorders, 32* (3), 319–325.

Kiyohara, K., Tamai, H., Takaichi, Y., Nakaqawa, T., and Kumagai, L.F. (1989). Decreased thyroidal triiodothyronine secretion in patients with anorexia nervosa: Influence of weight recovery. *American Journal of Clinical Nutrition, 50* (4), 767–772.

Klostermann, B.K., Slap, G.B., and Nebrig, D.M. (2005). Earning trust and losing it: Adolescents' views on trusting physicians. *Journal of Families Practice, 54* (8), 679–687.

Kurlan, R., and Kaplan, E.L. (2004). The pediatric autoimmune neuropsychiatric disorders associated with streptococcal infection (PANDAS) etiology for tics and obsessive-compulsive symptoms: Hypothesis or entity? Practical considerations for the clinician. *Pediatrics, 113* (4), 883–886.

Lai, K.Y., de Bruyn, R., Lask, B., Bryant-Waugh, R., and Hankins, M. (1994). Use of pelvic ultrasound to monitor ovarian and uterine maturity in childhood onset anorexia nervosa. *Archives of Disease in Childhood, 71,* 228–231.

Lantzouni, E., Frank, G.R., Golden, N., and Shenker, R.I. (2002). Reversibility of growth stunting in early onset anorexia nervosa: A prospective study. *Journal of Adolescent Health, 31* (2), 162–165.

Lupoglazoff, J.M., Berkane, N., Denjoy, I., Maillard, G., Leheuzey, M.F., Mouren-Simeoni, M.C., et al. (2001). Cardiac consequences of adolescent anorexia nervosa. *Archives Mal Coeur Vaiss, 94* (5), 494–498.

Majer, M., Ising, M., Kunzel, H., Binder, E.B., Holsboer, F., Modell, S., et al. (2004). Impaired divided attention predicts delayed response and risk to relapse in subjects with depressive disorders. *Psychological Medicine, 34* (8), 1453–1463.

Mason, H., Allan, R., Hugo, P., and Lask, B. (2006, September). Pelvic ultra-sonography in anorexia nervosa: What the clinician should ask the radiologist and how to use the information provided. Retrieved October 26, 2006. *European Eating Disorders Review.* DOI 10.1002/erv.719.

Miller, K.J. (2005). Executive functions. *Pediatric Annals, 34* (4), 310–317.

Misra, M., Miller, K.K., Bjornson, J., Hackman, A., Aggarwal, A., Chung, J., et al. (2003). Alterations in growth hormone secretory dynamics in adolescent girls with anorexia nervosa and effects on bone metabolism. *Journal of Clinical Endocrinology and Metabolism, 88* (12), 5615–5623.

Mont, L., Castro, J., Herreros, B., Pare, C., Azqueta, M., Magrina, J., et al. (2003). Reversibility of cardiac abnormalities in adolescents with anorexia nervosa after weight recovery. *Journal of the American Academy of Child and Adolescent Psychiatry, 42* (7), 808–813.

Morris, L.G., Stephenson, K.E., Herring, S., and Marti, J.L. (2004). Recurrent acute pancreatitis in anorexia and bulimia. *Journal of the Pancreas, 5* (4), 231–234.

Munoz, M.T., and Argente, J. (2002). Anorexia nervosa in female adolescents: endocrine and bone mineral density disturbances. *European Journal of Endocrinology, 147* (3), 275–286.

Munoz, M.T., Morande, G., Garcia-Centenera, J.A., Hervas, F., Pozo, J., and Argente, J. (2002). The effects of estrogen administration on bone mineral density in adolescents with anorexia nervosa. *European Journal of Endocrinology, 146* (1), 45–50.

Neumark-Sztainer, D., Story, M., Resnick, M.D., and Blum, R.W. (1997). Adolescent vegetarians. A behavioral profile of a school-based population in Minnesota. *Archives of Pediatric and Adolescent Medicine, 151* (8), 833–838.

Nicholls, D., Chater, R., and Lask, B. (2000). Children into DSM don't go: A comparison of classification systems for eating disorders in childhood and early adolescence. *International Journal of Eating Disorders, 28* (3), 317–324.

Nussbaum, M., Baird, D., Sonnenblinck, M., Cowan, K., and Shenker, I.R. (1985). Short stature in anorexia nervosa patients. *Journal of Adolescent Health Care, 6* (16), 453–455.

O'Brien A., Hugo, P., Stapleton, S., and Lask, B. (2001). Anorexia nervosa saved my life – coincidental anorexia nervosa and cerebral meningioma. *International Journal of Eating Disorders, 30*, 246–249.

Olivares, J.L., Vazques, M., Fleta, J., Moreno, L.A., Perez-Gonzalez, J.M., and Bueno, M. (2005). Cardiac findings in adolescents with anorexia nervosa at diagnosis and after weight restoration. *European Journal of Pediatrics, 164* (6), 383–386.

Palla, B., and Litt, I.F. (1988). Medical complications of eating disorders in adolescents. *Pediatrics, 81* (5), 613–623.

Panagiotopoulos, C., McCrindle, B.W., Hick, K., and Katzman, D.K. (2000). Electrocardiographic findings in adolescents with eating disorders. *Pediatrics, 105* (5), 1100–1105.

Paxton, S.J., Schutz, H.K., Wertheim, E.H., and Muir, S.L. (1999). Friendship clique and peer influences on body image concerns, dietary restraint, extreme weight-loss behaviors, and binge eating in adolescent girls. *Journal of Abnormal Psychology, 108* (2), 255–266.

Ravelli, A.M., Helps B.A., Devane, S.P., Lask, B.D., and Milla, P.J. (1993). Normal gastric antral myoelectrical activity in early onset anorexia nervosa. *Archives of Diseases of Childhood, 69* (3), 342–346.

Rigotti, N.A., Neer, R.M., and Skates, S.J. (1991). The clinical course of osteoporosis in anorexia nervosa: A longitudinal study of cortical bone mass. *Journal of the American Medical Association, 265* (9), 1133–1138.

Rogol, A.D. (1998) Leptin and puberty. *Journal of Clinical Endocrinology and Metabolism, 83* (4), 1089–1090.

Rome, E.S., and Ammerman, S. (2003). Medical complications of eating disorders: An update. *Journal of Adolescent Health, 33* (6), 418–426.

Root, A.W., and Powers, P.S. (1983). Anorexia nervosa presenting as growth retardation in adolescents. *Journal of Adolescent Health Care, 4* (1), 25–30.

Ruuska, J., Kaltiala-Heino, R., Rantanen, P., and Koivisto, A.M. (2005). Psychopathological distress predicts suicidal ideation and self-harm in adolescent eating disorder outpatients. *European Child and Adolescent Psychiatry, 14* (5), 276–281.

Shamim, T., Golden, N.H., Arden, M., Filiberto, L., and Shenker, I.R. (2003). Resolution of vital sign instability: An objective measure of medical stability in anorexia nervosa. *Journal of Adolescent Health, 32* (1), 73–77.

Sherman, P., Leslie, K., Goldberg, E., Rybczynski, J., and St. Louis, P. (1994). Hypercarotenemia and transaminitis in female adolescents with eating disorders: A prospective, controlled study. *Journal of Adolescent Health, 15* (3), 205–209.

Sokol, M.S. (2000). Infection-triggered anorexia nervosa in children: Clinical description of four cases. *Journal of Child and Adolescent Psychopharmacology, 10* (2), 133–145.

Solomon, S.M., and Kirby, D.F. (1990). The refeeding syndrome: A review. *Journal of Parenteral and Enteral Nutrition, 14* (1), 90–97.

Steinhausen, H.C. (2002). The outcome of anorexia nervosa in the 20th century. *American Journal of Psychiatry, 159* (8), 1284–1293.

Stock, S.L., Goldberg, E., Corbett, S., and Katzman, D.K. (2002). Substance use in female adolescents with eating disorders. *Journal of Adolescent Health, 31* (2), 176–182.

Stoving, R.K., Hangaard, J., and Hagen, C. (2001). Update on endocrine disturbances in anorexia nervosa. *Journal of Pediatric Endocrinology and Metabolism, 14* (5), 459–480.

Stoving, R.K., Veldhuis, J.D., Flyvbjerg, A., Vinten, J., Hangaard, J., Koldkjaer, O.G., et al. (1999). Jointly amplified basal and pulsatile growth hormone (GH) secretion and increased process irregularity in women with anorexia nervosa: Indirect evidence for disruption of feedback regulation within the GH-insulin-like growth factor I axis. *Journal of Clinical Endocrinology and Metabolism, 84* (6), 2056–2063.

Swedo, S.E., Leonard, H.L., Garvey, M., Mittleman, B., Allen, A.J., Perlmutter, S., et al. (1988). Pediatric autoimmune neuropsychiatric disorders associated with streptococcal infections: Clinical description of the first 50 cases. *American Journal of Psychiatry, 155* (2), 624–627.

Swenne, I. (2004). Weight requirements for return of menstruations in teenage girls with eating disorders, weight loss and secondary amenorrhoea. *Acta Paediatrica, 93* (11), 1449–1455.

Swenne, I. (2005). Weight requirements for catch-up growth in girls with eating disorders and onset of weight loss before menarche. *International Journal of Eating Disorders, 38* (4), 340–345.

Theintz, G., Buchs, B., Rizzoli, R., Slosman, D., Clavien, H., Sizonenko, C., et al. (1992). Longitudinal monitoring of bone mass accumulation in healthy adolescents: Evidence for a marked reduction after 16 years of age at the levels of lumbar spine and femoral neck in female subjects. *Journal of Clinical Endocrinology and Metabolism, 75* (4), 1060–1065.

Ulger, Z., Gurses, D., Ozyurek, A.R., Arkan, C., Levent, E., and Aydogdu, S. (2006). Follow-up of cardiac abnormalities in female adolescents with anorexia nervosa after refeeding. *Acta Cardiologica, 61* (1), 43–49.

Waldholtz, B.D., and Andersen, A.E. (1990). Gastrointestinal symptoms in anorexia nervosa. A prospective study. *Gastroenterology, 98* (16), 1415–1419.

Welt, C.K., Chan, J.L., Bullen, J., Murphy, R., Smith, P., DePaoli, A.M., et al. (2004). Recombinant human leptin in women with hypothalamic amenorrhea. *New England Journal of Medicine, 351* (10), 987–997.

Wentz, E., Gillberg, I.C., Gillberg, C., Råstam, M., and Carina, G. (2005). Fertility and history of sexual abuse at 10-year follow-up of adolescent-onset anorexia nervosa. *International Journal of Eating Disorders, 37* (4), 294–298.

Wolfe, B.E., Metzger, E.D., Levine, J.M., and Jimerson, D.C. (2001). Laboratory screening for electrolyte abnormalities and anemia in bulimia nervosa: A controlled study. *International Journal of Eating Disorders, 30* (3), 288–293.

Wonderlich, S.A., Brewerton, T.D., Jocic, Z., Dansky, B.S., and Abbott, D.W. (1997). Relationship of childhood sexual abuse and eating disorders. *Journal of the American Academy of Child and Adolescent Psychiatry, 36* (8), 1107–1115.

8 Eating disorders and the brain

Ian Frampton and Anna Hutchinson

Introduction

Why is the brain important in eating disorders? At first glance, it may seem strange to be thinking about neuroscience at all. Surely eating disorders are a consequence of psychosocial pressure and cultural expectations for thinness and attractiveness, rather than anything to do with neurobiological abnormalities?

At a fundamental level, of course, we do need to invoke biological mechanisms to account for the processes and consequences of restricting food intake (weight loss, changes in appetite and the biological consequences of starvation, for example) and the processes of cognitive bias (believing oneself to be fat or too heavy) that are pathognomic to anorexia nervosa. However, recent advances in the neurosciences indicate that neurobiological mechanisms may also play a more fundamental role in the genesis and maintenance of eating disorders.

This perspective suggests that the characteristic repetitive restricted eating behaviours and intrusive thoughts about weight and shape in anorexia nervosa makes the disorder a prime candidate for neuropsychological modelling. Such models aim to account for how the surface features of the disorder relate to underlying information processing deficits. The characteristic overvalued ideas about weight and shape and restricted eating behaviour have obvious information processing parallels (in *flexible thinking* or *behavioural inhibition*, for example). Modelling them in neuropsychological terms may help our understanding and treatment.

Importance of a developmental perspective

Building neuropsychological models of eating disorders provides an opportunity to take a developmental perspective. From a neuroscience perspective, studying and ultimately helping children with eating disorders requires us to take account of the child's developing brain and cognitive skills, and how these might be affected by, as well as effect, starvation. Developmental neuropsychology is fundamentally not just about applying adult neuropsychology to little people and has a distinct basis in developmental psychology and developmental cognitive neuroscience (Johnson, 2005).

Nevertheless, because of the paucity of neuroscience research focusing solely on the early onset group, it will be necessary to draw cautiously on the adult neuropsychology literature, remaining mindful of the potential pitfalls of applying adult findings to children. Thus neuropsychological models aiming to account for the generation and maintenance of overvalued ideas about weight and shape and restricted eating should be able to explain how normal ways of thinking and behaving relate to the development of the disorder. Equally, taking a developmental perspective might challenge the adult-oriented assumption, derived mainly from cognitive models of psychopathology, that restricted eating is a consequence of concerns about weight and shape. In the early years of a child's development, behaviour tends to emerge before thoughts. So we cannot immediately discount the possibility that children might give up eating first, and then adopt beliefs about fear of fatness or weight gain as secondary sense-making phenomena to account for their behaviour. Developmental models should be able to account for either possibility.

For this review, we draw therefore on studies of both adult and childhood onset eating disorders, taking into account what we know about related and comorbid disorders such as obsessive compulsive disorder (OCD) and depression where helpful. Although this book aims to encompass all early onset eating disorders, because bulimia nervosa (BN) is much rarer in the early onset group and arguably a different disorder, and because there is almost no research into neuropsychological functioning in other eating disorders, we restrict the present review to early onset anorexia nervosa (EOAN).

Theoretical basis

Models implicating neurobiological or neuropsychological deficits should begin from a psychological theory that generates testable hypotheses. This approach can be distinguished from a 'battery' approach to neuropsychological assessment whereby a large number of assessments are made (frequently without statistical control for multiple comparisons) without any a priori prediction about expected pattern of deficits. At the most basic level, at least two possible explanations for neuropsychological deficits in eating disorders exist. The first is that the characteristic behavioural and cognitive features of EOAN could arise as a consequence of underlying neuropsychological abnormalities. The second is that eating disorder symptoms, such as maintained low weight, could themselves be the cause of disruption in neural mechanisms. Subsequently this might lead to interference with mental functioning, and hence neuropsychological deficits. In addition, theory underpinning neuropsychological models of EOAN should be able to account for the developmental and natural history of the disorder. EOAN itself may be a final common pathway emerging from a variety of predisposing and precipitating factors, and models should encompass this broad heterogeneity.

Finally, an adequate theoretical neuroscience model of EOAN must predict the direction of the relationship between the neurobiological abnormalities that have been empirically reported, the consistently found neuropsychological functioning deficits and the core cognitive and behavioural psychopathology.

Figure 8.1 shows three possible candidate models. In Figure 8.1a underlying neurobiological abnormalities (revealed by the neuroimaging studies reviewed below) have independent effects on neuropsychological functioning and psychopathology. In this model, neuropsychological deficits are simply 'markers' of underlying neurobiological abnormality (suggesting that neuropsychological assessment might be helpful as a cheap alternative to imaging in the absence of neuroimaging facilities!).

The second candidate model (Figure 8.1b) predicts that neuropsychological deficits mediate between the underlying neurobiological abnormalities and core psychopathology, with independent effects on behaviour and cognition (an attractive proposition for a neuroscientist, since these phenomena have different temporal and spatial realisation in the brain).

The third candidate model (Figure 8.1c) attempts to capture the implicit approach adopted by much of the research effort, which suggests that overvalued ideas about weight and shape lead to restricted eating, which in turn affects neurobiological functioning (due to the effects of starvation) and thus neuropsychological functioning. Of course, this 'causal' model still needs to account for why some individuals are more susceptible to developing overvalued ideas about weight and shape than others, whereas the first two predict that individuals who go on to develop EOAN may have a predisposing neurobiological vulnerability.

Proposed neuropsychological deficits should correlate with symptom severity (unless the model predicts that the deficit reflects an underlying trait). Models should also be able to account for why cognitions and behaviours in EOAN are relatively restricted (to food rather than fluids, and concerns typically about the size of trunk and thighs rather than other body parts). Why these symptoms and not others? Finally, proposed neuropsychological deficits should be specific to AN, and so studies should control for intelligence, comorbid depression and the presence of other anxiety disorders and OCD which can affect test results (Christensen, Kim, and Dysken, 1992; Tallis, 1997).

In the remainder of this chapter, we explore the brain structures that are important in eating. As above, we differentiate three levels at which eating disorders can be described: neurobiological abnormalities, neuropsychological functioning and eating disorder psychopathology. We then discuss the recent advances in neuroimaging technologies which have helped us to become much clearer about neurobiological abnormalities in AN. We go on to review

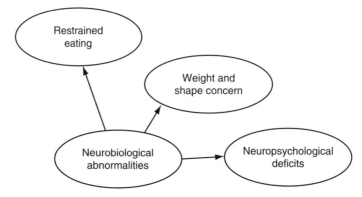

Figure 8.1a Hypothesised independent effects of underlying neurobiological abnormalities on neuropsychology and psychopathology.

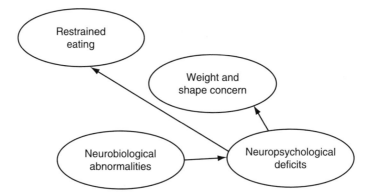

Figure 8.1b Alternative formulation suggesting that neuropsychological deficits mediate between neurobiological abnormalities and psychopathology, potentially with independent effects on restrained eating behaviour and eating disorder psychopathology.

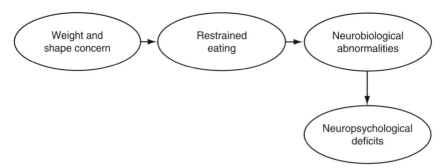

Figure 8.1c Causal model suggesting that cognitive deficits come first and lead to restrained eating, which in turn causes neurobiological abnormalities and neuropsychological deficits.

the evidence that there is some form of neuropsychological deficit in at least a subset of patients with EOAN, and the implications of these findings for understanding the aetiology and/or maintenance of the condition. Finally, we conclude with a summary and point to potential future directions for research and treatment.

The brain in eating

To answer the question 'What part of the brain is involved in eating?' it would be a lot easier to begin by specifying those parts of the brain that are not implicated. This would be a very short list indeed. Eating meets a primary need to sustain life. As such it falls under the control of a vast number of brain structures, from instinctive behavioural macros that drive unconscious behaviour through to the highest level cognitive representations of how to behave in complex social situations such as not snaffling all the canapés at the departmental Christmas party.

From the outset it is important to clarify that we are grossly oversimplifying the situation in ascribing specific functions to individual parts of the brain. Recent advances in the neurosciences have helped us to understand how performance of even the simplest task requires the integrated functioning of a vast number of structures and the connections between them. These so-called connectionist models of cognitive functioning place at least as much emphasis on the connections between structures as on the structures themselves. This has led to the development of disconnection theories of a range of psychiatric disorders including schizophrenia.

Having presented this caveat, Table 8.1 summarises the principal neural structures potentially involved in anorexia nervosa, based on Nunn, Gordon, Frampton, and Lask (2006). Many of the structures proposed by Nunn and colleagues are consistent with the model developed by Connan, Campbell, and Katzman (2003) which emphasises the involvement of the limbic system and prefrontal cortex in AN.

Neuroimaging studies in EOAN

Having identified which brain structures appear to be important in eating and its disorders, the obvious next stage is to use neuroimaging technology to look at their structure and function both at low weight and following weight restoration. Taking this prospective approach has enabled researchers to address, in part, the fundamental question about whether any abnormalities are more likely to be secondary to the disorder, or pre-existing and therefore potentially causal. From a methodological perspective, the low incidence of EOAN presents a problem in eating disorder research in proving that abnormalities in brain functioning cause the disorder. We would need to design a prospective study to scan a very large number of children at a young age before eating disorder psychopathology starts to emerge, to look for

Table 8.1 Proposed relationship between eating disorder characteristics, neural structure and function (after Nunn et al., 2006).

Eating disorder characteristics	Key neural structures	Key functions
Core psychopathology		
Morbid preoccupation with weight and shape	Somatosensory cortex Amygdala Frontal cortex	Body size evaluation Threat detection Information processing
Distorted body image	Somatosensory cortex Hippocampus Frontal cortex	Body size evaluation Contextual memory Information processing
Restricted food intake	Hypothalamus Striatum Frontal cortex	Appetite and satiety Reward value of eating Goal directed behaviour
Associated features		
Low self-esteem, shame and disgust	Insular cortex Limbic system Frontal cortex	Disgust Linking bodily experience to feelings and thoughts Information processing
Drive for thinness	Striatum Frontal cortex	Reward Goal-directed behaviour
Common comorbid features		
Obsessions and compulsions	Striatum Frontal cortex	Compulsive behaviours Obsessional thoughts
Anxiety	Amygdala Hippocampus	Threat detection Contextual memory
Depression	Hippocampus Frontal cortex	Contextual memory Information processing
Impaired visuospatial skills	Parietal cortex Hippocampus	Visual association processing Long-term visual memory
Impaired executive functions	Frontal cortex	Cognitive inhibition
Empathy impairment	Limbic system Frontal cortex	Linking bodily experience to feelings and thoughts Information processing
Anosognosia	Somatosensory cortex Frontal cortex	Body evaluation Information processing
Raised pain threshold	Thalamus Insular cortex Somatosensory cortex	Pain processing Pain processing Body evaluation

both structural and functional abnormalities that predict the subsequent emergence of anorexia nervosa or other eating disorders.

Structural imaging studies

The technology to scan the detailed internal structure of the brain has been available for several years. Computed tomography (CT) scans use digital geometry processing to generate a three-dimensional image of the brain from a large series of two-dimensional X-ray images. More recently, magnetic resonance imaging (MRI), using the safe application of a fast-switching electromagnetic field together with radio frequency (RF) waves, has been used to create very detailed maps of the micro-structure of the brain, with higher levels of spatial resolution than CT.

Studies using structural scanning technology have consistently shown ventricular enlargement which decreases with refeeding, both in mixed populations of adults and adolescents (Palazidou, Robinson, and Lishman, 1990), and in early onset AN (Katzmann, Zipursky, Lambe, and Mikulis, 2003). The findings suggest that the changes may be due to neuronal damage secondary to malnutrition, with possible regeneration of myelin accounting for the general reversibility (Artmann, Grau, Adelmann, and Schleiffer, 1985).

Functional imaging studies

More recently, functional imaging techniques have been developed that enable us to observe how the brain is functioning, either at rest or in response to specific sensory stimulation such as being shown a series of pictures of highly calorific foods. One of the first types of functional imaging techniques developed was a variant of CT scanning using single positron emission computed tomography (SPECT) to explore regional cerebral blood flow. This technique shows which parts of the brain are hypoperfused (receiving less blood flow, and thus considered to be less active) than more active parts of the brain receiving more blood flow.

Functional neuroimaging studies in EOAN using SPECT (Chowdhury, Gordon, Lask, Watkins, Watt, and Christie, 2003; Gordon et al., 1997) have consistently shown evidence of hypoperfusion in the temporal region, predominantly antero-medial, but also stretching to the frontal and parietal lobes and the striatum in some instances. This hypoperfusion, a reflection of hypometabolism, appears to be significantly correlated with impaired visuo-spatial memory and impaired executive functioning, specifically in the area of cognitive inhibition (Hutchinson, Frampton, Chowdhury, Watkins, Gordon, and Lask, 2006; Lask et al., 2005).

The key finding emerging from these studies is that there is unilateral reduction of blood flow in the temporal lobe and/or associated areas in about 75 per cent of patients with early onset AN. While these studies need to be replicated, present knowledge indicates that there is no association between this reduction in blood flow and cerebral dominance, nutritional status, length of illness, mood or eating disorder psychopathology. However, it appears that there may be a significant association between reduced blood flow and impaired visuo-spatial ability, impaired complex visual memory and enhanced speed of information processing.

There have been no other reports of functional neuroimaging conducted on younger patients with AN. However, Råstam et al. (2001) reported on the use of SPECT on 21 adult patients seven years after their predominantly adolescent onset of AN. They found reduced blood flow in the temporal or associated regions in 14 patients (66 per cent) with no correlations between reduction in blood flow and current BMI, lowest ever BMI, any residual eating disorder psychopathology, or IQ.

Taken together, functional neuroimaging studies of mixed populations (child, adolescent and adult) using SPECT report inconsistent findings, with some studies reporting no abnormalities, others noting hypermetabolism, and yet others hypometabolism. There are a number of possible explanations for these contrasting findings: (a) mixed age range; (b) use of different equipment; (c) different methods of interpretation of the imaging; (d) failure to control for emotional arousal; (e) comorbidity; (f) whether the imaging was conducted before or after a meal; (g) other methodological problems associated with functional neuroimaging.

Nevertheless, the functional changes reported do require explanation. It is unlikely that unilateral and localised hypoperfusion would result from starvation factors alone. The persistence of reduced regional cerebral blood flow at follow-up, independent of such variables as previous or current nutritional status and eating disorder psychopathology (Lask, Gordon, Christie, Frampton, Chowdhury, and Watkins, 2005; Rastam et al., 2001) suggests that the hypoperfusion is likely to be either a primary phenomenon or a result of starvation that is slow to reverse, or is actually irreversible. The combination of reduced regional cerebral blood flow and its possible association with impairments of cognitive function, independent of nutritional status, point to both cortical and subcortical components indicating a systemic rather than a focal abnormality. As we have described above, it is much more likely that the neurobiological abnormalities underlying eating disorders will turn out to be a subtle impairment in a complex neural network of structures and connections, rather than a 'hole in the head' specific deficit in one part of the brain.

Chowdhury et al. (2003) have argued that the neural circuit most likely to account for the characteristic features of AN as well as this pattern of reduced blood flow and impaired cognitive functioning is the limbic system. This set of interlinked structures includes the temporal lobe and adjacent structures, such as the hypothalamus, amygdala, thalamus and hippocampus. It is important in emotion and appetite regulation, memory, motivation and perception.

Developments of MRI techniques have also enabled us to see how blood oxygen levels in the brain change in relation to sensory stimulation with pictures or sounds. This technique also measures blood oxygen levels and identifies structures that have higher levels of activation in response to specific tasks. In studies of adults with AN using functional MRI (fMRI), Uher, Brammer, Murphy, Campbell, Ng, Williams, and Treasure (2003) showed that in response to pictures of high calorie foods such as cake, individuals who had recovered from AN continued to show increased medial prefrontal and anterior cingulate activation, as well as a lack of activity in the inferior parietal lobule, compared with healthy control subjects. They also showed that increased activation of the right lateral prefrontal, apical prefrontal, and dorsal anterior cingulate cortices differentiated these recovered subjects from chronically ill patients. They showed that group differences were specific to food stimuli, whereas processing of general emotional stimuli did not differ between groups. The authors concluded that separate neural correlates underlie trait and state characteristics of AN and that different patterns of activation are associated with good or poor outcome, possibly reflecting heterogeneous subtypes.

Similarly, Seeger, Braus, Ruf, Goldberger, and Schmidt (2002) used fMRI in combination with a computer-based life image distortion technique to show adult female anorectic patients and healthy controls digital pictures of their own body image, individually distorted by themselves. They showed that for patients with anorexia nervosa, stimulation with their own body image was associated with more activation in the right amygdala, the right fusiform gyrus and the brainstem region compared with controls and concluded that their preliminary findings indicate an activation of the brain's 'fear network'. They suggested that future research should examine body image distortions in anorectic patients using fMRI to further evaluate the course of this disturbance in a longitudinal approach.

Neurotransmitter imaging studies

As well as exploring brain structure and functioning using CT and MRI, neuroimaging technologies have also been developed to look at the activity of neurotransmitter chemicals in the brain in eating disorders. These chemicals carry signals across the synapse from one brain cell to the next. Using radioactive tracers or ligands injected into the bloodstream that attach themselves to specific neurotransmitters, it is possible to detect the amount of this neurotransmitter's activity using positron emission tomography (PET).

Kaye et al. (2005) have summarised several studies using imaging with radioligands specific for the neurotransmitters serotonin (5HT) and dopamine (DA). These studies have shown abnormalities in the amount of serotonin (5HT) and dopamine (DA) in the synapse in adults with eating disorders, associated with characteristics such as harm avoidance, behavioural inhibition and self-control. These findings are important as serotonin (5HT) is thought to play a role in behavioural inhibition and is involved in the regulation of many biological systems including feeding behaviour and emotion processing. High levels of 5HT have been associated with inflexibility and obsessive compulsive disorder (Baxter et al., 2000) which has striking levels of comorbidity with AN. Conversely, dopamine has been associated with the regulation of attention and behaviour, motor activity, reward sensitivity and novelty seeking, all potential candidates for involvement in AN.

Kaye et al. (2005) caution that the 5HT and DA systems are highly complex and so disturbances of these components may reflect complex dysregulation of neuronal systems, rather than a simple causal mechanism. They suggest that although these imaging technologies tend to be a one-time, static measure, they can inform about the activity of 5HT and DA in brain regions, and thus aid in the identification of circuits contributing to AN. Used in combination with fMRI, future studies can help us to understand the dynamic relationship of symptoms such as abnormal feeding to the function of brain regions. For example, disturbances of DA suggest alterations in the modulation of salient stimuli, motivation and reward systems for food in the brain. Future fMRI studies can help to explore how individuals with AN and controls activate different brain regions in response to rewarding tasks.

Neuropsychological factors

Comprehensive reviews of neuropsychological functioning in eating disorders have been conducted recently by Duchesne, Mattos, Fontelle, Veiga, and Apporlinario (2004), Tchanturia, Campbell, Morris, and Treasure (2005), Southgate, Tchanturia, and Treasure (2005), and Ryan, Øveras, and Frampton (2006). Rather than list findings from the literature here, we have identified two distinct areas where links between neurobiological abnormality, neuropsychological functioning and eating disorder psychopathology have been made, and where there have been contributions from researchers working specifically in EOAN.

Visuospatial deficit models

The theory that visuospatial deficits might contribute to EOAN is plausible, since there is an obvious connection between distorted body image and eating disorder psychopathology. Visuospatial skills are required to perceive and manipulate objects in two and three dimensions (Rauch and Savage, 1997) and to put visual information together in a gestalt to see the 'big picture' (rather than focusing on individual elements in a sequence as in linguistic processing). Such skills are associated with the Performance Scale of IQ tests such as the WAIS-III and WISC-III-UK. From the perspective of adult neuropsychological theory, deficits in Performance Scale relative to Verbal Scale tasks are suggestive of right hemisphere dysfunction.

However, from a developmental neuropsychology perspective, so-called

Verbal-Performance (V-P) discrepancies are associated with range of neuro-developmental disorders, including autism or Tourette's syndrome. It has been argued that V-P discrepancies in which verbal skills are superior to performance skills illustrate how neuroplastic factors in the developing brain preserve verbal over nonverbal skills (Goodman and Yude, 1996). Brain areas (particularly in the right hemisphere in right-handed individuals) that are normally destined to subserve visuospatial functions may also have a 'shadow' potential to take on language functions. Where early disruption forces reorganisation, areas destined for visuospatial functions can be 'colonised' by language processes, with the resulting crowding out of subtle visuospatial skills.

It is therefore interesting that neuropsychological studies have consistently identified abnormalities in visual spatial processing in anorexia nervosa. For example, Thompson (1993), Kingston, Szmukler, Andrews, Tress, and Desmond (1996), Jones, Duncan, and Brouwers (1991) and Gillberg, Gillberg, Råstam, and Johanson (1996) have all reported that AN groups performed significantly worse than control groups on visual perceptual tasks including the Picture Completion and Object Assembly subtests of the Wechsler Adult Intelligence Scale (Revised) or on the Rey-Osterreith Complex Figure. Also Fowler and colleagues (2005) recently reported impairments on tests of spatial recognition and rapid visual information processing in adults with AN, as measured by the Cambridge Neuropsychological Test Automated Battery (CANTAB).

Alternative measures of visuospatial abilities have also yielded significant results. Hamsher, Halmi, and Benton (1981) found over 25 per cent of a sample with AN were deficient on the Benton Visual Retention Test (BVRT) on admission, whilst Palazidou et al. (1990) reports a significant difference between the anorexic and control groups on the visual spatial ability subtest of the Bexley Maudsley Automated Psychological Screening Battery. Maxwell, Tucker, and Townes (1984) found that those with AN did not differ significantly from controls when drawing a complex design from a model (Aphasia Screening Test) but their pictures were much oversimplified and distorted. This could be indicative of a deficit in either spatial processing or short-term visuospatial memory. More research is needed to clarify and better understand these findings. Although no research has yet reported any correlation between body mass index (BMI) and neuropsychological deficits and most of these studies have failed to find a relationship between depression and cognitive performance, future studies still need to control for such variables (Hamsher et al., 1981; Kingston et al., 1996; Szmukler, Andrews, Chen, and Stanley, 1992).

It is not yet known how visuospatial processing might be related to eating disorder symptoms. A current limitation of previous research is that there is a lack of any coherent model to explain how these disturbances might be related to the onset, maintenance or exacerbation to such symptoms as body image disturbance. It may be that within the western cultural climate someone with a tendency to perceive their body as being larger than it is, whether due to visuospatial deficits or other disturbances, will be particularly vulnerable to attempting to restrict their food intake. When associated with other variables, such as low self-esteem, this in turn leads to a greater risk of developing an eating disorder. Severity of any eating disorder appears to be increased if there is body image disturbance, as well as risk of relapsing once recovered.

Although intuitive links have been made between these visuospatial deficits and body image disturbance, there are no existing studies that examine both variables together within this population. Additionally, to date no research has been conducted that attempts to examine whether perceptual and attitudinal aspects of body image might be related to each other. In conclusion, the neuropsychological and neurological deficits found in some people with AN may be crucial to the clinical features of this condition, such as body image disturbance, rather than simply a sign of unrelated abnormalities within the brain. Future research should therefore explore visuospatial abilities (specifically visuospatial memory, object recognition and spatial perception), and both attitudinal and perceptual measures of body image disturbance in order to identify whether there are any relationships between these variables.

Executive functioning deficit models of EOAN

The term 'executive functioning' (EF) encompasses a wide range of skills needed to solve problems. These include goal-directed behaviour, maintenance of a cognitive set of representations of the problem to be solved, inhibition of automatic responding and sustained attention. These functions have been localised to the orbital and dorsolateral region of the prefrontal cortex (Lezak, 1995).

From a developmental neuropsychology perspective, Pennington and Ozonoff (1996) have reviewed the potential contribution of executive functioning deficits to a range of disorders including autism and hyperkinetic disorder. Several studies have explored the emergence of EF skills in normal and clinical populations of children following meningitis infection and girls with Turner syndrome (Romans, 1997). In the following section we review the neuropsychological evidence of impairment in inhibition and set shifting in anorexia nervosa.

Behavioural and cognitive inhibition

Evidence from ethology suggests that most species will be prompted by the presence of food to eat it. In an uncertain world when it is not clear where the next meal might be coming from patients with anorexia nervosa have an enhanced ability to inhibit such behaviours. Much has been learned in recent years about the neurobiological basis of behavioural inhibition, both in normally developing and brain injured populations, and we review these advances below. We attempt to integrate these findings with the neuro-psychology literature in AN and propose that individuals who go on to develop anorexia nervosa in the context of specific precipitating factors may have an underlying neurobehavioural bias towards enhanced behavioural inhibition. On the other hand, there is also evidence that individuals with anorexia nervosa have impaired cognitive inhibition, in the sense that they are prone to overvalued ideas of the importance of body weight and shape to self-concept (Shafran and Somers, 1998). One possibility is that the core psychopathology of anorexia nervosa reflects impairment in neural networks that inhibit cognitive biases.

The study of inhibition has been consistently linked, experimentally and theoretically, to specific brain regions within the prefrontal cortex. Adults with frontal lobe damage frequently persevere with unsuccessful strategies or responses to tasks, suggesting that they are having problems with inhibiting ongoing behaviour and generating a more appropriate response (Dennis, 1991). In this sense inhibition is essential for control, and thus purposeful goal-directed activity. Many patients with frontal lobe damage are reported as having problems inhibiting their responses to external or internal stimuli when appropriate (for example, see Shimamura, Berry, Mangels, and Rusting, 1995).

Henson, Shallice, Josephs, and Dolan (2002) recently demonstrated, through the use of fMRI, that there may be distinct regions within the pre-frontal cortex that serve different inhibitory functions. Results from their study suggest that the left inferior frontal regions are associated with verbal fluency and the ability to initiate a search for appropriate responses, whilst the frontopolar regions appear to be associated with the ability to override external stimuli and follow internalised response rules. Both skills are essen-tial in order to inhibit and 'disinhibit' responses to external and internal stimuli when appropriate or functional.

Aron, Fletcher, Bullmore, Sahakian, and Robbins (2003) recently tested inhibition in 18 patients with lesions of the right frontal lobe. They used a traditional test of behavioural inhibition – the 'Go-No-Go task' and found, in line with previous research, that their patients had more difficulty inhibiting their responses than did the healthy controls. MRI scans of the patients' brains demonstrated a correlation between damage to the inferior frontal gyrus and the response times for the no-go trials, suggesting that this region is also critical for response inhibition. Thus damage to frontal brain regions appear to result in deficits in inhibitory ability. In the context of brain injury, these deficits present as traditional executive functioning impairments, with patients unable to control both their thinking (cognitive inhibition) or behaviours (behavioural inhibition).

In eating disorders, more subtle deficits in executive functions have been demonstrated than those seen in acquired brain injury. Ohrmann et al. (2004) have demonstrated impaired performance of participants with AN on a 'Go-No-Go and Stop' task compared to matched controls. Similarly,

Kaye et al. (2005) used the Matching Familiar Figures Task (MFFT) as a measure of cognitive response style, since it is possible to respond to this task with an impulsive style (associated with a high rate of speed-error trade-offs) or a reflective style (taking longer to make a response but being more accurate). In both studies, participants with the restricting subtype of AN adopted a reflective cognitive response style, whereas individuals with the binge-purging subtype typically showed the opposite response style, making inaccurate responses with short reaction times.

Set shifting

The second component of executive functioning, set shifting, refers to the ability to mentally switch from one way of thinking to another, in response to changing task demands. The possibility that the set-shifting component of executive functioning might be impaired in EOAN is intriguing, since neuropsychological deficits in this domain are associated with cognitive inflexibility (the tendency to adopt concrete and rigid approaches to problems) and behavioural inflexibility (the tendency to perform perseverative or stereotyped behaviours). In the case of anorexia nervosa, the total and inflexible preoccupation with weight and shape-related issues and a totally rigid approach to eating are obvious parallels with these information-processing styles.

A number of studies with adult populations using tasks such as the Wisconsin Card Sorting Test (WCST) and the Trail Making Test (TMT) which are both good measures of set shifting have reported impaired performance in AN samples (Bowers, 1994; Fassino, Piero, Daga, Leombruin, Mortara, and Rovera, 2002; Holliday, Tchanturia, Landau, Collier, and Treasure, 2005; Jones et al., 1991; Lauer, Gorzewski, Gerlinghoff, and Zihl, 1999; Tchanturia, Morris, and Brecelj Anderluh, 2004; Tchanturia, Serpell, Troop, and Treasure, 2001; Tchanturia et al., 2005). In the case of EOAN, Hutchinson et al. (2006) have demonstrated enduring impairment in TMT performance in a group of young people previously diagnosed with an eating disorder two to three years after weight recovery, suggesting that set-shifting problems may be an underlying state vulnerability for developing an eating disorder. Recently, Southgate et al. (2005) have shown that adults with a diagnosis of restricting subtype AN were significantly less flexible on set-shifting measures than individuals with a history of binge-purging subtype, demonstrating a link between neuropsychological functioning and psychopathogy.

Neuropsychological deficits in AN: cause or effect?

Research thus far suggests that neuropsychological and neurological deficits certainly could precede the onset of AN in some individuals, based on the fact that although many neuropsychological abilities appear to improve with refeeding in AN, some deficits – namely visuospatial/sensory and set-shifting and inhibitory abilities – do not (e.g. Green, Elliman, Wakeling, and Rogers, 1996; Grunwald et al., 2001; Tchanturia et al., 2004). It is worth considering that other groups that have experienced extreme weight loss, hypoglycaemia and/or inadequate nutritional uptake, such as extreme dieters, prisoners of war and people with diabetes, frequently do recover all functioning once they are no longer malnourished.

Additionally, these groups show similar but slightly different patterns of deficits to those found in AN. POWs, extreme dieters and those with diabetes mirror the AN population with regard to their impaired and recovering executive functioning. However, it seems that the apparently consistent deficit in the visuospatial domain is unique to people who have experienced starvation due to AN (see Mathias and Kent, 1998). Once more we point to the parallel findings of impaired executive functioning and visuospatial skills in a variety of pervasive developmental disorders, as well as OCD and attention deficit/hyperactivity disorders, in children (see Watanabe et al., 2005). Such a similar pattern of impairments between EOAN and well-defined developmental disorders suggests that EOAN may also follow some form of neurodevelopmental course, at least in a subset of cases.

Adolescence – a critical period in brain development

A second possibility is that the neuropsychological and neurological deficits do not precede the illness and are simply the end result of having experienced malnutrition at a specific point in development. The above studies into malnutrition were conducted with adult participants. For teenage onset anorexia, it may be that experiencing malnutrition during a critical period of hormonal and neurological development, perhaps alongside body shape changes, might lead to these observed impairments. Thatcher (1992) has demonstrated with EEG data that neurons in the frontal lobes of the brain appear to go through bursts of growth, both in the number of cells and in the extent of their connections with each other during the first few years of life and again during adolescence. During these peak periods of synaptic growth, cognitive abilities may be temporarily impaired, by the excess number of new synapses being formed (McGivern, Andersen, Byrd, Mutter, and Reilly, 2002).

While as yet there is little research into the impact of puberty and adolescence on visuospatial functioning, there is growing empirical evidence of impairment in frontally mediated skills during this time of development. For example, the role of the frontal lobes in recognising and understanding other people's emotions is well documented (see Frith and Frith, 1999). McGivern, Andersen, Byrd, Mutter, and Reilly (2002) have demonstrated that reaction times for judging facial emotions were significantly longer in a group of 11- and 12-year-old children than they were for the same group when tested the previous year. A similar study looking at unfamiliar face recognition in late childhood and adolescence found that these skills seemed to be impaired between the ages of 11 and 14 years of age, after which improvement occurs (Carey, Diamond, and Woods, 1980).

Thus, as the frontal areas continue developing into adolescence, young people who already have a predisposing bias towards enhanced behavioural inhibition may now be at risk of developing an opposite bias, i.e. reduced cognitive inhibition. In consequence it may be more difficult to inhibit socially imposed beliefs regarding weight and shape. If this were the case, the individual would be 'flooded' with conscious negative ideas relating to the self and the body. Those with enhanced behavioural inhibition might attempt to 'neutralise' these thoughts via altering their eating behaviours, which if successful could lead to a self-maintaining cycle of thinking and behaviour as seen in AN.

If this pattern of impaired cognitive and enhanced behavioural inhibition exists during the final cycle of synaptic growth and reorganisation during adolescence, then it is conceivable that these biases might become a stable part of that person's neuropsychological functioning into adulthood. Equally, this model could account for the fact that adolescence is in a risk period for a range of neurodevelopmental disorders that implicate executive dysfunction, including obsessive compulsive disorder and early psychosis.

There is clearly more work needed to help us understand the role of adolescence in neuropsychological development (and vice versa), both within clinical and normally developing populations. Future work, including prospective studies, is needed to clarify whether an individual who goes on to develop AN is neuropsychologically predisposed from early life to developing specific cognitive and behavioural biases, or as suggested above these become 'hard wired' if encountered during later critical stages of brain development.

Neuropsychological models

Based on the research reviewed above, Nunn et al. (2006) have hypothesised that AN might emerge as a final pathway of interactions between predisposing and precipitating factors. Within specific setting conditions such as sociocultural pressures to be thin and a driven and perfectionist personality, a neural circuit imbalance may be triggered by such factors as puberty, dieting, weight loss and various stressors. The consequent imbalance allows the emergence of the characteristic features of AN. They suggest that this imbalance may be centred around the insular cortex, a structure that is important in regulating the activity of the neocortex and limbic system and communications between them. Thus children at risk of developing anorexia nervosa may have an underlying impairment or dysfunction of the insula which constrains its ability to modulate these networks. It is intriguing that the insula lies medial to the temporal lobe and it is in this area that the abnormalities in regional cerebral blood flow are most commonly noted (Chowdhury et al., 2003; Gordon, Lask, Bryant-Waugh, Christie, and Timimi, 1997; Lask et al., 2005). Equally intriguing is the fact that a proportion of patients with EOAN have no abnormalities of cerebral perfusion or neuropsychological function-ing, raising the possibility that there may be more than one type of early onset AN, as has also been proposed by Råstam et al. (2001).

Connan et al. (2003) have elaborated an alternative model of eating disorders that incorporates a developmental perspective within a compre-hensive biopsychosocial framework. In their neurodevelopmental model, a complex interaction between multiple genetic factors, early life experience and environment around the time of puberty may confer specific risk for AN through impaired regulation of emotion and appetite. They propose that poor regulation of the stress response and impaired functioning of the hypothalamic-pituitary-adrenal (HPA) axis makes vulnerable individuals susceptible to chronic stress and maladaptive coping strategies (including impaired emotional, cognitive and social functioning), mediated by genetic and environmental influences. They propose that these underlying neurobiol-ogical abnormalities interact with impaired neuropsychological functioning in a critical period of adolescent development to produce and maintain the characteristic cognitive and behavioural psychopathology of eating disorders.

A third alternative hypothesis has been proposed by Steinglass and Walsh (2006) who make links between specific neurocognitive disturbances in indi-viduals with OCD and potential neural mechanisms mediating both these and the psychological disturbances. They argue that similar disturbances, involving neural circuits between the cortex and the basal ganglia, may be present in individuals with AN.

Further research is required to test these hypotheses. A testable paradigm needs to be constructed that allows for the exploration of the relationship between brain metabolism and the cognitive processes most relevant to AN. Of particular interest would be a study that sought to investigate the relation-ship between the distorted body image that is pathognomonic to anorexia nervosa and the findings of impairments of visuospatial abilities and complex visual memory reviewed above. The use of functioning imaging techniques would allow for both activation and prospective studies whilst controlling for relevant variables such as age at onset, length of illness, sex, mood, nutritional status, eating disorder psychopathology and comorbidity.

Neuropsychological assessment

Researchers exploring a wide variety of disorders have called for the develop-ment of more sophisticated approaches to psychotherapy, whereby interven-tions are amended as appropriate to each patient's cognitive abilities, strengths and weaknesses in order to increase the chance of a treatment being effective (Steinglass and Walsh, 2006). There is evidence to suggest that neuropsycho-logical performance may be related to outcome in AN (Hamsher et al., 1981; Kingston et al., 1996), with individuals who are impaired on more than one domain being statistically more likely to have poorer outcome. Identifying children who fit such a potential 'neurodevelopmental subtype' (Hutchinson et al., submitted) may therefore be important in treatment and prognostic planning. It seems that neuropsychological testing should be an important component of any assessment of a child presenting with EOAN.

Another reason for conducting a neuropsychological assessment is to help identify young people who fit the classic AN profile of being academic overachievers. Research has shown that young people with AN typically have worked diligently in school to achieve good grades and make impressive academic progress, beyond the level predicted by their cognitive ability. Bruch (1973) originally described a tendency for concrete thinking with a perfectionist and compulsive attitude towards scholastic achievement. Subsequent studies have confirmed average-range IQ using global measures of intellectual functioning, contrasted with overachievement in attainment measures particularly in reading and spelling (Hamsher et al., 1981; Mathias and Kent, 1998; Touyz, Beumont, and Johnstone, 1986). It is therefore helpful to identify those children presenting with eating disorders who have been striving to produce good grades beyond their predicted ability level, and to encourage a more realistic level of expectation from teachers, parents and young people themselves.

Treatment implications

As mentioned briefly above, taking a neuropsychological perspective may encourage the development of novel treatment strategies in AN. The theoretical and functional models presented above, if proven, may point to novel pharmacological treatment to modulate the activity of serotonin and dopamine neurotransmitter systems. The implication of the HPA axis in Connan et al.'s (2003) model points to medical treatments targeting noradrenaline and its precursors.

From a psychological treatment perspective, the elucidation of set-shifting and inhibition deficits in AN has already led to the development of novel cognitive remediation treatment. This approach, grounded in neuropsychological theory, adapted from work with adults with acquired brain injury and initially applied in the context of early psychosis (Wykes, 1998), has recently been extended by Tchanturia et al. (2005) to apply to eating disorders. In a series of structured sessions, patients are invited to work on cognitive tasks to improve their ability to shift cognitive perspective (for example, by looking at visual illusions that contain two embedded images and to shift between them).Through repeated practice and reflection on the process, patients are encouraged to adopt more flexible thinking styles in their everyday life.

Results from early trials of this intervention are promising (Davies and Tchanturia, 2005), with participants reporting a high degree of satisfaction and enjoyment with the tasks. In particular, taking the focus away from endless discussion over food and eating creates the possibility for making therapeutic progress in other areas. Patients report that they are making connections between the tasks and their everyday experiences, and the results of controlled trials in schizophrenia are positive (Wykes, 1998). As we improve our understanding of how visuospatial processing might be related to body image in EOAN, it seems possible that unique treatments aiming to either modify or circumnavigate patient's visuospatial ability could also be developed.

Finally, the emphasis on emotion-processing deficits highlighted in the models of Connan et al. (2003) and Southgate et al. (2005) implies that psychological approaches to improving emotion recognition and expression may be appropriate for use with this client group. Such 'mindfulness' approaches to enhancing and regulating subjective emotional experience have been developed in a range of other psychiatric disorders and may be applicable to AN.

Conclusions

Neuropsychological models may be very helpful in developing our understanding of anorexia nervosa. Restricted behaviours and disinhibited thoughts have obvious information-processing parallels, and a strong neuropsychological theory would posit core processing deficits (in perseveration or cognitive inhibition, for example), which can account for the psychopathology of eating disorders. Weaker models might make comparisons between neuropsychological deficits and the phenomenology of AN, without suggesting that they are somehow causal.

The development of neuropsychological models of AN has tended to follow trends in neuropsychology research, beginning with a focus on visuospatial deficits and more recently encompassing executive dysfunction. Early experimental studies were flawed by design weaknesses including use of non-clinical control groups, failure to control for multiple comparisons, poor selection of clinical cases and lack of underlying theory guiding experimentation. More recent studies have addressed some of these weaknesses and links with other areas of neuroscience research, including structural and functional neuroimaging, have strengthened theory and experimental design.

One of the key areas where neuropsychological models may become increasingly helpful is in the delineation of subgroups within EOAN. Neuropsychology may be helpful in defining subgroups of patients, based on common neuropsychological profiles, who will be predicted to have more complex and enduring problems. Functional neuroimaging tasks that include measures of specific neuropsychological functions may be particularly useful for detecting neuroanatomical characteristics that distinguish EOAN subgroups (Lask et al., 2005). From a developmental neuropsychology perspective, early identification and intervention during childhood and adolescence, when these cognitive skills would normally be maturing, may provide new opportunities to prevent young people with EOAN facing a chronic and debilitating disorder.

References

Aron, A.R., Fletcher, P.C., Bullmore, E.T., Sahakian, B.J., and Robbins, T. W. (2003). Stop-signal inhibition disruption by damage to right inferior frontal gyrus in humans. *Nature Neuroscience, 6*, 115–116.

Artmann, H., Grau, H., Adelmann, M., and Schleiffer, R. (1985). Reversible and non-reversible enlargement of cerebrospinal fluid space in AN. *Biological Psychiatry, 23*, 377–387.

Baxter, L.R., Ackermann, R.F., Swerdlow, N.R., Brody, A., Sacena, S., Schwartz, J.M., et al. (2000). Specific brain system mediation of obsessive-compulsive disorder responsive to either medication or behaviour therapy. In W.K. Goodman, M.V. Rudorfer, and J.D. Maser (Eds.), *Obsessive-compulsive disorder: Contemporary issues in treatment* (pp. 573–609). Mahwah, NJ: Lawrence Erlbaum Associates, Inc.

Bowers, W. (1994). Neuropsychological impairment among anorexia nervosa and bulimia patients. *Eating Disorders, 2* (1), 42–46.

Bruch, H. (1973). *Eating disorders: Obesity, anorexia and the person within*. New York: Basic Books.

Carey, S., Diamond, R., and Woods, B. (1980). Development of face recognition: A maturational component? *Developmental Psychology, 16*, 257–269.

Chowdhury, U., Gordon, I., Lask, B., Watkins, B., Watt, H., and Christie, D. (2003). Early-onset anorexia nervosa: Is there evidence of limbic system imbalance? *International Journal of Eating Disorders, 33*, 388–396.

Christensen, K.J., Kim, S.W., and Dysken, M.W. (1992). Neuropsychological performance in obsessive-compulsive disorder. *Biological Psychiatry, 3*, 14–18.

Connan, F., Campbell, I.C., and Katzman, M. (2003). A neurodevelopmental model for anorexia nervosa. *Physiology and Behaviour, 79*, 13–24.

Davies, H., and Tchanturia, K. (2005). Cognitive remediation therapy as an intervention for acute anorexia nervosa. *European Eating Disorders Review, 13*, 311–316.

Dennis, M. (1991). Frontal lobe function in childhood and adolescence: A heuristic for assessing attention regulation and executive control. *Developmental Neuropsychology, 7*, 327–358.

Duchesne, M., Mattos, P., Fontelle, L. F., Veiga, H., and Apporlinario, J. C. (2004). Neuropsychology of eating disorders: A systematic review of the literature. *Revista Brasileira de Psiquiatria, 26* (2), 107–117.

Fassino, S., Piero, A., Daga, G. A., Leombruin, P., Mortara, P., and Rovera, G. G. (2002). Attentional biases and frontal functioning in anorexia nervosa. *International Journal of Eating Disorders, 31* (3), 274–283.

Fowler, L., Blackwell, A.D., Jaffa, A., Palmer, R., Robbins, T.W., Sahakian, B.J., et al. (2005). Profile of neurocognitive impairments associated with female in-patients with anorexia nervosa. *Psychological Medicine, 36* (4), 517–527.

Frith, C.D., and Frith, U. (1999). Interacting minds – a biological basis. *Science, 286*, 1692–1694.

Gillberg, I., Gillberg, C., Råstam, M., and Johanson, M. (1996). The cognitive profile of anorexia nervosa: A comparative study including a community based sample. *Comprehensive Psychiatry, 37* (1), 23–30.

Goodman, R., and Yude, C. (1996). IQ and its predictors in hemiplegia. *Developmental Medicine and Child Neurology, 38*, 881–890.

Gordon, I., Lask, B., Bryant-Waugh, R., Christie, D., and Timimi, S. (1997).

Childhood-onset anorexia nervosa: Towards identifying a biological substrate. *International Journal of Eating Disorders*, *21*, 159–165.

Green, M. W., Elliman, N. A., Wakeling, A., and Rogers, P. J. (1996). Cognitive functioning, weight change and therapy in anorexia nervosa. *Journal of Psychiatric Research*, *30*, 401–410.

Grunwald, M., Elliman, C., Assmann, B., Daphne, A., Krause, W., Busse, F., et al. (2001). Deficits in haptic perception and right parietal theta power changes in patients with anorexia nervosa before and after weight gain. *International Journal of Eating Disorders*, *29*, 417–428.

Hamsher, K.S., Halmi, K.A., and Benton, A.L. (1981). Prediction of outcome in anorexia nervosa from neuropsychological status. *Psychiatry Research*, *4*, 79–88.

Henson, R.N.A., Shallice, T., Josephs, O., and Dolan, R.J. (2002). Functional magnetic resonance imaging of proactive interference during spoken cued recall. *NeuroImage*, *17*, 543–558.

Holliday, J., Tchanturia, K., Landau, S., Collier, D., and Treasure, J. (2005). Is impaired set-shifting an endophenotype of anorexia nervosa? *American Journal of Psychiatry*, *162* (12), 2269–2275.

Hutchinson, A., Frampton, I., Chowdhury, U., Watkins, E., Gordon, I., and Lask, B. (2006). *Is early onset anorexia nervosa a neurodevelopmental disorder – a follow-up study.* Manuscript submitted for publication.

Johnson, M. (2005). *Developmental cognitive neuroscience* (2nd ed.). Oxford: Oxford University Press.

Jones, B. P., Duncan, C., and Brouwers, P. (1991). Cognition in eating disorders. *Journal of Clinical and Experimental Neuropsychology*, *13* (5), 711–728.

Katzmann, D.K., Zipursky, R.B., Lambe, E.K., and Mikulis, D.J. (1997). A longitudinal magnetic resonance imaging study of brain changes in adolescents with AN. *Archives of Paediatric and Adolescent Medicine*, *151*, 793–797.

Kaye, W.H., Frank, G.K., Bailer, U.F., Henry, S.E., Meltzer, C.C., Price, J.C., et al. (2005). Serotonin alterations in anorexia and bulimia nervosa: New insights from imaging studies. *Physiological Behaviour*, *85* (1), 73–81.

Kingston, K., Szmukler, G., Andrews, D., Tress, B., and Desmond, P. (1996). Neuropsychological and structural brain changes in anorexia nervosa before and after refeeding. *Psychological Medicine*, *26*, 15–28.

Lask, B., Gordon, I., Christie, D., Frampton, I., Chowdhury, U., and Watkins, E. (2005). Functional neuroimaging in early-onset anorexia nervosa. *International Journal of Eating Disorders*, *37* (S1), S49–S51.

Lauer, C.J., Gorzewski, B., Gerlinghoff, M., and Zihl, J. (1999). Neuropsychological assessments before and after treatment in patients with anorexia nervosa and bulimia nervosa. *Journal of Psychiatric Research*, *33*, 129–138.

Lezak, M. (1995). *Neuropsychological assessment* (3rd ed.). New York: Oxford University Press.

Mathias, J. L., and Kent, P.S. (1998). Neuropsychological consequences of extreme weight loss and dietary restriction in patients with anorexia nervosa. *Journal of Clinical and Experimental Neuropsychology*, *4*, 548–564.

Maxwell, J.K., Tucker, D., and Townes, B. (1984). Asymmetric cognitive function in anorexia nervosa. *International Journal of Neuroscience*, *24*, 37–44.

McGivern, R.F., Andersen, J., Byrd, D., Mutter, K.L., and Reilly, J. (2002). Cognitive efficiency on a match sample task decreases at the onset of puberty in children. *Brain and Cognition*, *50*, 73–89.

Nunn, K., Gordon, I., Frampton, I., and Lask, B. (2006). *The fault, Horatio, is not in her parents, but in her insula: A neurobiological hypothesis to explain the common features of anorexia nervosa.* Manuscript submitted for publication.

Ohrmann, P., Kersting, A., Suslow, T., Lalee-Mentzel, J., Donges, U., Fiebich, M., Arolt, V., Heindel, W., and Pfleiderer, B. (2004). Proton magnetic resonance spectroscopy in anorexia nervosa: Correlations with cognition. *Neuroreport, 15* (3), 549–553.

Palazidou, E., Robinson, P., and Lishman, W.A. (1990). Neuroradiological and neuropsychological assessment in anorexia nervosa. *Psychological Medicine, 20,* 521–527.

Pennington, B.F., and Ozonoff, S. (1996). Executive functions and developmental psychopathology. *Journal of Child Psychology and Psychiatry, 37,* 51–87.

Råstam, M., Bjure, J., Vestergren, E., Uvebrant, P., Gillberg, I., Wentz, E., et al. (2001). Regional cerebral blood flow in weight-restored anorexia nervosa: A preliminary study. *Developmental Medicine and Child Neurology, 43,* 239–242.

Rauch, S.L., and Savage, C.R. (1997). Neuroimaging and neuropsychology of the striatum. Bridging basic science and clinical practice. *Psychiatric Clinics of North America, 20* (4), 741–768.

Romans, S.M. (1997). Executive function in girls with Turner syndrome. *Developmental Neuropsychology, 13,* 23–40.

Ryan, J., Øverås, M., and Frampton, I. (2006, October). *The Ravello profile.* Paper presented at the Eating Disorders Research Consortium, Cambridge, UK.

Seeger, G., Braus, D.F., Ruf, M., Goldberger, U., and Schmidt, M.H. (2002). Body image distortion reveals amygdala activation in patients with anorexia nervosa – a functional magnetic resonance imaging study. *Neuroscience Letters, 362,* 25–28.

Shafran, R., and Somers, J. (1998). Treating adolescent obsessive-compulsive disorder: Applications of the cognitive theory. *Behaviour Research and Therapy, 36* (1), 93–97.

Shallice, T. (1988). *From neuropsychology to mental structure.* Cambridge: Cambridge University Press.

Shimamura, A.P., Berry, J.M., Mangels, J.A., and Rusting, C.L. (1995). Memory and cognitive abilities in university professors: Evidence for successful aging. *Psychological Science, 6,* 271–277.

Southgate, L., Tchanturia, K., and Treasure, J. (2005). Building a model of the etiology of eating disorders by translating experimental neuroscience into clinical practice. *Journal of Mental Health, 14* (6), 1–14.

Steinglass, J., and Walsh, B.T. (2006). Habit learning and anorexia nervosa: A cognitive neuroscience hypothesis. *International Journal of Eating Disorders, 39* (4), 267–275.

Szmukler, G., Andrews, D., Chen, L., and Stanley, R. (1992). Neuropsychological impairment in anorexia nervosa before and after refeeding. *Journal of Clinical and Experimental Neuropsychology, 14* (2), 347–352.

Tallis, F. (1997). The neuropsychology of obsessive-compulsive disorder: A review and consideration of clinical implications. *British Journal of Clinical Psychology, 36,* 3–20.

Tchanturia, K., Campbell, I.C., Morris, R., and Treasure J. (2005). Neuropsychological studies in anorexia nervosa. *International Journal of Eating Disorders, 37,* S72–S76.

Tchanturia, K., Morris, R., and Brecelj Anderluh, M. (2004). Set shifting in anorexia nervosa: An examination before and after weight gain, in full recovery and in relationship to childhood and adult OCPD traits. *Journal of Psychiatry Research, 38,* 545.

Tchanturia, K., Serpell, L., Troop, N., and Treasure, J. (2001). Perceptual illusions in eating disorders: Rigid and fluctuating styles. *Journal of Behavior Therapy, 32,* 107–115.

Thatcher, R.W. (1992). Cyclical cortical reorganization during early childhood development. *Brain and Cognition, 207,* 24–50.

Touyz, S.W., Beumont, P.J., and Johnstone, L.C. (1986). Neuropsychological correlates of dieting disorders. *International Journal of Eating Disorders, 5* (6), 1025–1034.

Uher, R., Brammer, M.J., Murphy, T., Campbell, I.C., Ng, V.W., Williams, S.C., et al. (2003). Recovery and chronicity in anorexia nervosa: Brain activity associated with differential outcomes. *Biological Psychiatry, 54* (9), 934–942.

Watanabe, K., Ogino, T., Nakano, K., Hattori, J., Kado, Y., Sanada, S., et al. (2005). The Rey-Osterrieth Complex Figure as a measure of executive function in childhood. *Brain and Development, 27,* 564–569.

Wykes, T. (1998). What are we changing with neurocognitive rehabilitation? Illustrations from two single cases of changes in neuropsychological performance and brain systems as measured by SPECT. *Schizophrenia Research, 34,* 77–86.

9 Overview of management

*Bryan Lask and Rachel
Bryant-Waugh*

Introduction

The treatment of eating disorders in childhood and adolescence presents
many challenges. Patients with anorexia nervosa are terrified by the thought
of eating and weight gain, overwhelmed with self-disgust and often suffering
from comorbid depression and/or obsessive compulsive disorder. In addition they may have specific cognitive impairments (see Chapter 8). Their
inadequate diet frequently gives rise to serious physical complications, which
in turn may exacerbate the psychological problems. As part of this vicious
cycle these problems may be compounded by the fact that many patients do
not accept that they are ill and have not chosen to enter treatment. Similarly
with the other early onset eating disorders there are significant psychological
problems, and commonly cognitive and physical complications. The disorders
have a complex pathogenesis and the potential for a poor outcome.

Clearly, therefore, a rapidly initiated treatment programme is indicated. In
all but the mildest cases this will need to be both intensive and comprehensive. This chapter offers an overview of such a programme as provided in our
own work contexts, and in subsequent chapters some of the more specific
treatments are described in depth. It is acknowledged that resources vary
between services, but it should be possible to provide the key components of
the programme with relatively few staff.

There is no one treatment of choice and typically combinations of treatment are needed (NICE, 2004). The choice of specific therapies is in practice
determined as much by availability as by need. However, regardless of
what disciplines and therapies are available, good teamwork is essential. It
is equally important that the parents should be involved, the principle
being that the clinician's task is to help the parents help their daughter to
overcome the eating disorder. A therapeutic alliance is vital to a successful
outcome. Individual therapies such as motivational enhancement and cognitive behavioural therapy are likely to be required and psychodynamic psychotherapy may be indicated when psychopathology is so deeply entrenched that
a more in-depth approach is required. Input from nutritionists, physiotherapists and teachers adds to the chances of a good outcome. Finally, there needs

to be a focus on the eating behaviours of patients and the skills that parents are required to learn in order to support their daughters at meals. On inpatient services this is normally provided by nursing staff. Teams need to decide who will provide this essential aspect of the treatment in the absence of nurses, for example in an outpatient service.

Teamwork

The management of any childhood disorder requires collaboration between the child, parents and all the clinicians involved. The tendency of some early onset eating disorders to be associated with both resistance to treatment and severely compromised physical health makes such collaboration far more difficult than in most other forms of illness. At presentation it is not at all uncommon for the child/adolescent to appear to be in charge, with the parents trying to ensure their child is eating adequately and at the same time trying to avoid upsetting her. Commonly they end up achieving neither. In consequence parents are frequently bewildered by their daughter's change in behaviour and apparent self-destructiveness and overwhelmed by frustration and anxiety. It is all too easy for clinicians to then take over control. Whilst in some ways this may be necessary, the danger is that in so doing the parents feel marginalised and even more disempowered.

In such circumstances it is essential to address the issues of leadership, roles and responsibilities, between the parents themselves, between the parents and the clinical team, and within the clinical team. On an outpatient basis the parents should be in charge as they spend up to 24 hours per day with their daughter. When she is well enough to share some responsibility she should be encouraged to do so, with the aim of her eventually taking age and culturally appropriate responsibility for her eating. Throughout, the clinicians should be available as consultants, counsellors and advisers, their prime tasks being to support the parents in their efforts to help their daughter overcome her illness and to offer specific input such as nutritional counselling and various forms of therapy (see below). The specifics of working with the parents are discussed further below and in Chapter 12.

The situation differs in residential settings. Far more people become involved in the child's care and the potential for miscommunication, confusion and splitting is enormous. Indeed, these phenomena are likely to be the norm in early onset anorexia nervosa (EOAN). At the core of the illness is confusion and contradiction, both of which are likely to be experienced not only by the patient but also by her parents and the clinical team. It is almost inevitable therefore that splitting will occur as different people experience and identify with different aspects of the child.

In these circumstances the question of leadership is vital and it needs to be clear who is in charge. That person should have a good knowledge of early onset eating disorders, be able to work effectively with colleagues to adopt a comprehensive approach to assessment and treatment and be willing to work collaboratively with the parents (see Chapter 12). Once assessment is complete a treatment plan should be constructed, with the aims, content, roles and responsibilities of all involved clearly outlined. Each of these components plays an important part in the recovery process, but if not clearly defined can obstruct recovery. The aims should be formulated on the basis of the comprehensive assessment and ideally should exceed the restoration of weight. These aims may of course include refeeding and restoration of overall physical health, but should also include enhancing motivation to maintain healthy weight and cessation of compensatory behaviours. In addition attempts should be made to establish and address a shared understanding of underlying problems, and for there to be a resumption of normal and age-appropriate behaviour, whilst the child and parents gradually take back responsibility.

Each person on the team, including the parents, needs to be clear regarding their roles since confusion and overlapping of roles commonly occurs. All too often team members reach beyond their remit: for example, several people on a team might participate in some form of individual work involving exploration and discussion of the child's feelings and behaviour. This cannot be helpful to the child or to the recovery process. Nutritional advice, rather then psychotherapy, would be the preserve of the dietitian; family therapy the preserve of the family therapist; physical assessment and use of medication the preserve of the physician; and meal support the preserve of the nursing staff. Role clarification needs to be achieved at the start of the treatment process if the intensification of confusion and splitting is to be avoided.

A linked theme is that of responsibility. The potential for severe harm that accompanies some of the eating disorders places an enormous burden upon parents and clinicians. Clinicians often feel challenged by the potential of failing their patients and even at times impotent in the face of treatment resistance. In consequence they redouble their efforts. The problem with this is that the child may react by intensifying her resistance and the parents by relinquishing any residual responsibility. This process is quite the opposite to what should be achieved – a collaborative approach to overcoming the illness with shared responsibility for so doing.

The necessary consideration of the involvement of the wider community – the illness network (Lask and Fosson, 1989) – makes matters even more complex. Within the family are the grandparents, who can be particularly influential, as well as siblings, aunts and uncles. Additionally there is often involvement of other clinicians not on the immediate team, such as the family doctor, community-based mental health professionals, and many others such as teachers. Each of these people may have contact with and influence upon the child. In consequence they all need to be taken into account, to some degree, when constructing a treatment plan.

The content of the treatment plan will differ from case to case and will be discussed further below. Once it has been agreed, it is useful to document the decisions so that there is less potential for misunderstanding, confusion and splitting. Everyone, including the parents and child, should as much as possible contribute to drawing up the treatment plan and therefore have access to its documentation.

Consistency is a key ingredient to a successful treatment programme. Consistency can be considered at two levels: consistency between individuals and consistency over time. For example, the parents need to be consistent between each other in their approach to their child's management. It won't help the child if the father takes one approach, perhaps a coercive one, and the mother adopts the opposite. Even if they adopt a similar approach, there is a danger that they will not persevere with the approach and resort to a change before it has had a chance to have an effect. Change can take a long time and in many cases will only occur in the context of a consistent approach to management. Therefore consistency between carers and consistency over time are both necessary. This applies equally to consistency between the parents and the clinical team and within the clinical team. With so many people involved this becomes a difficult aim to achieve and yet an important one. Much recovery is hampered by inconsistency.

It is wise to hold regular reviews to ascertain what progress has been made. For those who are very unwell this may need to occur very frequently, although the treatment plan should not necessarily be changed simply because of lack of progress. Changes to the plan should be made only if there is obvious deterioration or a failure to progress after a number of weeks. It should also be noted that when initiating refeeding it is not always possible to start with a weight-restoring diet. For example, if a child has previously been consuming only 600 calories daily then she will only be able to tolerate gradual increments (see below and Chapter 11) of approximately 200–300 calories every three days. This means that it will take at least two weeks before weight gain can occur.

The management of early onset eating disorders is complex, frustrating and challenging. Often the least experienced at managing eating disorders, parents or junior nurses, are in the front line. In consequence it is important to ensure sufficient support for those in such positions in the form of frequent counselling for parents and regular supervision for staff. Regular opportunities for continuing education should be integral to any eating disorders treatment programme.

Creating a therapeutic alliance

Successful treatment is dependent upon the creation of a therapeutic alliance, the essence of which is working *with* the patient, not *against* her. It is the clinician's task to help the parents help their daughter to fight her eating disorder, not to fight her. All too often parents and clinicians enter a struggle with the child instead of with the eating disorder. This theme is developed further below (see externalisation).

The key components in creating the therapeutic alliance include adopting a facilitative therapeutic stance, the provision of information, collaboration with the parents (see below and Chapter 12), avoiding coercion as much as possible, using externalisation, acknowledging and exploring fears and contradictions, and focusing on motivation.

It is not always possible to effect a therapeutic alliance with younger patients with anorexia nervosa early in the treatment process. Their fear and denial are often too strong. However, by ensuring a good working relationship with and between the parents and the implementation of appropriate treatment for the child, an alliance is usually gradually formed. Those young patients with other eating disorders such as bulimia nervosa (BN) and food avoidance emotional disorder (FAED), and some older children with selective eating are generally more likely to want treatment and may therefore be easier to engage in a therapeutic alliance.

Therapeutic stance

All too often clinicians are so challenged by the eating disorder that they adopt a coercive and confrontational approach, which in turn creates further resistance and a vicious cycle. An appropriate therapeutic stance consists of:

- supportiveness
- warmth
- respect
- empathy
- honesty
- acceptance
- curiosity
- humility
- flexibility.

Supportiveness is the antithesis of coercion. In the context of resistance to treatment in a serious illness such as anorexia nervosa, the ensuing anxiety and frustration commonly lead to coercion. In turn coercion is likely to lead to further anxiety and/or resistance on the patient's part. This is hardly surprising if the eating difficulties are conceptualised as phobic avoidance, which certainly seems to be the case in anorexia nervosa and functional dysphagia. If someone with a snake phobia were forced to touch a snake the anxiety and resistance would be intense. In any event coercion only deals with the particular moment and does not promote resolution of the underlying difficulties.

Supportiveness is integral to a successful therapeutic alliance. Only in the rarest of situations is it necessary to coerce or force a child/adolescent to eat. There are many ways of helping young people with eating disorders to eat which involve collaboration rather than coercion. These are discussed below under the headings of externalisation, motivation and restoration of healthy eating.

Other components of the therapeutic alliance such as warmth, respect, empathy and honesty should require no elaboration. Curiosity is non-judgemental interest in the child's behaviour, thoughts, feelings, perceptions and attitudes and an ability and willingness to discuss these as and when she wishes to do so. Curiosity is important when the child persists in behaving in destructive ways. The clinician's attempts to understand are likely to be more productive than being cross or punitive. Acceptance involves acknowledgement of the child's experiences as being valid representations of her sense of self. Humility is the ability to acknowledge when we do not have a full understanding of the situation nor all the answers. Flexibility is the ability to adopt different approaches as required. For example, motivational enhancement (see Chapter 10) requires a completely different approach from that needed to explain and implement an adequate refeeding programme (see below).

Provision of information

Explanation and education form an essential part of the management of the eating disorders. Parents and child need a clear statement about the diagnosis, the course and complications of the condition, possible perpetuating factors and proposed treatment. Parents are understandably eager to understand the cause of their child's illness, but this rarely proves fruitful. Given the multifactorial aetiology of the eating disorders (see Chapter 5), we are extremely unlikely to understand the detailed pathogenesis of one particular person's eating disorder. It generally proves more useful to focus on those factors that may be maintaining the problem and to find ways of overcoming them.

Parental understanding of the seriousness or otherwise of their child's problem is very variable. For example, in anorexia nervosa some parents are stunned to discover how ill their child has become. In other instances they have had considerable difficulty convincing clinicians to take their child's eating difficulties seriously. In contrast, parents of selective eaters are often convinced that their child has suffered, or will suffer, irreversible damage because of their limited range of foods. These worries may occur despite the fact that their child is obviously in very good health.

We find it helpful to adopt a clear method of conveying our understanding of the situation. This varies depending upon the diagnosis and its implications. In anorexia nervosa, having completed the initial assessment, we might make a statement such as:

> As you are probably aware Alison has anorexia nervosa. You have probably read and heard quite a bit about this illness, but we think it might be helpful to explain it to you in some detail. It is hard to take everything in at once so we will provide you with information in writing and we will be happy to answer any questions at any time.

Anorexia nervosa is a mean and mysterious disorder, which plays a lot of tricks and can be difficult to overcome. It makes Alison think she is fat when actually she is very thin, it makes her feel guilty when she eats, and it makes her see herself as a bad and useless person. It can even make her feel like it's her friend. It really can dominate her thoughts, feelings and behaviour.

No one fully understands how it occurs but certainly there is no single cause and many different factors come together to create it. Parents sometimes wonder if it is something they have done wrong but there is no evidence that parents cause anorexia nervosa. It is actually more useful to try and identify what keeps it going, for this is usually something that we can tackle together. As parents you are in a strong position to help your daughter overcome it and that is why we will work closely with you to help you.

Meanwhile, it is important to acknowledge that it is a serious illness and at least one-third of young people with anorexia nervosa don't make a full recovery. It can delay growth, impair development and fertility, and lead to osteoporosis and many other complications. Some people become desperately ill. Occasionally patients die from this illness. That is why we take it so seriously and why we must all work closely together to help her fight the illness.

Fortunately we do know some of the factors that contribute to recovery. The children who do well are those whose parents are able to work well *together*, and are able to work *with us* to ensure their child's health. It is often a long hard struggle because the anorexia nervosa makes people so desperate to avoid gaining weight that they often resort to a wide range of methods to stay dangerously thin. These include not only avoiding food, but also inducing vomiting, taking laxatives, and excessive exercising. You may think your daughter hasn't or wouldn't do these things but most people with anorexia nervosa from time to time use other methods beside food avoidance. So it will be necessary for a while for you to take responsibility for your daughter's health care, including what she eats. You will need to ensure that she doesn't vomit after meals, or use laxatives, or take excessive exercise. However, if you as parents can resolve to work together, and with us, to ensure her health, then we will all be doing everything we can to ensure a full recovery.

When you leave here today it is very likely that she will tell you that we have got it all wrong and that we don't understand. She may promise to eat properly and beg you to give her a chance. It is important for you to understand that this is likely to be the 'anorexia' speaking. It really is like 'the enemy within' and it will fight all your efforts to overcome it. You will need to be strong and determined; at least as strong and as determined as the 'anorexia'. We will all have to fight together if we are to win.

This sort of statement can be adjusted to suit the circumstances, and may be addressed predominantly to the parents or shared equally between child and parents. Using the child's name, rather than 'your daughter' probably has a greater impact. The analogy of a battle against a vicious and deceitful enemy is deliberately chosen for two reasons. First, this is so often just how it feels to all concerned. Second, it is useful to 'externalise' the problem so that the child does not feel even more persecuted (see below). So often the parents believe that their daughter has deliberately chosen to behave this way, and respond accordingly by getting into fights with her. This is hardly helpful to a young person who is already in distress. It feels better to all concerned 'if we can all work together to fight the illness'.

The message we communicate to parents of children with selective eating is obviously quite different. It would usually sound something like this:

> We are pleased to be able to tell you that your son's condition is nothing more serious than what we call selective eating. This is a condition with which we are very familiar and is far more common than is generally realised and fortunately far less serious than you have probably feared. Basically it is an extension of that normal phase you see in toddlers known as food faddiness. Most toddlers go through such a phase but usually grow out of it. Selective eaters seem to take much longer to grow out of it but fortunately almost all of them do so in their teenage years.
>
> It rarely does any harm and as you can see your son is thriving. He is of normal weight and height for his age and shows no evidence of ill health. It is amazing how children can thrive on such a *narrow* range of foods, but obviously they are having perfectly adequate *amounts* of food and usually getting all the necessary nutrients.
>
> The important thing to do here is just let him get on and eat what he likes rather than trying to make him eat foods he doesn't like. If you do try to make him eat foods he insists he does not like, this is likely to make the situation worse rather than better. I expect you have already discovered that for yourselves. He won't come to any harm and when he is ready he will gradually start trying other foods. No treatment is necessary at present but when he says he would like some help, we would be happy to offer it.

Again the message can be adjusted to fit the circumstances. In those rare instances when selective eating does impair growth or have a serious negative impact on family or social functioning, we might offer a treatment programme including parental counselling and/or family work (Chapter 12) and cognitive behavioural therapy (Chapter 13).

Most parents seem to find this approach very helpful and appear grateful to us for being so clear and direct. Often they state that they have not previously been given any clear explanation of what is wrong. Understandably they also seem to value the opportunity to share the responsibility for their child's care.

We give all parents written information about eating disorders and recommend other reading. The handouts have proved so useful that we have now published a parent's guide to eating disorders (Bryant-Waugh and Lask, 2004). At the next meeting we ensure sufficient time to answer further questions and discuss areas of concern or uncertainty. In our experience it has proved invaluable to provide this information and to allow considerable time for questions and concerns to be raised early in our contact with families. Otherwise unresolved anxieties can interfere with the process of treatment. Once the parents feel fully informed we can then move on to ensure that the adults take responsibility for tackling the eating disorder.

Collaboration with the parents

Four important aspects of the eating disorders are:

1   Their potential for severe damage to health.
2   The anxiety this engenders.
3   The patient's frequent lack of insight.
4   Battles around control.

It is possible, therefore (as is commonly the case in anorexia nervosa), that the child or teenager may be seriously ill, have little insight into her condition and yet she fights vigorously to retain control over what she eats. Unsurprisingly, this exacerbates parental anxiety and the parents may find it hard even to think clearly, let alone to act firmly and consistently. In consequence one of the first clinical tasks, be it that of the physician, nurse, psychologist or family therapist, is to contain parental anxiety. The temptation to deal first with other matters such as exploring family history or offering management advice is best avoided. Containing parental anxiety is done first by acknowledging the anxiety and encouraging expression and exploration of their concerns. Assurance is offered that we will provide as much support to the child and parents as is necessary and that we will be focusing on ensuring restoration of health. This process of containment gradually allows parents to think more clearly and to consider more calmly their options. The provision of information, as outlined in the previous section, runs in parallel with and assists this process.

People with anorexia nervosa often feel they have little control over their lives, and that two areas in which they can have control are their food intake and their weight. An understandable reaction is to over-control food intake, with a resultant sense of achievement. This ability to control food intake and body shape and size is so satisfying that it can develop an addictive quality. However, its health and life-threatening nature demands intervention.

For this reason it is vital that the adults responsible for the young person's welfare take charge. In the case of anorexia nervosa this will often appear to be against the child's apparent wishes. Giving a clear message that parents/adults should be taking charge can be even harder for the child as this is so commonly a change of approach. Previously the parents may have colluded with their daughter's weight loss, either by not having noticed just how much weight she had lost, or by not intervening firmly enough once the weight loss had become obvious. Understandably parents may have considered that the weight loss was due to physical ill health and seek alternative explanations to self-starvation. Also, even when the weight loss becomes apparent parents are often loath to take a firm approach for fear of upsetting their daughter. Commonly young people with anorexia nervosa become very angry when any attempt is made to discuss their eating habits and their weight. It is clear then that a key feature of management is that the adults responsible for the child's welfare take firm control. A clear statement to this effect should be made to the parents at an early stage, for example:

> You can see that Alison is very ill, having lost nearly a third of her body weight. You can also see that that she does not accept that she is ill. If this is allowed to continue unchecked, she will get worse and may even die. Therefore, as from this moment it is *not* appropriate for Alison to continue taking responsibility for her health and diet. She has shown you that she cannot do that safely. You must make a decision as to how you want to proceed from here, but it would be unwise to be influenced by Alison's protests. These protests are coming from the anorexia nervosa.

At this stage it is likely that Alison will indeed be protesting, but if not she will almost certainly start to once discussion turns to her required food intake, for this is likely to be substantially greater than her current intake. The child may challenge the right of clinicians to dictate such terms or the right of her parents to take control, or she may start crying or screaming. Whatever the topic of discussion at the time the protest commences, it is important to demonstrate the battle for control to the parents, and to help them recognise the need for them to help their daughter to fight the eating disorder rather than to fight everyone else. This does not mean that the parents should take control over all aspects of their daughter's life, but specifically those concerning her health. It is important that she retains control in other areas of less immediate importance, such as the choice of clothing, hobbies, or friends.

This is a useful time to reiterate the importance of the parents working together, offering mutual support and agreeing a consistent plan of management. It is not at all unusual for parents to be in conflict over various issues, but particularly in relation to how to handle the eating disorder. One parent may feel unsupported or that the other is too strict or too lax. Frequently, the child is sided with one parent against the other. Clearly, the parents cannot be helpful to their daughter for as long as they are in disagreement.

Issues over which the parents may disagree, and therefore need help to resolve, include how to help their daughter to eat, whether or not they wish to accept treatment, and whether or not their child should be admitted to hospital. The clinician's role here is not to take sides but rather to offer advice, and to help the parents to reach agreement, preferably without being influenced by their daughter's protests.

It is sometimes difficult to feel sympathetic towards a child who has what initially appears to be a self-inflicted problem, who denies that she is ill and angrily rejects all attempts to help. Nonetheless, it is obviously important to acknowledge her distress, and a statement along the following lines may be helpful:

> Alison, I know that just now you are feeling very angry with me because of what I have said to your parents, and angry with them for listening to me. You may not believe me but I do understand not only how angry you may be, but also that you may be worried about what has happened to you, and whether everything will get completely out of control. If your parents want me to, I will help them to get you well again. We are not going to let you die and nor will we let you get overweight. Now if you have any questions I will do my best to answer them.

Often at this point the child renews her protests or turns to her parents for support. It is helpful to note whether the parents are able to adopt a firmer and more united stance when this happens. If necessary the clinician can demonstrate how their daughter continues to control the situation by her protests or distress, and reiterate the need for her parents to take responsibility and not give way on life-threatening matters. It is always helpful to frame this as parents joining with their daughter in the fight against the illness rather than against her.

As treatment proceeds successfully there should be a gradual return of responsibility to the child so that ultimately she is taking full responsibility for her eating and health. The timing is crucial in that giving too much responsibility too soon almost always delays recovery. The emphasis is on 'gradual', with a degree of trial and error in the process.

It is important to emphasise that not all children with eating disorders will need such a vigorous approach. Indeed, selective eaters for example (see Chapter 3) are rarely physically ill and the parents may need help to allay their anxieties and to accept that their child is not ill (see earlier). Some children with FAED lose as much weight as those with anorexia nervosa and their parents will need to adopt a similar approach. Others, however, are less ill and may benefit more from their parents adopting an approach that is less focused on eating and more on their underlying sadness or anxiety.

Similarly children with functional dysphagia need an approach that tackles their dread of vomiting, choking, or suffocating. Coercion to eat will have the most dramatic adverse effects. Parental responsibility here is to ensure their child receives the appropriate help needed to overcome the fears and is encouraged to progress at the right pace.

Bulimia nervosa requires yet another approach, in that most young people with this disorder accept that they have a problem and want help. Often, however, their parents have taken to monitoring all their activities in an attempt to stop them from bingeing or vomiting. Although it is perfectly reasonable for parents to try to help, it is usually more helpful if they do so by agreeing a plan not only between each other but also with their daughter. People with bulimia nervosa are usually far more able to accept help than those with anorexia nervosa, and are able to explore with their parents strategies to help them resist the urge to binge and purge.

Externalisation

All too often young people with eating disorders are considered to be choosing to behave as they do and that if they so wished they could revert to normal eating and behaviour. A teenage girl with anorexia nervosa is often thought simply to be responding to media and peer group pressure and that persuasion and coercion should be sufficient to get her to 'see sense'. When these prove insufficient, anger and frustration ensue. In turn the teenager herself experiences a multitude of conflicting thoughts and feelings, which in sum leave her feeling confused and frightened. Similarly, the difficulties experienced in swallowing by those with functional dysphagia, or in trying new foods by those with selective eating, may be responded to with persuasion or coercion, with subsequent increased resistance by the child.

Externalisation is the process of making a clear distinction between the child and the illness. Many people with anorexia nervosa are able to make such a distinction for themselves, for example by talking about 'my anorexia', 'the anorexic voice', or 'my thoughts'. Others lack such awareness and cannot perceive themselves as ill. The same may apply to parents, with some being fully aware that their daughter is ill, but others seeing their daughter as having complete control over her behaviour and choosing to behave in the way she does.

The utilisation of externalisation involves explaining to the child and parents that just as a child with a chest infection does not choose to have a cough, a fever and pain when breathing, so the child with anorexia nervosa does not choose to see herself as fat and to become terrified of weight gain. Instead, just as the chest infection is conceptualised as a distinct entity so is 'the anorexia'.

It is helpful for the clinician to reiterate that 'my job is to help your parents to help you to fight the anorexia'. When a child with anorexia nervosa appears vigorously to be resisting attempts to help her or is expressing terror at the thought of having to eat, the clinician (or parent) can say something along the lines of 'the anorexia is giving you a particularly hard time today' or 'the anorexic voice sounds really strong just now'.

Externalisation may be used during any conversation: for example, when a child says, 'I can't eat, I am too fat', a helpful reply can be, 'Is that you or your anorexia speaking?' When things are going well it is useful to make a comment such as, 'Seems like you are getting the better of the anorexia today.'

Initially such comments may irritate the child (as do most comments) but in time they become more acceptable and appear to help. Gradually she starts using the same 'language'. The parents often value such an approach, not only because they can begin to understand that their child is indeed gripped by an illness, rather than being difficult, but also it gives them a language with which to speak to her.

Motivation

It is important to consider the child's motivation, as their stage of readiness for change will determine to some extent the treatment. A child in 'pre-contemplation', without insight and with determined resistance to change, requires a totally different approach to management from that required by a child in 'action' or 'maintenance' who is eager for help. The more motivated the child, the more responsibility she should have for her treatment programme. Assessment and enhancement of motivation are discussed in depth in Chapter 10.

The implementation or restoration of healthy eating patterns is one of the main goals of treatment for nearly all the eating disorders. However, this should be distinguished from refeeding, i.e. ensuring adequate nutrition and hydration. This is only indicated when there is evidence of nutritional deficiency such as electrolyte deficiency, dehydration, circulatory failure, or growth delay as might be found in anorexia nervosa, functional dysphagia, FAED, and pervasive refusal syndrome. Young people with bulimia nervosa are generally at normal weight and the main risks are of electrolyte imbalance and complications of recurrent vomiting. Selective eaters rarely show evidence of physical complications and early restoration of healthy eating patterns is not necessary. Indeed, it tends to occur spontaneously during the teenage years and there is usually no need for treatment unless the child specifically requests it.

This distinction between refeeding and regularising eating patterns is of considerable importance. Refeeding must take priority when physical well-being is at risk. How, when or what a young person eats and drinks is far less important than that she eats and drinks sufficiently to restore physical health. Selective eaters are a good example of the fact that a seemingly inadequate and unhealthy diet can actually be perfectly adequate and healthy.

When indicated, refeeding may be achieved orally, by feeding through nasogastric or more rarely gastrostomy tubes. The decision on how to proceed is made on the urgency of the situation. When a child is severely dehydrated or has electrolyte deficiency, a delay of more than a few hours can be dangerous. In consequence, it is reasonable to spend some time encouraging and helping the child to eat and drink, but if there is no immediate success further delay in instituting artificial feeding is not advisable. Fortunately, most children do not require artificial feeds and respond over time to encouragement to resume sufficient nutritional intake.

Whether this is best achieved by a graded refeeding programme (see later and Chapter 11) or trying to impose a normal diet immediately is debatable. In fact, it really does not matter at this stage how, when, or where calories are consumed, so long as the intake is adequate. In general, however, children whose weight loss is not too severe, whose illness is of recent onset, and who are being treated on an outpatient basis, should be encouraged to resume a normal eating pattern and diet as soon as possible. For children whose weight loss is substantial or long lasting, it may be easier and safer for them to resume eating if offered a graded refeeding programme.

Graded refeeding

The full details of such a programme are described in Chapter 11. When dietary intake has been very low it is best to start with a slight increase on the current calorie total. Initially this may mean fewer than 1000 calories daily for a few days. Once the child is used to having slightly more there can be further increments of 200–300 calories every two to three days. How the diet is constituted can be determined by discussion between child, parents and a dietician. Although it is important to try to include foods that the child likes and are appealingly presented, it is also important that the adults take ultimate responsibility for determining the diet. (A useful tip is that a small portion served on a large plate is more likely to be consumed than the same portion served on a small plate!)

The dietician is an invaluable member of the clinical team. Her role is to act as a consultant to the parents and other members of the clinical team. She can be particularly helpful in a number of ways including:

- planning an intake acceptable to the child
- increasing the intake gradually as food becomes less 'scary'
- recommending substitutions as necessary
- emphasising the essential nutrients
- advising regarding supplements such as high calorie drinks.

We do not believe that the dietician should offer individual support and counselling to this younger age group. The potential for splitting is far too high and we have seen time and again children who mislead the dietician with regard to what they are actually eating and then mislead their parents or the clinicians with regard to what the dietician has said. It is far better for the dietician to be a consultant to the parents and team advising on the meal plan (see Chapter 11).

Nasogastric and gastrostomy feeding

When the child's physical state demands immediate refeeding and if this cannot be achieved orally, a nasogastric feeding programme should be implemented. Such a programme is carefully co-ordinated with liaison between medical and nursing staff and the dietician. The aim should be to ensure the child is receiving an adequate diet and preferably in the region of 2000–3000 calories daily. It is usually helpful to tell the child exactly what the planned intake will be and to say that any amount taken by mouth will be deducted from the 24-hour total nasogastric feed (see Chapter 11).

Nasogastric feeding of young people with eating disorders does cause some concern with regard to the infringement of rights and the mistaken view that this is force-feeding. If a child has a life-threatening illness and is unable to consume sufficient nutrition, there is general agreement within paediatric practice that artificial feeding by nasogastric tube is perfectly acceptable and no one would consider such action as infringing the child's rights. However, because anorexia nervosa and some of the other eating disorders present with the child refusing to eat sufficiently, anxieties then arise about overruling the child's wishes. Such views are based on an underlying misunderstanding of the psychopathology, which renders the child just as unable to eat adequate amounts as a child with any illness that impairs the appetite. If the child's life or long-term health is put at risk by the diminished intake, then whatever the underlying illness, remedial action has to be taken (see Chapter 17 for a fuller discussion of the ethical issues).

The intended course of action should always be discussed with the child and her parents and their agreement sought. Surprisingly, it is very rare for a child to refuse. It seems that most children in these circumstances are relieved that the responsibility for eating is taken away from them, at least temporarily. As much as possible they should always be given choices about who passes the tube, where and with whom present. If a child does strongly object to nasogastric feeding, in a few extreme cases she can be offered the alternative of intravenous feeds (see later), although there are considerable risks related to this that also need to be taken into account.

There is some debate as to whether or not nasogastric feeds should be administered at night. The advantage of night feeding is purported to be that the child can lead as normal a life as possible during the day without being perceived as being different from others. This potential advantage is often outweighed by the possibility of her interfering with the feeds during the night. Further, whether or not repeated passing of the tube each evening is useful is unclear. Some children find it aversive and quickly opt to eat adequate amounts by mouth, whereas others very quickly adapt to it and pass their own tubes. Other disadvantages of overnight feeds include the discomfort associated with being fed while lying in bed and the fact that it is physiologically unnatural to be fed overnight. On balance, it is likely that daytime bolus feeding is more likely to hasten a normal eating pattern than overnight feeding. Occasionally, children can seem to become dependent on the tube and make no effort to eat normally:

> Hannah, 12, was admitted to hospital having lost 52 per cent of her weight over a 12-month period. Her physical state was such that artificial feeding was essential. She refused to eat or drink anything by mouth for a further 18 months. All efforts to withdraw nasogastric feeding failed. Eventually, Hannah started eating normally after living with a foster family for six months.

Such circumstances are unusual and possibly in her case related more to her fear of returning to her family than to dependency on the tube. There is no evidence that long-term dependency on tube feeding does occur. In general, however, nasogastric tube feeding should be seen as a life-saving measure, preferably to be used for time-limited periods.

In extreme circumstances gastrostomy feeding may need to be considered. The indications for such an approach would be the same as those for naso-gastric feeds but with the added complication that the patient is actively resisting the feeds to the point of fighting against them and withdrawing the tube herself. Gastrostomy feeds are easier to administer under such circum-stances and it is much harder for the patient to withdraw the tube which is much more easily secured.

Finally, an audit of child and parent responses to nasogastric tube feeding has shown that in retrospect the vast majority of children who had been tube-fed and their parents were grateful that such action had been taken and had few regrets (Neiderman, Richardson, Farley, and Lask, 2001). The fact that the treatment was perceived as lifesaving far outruled any concerns about its intrusiveness. Their main criticism related to the manner in which the topic was raised, noting that all too often it had been presented punitively. Neiderman, Zardy, Tattersall, and Lask (2000) have described the successful use of gastrostomy feeding in these extreme circumstances.

Intravenous feeding

Intravenous feeding may on very rare occasions be used as an alternative to nasogastric feeds. All necessary nutrients are fed directly into a vein via an indwelling needle or catheter. The advantages are rapid rehydration and electrolyte replacement. The disadvantages are that it can only be imple-mented on a medical or paediatric ward and for short periods. Intravenous feeding is best reserved for the very rare times when immediate fluid or elec-trolyte replacement are required and the child can tolerate neither oral, nasogastric nor gastrostomy feeds.

Weight and target weights

In most of the early onset eating disorders, achieving and maintaining a healthy weight is invariably a matter of concern to parents, but it is only those young people with anorexia nervosa and bulimia nervosa who are unduly preoccupied with their weight. The others have unusual eating patterns for other reasons and are rarely concerned about their weight.

Thus, when considering what constitutes a healthy weight range the reac-tions are likely to differ depending upon the type of eating disorder. In anorexia nervosa there is such a preoccupation with and dread of weight gain that the clinician's reaction may reflect this. The temptation is either to distract the child from this theme, to fix a very specific target weight, or to become embroiled in endless discussions and negotiations about the target. Clinicians are often as preoccupied with a correct weight as are their patients.

We do not find any of these approaches in the least bit helpful. Attempting to determine a specific target is at best arbitrary as the ideal for any indi-vidual is determined by a number of factors including age, gender, height and genetic make-up. It is impossible to know prospectively what is right for any one individual. Furthermore weighing is an exact science and individual weight varies by up to one kilogram within any 24-hour period. How is it determined which end of this range is the 'correct' one? Even if a target is set, on the basis of population norms for age, gender, and height population, regardless of its arbitrariness this will then lead to considerable challenging and manipulation by the young person concerned. She may disagree with the target set and ensure that she stays below that point. Inpatients who want to avoid going home are even more likely to do that. Conversely she may wish to show that she has gained weight even though she has not, and does so by water-loading or concealing weights in her clothing or on her body. Some inpatients will achieve the target as quickly as they can so that they can be discharged home where they will lose the weight as quickly as they can.

For all these reasons we prefer to avoid completely the concept of a target weight. It is certainly possible to give the young person an idea of what constitutes a healthy weight range for someone of her age and height, but it is important to emphasise that we do not know if this will be right for her. Furthermore, we avoid getting into debates about this.

Instead, we use pelvic ultrasound scanning (see Chapter 7) to help deter-mine a healthy weight. Once the ovaries and uterus have reached the appropriate size, shape and appearance for age we know that they are mature and that the weight is satisfactory. In consequence we carry out regular pelvic ultrasound scans and advise the girl concerned of the findings. Most girls reach ovarian and uterine maturity at between 95 and 100 per cent weight–height ratios. However, some achieve maturity at much lower weights, whereas a few need to be higher. For example, twins Diana and Fiona, aged 13, both had a weight–height ratio of 130 per cent at the start of their illness. Menstruation ceased when the ratio dropped to 115 per cent and by the time they had reached 105 per cent both were very ill. With refeeding, menstruation resumed at 115 per cent.

If clinicians, like the patients, feel obliged to focus on weight and targets, it is more helpful to use the concept of anticipated weight gain. This can be done by plotting on a graph the anticipated weights on a monthly basis. This is illustrated in Figure 9.1 which shows that the current weight is 27 kg (weight–height ratio 75 per cent) and the estimated healthy weight range is between 34 and 36 kg (weight for height ratio 95–100 per cent). As weight recovery takes time (approximately 2 to 3 kg per month), and during the childhood and teenage years weight and height should be increasing as time goes by, the estimated weight range should take these factors into account. Therefore, in the case example in Figure 9.1, the projected weight after one month is 29.5 kg, after two months 32.3 kg, and after three months 35 kg. Thereafter, the projected weight will be between the two lines representing 95 and 100 per cent weight–height ratio. This can be quite confusing for a young person who is already very frightened by the prospect of weight gain and it is helpful to let her have a copy of the graph. This is obviously particularly important for boys, for whom pelvic ultrasound is inapplicable.

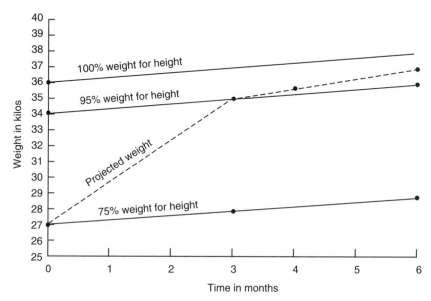

Figure 9.1 A sample growth chart (Lask, 1993, reprinted with permission).

Pelvic ultrasound examination can be repeated at approximately three-monthly intervals, and once maturity is shown on ultrasound no further weight gain is required. Menstruation usually commences or returns within three months of maturity being attained, but can take up to a year.

Family approaches

Working with the family, and especially the parents, is a sine qua non of the management of any child or adolescent with an eating disorder. The importance of collaborative work with the parents has been emphasised earlier in this chapter and family work generally is discussed in detail in Chapter 12.

Cognitive and behavioural therapy (CBT)

The cognitive and behavioural approaches to therapy are commonly used in the treatment of early onset eating disorders. They seem to be particularly helpful in bulimia nervosa, selective eating and functional dysphagia, but may also be used in the other eating disorders. A full account of these techniques is provided in Chapter 13.

Individual psychotherapy

Psychodynamically oriented psychotherapy has for some time been in common use in the treatment of early onset eating disorders. Its effectiveness has often been taken for granted in the absence of any evidence. Nonetheless in those instances where psychopathology is deeply entrenched it surely has a part to play. A full account of its application is provided in Chapter 14.

Group work

Group work is commonly used in inpatient units for the management of eating disorders. These include groups for children, teenagers and parents and can take the form of discussions, psycho-education, art, drama, dance, body awareness, and social skills training. There has been no evaluation of such approaches other than of multifamily groups (see Chapter 12). One of the main concerns is that such groups are commonly led by clinicians with little or no understanding or experience of group dynamics and group therapy. On inpatient units such groups may be led by 'whoever is available'. This is a worrying trend in that the subtlety and complexity of group phenomena are often neglected in such circumstances, which can hardly be to the benefit of the patients. The complexities of groups for children and adolescents and the techniques for leading such groups have been described by Behr and Hearst (2005: 203–219).

Physical activity and exercise

Physical activity and exercise play a major part in weight control in anorexia nervosa and sometimes in bulimia nervosa. Levels of activity may vary from marked inactivity (possibly relating to lowered mood) to damaging overactivity. Clinicians are often preoccupied with attempting to reduce overactivity as a means of trying to help reduce excessive calorie expenditure. However, little is known about how best to assess and manage pathological activity. Decisions are sometimes made in the absence of objective assessments and without consideration of the patient's physical and psychological need for exercise.

A number of therapies have been proposed for the treatment of overactivity. These physical therapies have an important part to play in the management of eating disorders in terms of providing controlled exercise programmes, muscle strengthening, relaxation, massage and body-awareness exercises. (a full account is provided in Chapter 15).

Medication

In the current state of knowledge, medication has but a small part to play in the management of eating disorders.

Appetite stimulants, vitamins and food supplements

It is debatable whether there are any true appetite stimulants, but in any event they would have little part to play given that, with the possible exception of FAED, there is rarely a true loss of appetite. Nor is there is any evidence that vitamin or mineral supplements enhance appetite. Deficiencies of these substances are usually rapidly remedied by the implementation of a normal diet. What little evidence exists suggests that supplementation is no more effective than a refeeding programme in overcoming the deficiencies (e.g. Lask, Fosson, Thomas, and Rolfe, 1993). However, Ayton (2004) has shown in an open trial that omega-3 polyunsaturated fatty acids (PUFAs) supplementation has led to symptomatic improvement (see also Chapters 7 and 11).

Anxiolytics and atypical antipsychotics

Anxiolytics and atypical antipsychotics have a very limited role. There is no evidence for their value in bulimia nervosa or anorexia nervosa, despite the fact that anxiety, phobias and obsessionality often accompany eating disorders. Anxiolytics, particularly alprazolam, may be of some help in functional dysphagia. They and atypical antipsychotics may also be helpful when used for short periods for those children suffering from extreme anxiety or distress associated with the eating disorder.

Antidepressants

Antidepressants do have a slightly more useful role in early onset eating disorders associated with depression. In many cases of depression accompanying anorexia nervosa, the depression lifts with adequate nutrition. However, in some instances the accompanying depression, associated with psychomotor retardation, feelings of guilt and worthlessness and biological changes such as poor sleep and diurnal mood variation, does not respond to nutritional rehabilitation. In these circumstances some of the selective serotonin reuptake inhibitors (SSRIs) such as fluoxetine do seem to have value. In addition the SSRIs have been shown to reduce the urge to binge in adults with bulimia nervosa (American Psychological Association, 1994), although this is yet to be shown in the younger population. In any event there is increasing restriction on the use of SSRIs in the under-18s because of an alleged increase in suicidal behaviour.

Caution should always be taken when using psychotropic medication in the younger population. It is wise to check for normal cardiovascular, hepatic and renal functioning, and to start with low doses building up slowly through weekly increments. Cessation of any such medication should be conducted gradually. A comprehensive overview of the use and abuse of medication in childhood and adolescence has been provided by Lask, Taylor, and Nunn (2004).

Treatment of low bone density and delayed growth

There are major concerns regarding the possibility of irreversibility of osteopenia and osteoporosis. The value of calcium and vitamin D supplementation has yet to be established (see Chapter 7) although various centres do use them. The recommended dose is 1500 mg calcium daily and 400 IU of vitamin D. The best treatment is adequate nutrition and weight-bearing exercise. Oestrogen supplementation should not be used in child or adolescent eating disorders as it has not been shown to have any value and may impair growth. Furthermore the associated monthly withdrawal bleeds are often misinterpreted as the resumption of menstruation. Biphosphonates, shown to be useful in post-menopausal osteoporosis, must not be used in females of child-bearing age because of their teratogenic potential.

In longstanding eating disorders with markedly delayed growth and/or puberty, growth hormone or oestrogens may be indicated (testosterone for boys) but generally hormonal treatment should be avoided in the younger population. The treatment of these disorders of the musculo-skeletal system should be left to specialists and not managed by physicians or psychiatrists who lack the relevant expertise.

Finally, it is worth cautioning against the use of laxatives when constipation is troublesome. This is best overcome by a combination of adequate diet and exercise. In particularly resistant constipation, laxatives may be inadequate and suppositories may be required. If they are to be used then adequate doses should be given and withdrawal must be gradual, as 'rebound' constipation is common.

Schooling considerations

Whatever the type of eating disorder and its severity, there will be a need to consider the child's schooling. It is always helpful to have information available from the school about the child's abilities, performance, peer relationships and eating behaviour. Schools may find it useful to know how to handle mealtimes, and of course schooling must be provided within the context of a hospital admission. It is also important to acknowledge that despite the fact that people with anorexia nervosa appear to be highly intelligent, in fact very commonly they have specific cognitive deficits (see Chapter 8) that make some of their school work harder for them than for others. This is rarely recognised and in practice means that such youngsters have to work even harder to achieve. Their determination, diligence and perfectionism give pleasure to the adults around them but often come at considerable cost. Schooling is discussed in detail in Chapter 16.

Consideration of hospitalisation

An early and important decision that needs to be made involves whether or not the child or teenager needs hospitalisation. A range of factors needs to be considered in making this decision, including the child's physical and mental state, the parents' anxieties and the availability of appropriate resources. In general, we give serious consideration to the possibility of hospitalisation under any of the following circumstances:

1   There is a rapid deterioration in physical status (see Chapter 7) as manifested by:

  • severe weight loss
  • dehydration
  • circulatory failure, as shown by low blood pressure, slow or irregular pulse rate, or poor peripheral circulation
  • electrolyte deficiency
  • persistent vomiting or vomiting blood.

2   Marked depression, suicidal ideation or intent.
3   Other major psychiatric disturbance.
4   Failed outpatient treatment.

In practice, this means that those young people most likely to need hospital admission are those with anorexia nervosa and pervasive refusal syndrome (which cannot be treated on an outpatient basis). Less commonly, admission may be necessary for those with bulimia nervosa, FAED and functional dysphagia. Selective eaters very rarely require admission.

The clinician's task is to advise the parents so that they can make an informed decision. It is perfectly reasonable to attempt a brief trial of out-patient treatment even for those who are seriously ill, but this should be very closely monitored. For those whose physical health is seriously compromised, progress should be reviewed on a day-by-day basis. If there is no immediate improvement the trial should be terminated and hospitalisation arranged.

It is also necessary to consider what resources are available. For urgent medical treatment such as rehydration or electrolyte replacement, admission to a paediatric unit is clearly appropriate. However, for the more long-term treatment of underlying emotional problems the emphasis in such a unit on immediate physical care makes admission less appropriate. In these circumstances if outpatient care has proved insufficient, admission to a unit that has some experience and expertise in the management of eating disorders in this age group should be considered. Ideally, there should be specialist units for young people with eating disorders, which can offer all aspects of the treatment required. However, there are very few such units. A possible compromise involves a short admission to a paediatric unit for medical emergencies as required, linked with intensive outpatient treatment for the psychological issues. Day-care programmes have been shown to be of value for adults (Freeman, 1991) and their use for the younger population warrants consideration if the practicalities can be overcome. Whatever programme is being considered, it must be remembered that such patients need highly skilled age-appropriate mental health treatment allied with close medical supervision.

Integrated treatment

It is beyond dispute that the management of all but the mildest cases of early onset eating disorders requires a comprehensive approach. This includes focusing on biological, social and psychological factors and requires a multi-disciplinary team. The team might include nurses, psychologists, psychiatrists, family therapists, psychotherapists, social workers, dieticians and physiotherapists or occupational therapists. Between them they can provide a comprehensive (physical, social and psychological) assessment and an integrated treatment, which might include parental counselling and/or family therapy, motivational enhancement therapy, cognitive behavioural therapy, psychodynamic psychotherapy, medication, meal plans, meal support, exercise activities and body-awareness programmes. Teachers should be consulted and advised with regard to school-related issues and they are essential for an inpatient programme. A social work input is necessary when neglect or abuse is suspected, or on the rare occasions when parents decline or in other ways resist treatment for their sick child. On such occasions the social worker can advise on the need for and if necessary organise a network meeting or case conference. It is important to share information and exchange views in such worrying circumstances before making decisions about management.

Such comprehensive teams are more likely to be available within an inpatient service, and the majority of children and adolescents with eating disorders are likely to be treated as outpatients. However, every effort should be made to ensure that the essential ingredients of the treatment programme are available, whatever the context. Generally it should be possible to provide the essential ingredients with even a relatively small team. It is our experience that early onset eating disorders become even more problematic as a result of the failure to acknowledge the need for and/or to implement appropriate treatment.

This links to the fact that just as important as professional title/grouping is that there are clinicians available who have experience and expertise in treatment of eating disorders. Patients and parents emphasise the importance of having confidence in the clinician, which is is so often connected to the clinician's experience. In clinics which lack a well-staffed multidisciplinary team the vital ingredient then becomes experience.

Stages of recovery

It is helpful to be aware of issues relating to both the pace and nature of change. The complexity and severity of eating disorders in young people, combined with the common resistance to change, are such that change is usually very slow. Furthermore, change is often accompanied by what initially appears to be deterioration. In anorexia nervosa particularly, but also with FAED, pervasive refusal syndrome, and sometimes other emotional disorders such as obsessive compulsive disorder, we have noticed specific patterns of behaviour which predominate at certain times. These are illustrated in Figure 9.2 and are usefully categorised as three stages. Stage 1 is that of the presenting problem, when the eating disorder is the predominant feature. The young person with anorexia nervosa tends to be preoccupied with weight and food intake almost to the exclusion of other considerations. With the possible exception of schoolwork, she shows no interest in anything else. She is unable to recognise that she has any problem other than that 'stupid adults are trying to make me fat'. A similar picture can be painted for other eating disorders. Once treatment is initiated, and usually within a few weeks, a slow improvement in the presenting problem occurs. On average after about six months it has almost resolved, providing the next stage of behaviour is tolerated.

This Stage 2 is one of increasing assertiveness and expression of very powerful, negative feelings, with an apparent absence of concern for those to whom the feelings are directed – most commonly the parents, but also clinicians. The young person behaves in a manner that is totally uncharacteristic and causes great distress to her parents. Indeed the parents may blame the clinician for 'turning their child into a monster'. This stage has now become so familiar to us as a necessary step to recovery that we not only predict it but

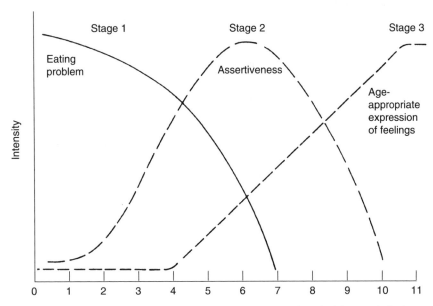

Figure 9.2 Stages of illness and recovery (Lask, 1993, reprinted with permission).

also positively welcome it. We advise the parents in advance along the following lines:

> If your child is to make a full recovery she will most likely go through a phase that you will probably find extremely difficult. This is a very trying phase indeed. She will be horrible to you and probably to us as well. You will be angry with us, and feel that we have made her worse. However, we will be pleased because this will mean that she is getting better. It is as if she has been unable to express these feelings and they have built up inside her almost to the point when she cannot eat. Once treatment starts, however, these feelings will come pouring out, almost like a volcano exploding. We will of course do our best to support you during this stage and it will come to an end. However, if you block her feelings, if you don't let her express them, or you punish her, she will withdraw and lock them up inside. You may then feel better but her eating problems won't resolve. Of course, you will need to set limits such as no breaking things or physical violence, but if you can tolerate the rest you will be helping her to recover.

As Stage 2 behaviour diminishes it is gradually replaced by a more age-appropriate expression of feelings. For example, the young person may express her anger directly at the person concerned, but within a few minutes is able to discuss it all in a relatively calm and rational manner. Once this behaviour predominates over eating problems and excessive negativism, Stage 3 has been achieved and the child is well on the way to complete recovery.

As can be seen from Figure 9.2, there is considerable overlap between these stages, leading to some confusion and much distress, especially when Stages 1 and 2 overlap in the first few months. However, it can be seen that this overlap is part of a process and so long as it can be tolerated there will be movement forward to recovery.

Some children, especially those who have been severely traumatised either by neglect or abuse, are likely to go through a stage of regression, before they enter Stage 2. They may behave like a child much younger than their years and even adopt quite infantile behaviour, such as drinking from a baby's bottle or wetting the bed. Again, tolerance of this and sympathetic understanding and support aids recovery.

Summary

There is no escaping the fact that the treatment of early onset eating disorders is both complex and challenging. A comprehensive approach to both assessment and treatment is mandatory. The formation of a therapeutic alliance with the parents and their daughter should be at the forefront of treatment. Teamwork, characterised by clarity of roles and responsibilities, consistency within the team, consistency between the team and the parents, and consistency over time, are all likely to enhance the outcome. Treatment that is relatively straightforward and focused is more likely to be of value than prolonged exploration of possible underlying causes. The enhancement of motivation as a specific focus of treatment is often overlooked yet appears to be a useful addition for those patients lacking insight and/or motivation. Underlying cognitive deficits should not be ignored and cognitive remediation techniques, focused on the deficits, rather than on the eating disorder symptoms, are showing considerable promise (Tchanturia, Campbell, Morris, and Treasure, 2005). Finally, change is likely to be slow and patience and empathy are necessary virtues.

References

American Psychiatric Association (APA, 1994). *Diagnostic and statistical manual of mental disorders* (4th ed.). Washington, DC: APA.

Ayton, A.K (2004). Dietary polyunsaturated fatty acids and anorexia nervosa: Is there a link? *Nutritional Neuroscience, 7* (1), 1–12.

Behr, H., and Hearst, L. (2005). *Group-analytic psychotherapy* (pp.203–219). Chichester: John Wiley.

Bryant-Waugh, R., and Lask, B. (2004). *Eating disorders in childhood and adolescence: A parent's guide.* Hove, UK: Psychology Press.

Freeman, C. (1991). Day treatment for anorexia nervosa. *British Journal of Bulimia and Anorexia Nervosa, 6,* 3–8.

Lask, B., and Fosson, A. (1989). *Childhood illness – the psychosomatic approach: Children talking with their bodies*. Chichester: John Wiley.

Lask, B., Fosson, A., Thomas, S., and Rolfe, U. (1993). Zinc deficiency and childhood onset anorexia nervosa. *Journal of Clinical Psychiatry*, *54*, 63–66.

Lask, B., Taylor, S., and Nunn, K. (2003). *Practical child psychiatry: The clinician's guide*. London: BMJ Books.

National Institute for Health and Clinical Excellence (NICE, 2004). *Eating disorders: Core interventions in the treatment and management of anorexia nervosa, bulimia nervosa and related eating disorders: A national clinical practice guideline*. London: NICE.

Neiderman, M., Richardson, J., Farley, A., and Lask, B. (2001). Naso-gastric feeding in early-onset eating disorders. *International Journal of Eating Disorders*, *29*, 441–448.

Neiderman M., Zardy, M., Tattersall, M., and Lask, B. (2000). Enteric feeding in early-onset anorexia nervosa. *International Journal of Eating Disorders*, *28*, 470–475.

Tchanturia, K., Campbell, I. C., Morris, R., and Treasure, J. (2005). Neuropsychological studies in anorexia nervosa. *International Journal of Eating Disorders*, *37*, S72–S76.

10 Motivational approaches

*Bryan Lask, Josie Geller and
Suja Srikameswaran*

The sun and the wind were having a dispute as to who was more powerful. They saw a man walking along and they had a bet as to which of them could get him to remove his coat. The wind started first and blew up a huge gale, the coat flapped but the man only fastened the buttons and tightened up his belt. The sun tried next and shone brightly making the man sweat. He took off his coat.

(Anonymous)

Introduction

The story of the sun and the wind highlights the importance of motivation. The wind's coercive approach simply increased the man's resistance to change; the sun's approach led the man to *want* to take off his coat.

Over the past decade, motivational approaches have received increased attention in eating disorder centres around the world. Their growing popularity is linked to the recognition that to be effective, it is necessary for clinicians to address the widespread problems of treatment refusal, resistance, dropout and relapse, which commonly occur in this patient population.

Motivational approaches have their origins in the substance misuse field and were initially based upon the observation that substance users commonly lack motivation to change. Central is the premise that only the client has the power to bring about substantive change and that resistance is not a trait that exists within a person, but rather something that characterises an interpersonal process (Miller and Rollnick, 2002). Motivational approaches are partially based upon the observation that directly attempting to influence behaviour in individuals who lack motivation can lead to increased resistance and to the absence of behavioural change (the sun and the wind).

Within the field of motivational approaches there are a number of terms in common use. Unfortunately, they are increasingly being used inconsistently and their meanings are often confused. Their original meanings have historical and research validity and in consequence we shall define and describe the concepts as they were originally intended. However, because clinicians do not use the terms exclusively in research or historical contexts, and because of the move away from their original meanings, we have chosen, for the purpose of this chapter, to use whenever possible the more generic term 'motivational approaches'.

Readiness and motivation for change

Readiness and motivation for change have been considered as related but distinct, constructs. While *motivation* was used to refer to an individual's desire and drive for change, the term *readiness* emphasised that change occurs as a result of an individual's capability for change (i.e. the patient has the skills to change), and faith that change is both possible and will produce a positive outcome. Together, readiness and motivation for change were seen as the product of desire, drive, capacity and beliefs about the outcome of change.

Motivational interviewing

Motivational interviewing (MI) was introduced as a person-centred clinical method for helping clients to resolve ambivalence about and to move ahead with change. MI is a collaborative approach that considers clients as experts about themselves and their experiences (Miller and Rollnick, 2002). It draws upon the client's own values, motivations, abilities and resources. It is influenced by the client-centred approach in its use of reflective listening and accurate empathy, and by humanistic psychotherapies in its premise that given the proper supportive environment people will naturally change in a healthy direction. In MI the role of the therapist is to foster a trusting, collaborative relationship in which the client can explore incentives and disincentives for a problem and recovery from a problem in a non-pressurised environment. The attitude and stance of the therapist are central to this approach and can be challenging for clinicians who are accustomed to using a more directive therapeutic style. In MI, rather than being a 'cheerleader' for change the therapist expresses few or no expectations of change.

Motivational enhancement therapy

Motivational enhancement therapy (MET) was initially designed as a brief treatment based upon principles of MI with the addition of clinical feedback provided to clients (Miller and Rollnick, 2002). In its original form, MET consisted of four sessions focusing on developing a trusting relationship with the client, providing detailed clinical feedback of assessment results, understanding the function of the problem and reviewing the advantages and disadvantages (pros and cons) of change. Now it is practised in many different contexts and formats.

Motivational approaches

Motivational approaches are characterised by a focus on the patient's wishes in regard to whether or not to relinquish a problem, be that a compulsive behaviour, an addiction, adherence to treatment or an eating disorder. Such approaches explore the competing incentives to change and to stay the same and have the ultimate aim of enhancing motivation to change. They are characterised by a collaborative relationship that places as much responsibility as possible in the hands of the patient and is devoid of argument or coercion. They are informed by a specific stance – the motivational stance.

Motivational stance

The motivational stance refers to the attitude and behaviour of the clinician toward the patient. Critical elements of the stance for the younger population include:

* *warmth, respect, empathy*: attitudes that are common to most therapies
* *honesty*: the therapist at all times being honest and ensuring that there are no negative consequences to the patient for being honest
* *acceptance*: communication of values and beliefs that foster the patient's self-acceptance
* *humility*: making no assumptions
* *curiosity*: non-judgemental interest
* *flexibility*: the ability to utilise a motivational stance alongside other strategies as determined by the patient's needs (e.g. around non-negotiables, see Chapter 9) and the ability to accept and work with the patient's frequent fluctuations between the various stages of change
* *low investment*: the clinician's therapeutic energy is not directed toward refeeding, weight gain or behavioural change but toward understanding the patient and helping to enhance her motivation. The agenda is curiosity not cure.

For a more general discussion of applications of the motivational stance to individuals with eating disorders, see for example, Geller, Brown, Zaitsoff, Goodrich, and Hastings (2003), Treasure, Katzman, Schmidt, Troop, Todd, and de Silva (1999), Vitousek, Watson, and Wilson (1998).

Transtheoretical model of change

The transtheoretical model of change (Prochaska and DiClemente, 1983) offers a framework for considering motivation/readiness in 'treatment-resistant individuals'. According to this model, motivation/readiness status can be described according to a series of stages:

1   *Pre-contemplation*: being unaware of a problem, or being unwilling to change.
2   *Contemplation*: being aware that there is a problem but unwilling to change.
3   *Preparation*: having the intention of changing soon.
4   *Action*: actively working to change.
5   *Maintenance*: working to prevent relapse.

For a clinical illustration of these stages, see the section on 'advantages and disadvantages' (p. 183). The stages are shown diagrammatically in Figure 10.1, which demonstrates an average time frame (in months) for the progression of an adolescent with anorexia nervosa through the stages, the tendency to move between them throughout the process and the overlap between them. It is important to emphasise that Figure 10.1 is an approximation and that there is considerable variation with some/patients progressing much more rapidly and others much more slowly. Occasionally relapse does occur with regression to earlier stages. However, in this younger population it is unusual to see regression all the way to pre-contemplation once action has been reached. Extensive research among individuals attempting to modify addictive behaviours has supported the utility of this model (e.g. Prochaska and DiClemente, 1983).

In the eating disorders, stages of change have been assessed using interview and self-report measures (Geller and Drab, 1999; Rieger and Touyz, 2006). Research both in adolescents and adults has shown that readiness tends to differ according to symptoms, with patients usually being most interested in making changes to binge symptoms and least interested in making changes to dietary restriction and the use of compensatory strategies (Geller, Cockell, and Drab, 2001). Consequently, in attempting to understand readiness and motivation, it is important for clinicians to ask questions about all aspects

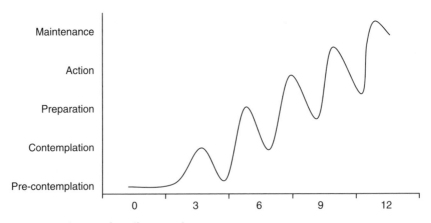

Figure 10.1 Stages of readiness to change.

of the disordered eating. Obtaining an accurate picture of readiness and motivation is useful because readiness scores have been shown to predict clinical outcome in adolescents and adults, including the decision to engage in intensive symptom reduction treatment, symptom change post-treatment, dropout and relapse (Geller et al., 2001; Geller, Drab-Hudson, Whisenhunt, and Srikameswaran, 2004). Without this information, clinicians may have difficulty recommending appropriate treatment that is suited to the patient's and family's needs.

Motivational approaches with children, adolescents and their parents

Motivational approaches for children and adolescents with eating disorders are based upon the same principles as those used for adults. There are many similarities in their application with the younger population but also some differences. These are generally determined by developmental issues such as the need to simplify language and concepts as well as the need to work closely with parents. In this section we present, discuss and illustrate some of the ways in which motivational approaches are applied when working with the younger population.

Although very little has been written about the application of motivational approaches for younger patients and their parents (e.g. Lask, 2003), they are of particular importance in the assessment and treatment of this population for a number of reasons. First, many of this age group are in pre-contemplation and either do not recognise they are ill or have no wish to change. It is common for them to be seeing a clinician because their parents have chosen that course of action and have not made this decision themselves. Resistance to treatment for an eating disorder in this age group is the norm. This is intensified by the age-appropriate tendency of adolescents to resist authority, to assert their rights to as much autonomy as possible and to assert the supremacy of their own views and values over those of adults. Finally, the developmental status of children and adolescents renders them far more vulnerable to the physical sequelae of an inadequate diet and therefore more liable to rapid physical decompensation (see Chapter 5).

Clinical applications

Motivational approaches incorporate a number of techniques. To describe these let us consider a fairly typical example of a teenager with anorexia nervosa being seen for the first time.

> Lisa, aged 14, presented to an early onset eating disorders pro-
> gramme with a history of food restriction and marked weight loss.
> Her parents said that they were concerned about her low weight,

moodiness, and overall health. They described Lisa as an over-achiever in all domains of her life – an excellent student at school, successful in her competitive gymnastics club and very popular. In response to their growing concern, Lisa's parents had tried a num-ber of techniques to get her to eat more, including persuasion, bribes and threats. On a few occasions her father had lost his tem-per and stormed out of the house. Both parents said they were sick with worry about her and feared that she might die. Lisa said, 'I like me the way I am. My parents are making a big deal out of nothing. Why won't they just leave me alone?'

Open questions

These are questions that do not require a yes or no answer, but rather allow for a wide range of answers. So instead of asking 'Do you think that you are too thin?' the clinician might ask Lisa 'What for you are the good things about being thin?' Other such questions include 'Can you tell me more about that?' and 'Can you help me to understand that better?' Such questions are not challenging and reflect the stance of curiosity.

Reflective listening

This involves repeating what the patient has said, using very slightly different words but retaining the essence of her reply. For example, Lisa answered the question 'What for you are the good things about being thin?' by saying 'I feel good about myself.' When asked to explain further, she said 'It makes me feel strong, like I have willpower', to which the clinician replied 'So, for you, being thin equals being strong and disciplined.' Such a response helped Lisa feel understood.

Affirmation

Should Lisa give a positive reply to the therapist's reflection above, this might be followed by 'It must feel great to be strong and disciplined.' Affirmation is warm and respectful validation of the patient's views and attitudes. It adds to the sense the patient may be experiencing of being listened to and understood and complements this with a sense of being accepted.

Tracking

This involves the therapist not having a specific agenda but rather following the patient's thoughts and feelings, regardless of what these are. It incorpor-ates the therapeutic stance of flexibility. For example, if after the therapist had said to Lisa 'It must feel great to be strong and disciplined' she had replied 'Yes', the therapist might ask another open-ended question such as 'Can you tell me more about that?' However, if Lisa had replied by saying 'It's not always great to be the strong one', the therapist might respond with a reflection such as 'So it sounds like there are times when it's not great to be strong.' Alternatively, had Lisa replied 'But I am not always as strong and disciplined as I should be', the therapist would need to utilise sufficient flexibility to track this change of 'direction'. A tracking reply might be 'Let me make sure I understand – you feel great about being strong and disciplined, but sometimes you worry that you are not as strong and disciplined as you want to be.' In essence tracking is staying on the same track as the patient wherever the track leads, even if that involves the patient talking about something seemingly completely unrelated to the eating disorder, such as her favourite music.

Exploring mixed feelings

Most people with anorexia nervosa have mixed feelings about their illness, especially in the stages of contemplation and preparation. For example, if Lisa were to be in contemplation she might say something like 'One part of my mind tells me to eat and the other tells me not to as I am too fat.' The therapist might respond to that by acknowledging empathically the ambivalence and asking her to talk more about 'these divided feelings'. The acknowledgement of ambivalence is in itself supportive but also allows for further exploration, especially in relation to the advantages and disadvantages of change.

The advantages and disadvantages

Central to the ambivalence so commonly seen in those with eating disorders are the competing advantages and disadvantages of the disorder. When those with anorexia nervosa are in contemplation, although they can see advantages and disadvantages to being thin, even one important advantage that restricting offers can outweigh many disadvantages. Examples of what they might say include:

- I feel in control.
- Being thin comforts me.
- I look good when I am thin.
- I feel good when I am thin.
- Eating gives me stomach pains; if I don't eat I don't get the pain.
- Eating makes me feel sick; if I don't eat I don't feel sick.
- I get a sense of achievement when I lose weight.
- I feel proud of myself when I lose weight.
- Not eating keeps stress away.
- I feel ashamed when I eat so not eating keeps that feeling away.

- I feel disgusted with myself if I see fat when I look in the mirror so if I am thin I don't have that problem.
- I feel special when I am thin.

When asked about possible disadvantages, those in pre-contemplation are usually unable to think of any. Once they have reached contemplation or beyond they are more able to mention disadvantages such as:

- I feel tired all the time.
- I feel cold even when it's hot.
- I don't have the energy I used to have.
- I get dizzy when I stand up.
- I can't lead my usual life.
- I am fed up with worrying about my weight and what I eat.
- I can't stop thinking about my weight and shape.
- People are always nagging me.
- My mum and dad are always freaking out.
- I worry about what's happening to my bones.
- I'm scared I may not be able to have children.
- I want to get back to my old self and not be worried all the time.

The balance between advantages and disadvantages varies depending upon the stage of readiness to change. In pre-contemplation, only advantages can usually be considered. In contemplation, disadvantages emerge and in preparation there is some sort of balance between them. In action and maintenance, the disadvantages outweigh the advantages. When using a motivational approach disadvantages are best discussed only if the patient mentions them or appears ready to consider them.

In Lisa's case she could initially only see advantages, saying she felt much fitter being thin, had just the right weight for her gymnastics and that her friends wished they could be like her. 'I feel much more in control – people are always trying to control me; this way it all feels much better.' She was clearly in *pre-contemplation*.

Initially her treatment explored the perceived advantages of restricting and the consequences of Lisa expecting herself to be strong and disciplined all the time. After some sessions, Lisa noted that she didn't have the same amount of energy that she used to have. She also became aware that this made it hard to convince herself and others that she was strong. Someone had mentioned that if she fell during her gymnastics she might break a bone: 'That worries me but I am not going to put on any weight 'cos I prefer myself the way I am' (*contemplation*).

A few weeks later she commented that her gymnastics coach had told her she was too thin and that she couldn't be successful if she didn't gain some weight. She felt she was working harder and harder to feel strong and disciplined, but the feeling of strength was eluding her. She was wondering how to cope with what was becoming obvious to her – 'that I need to gain weight but I am so worried about getting fat' (*preparation*).

Shortly after this, Lisa asked for help. She said she wanted to learn how to better communicate with her parents and friends. She was ready to try eating again. She had come to the conclusion that although she still wanted to be thin and considered herself overweight, she could also acknowledge that her low energy and unhappiness were spoiling her life. On balance she felt that it was better to find a way of coping with weight gain rather than maintaining a weight that was too low for her to be healthy (*action*).

As she resumed a normal diet and started gaining weight her anxieties increased and from time to time she was very upset and scared about being 'forced to eat'. Her parents discussed with her different ways in which they could help her to cope with her distress. She chose to have her mother holding her hand during each meal and for her father not to be in the room (*maintenance*).

Summarising

Just as reflective listening involves repeating what the patient has just said, using very slightly different words but retaining the essence of her reply, summarising involves a reflection of the essence of what the patient has been saying throughout the session. For example, in Lisa's case toward the end of their fourth meeting the therapist said: 'Let me see if I have understood what you have been saying. It seems like you want to be thin because it helps you feel good about yourself, you feel much stronger and disciplined, and fitter being thin, have just the right weight for your gymnastics and you feel much more in control. You feel your parents are making an unnecessary fuss and wish they would get off your back. Is that approximately right'? Lisa nodded her agreement, at which the therapist asked if there was anything he had forgotten or got wrong. Lisa reminded the therapist that she had told him that her friends wished they could be like her but also that she was a bit worried about the danger of breaking a bone.

Summarising has many advantages. It helps the patient feel listened to, understood and acknowledged, allows her to correct the therapist when mistakes are made or particular points are forgotten and to reflect upon what she has been saying. The option of summarising from time to time also encourages the therapist to focus even more on what is being said, which in turn enhances the chances of understanding and remembering.

Draining

Patients often feel that they are not understood and are overwhelmed by the demands of the illness. Draining is a technique designed to help with these phenomena, and involves a thorough exploration of the advantages of the illness (e.g. feeling proud, having a sense of achievement, feeling in control, feeling attractive). The purpose of the draining technique is to explore all ways in which eating disorder symptoms may be helpful. Without this shared understanding the patient's energy is often spent protecting the status quo, and they are left stuck and pre-contemplative. Increased understanding can set the stage for consideration of alternatives and possibly discussion of the disadvantages of their illness. Critical to draining is the therapist placing no pressure on the patient and conveying that they have all the time in the world to listen to what the patient has to say. The process of draining will not only leave patients feeling understood by the therapist, but they will also have a better understanding of themselves, and much of the shame and guilt of their disorder will be alleviated. In Lisa's case part of the conversation went along these lines:

Therapist: You have said that there are many good things for you in losing weight – I wonder if we can just discuss them a bit more.

Lisa: Well I have already told you I feel more in control if I don't eat and my friends envy me.

Therapist: More in control?

Lisa: Yes, I eat what I want and if I don't want to eat then I don't, and no one can control me. I am fed up with people always telling me what to do and when.

Therapist: Who is controlling you?

Lisa: My dad especially and he's always commenting on my weight – first he said I was getting fat, now he's saying I am too thin. Why can't he leave me alone? It's my body not his!

Therapist: So your dad tries to control you by commenting on your weight.

Lisa: Yes and it pisses me off – he's always done that, ever since I can remember.

Therapist: So one of the good things in not eating is that you can control your dad.

Lisa: Yes. He is such a control freak and he needs to know what it's like.

Therapist: Seems like having some control over him is a really good feeling.

Lisa: You bet.

Therapist: Can you tell me about some of the other good things about being more in control.

Lisa: I feel stronger in myself.

Therapist: Stronger?

Lisa: Yes, I feel really powerful and like I can do anything.

The conversation continued along these lines for another ten minutes. The therapist is using motivational techniques such as open questions, reflective listening, affirmation and tracking. In addition he is encouraging Lisa to talk as much as possible about the particular theme of control. Eventually he asks if there is anything else Lisa wants to say about being in control:

Lisa:	No.
Therapist:	Sure?
Lisa:	I think so.
Therapist:	Well we can always come back to control whenever you want. Meantime you also mentioned earlier on that your friends envy you.
Lisa:	They all want to be thin, all girls do. I don't think I'm the thinnest but I seem to get the most attention.
Therapist:	Attention?
Lisa:	Katie's always going on about how she'd like to be as thin as me and has tried but can't do it – she keeps asking how I do it.
Therapist:	How does that feel for you?
Lisa:	Good – like I am better than her.
Therapist:	Better?
Lisa:	Well she's very smart and pretty and everyone admires her and I always felt envious of her, but now it's like the other way round.
Therapist:	Sounds like that feels really good for you.
Lisa:	Uh huh.
Therapist:	So being thin helps you feel in control and admired. Are there any other things that make you feel good about yourself?
Lisa:	When I do well in school.
Therapist:	Yes, your mum mentioned that you are an excellent student! What do you like most about school?
Lisa:	I like it when I work hard on something and get top marks.
Therapist:	It sounds like school is something that you are really good at and provides a sense of accomplishment. Is there anything else that makes you feel good about yourself?
Lisa:	Yes, gymnastics!
Therapist:	Ya, I can see from the smile on your face that gymnastics is a good thing in your life. What is it about gymnastics that makes you feel good about yourself?
Lisa:	I love winning competitions; I love being able to do a perfect landing.
Therapist:	Sounds like there are lots of things about gymnastics that make you feel good about yourself . . . What else?

The conversation proceeds along these lines giving Lisa the chance to say all she wants about why she loves gymnastics. Lisa is then 'drained' of other things that make her feel good about herself, including spending time with friends, horseback riding and taking care of her little sister.

After a while Lisa reflects, 'Gymnastics is the biggest thing for me. Trouble is, although I look better now since I got thin, I don't seem to be as strong as I used to be. Do you think my strength will come back?'

At some point the therapist needs to make a decision as to whether to try to continue the draining about things that make Lisa feel good about herself or invite Lisa to talk about the disadvantage of being thin. If the therapist focuses exclusively on the disadvantages, there is the danger of Lisa feeling controlled and even coerced. However, once Lisa has hinted at disadvantages it is useful to follow up with open questions about them.

Transfer

This involves exploring other areas of the patient's life, to which the advantages of AN might be applied; for example, feeling in control and feeling special. This allows the patient to consider how she might achieve the good feelings associated with maintaining a low weight without having to endanger her health. In Lisa's case:

Therapist: You have said how important it is to you to have control and that you only seem to have it through not eating.

Lisa: Yes, I never have control.

Therapist: So in what parts of your life would you like control?

Lisa: My dad's always telling me what to do, what to wear, who I can see, when I've got to be home.

Therapist: Sounds very annoying.

Lisa: He never lets up. He's got some sort of hang-up.

Therapist: So what would you like to tell him?

Lisa: To leave me alone and mind his own business.

Therapist: Mind his own business. . . .

Lisa: Yeh, why does he have to interfere so much?

Therapist: Why do you think?

Lisa: Well I know he loves me and he worries about me but he has a funny way of showing it.

Therapist: So how would you like him to show it?

Lisa: Well he could stop nagging me for a start.

Therapist: I wonder if you could ask him to stop.

Lisa: He wouldn't listen.

Therapist: So he doesn't listen when you ask him to stop, and he doesn't listen when you restrict – sounds like neither strategy is working.

Lisa: Yeh, nothing works with him.

Not all children or adolescents are as co-operative or willing to speak as Lisa. Many young patients with eating disorders are angry, denying or silent and the application of a motivational approach in such scenarios is associated with many challenges. In the following section examples are given of how to work motivationally with Sunita, an angry 16 year old, Pat, a 15 year old in pre-contemplation and Sue, a silent 13 year old.

Jane, 16

Therapist:	Hi Jane – good to see you.
Jane:	It's not good to see you – it's a waste of time.
Therapist:	A waste of time?
Jane:	What's the point – you just want me to put on weight, just like everyone else does. You all pretend you care and want to help but all you really want is to turn me into a fat pig.
Therapist:	A fat pig?
Jane:	That's what you all want. No one cares about what I want.
Therapist:	You seem very angry today.
Jane:	I don't seem angry – I am angry.
Therapist:	Can you help me to understand some of what's making you so angry?
Jane:	I've already told you, just now. Don't you listen to anything I say? Obviously you can't understand if you don't listen.
Therapist:	Any possibility of another chance?
Jane:	What's the point?
Therapist:	So it's all pointless?
Jane:	Congratulations, at least you got that right.
Therapist:	So maybe I can try a bit more?
Jane:	That's up to you.
Therapist:	Well I'm hoping we can work on this together.
Jane:	That would be a first.
Therapist:	So no one wants to work *with* you?
Jane:	They say they do but they're all liars.
Therapist:	That sounds really hard for you if you can never believe anyone.
Jane:	It's hardly surprising I get so angry with everybody.
Therapist:	No, not surprising at all – I would feel very angry if I thought everyone was lying to me.
Jane:	Would you?
Therapist:	Absolutely.
Jane:	So why can't you all be honest and just admit you want to fatten me up?
Therapist:	I'm wondering what's so awful for you about people wanting you to put on weight.
Jane:	It's up to me what weight I should be, not all you apologies for doctors and psychologists.
Therapist:	Yes, of course you should decide what weight you should be.
Jane:	So why don't you all just let me be 38 kilos. I keep telling you that's what I want to be.
Therapist:	How would it be if you weighed more?
Jane:	Awful, really awful, and I am NOT going to put on weight.

Therapist:	Because?
Jane:	Because I'd be fat and ugly and disgusting.
Therapist:	So putting on weight means being fat, ugly and disgusting.
Jane:	Wow, you are listening.
Therapist:	Can you tell me a bit more about disgusting?
Jane:	Fat is disgusting. It shows you are greedy and it looks gross.
Therapist:	Gross?
Jane:	Yes, like a fat pig.
Therapist:	So can I just check I've understood correctly – you can't trust anyone because they are all liars and all they really want is to make you put on weight. And if you do that you will be fat, ugly and disgusting.
Jane:	Have you been taking lessons or something?
Therapist:	So I got something right for a change?
Jane:	For a change!
Therapist:	Okay, whilst I am on a roll, can I try to understand a bit more?
Jane:	If you want.

At this point Jane's anger seems to be subsiding, associated with the therapist taking her anger full on, acknowledging and affirming it. By continuing in the same vein it should be possible for Jane and the therapist to have a useful conversation around readiness and motivation (or lack of them).

Pat, 15

FIRST MEETING

Therapist:	Hi Pat, nice to meet you.
Pat:	Why am I here?
Therapist:	What did your parents tell you?
Pat:	Dunno.
Therapist:	Okay – they told me they were worried about you not eating and losing a lot of weight.
Pat:	Where do they get that idea from?
Therapist:	I guess we will have to ask them.
Pat:	They're stupid.
Therapist:	Sometimes parents can seem very stupid.
Pat:	They just imagine things. I am eating fine.
Therapist:	So it must be strange for you that they say you aren't.
Pat:	Well I eat normally, just the same as my sister and my friends.
Therapist:	So how can you convince your parents there is nothing to worry about?
Pat:	I don't know – you tell them.
Therapist:	Well that would be hard for me to do as I don't know anything about your eating.

Pat:	Well do you think I am too thin? They say I am but I know they are lying.
Therapist:	Lying?
Pat:	Yes, they know how much I hate being fat so they pretend I am not.
Therapist:	What do you hate about being fat?
Pat:	It's yukky, gross, horrible.
Therapist:	Can you tell me more about that?
Pat:	No one wants to be fat. They all look at you and laugh at you.
Therapist:	What do they say?
Pat:	Oh I don't know. Why do you ask all these questions?
Therapist:	Well I am trying to understand how it is for you. It seems like you are having a very tough time at the moment.
Pat:	No one believes me and they are just trying to make me fatter.
Therapist:	I am wondering how things would be better for you if you could be the size you wanted.
Pat:	The thinner you are the more popular you are – the thin girls are much more popular.
Therapist:	That sounds like you don't feel you are popular.
Pat:	Well I am not – most of the girls in my class hate me.
Therapist:	You reckon that if you could be the size you want they are more likely to like you.
Pat:	Dunno.
Therapist:	Well it's important to feel liked.
Pat:	I wouldn't know.
Therapist:	Well may be I can try to understand all this better. Can you tell me some other good things about being thinner?
Pat:	I'd be more successful. All the people on the telly are thin. . . .
Therapist:	And in the magazines.
Pat:	Yeh, everywhere. You just can't get anywhere if you're fat and no one likes you and you feel stupid.
Therapist:	Maybe I can just check that I have understood – you are worried about being fat but your parents say you are too thin and that you need to put on weight. The idea of being fat is yukky. People would look at you and laugh at you and you can't be popular and successful, you would just be stupid. Is that roughly how you see it?

In this dialogue the therapist has made no attempt to convince Pat she is thin, nor got into any arguments with her, despite her lack of insight. Instead he has simply tracked her thoughts and feelings, using curiosity, open questions, reflection, affirmation and summarising. This has facilitated a conversation about the perceived advantages for her in being thin and the disadvantages of being fat. Continuation of the dialogue over a number of meetings was associated with a gradual transition to contemplation.

Sue, 13

SECOND MEETING

Sue is sitting silently, her head bowed and her face hidden behind long hair. The therapist, who is sitting a metre away from her and at an angle to her, is speaking slowly, with long pauses.

Therapist:	Good to see you again, Sue.
	Sue remains silent.
Therapist:	I am wondering how things have been since we last met.
	Sue remains silent.
Therapist:	Seems like you don't want to talk today.
	Sue shrugs her shoulders.
Therapist:	That's okay and of course you don't have to if you don't want to.
	Sue remains silent.
Therapist:	Sue, I am not expecting you to talk and that's absolutely fine. If you want to say anything, of course you can, but as I said I am not expecting you to.
	Sue remains silent.
Therapist:	But you know I have this funny habit of thinking aloud and I hope you won't mind if I do this now.
	Sue shrugs her shoulders.
Therapist:	And what I am thinking is that Sue really doesn't want to be here today and it's all a waste of time.
	Sue gives no response.
Therapist:	And that she wishes everyone would just leave her alone to get on with her life how she wants . . . that it's a complete pain when people interfere and tell her what she should and should not do . . . and no one will ever understand her properly . . . I think that's a horrible situation to be in.
	Sue shows an almost imperceptible nod of her head.
Therapist:	And it's even worse because people are trying to make her put on weight when she desperately wants to lose weight.
	Sue turns her head very slightly toward the therapist.
Therapist:	So, I am wondering what I can do to be helpful.
	Sue gives no response.
Therapist:	I am not even sure if it's okay to continue thinking aloud.
Sue:	[irritated mumble] Whatever.

After an initial and almost complete unresponsiveness, Sue's nonverbal responses indicate a grudging interest in what is being said. The use of the third person, talking about Sue as if she is not there, rather than addressing her directly, is deliberate. Because it is indirect it takes the pressure off Sue to respond. Any pressure is experienced as coercive and the natural response is to resist. The therapist can continue in this manner, being especially sensitive to the nonverbal communications, cautious about saying too much and ensuring adequate time between each comment for Sue to consider what is being said.

Including parents

A potential problem in utilising motivational approaches when working with children and adolescents is that the parents may be excluded. Consequently they may not be able to understand the therapeutic aims. The child may convey to her parents that the therapist is being supportive of her maintaining a low weight and there is every possibility of inconsistency in what is said. Therefore it is far better to include the parents in the therapeutic process. This has the advantage of helping them to understand better what is driving their daughter to starve herself and learning how best to talk with her.

Sara, 15, has had AN for about six months and the following dialogue occurred during the initial assessment when her parents were present:

Therapist: I am wondering if you could help me to understand a bit more about your wish to lose weight.

Sara: I am just so fat, I've got to lose weight; I look disgusting and . . .

Father: Sara, I've told you so many times, you aren't fat, you are desperately thin.

Therapist: Maybe we can just let Sara explain to us how it is for her, then you can let me know how you see things. Is that okay?

Father: Okay.

Therapist: You were saying Sara that you feel you look disgusting . . .

Sara: Yes, I've got all this fat and I hate myself. I am so ugly.

Mother: Darling you aren't ugly – you are the most beautiful girl in the world.

Therapist: Again it may be helpful if we just let Sara say what she thinks first. Then we can discuss it further. Sara, sorry, you were saying you hate yourself.

Sara: Anyone this fat would hate themselves.

Therapist: Can you tell me more about ugly and hating yourself?

Sara: If you eat too much you get fat and ugly and that means you are greedy and disgusting.

Father: But she doesn't eat too much . . .

Therapist: Maybe you can help your parents understand how it feels to be you.

Sara: What's the point – they don't listen.

Therapist: Well maybe I can help them to listen.

Sara: They never do.

Therapist [to Sara and parents]: How about we all try to work on this together?

Father: That's why we came here but Sara has got to be honest, she never . . .

Therapist: Well I think the best way forward is that we let Sara explain how she sees things. Then each of you can have your turn . . .

Mother [to therapist]: He gets so worried about her.

Therapist: I think everyone has their own worries and we should make sure everyone has a chance to share them and feel understood. Sara, you were saying that you are desperate to lose weight, that you feel fat, ugly and disgusting, and that you hate yourself . . .

Sara: And no one understands. I can't eat more – it will ruin my life . . . Father leans forward to speak.

Therapist: Can you explain to your parents how it would ruin your life, and [to parents] can you just let her tell you about that?

Sara: You don't understand how I hate being fat. You don't even believe me and I do eat and I know you think I throw up all the time but I don't . . .

Father: You know that's not true. We can smell it in the bathroom . . .

Therapist: I tell you what Sara, maybe we should let your dad have his say first, so he can get it off his chest, and then maybe your mum, then you can have your say? Or would you prefer mum to have her say first? Sara shrugs.

Therapist: Who wants to go first?

Mother: He should.

Therapist [to Sara and father]: Okay? Both nod.

Therapist [to father]: You are obviously very worried about Sara . . .

Father: If she carries on like this she will die. I can't bear to see her looking so ill and inflicting it on herself. She looks like something out of Belsen. We've got to do something.

Therapist: It must be awful for you seeing this happening.

Father: You can't imagine, you feel so helpless and all she does is fight us when we try to help . . .

Sara: You don't help, you just get angry and yell at me . . .

Therapist: How about we let him finish Sara, then you can tell him where he got it wrong.

Sara: Okay.

Therapist: Sounds like the biggest problem is that you feel she's going to die and that you feel there is nothing you can do to help her.

Father: Any father would feel that way. It's dreadful seeing her this way.

The therapist continues to encourage Sara's father to 'offload' his concerns, using the same stance and similar techniques, especially open questions, affirmation, reflection, tracking and draining. Later:

Father:	I hope you've been listening Sara and that you'll listen to the doctor.
Sara:	Can I speak now?
Therapist:	Yes, maybe you can tell dad where you reckon he got it wrong, and maybe also any bits he got right.
Sara:	Well for a start I don't make myself sick, it was just once or twice and he thinks it's after every meal. And I don't do all those press-ups, I just want to have a flat tummy. What's wrong with that?
Therapist:	Maybe you can explain to dad about the flat tummy . . .
Sara:	Everyone wants a flat tummy . . .

And so the dialogue proceeds. Later Sara's mother is encouraged to give her account. When there is considerable interruption, as illustrated above, the therapist can help the family to decide who should 'go first', promising that everyone can have their say. It can take several sessions for progress to be made and it's important for everyone to be aware of this time frame. It can be helpful for the therapist to educate parents about research on readiness and motivation, including evidence suggesting that changing for others is associated with relapse. This can help parents recognise that pushing too hard can be counterproductive.

There can be a fine line between working motivationally with child and parents together and more conventional family therapy with its focus on family relationships (see Chapter 12). There need be no rules about what should be the primary focus, but generally speaking in the early stages of the assessment process it is likely to be more helpful to focus on motivation, although the experienced therapist should be sufficiently skilful and flexible to be able to work on both.

Integrating motivational approaches with other aspects of treatment

Motivational approaches are not an exclusive treatment but rather a complement to other approaches. Whilst motivational approaches can be used as a specific therapy, just as might be family therapy (Chapter 12), cognitive behavioural therapy (Chapter 13) or psychodynamic psychotherapy (Chapter 14), they can also be used alongside other therapies and integrated into the whole treatment regimen. It is perfectly reasonable to combine motivational approaches with, for example, the use of externalisation. This is particularly pertinent at meals and other times when compensatory behaviours such as purging or excessive exercising are being used. Once a treatment plan, including the non-negotiables, has been agreed, every effort should be made to avoid getting caught up in the inevitable arguments. Rather the motivational stance can be adopted as illustrated in the following example. Jenny, 14, with AN, in contemplation, is finding it very hard to adhere to the agreed meal plan:

Jenny: I can't eat all this – it's far too much. They've given me far more than I need. I'm not eating all this.

Nurse: It's really hard for you to eat all you need.

Jenny: I don't need this much – can't you hear me?

Nurse: Yes, I can hear you Jenny and I am sorry you are so upset.

Jenny: Then do something about it. I don't need to eat this much.

Nurse: Seems like the anorexia is giving you a really tough time today.

Jenny: It's nothing to do with anorexia, I just don't need this much.

Nurse: We have already agreed your meal plan and this is part of it, so I am wondering how I can help you to eat it.

Jenny: You can't – you're just useless. We agreed I only needed half a potato so why have they given me a whole one.

Nurse: It must be awful for you to be so worried about half a potato.

Jenny: So would you be if they lied to you about what they were going to give you.

Nurse: I see how upset you are and I know you are terrified of putting on weight, but this is what has been agreed and it's not going to help for us to argue. I wonder what else I can do to help you with this.

Jenny: If I eat this can I have more exercise time afterwards?

Nurse: I know you don't see it this way but I see your anorexia really getting at you today. I wonder what would be the worst thing for you about finishing this meal?

Jenny: Then I would have given in to you all and let myself down.

Nurse: Given in and let yourself down?

Jenny: Yes, I promised myself I wouldn't give in to you all.

Nurse: I can see how awful that feels to you.

Jenny: So why don't you do something about it?

Nurse: Well I was thinking how difficult it must be to have anorexia telling you one thing and us all telling you the opposite. It sounds like being pulled two ways at once.

Jenny: Yes, that's just it, so why don't you all stop pulling me and let me do what I want.

Nurse: I guess that would be us giving into the anorexia and letting it get the better of you.

Jenny: I don't want anyone getting the better of me.

Nurse: Absolutely. So what can we do to make sure the anorexia doesn't?

Jenny: Do you promise I won't put on weight?

Nurse: Anorexia doesn't want you to put on weight; but what do *you* want for yourself – to be tormented by anorexia and the fear of weight gain or to get out of here and get on with a normal life?

Jenny: Yes, I just want to get out of here.

Nurse: And to do that you need to be able to show your parents you can eat okay and they have nothing to worry about. So how can I help you to do that?

The nurse avoids arguing about content (either of the meal or other aspects of the eating disorder) and instead uses a motivational stance and externalisation. There are many variations on this approach, the detail of which can be adapted to suit the circumstances. For example after the meal Jenny may be determined to exercise excessively to compensate for her calorie intake:

Jenny: I've got to go for a walk now and I know you'll say no, but please, please let me.

Nurse: It's hard to have to wait for your walk.

Jenny: I am getting so fat.

Nurse: As we have already all agreed that you have to wait an hour for the walk, let's talk instead about how it feels to have to wait.

Jenny: Why do you torment me?

Nurse: I think it's the anorexia that torments you. Seems like it never leaves you alone for a minute. What's the worst thing it says to you?

Jenny: That I am a fat, disgusting pig.

Nurse: Wow, that's quite some insult.

Jenny: Well I am.

Nurse: It sounds as if you feel that taking a walk now may help you feel less fat and disgusting.

Jenny: Now you're at last beginning to understand so why don't you let me do what I need to?

Nurse: Can you help me to understand why it's so hard to wait an hour?

Other eating disorders

The focus in this chapter has been on the use of motivational approaches for AN. However, they are also applicable for the other eating disorders. For example, the resistance to trying new foods in selective eating, or to swallowing in functional dysphagia, or to eating more in food avoidance emotional disorder can all be explored using the motivational stance and similar techniques to those described above. All the same principles apply including parental involvement.

Conclusions

Motivational approaches focus on the patient's wishes in regard to whether or not to relinquish the eating disorder. Once motivation has improved there is more willingness to accept treatment for the eating disorder. They can be used in all age groups and for all eating disorders. The main aims are to enhance motivation rather than reduce symptoms. The approaches are characterised by a collaborative relationship that places as much responsibility as possible in the hands of the patient. In particular they avoid the use of challenge or coercion. Moving through the stages of readiness to change can be a slow process with much fluctuation between the stages. The therapeutic stance requires sufficient patience and flexibility to accommodate to these quite often dramatic fluctuations. Motivational approaches can and indeed should be used throughout the treatment process. They can be used in combination with many other treatments and might better be seen as a treatment principle rather than a stand-alone treatment.

When applied to children and adolescents it is important to include the parents in the treatment process so that they can better understand their daughter's illness, her ambivalence and help her with the battle against it. Although not yet empirically evaluated in the younger population, clinical experience suggests that the motivational approach is of considerable value and should be available in any early onset eating disorder programme.

References

Geller, J., Brown, K.E., Zaitsoff, S.L., Goodrich, S., and Hastings, F. (2003). Collaborative versus directive interventions in the treatment of eating disorders: Implications for care providers. *Professional Psychology: Research and Practice, 34,* 406–413.

Geller, J., Cockell, S.J., and Drab, D. (2001). Assessing readiness for change in anorexia nervosa: The psychometric properties of the readiness and motivation interview. *Psychological Assessment, 13,* 189–198.

Geller, J., and Drab, D. (1999). The readiness and motivation interview: A symptom-specific measure of readiness for change in the eating disorders. *European Eating Disorders Review, 7,* 259–278.

Geller, J., Drab-Hudson, D., Whisenhunt, B.L., and Srikameswaran, S. (2004). Readiness to change dietary restriction predicts short and long term outcomes in the eating disorders. *Eating Disorders: The Journal of Treatment and Prevention, 12,* 209–224.

Lask, B. (2003). Motivating children and adolescents to improve adherence. *Journal of Pediatrics, 143* (4), 430–433.

Miller, W.R., and Rollnick, S. (2002). *Motivational interviewing: Preparing people for change.* New York: Guilford Press.

Prochaska, J., and DiClemente, C. (1983). Stages and processes of self-change of smoking: Towards an integrative model of change. *Journal of Consulting and Clinical Psychology, 51,* 390–395.

Rieger, E., and Touyz, S. (2006). An investigation of the factorial structure of motivation to recover in anorexia nervosa using the anorexia nervosa stages of change questionnaire. *European Eating Disorders Review, 14,* 269–275.

Treasure, J., Katzman, M., Schmidt, U., Troop, N., Todd, G., and de Silva, P. (1999). Engagement and outcome in the treatment of bulimia nervosa: First phase of a sequential design comparing motivational enhancement therapy and cognitive behavioural therapy. *Behaviour Research and Therapy, 37,* 405–418.

Vitousek, K., Watson, S., and Wilson, G.T. (1998). Enhancing motivation for change in treatment-resistant eating disorders. *Clinical Psychology Review, 18,* 391–420.

11 Nutrition and refeeding

Melissa Hart

Introduction

This chapter deals with nutritional assessment and the establishment and maintenance of adequate nutrition and healthy eating patterns. Such components of management are best provided by a dietitian, although not all services have access to one. The role of the dietitian may vary depending on many factors including the expertise of the dietitian involved, the role of other members of the team, the needs of each individual patient and the overall treatment plan.

Assessment

A prerequisite of nutritional intervention is a comprehensive assessment. Key components of the assessment include creating a therapeutic alliance (see Chapter 9), involvement of parents (see Chapter 12) and assessment of nutritional intake and eating patterns. The therapeutic alliance is a key issue in nutrition intervention and essential in fostering a collaborative working relationship over time. A collaborative experience with a dietitian can be invaluable for anyone with an eating disorder, and may mean the patient will seek appropriate nutritional assistance when ready to make further change. The therapeutic alliance can, however, be hindered by an overemphasis on weight and food intake. At times of heightened clinician anxiety or frustration, it can be easy to become more directive and to focus more intently on weight gain or increased oral intake. Similarly, dietitians who are well versed in advising patients to increase physical activity and reduce dietary fat and energy may find it difficult to give the 'near enough eating is good enough' message (Beumont, Beumont, Touyz, and Williams, 1997).

A focus on weight and nutrition can be perceived by the patient as intrusive, challenging and of no immediate benefit. She may also be anticipating that the nutrition intervention will involve '*making* me eat' and '*making* me fat'. If this is not handled sensitively it may lead to an increase in resistance and power struggles. Bearing this in mind may also assist in ensuring our own expectations of change or adherence to the nutrition plan remain realistic.

One of the most important aspects of the nutrition assessment is how the interview is conducted. The style of interviewing will influence the amount and accuracy of the information obtained and may either foster or damage the therapeutic alliance. The interview should aim to proceed in the least threatening way possible, and questioning should be sensitive, empathic and validating (see Chapters 9 and 10 for further discussion of these issues). Early in the interview an enquiry of how the patient feels about discussing food and eating can be helpful. It is also important to gain some understanding during the interview of whether she feels there are certain aspects of her eating that she would like to change. This can assist in clarifying her aims and motivation.

Parental involvement

Parents or carers have a key role in assisting their daughter with her eating and are an essential source of knowledge regarding her eating history. In the nutritional management of children and adolescents with AN, carers should be included in any dietary education or meal planning (NICE, 2004).

Consequently parents should always be involved in the assessment process, including clarifying past and current eating behaviours and changes in eating over time. Family views on what constitutes normal, healthy eating and their attitudes to dieting should be ascertained. Food preparation practices should be clarified, including how food is purchased, who is responsible for meal preparation and how much influence over purchasing or preparation of food their daughter has. It is helpful to know about such activities as types of meals and snacks consumed, whether the family eats at the dinner table, whether meals are eaten together as a family and how family members react to restrictive or chaotic eating. Finally, it is also useful to determine whether and how family eating practices have changed during the illness.

Assessment of nutritional intake and eating behaviour

Assessing current and past dietary behaviour can assist in establishing a more realistic and physically safe nutrition plan. This will involve consideration of the factors influencing eating and assessment of the nutritional adequacy of the diet and behaviours around eating.

Factors influencing food choice and eating behaviour

Factors which influence eating and nutrition should be considered as part of assessment and may include stages of growth and development, food availability, family beliefs and practices, socioeconomic pressures and sociocultural influences.

Many biological influences on eating arise during childhood. Children experience continual growth each year and relatively high nutrient requirements in relation to size (McVeagh and Reed, 2001; Patchell, 2000). A high quality diet is required to achieve optimal growth and development during this time. Many children may have small appetites, however, and selective food refusal and food fads are often seen.

The nutritional requirements of adolescence are also high due to the growth spurt and physical maturation. This is a nutritionally vulnerable period of life, with a greater demand for nutrients and a period of psychosocial and developmental change (McVeagh and Reed, 2001; Patchell, 2000). Adolescence is a period of striving for independence and having a stronger need to conform with peers regarding food choices and eating behaviours. There may be increased interest in dietary fads and dieting behaviours. Body image dissatisfaction is also common. Typical adolescent eating behaviour may include missing meals, snacking to accommodate the higher energy requirements, increased fast food intake and consumption of high energy foods, including foods high in fat, soft drinks and sports drinks (Patchell, 2000).

Many other factors affecting eating need to be considered. Foods available in the home, in schools and in fast food restaurants can directly affect food choices, along with family dietary patterns and beliefs. Socioeconomic influences may include economic status, education of parents or carers, family structure, ethnic origin and social attitudes (Patchell, 2000). Advertising, portrayal of slimness in the media and fashion and body shape beliefs of family and friends may also influence body image concern and dieting behaviour (McVeagh and Reed, 2001).

Use of diet histories to assess nutritional intake and eating behaviour

Diet histories are often used by dietitians to assess the nutritional adequacy of the diet, to provide a detailed description of eating behaviour and to explore attitudes and beliefs towards food and eating of the patient and family. The diet history provides an opportunity to explore the quality of nutrition in the diet. A focus of enquiry should include the adequacy of specific nutrient intakes and food groups. Restriction or exclusion of dietary fat, total energy, carbohydrates, protein foods and fluids may be evident. Alternatively, intakes of these could be excessive if the patient is bingeing. The contribution of vitamin and mineral supplements to dietary intake should be assessed. Dietary fibre intake may be low or high due to excessive use of high fibre foods. Foods containing iron, folate and vitamin B_{12} may be reduced. Artificially sweetened substances (including chewing gums and sweets) may have a laxative effect and their use ascertained.

The regularity of meals and snacks or presence of chaotic eating behaviours throughout the day will also need to be determined. Periods of restriction or unusually large intake should be explored. Clarifying the changes in eating behaviour that have occurred over time (including types and quantities of foods or fluids) may also provide useful information regarding the development of thoughts associated with specific foods or nutrients. Vegetarianism, 'dislike' of certain foods and 'allergies' to specific foods may be reported. The timing and context of such occurrences need to be ascertained. If they arose after the onset of the eating disorder, they may be part of the eating disorder psychopathology rather than true vegetarianism, dislikes or allergies. Other behaviours that can provide useful information include calorie counting, recording, weighing or measuring food or fluid, arranging food in a certain way, excessive use of condiments, cutting food into small pieces, fiddling with food on the plate, or keeping a food diary. Finally, compensatory behaviours should also be explored. Restricting, bingeing and purging as well as excessive exercise may all directly influence nutritional status and requirements. It should be borne in mind that past bingeing or purging practices may re-emerge during treatment.

Management

Key components of nutritional management include involvement of the patient and her parents, meal planning and refeeding and developing healthy eating attitudes and behaviours.

Involvement of the patient

It is important that the change process is as patient centred as possible with plans being developed both with her and her parents. As such an essential aspect of the process is the therapeutic alliance (see above and Chapter 9).

It is unwise to avoid launching into nutritional treatment when the patient's readiness and motivation for change have not been addressed. This raises the likelihood of further resistance. An example of this may be the provision of education on nutrition and normal eating when the patient is clearly stating that she does not want to hear about nutrition and has no intention of beginning to eat. Once goals have been agreed, a useful way forward is to ask such a question as: 'If you were able to begin to move towards these goals, how would you like to do this?'

A conversation may occur such as:

> One of the goals you had mentioned is to be able to have a healthy body to do all the fun things that you like, like going horse riding and going out with friends. What do you think would need to change for that to be able to actually happen?

She might suggest a change that could assist in improving her energy levels such as being able to have some breakfast. A response may be something like:

> If you were to consider being able to have some breakfast each day,

what do you think would be a comfortable way of doing that? Is that something you might be able to try over the next week?

The dialogue needs to be focused as much as possible on what she thinks she can achieve and how she might achieve it.

Parental involvement

Parents are important members of the treating team and active participants in nutrition treatment, especially at home. Deciding and agreeing on approaches to managing nutrition at home should as much as possible be a collaborative process between patient, parents, dietitian and other members of the team. Decisions may be made about such issues as the types and quantity of foods to be eaten, the timing of mealtimes and snacks, where foods will be eaten, the time allowed for meals and snacks, who is to attend mealtimes and how difficulties around mealtimes will be managed. Strategies may also need to be made for managing bingeing, vomiting and exercise.

The type of information provided to parents should depend upon the needs of each family. Educational topics may include the healthy lifestyle approach to food and physical activity (as opposed to the dieting approach), nutritional requirements for age and stage of development, what is normal, healthy eating and creating a positive eating environment. Other discussions may include ways to assist the child in recovery by being mindful of imparting 'healthy' as opposed to 'dieting' messages (see below 'developing healthy eating behaviours'), and ensuring that other family activities are not displaced by an overemphasis on food and eating.

Healthy eating and dietary education

Healthy eating can be difficult to define and varies between individuals. Food beliefs, emotions, access to food, cultural background, stage of development and individual physical differences may all determine what constitutes normal, healthy eating for each individual. There are many factors involved in considering normal, healthy eating:

- maintaining a healthy body through eating in a relaxed and flexible way
- consuming a reasonably adequate nutritional intake
- eating a wide variety of foods
- eating regular meals and snacks that would be considered normal in type and amount (this may mean eating three meals per day or eating smaller amounts at more frequent time intervals throughout the day)
- eating in a way that responds to internal cues of hunger and satiety
- choosing foods that are desired or liked and eating them without guilt
- consuming a regular, healthy amount of 'junk' food without significant feelings of guilt

- eating out socially with minimal anxiety
- avoiding compensatory behaviours
- eating meals that would be considered culturally appropriate in different social contexts (such as religious celebrations or birthdays).

It is also important to consider what is not normal, healthy eating. This includes:

- counting calories or fats
- measuring or weighing what is eaten
- spending a large proportion of the day thinking about food, eating or body weight
- eating having much more significance than other activities
- continually following a rigid eating plan
- having rigid rules around eating
- using supplements in place of whole foods.

Any change in eating behaviour should work towards a normal, healthy outcome. Small but regular changes towards healthy eating should be made to allow for physical and psychological adjustment. A good place to start may be working towards being able to include some foods regularly throughout the day. This may progress to including foods from each of the food groups, and gradually being able to consume the amounts required within food groups to sustain health and growth. Finally, the focus may move to being able to eat regular (though not excessive) amounts of junk food and eating out socially without feelings of guilt (e.g. at the movies, eating junk food at a friend's party or having take-away meals with friends).

Offering choice may reinforce the importance of variety and flexibility in eating and may also allow the patient to take more responsibility around eating. Providing a range of choice in non-safety related areas may also improve the treatment alliance. If, however, in the face of choice and negotiation, patients become increasingly anxious or demanding, the number of choices and the negotiations offered may need to be reduced.

Some components of treatment may be considered as 'non-negotiable' (see Chapter 9). 'Non-negotiables' may include weekly weight gains and consuming a specified amount of nutrition at meals and mid-meals. Lengthy discussions and negotiations around this should be dissuaded to avoid collusion with the eating disorder and increasing disordered eating thoughts and behaviours. Choice, however, can be offered around the *process* of refeeding. What can be negotiable (within reason) is how the nutrition plan may be achieved (e.g. which would be more preferable for the patient to consume – a larger volume of food at mealtimes or the use of supplements or more energy-dense foods?). Options for refeeding can be discussed, including consuming food and fluid orally with the assistance of a menu plan, use of oral nutritional supplements or nasogastric feeding. If nasogastric feeding is likely to be required, a time-limited trial of oral feeding could be offered. Time will need to be allocated to talking about this and in providing the opportunity to consume food and fluids orally before proceeding with nasogastric feeding. A conversation regarding refeeding may be something like:

> We are *very* concerned for your health and would like to work towards improving this. To do this we need to improve your nutrition and weight, which I know is going to be very difficult for you. This is something that we simply *cannot* negotiate on. What we can do though is to talk about how you would like this to happen.

Other areas requiring consideration include the use of low fat and diet products, patient dislikes and vegetarianism. Being able to consume full fat products (such as regular fat dairy products or margarine) are considered as part of normal, healthy eating and are not dissuaded. Some treatment settings will not allow the use of low fat products for patients, while others allow a transition period between use of low fat and full fat products. The use of 'diet' products is generally not recommended for patients with eating disorders. Specific foods may not have been 'disliked' prior to the onset of the eating disorder, though have become a 'dislike' subsequently. Similarly, the patient may have become a vegetarian or developed 'allergies' to specific foods (such as cheese) during the course of the eating disorder. In such instances this may be more a component of the eating disorder and would need to be worked through as part of recovery. Potential food allergies should be discussed with the medical team to ensure physical safety.

Conveying key principles of healthy eating behaviour is also important. People with an eating disorder may be well versed in dieting and continual self-questioning of their own dietary intake and physical activity. As clinicians we need to be mindful when communicating nutrition messages that we convey healthy approaches towards eating and physical activity, rather than reinforcing dieting or rigid thinking. For example, rather than encouraging thoughts such as 'Have I had too much fat or too many calories?', a healthier way of thinking about dietary intake would be 'Have I had enough of the good, healthy foods such as breads and cereals, dairy, fluids and so forth?' With this in mind, important principles to convey would include:

- appreciation of body diversity and individuality
- thinking in food terms as opposed to nutrients or calories
- aiming for a healthy lifestyle approach to living with everything in moderation, as opposed to a 'dieting approach'
- an appreciation of the influences on eating behaviours that young people face (psychological issues, family dietary beliefs and practices, peer influence, media and socioeconomic issues).

Many psychological symptoms and social behaviours attributed to eating disorders are the result of starvation and return to normal with restoration of a healthy body weight. This does not, however, automatically alleviate abnormal eating or disturbed attitudes towards food and weight (Windauer, Lennerts, Talbot, Touyz, and Beumont, 1993). Ongoing nutritional care may assist patients to establish sustainable and appropriate eating behaviour. This may be enabled by the provision of education and facilitating gradual, stepwise changes towards healthy eating.

Nutrition education is an ongoing process and may be used to support positive and sustainable behaviour change. People with an eating disorder may have varying levels of knowledge regarding food, nutrition, health and weight. Ideas may have become distorted over time and knowledge may be highly selective and obtained from dubious sources (Beumont et al., 1997). Provision of appropriate information can assist with reducing misconceptions around eating and reducing fears associated with improved oral intake.

The type of information provided will depend upon the level of knowledge, the information requested and the patient's stage of treatment. Early in an admission, education to assist with reducing fear around eating and weight gain would be appropriate. This may include explaining expected weight fluctuations due to fluid shifts and glycogen storage, understanding potential physical feelings such as gastric discomfort and the effect of metabolic changes on nutritional requirements. Education may then progress to the effects of poor nutrition on physical and mental health, defining normal, healthy eating, the role of food groups in health, nutritional requirements to maintain health and energy balance. Finally, helpful information may include establishing regular eating patterns, meal planning, responding to hunger and satiety, establishing flexibility in eating, social eating, defining a healthy amount of 'junk' food and longer term maintenance of healthy nutrition.

Establishing gradual changes towards the longer term goals of normal, healthy eating should be patient centred. Consideration should be given to the agreed goals and phase of treatment. Regular short-term plans should be established and communicated clearly to all involved. This may include, for example, gradually increasing the type or quantity of foods included at meal-times or snacks, gradually introducing feared foods, being able to eat at the dinner table with others, reducing compensatory behaviours or being able to attend social occasions involving food.

Refeeding

Refeeding involves replenishment of adequate nutrition and hydration and is indicated when there is evidence of significant weight loss, delayed growth, nutritional deficiency, dehydration, circulatory failure or electrolyte disturbances. The primary and immediate aim of refeeding is to alleviate the shorter and longer term physical and psychological sequelae of malnutrition and restore normal growth. The first stage of treatment should focus on the correction of hypoglycaemia, electrolyte disturbance and dehydration and stabilisation of cardiovascular function (Royal College of Psychiatrists, 2005). The second stage is the correction of nutrient deficiencies and the third is correction of body composition. Vigorous efforts to achieve weight gain in the early stages have potential dangers and may be psychologically intolerable to the patient.

A dietitian is best placed to determine the nutritional requirements at different stages of weight restoration. Consideration will need to be given to requirements for total energy intake and intakes of fat, protein, carbohydrates, fluids, fibre, vitamins, electrolytes and minerals. Total energy intakes are important for normal growth and development and are particularly important for those requiring refeeding. Determining appropriate energy requirements for weight gain can be difficult, however, due to physical changes occurring during refeeding (including metabolic rate), actual energy consumed and actual energy lost (through activity or purging behaviours).

Other nutrients that will need to be considered include protein, carbohydrates, fluids, fibre, vitamins and minerals. Protein is essential for normal growth and development and may be compromised in people with an eating disorder. Carbohydrates are the body's preferred source of energy and should be consumed regularly throughout the day. Fluid is essential for survival and patients may become acutely unwell with restricted fluid intake.

Consideration should be given to the dietary fibre requirements and the gradual reintroduction of fibre in those with low intakes. A range of vitamins and minerals will also need to be considered. In the malnourished, a multivitamin and mineral supplement may be used to assist in repletion. Electrolyte supplementation is often required and micronutrient supplementation is recommended. However, iron supplements may be dangerous during the early stages of treatment (Royal College of Psychiatrists, 2005).

Medical requirements of refeeding may determine how directive refeeding will need to be and how much room there is for offering choice and negotiation. A more directive approach will be indicated for a patient at high risk of medical compromise, whereas a more collaborative stance may be adopted for less urgent situations.

Consideration should be given to the quantity of nutrition that the patient has been able to consume. The amount of nutrition the child may tolerate, both physically and psychologically, should also be assessed before proceeding with refeeding. When refeeding commences the initial calorie intake should be based upon the average daily consumption in the previous week or two. Generally it is wise to have an increase of only about 200 to 300 calories. Anything greater increases the risk of refeeding syndrome, based upon hidden biochemical deficiencies (see Chapter 7 for fuller explanation and below for management) and may in any event be either physically or psychologically intolerable. This may mean starting with a diet of only 600 to 900 calories per day with caloric intake spread throughout the day to minimise excessive nutritional load. In the case of nasogastric feeding or other forms of enteric feeding (see below) this would involve continuous 24-hour feeds (Beumont et al., 1997; Brooks and Melink, 1995).

A meal plan may be a useful way to provide structure for the day's eating and guidance around the timing and content of meals and snacks. Meal plans are not suitable for every patient and consideration should be given to the needs of each individual. If the meal plan contributes to increased rigidity or preoccupation with eating, increased anxiety or family conflict, its use should be reconsidered. Establishing the meal plan should also be a process that is facilitated (rather than imposed) by the dietitian. In constructing a meal plan there are a few key points to keep in mind:

1 Involve regular meals and snacks.
2 Meals and snacks should be appropriate in type, content and timing (timing will need to take into consideration the normal family routine).
3 Allow for variety, flexibility and spontaneity in eating.
4 Include foods from each of the food groups.
5 Provide structure for the day's eating.
6 Involve the patient and parents.

A sample meal plan for a healthy, moderately active adolescent is provided below. Obviously the content will need to be adjusted for those on a very restricted intake with the aim of a gradual increase in calorie intake every few days.

Sample Meal Plan

Breakfast (between 6.30 and 8.30 am)
1 bowl of cereal with milk
1–2 slices of toast (or 1–2 slices of fruit toast, ½–1 average bread roll or ½–1 breakfast muffin) with margarine and spread (or no cereal and 2–4 toast)
1 glass of juice

Morning tea (roughly halfway between breakfast and lunch)
1–2 snacks and 1 glass water

Lunch (between 12 and 1.30 pm)
1–2 sandwiches or bread rolls with filling (e.g. meat, cheese and salad)
Piece of fruit or tub of yoghurt
1 glass water

Afternoon tea (roughly halfway between lunch and dinner)
1–2 snacks and 1 glass water

Dinner (between 5.30–7.30 pm)
¼ plate meat, fish, chicken or alternative
¼ plate potato/rice/pasta/bread
½ plate mixed vegetables
dessert (e.g. tinned fruit and custard/yoghurt/ice cream)
I glass water

Supper
I–2 snacks and I glass water

Snacks
Piece of fruit, I tub of yoghurt (approx 200 g), 4 crackers with cheese, I glass of milk, a handful of dried fruit and nuts, ½ sandwich or I slice of toast

Extras/treats
50 g packet of chips or 60 g bar chocolate 3 times per week
Take-away meal or meal out (e.g. fish and chips) once per week

Meal plans can lead to splitting and important steps need to be taken to minimise this happening. One important aspect of meal planning is documenting and communicating the plan clearly for the young person, parents and other members of the treating team. This may also include sending the documented meal plan to the general practitioner for outpatients.

Nutritional intake can be increased by gradual amounts (usually about 200–300 calories) every third day until the final requirements have been met. Less emaciated patients who have been tolerating reasonable amounts of nutrition may be commenced on a higher nutritional intake (Beumont et al., 1997). It should be borne in mind that until calorie intake reaches between 1500 and 2000 daily, weight is unlikely to increase and may even drop in the early stages of refeeding. This is simply a reflection of an inadequate diet and, providing physical health is not immediately endangered, should be tolerated. If the patient is at immediate risk of severe physical decompensation then a higher intake will be necessary, but this should be supervised by a paediatrician. Also it should be remembered that some apparent weight gain may simply be a consequence of rehydration.

A weekly weight gain of 0.5 to 1.0 kg is suggested for inpatients and 0.5 kg for outpatients. However, energy requirements may also increase after the first few weeks of refeeding due to increases in the metabolic rate and increased physical activity. They may be as high as 3500 to 4500 calories depending on individual requirements (Andersen, Bowers, and Evans, 1997). Once an adequate weight has been achieved, nutritional intake can be reduced accordingly.

When possible, interventions should be aimed at fostering normal, healthy eating behaviour, such as sitting at the dinner table to eat, consuming appropriate types and quantities of foods at meal and snack times, eating within an acceptable time period, avoiding compensatory behaviours after eating and maintaining adequate weight. However, restoration of physical well-being is the top priority and this should be achieved by whatever means the patient finds tolerable. Refeeding can be a highly distressing process and means for minimising distress should be always be considered. The level of distress should be monitored and a collaborative stance around ways to minimise distress for the young person should be adopted.

The route of refeeding

Oral refeeding is the preferred option and should always be offered as a first choice. However, some patients simply cannot manage an adequate calorie intake orally. In such cases enteral feeding (e.g. nasogastric or even gastrostomy) may be necessary. In some situations, patients may actually prefer the assistance of nasogastric feeding and feel they simply cannot consume the required amount of nutrition orally.

Oral refeeding

Oral feeds would normally consist of a combination of food and drinks. The amount and type of nutrition required will be determined by the urgency of the situation (e.g. dehydration or medical instability) and the amount the child has been able to manage over the preceding few days or weeks (having realistic expectations). The nutrition plan should be appropriate in timing, type and quantity for normal eating, and higher energy choices may be added to allow for weight gain. Once acceptable growth has been achieved, higher energy choices can be reduced.

The degree of choice offered during refeeding will depend upon the urgency of the situation. For example, if a patient has consumed one apple per day and minimal fluids over the preceding two weeks, there will be a higher risk of medical compromise and less opportunity for offering choice. For a patient who has been consuming half of all meals and is medically stable, increased choice may be offered.

The boundaries of choice will need to be clear and the meal planning should remain a guided process. For a child at high risk of medical compromise, for example, there may be a specified period of time (e.g. the next eight hours) to consume a predetermined amount of food and fluid at each meal and snack time. The requirements may be something like five cups (5 × 250 ml) of fluid and a specific amount of food at each meal (e.g. half portion of protein, half sandwich, half serving of cereal with milk or one tub of yoghurt). Requirements will need to be very clear for all involved, along with what will need to happen if the patient is unable to achieve this. A decision will need to be made with the team and clearly communicated to the patient and family as to the action required if the nutrition plan is not able to be achieved. For a patient who is at a low risk of medical instability, more choice may be offered. The patient may need to consume three healthy meals each day, for example, and there could be choice around how this could be achieved.

The amount, type and timing of food and fluid decided should be documented in a menu plan and made clear to everyone involved. Time should be spent with the parents or carers and staff to ensure clarity in approach towards refeeding and to avoid potential splitting.

Oral nutritional supplements

Oral supplements can be helpful when beginning oral refeeding or when moving from nasogastric feeding. They may be an easier alternative to increased oral intake and less invasive than nasogastric feeding. In the early stages of refeeding and once nearing a healthy weight, energy intakes can be so substantial that patients find it difficult to ingest enough food orally to meet nutritional requirements (Russell, Baur, Beumont, Byrnes, and Zipfel, 1998). Nutrient-dense oral supplements, such as high energy drinks and puddings, can be a useful and acceptable solution. Supplements may be added to food intake as a high energy extra, then gradually reduced for weight maintenance.

When progressing from nasogastric feeding, oral supplements can be a useful transitional step. Supplements may be offered as a complement to or in place of enteric feeds, as a way of encouraging improved oral intake and reducing reliance on the nasogastric feed. A system may be documented whereby a predetermined amount will be deducted from the nasogastric feed for each specified quantity of oral supplement consumed. The plan should, however, include a plan for consuming oral foods as early as is practical.

Nasogastric feeding

Nasogastric (n-g) feeding is sometimes quite wrongly equated with 'forced feeding'. Forced feeding is literally that – feeding by physical force, against the patient's wishes. It is extremely rarely required providing the patient's eating disorder is managed appropriately, with a good therapeutic alliance, the use of externalisation and the motivational approach (see Chapters 9 and 10). Nasogastric feeding is indicated when oral intake is inadequate, despite all attempts to render it tolerable. Occasionally patients prefer nasogastric feeds, sometimes because they simply feel unable to eat adequately and other times because those with AN feel less guilty. When a patient states a preference for n-g feeds she should be supported until such time as her medical state has improved. An audit of children and adolescents who had undergone n-g feeding for AN showed that although many of them initially found it an unpleasant experience, the majority were grateful that it had been carried out (Neiderman, Zardy, Tattersall, and Lask, 2001).

Nasogastric feeds may be commenced as the sole source of nutrition or accompanied by oral nutrition if the child can so manage. Feeds are usually commenced at a low, continuous rate to reduce the nutritional load and gradually increased as tolerated. Once patients are tolerating an adequate amount of feed, feeding may then become intermittent (e.g. overnight) or may progress to bolus feeding (administering a particular volume of feed at regular intervals). Overnight feeding (e.g. from 7 pm to 7 am) may be used as a step towards bolus feeding. This may allow for increased appetite during the day and prove to be an acceptable step towards bolus or oral feeding. There may, however, be increased opportunity for tampering with overnight feeding. Patients may alternatively move directly from continuous to bolus regimens. Bolus feeding can be given at meal and snack times to mimic physiologically normal eating patterns.

Plans for progressing to oral feeding should form an ongoing component of the nutrition plan. Improved oral intake and normal, healthy eating should be encouraged and facilitated wherever possible. A plan may be negotiated, for example, that if the young person is able to consume a quarter of each meal orally for three consecutive days, this is good evidence of being able to manage more nutrition orally. The nasogastric feed may then be reduced accordingly. The plan may then progress to attempting half of the meals and so forth. Once the patient is consuming a full meal plan, a three-day trial may commence for ceasing the nasogastric feed while leaving the nasogastric tube in situ. The tube may then be removed and a trial of full oral feeds resumed.

Gastrostomy feeding

A gastrostomy is the insertion of a tube into the stomach for the purpose of administering feeds direct to the stomach. They are very rarely indicated in eating disorders, although quite commonly used in certain chronic diseases such as cystic fibrosis. However, in some severe circumstances, especially in AN, they may be lifesaving. Some patients with AN may be so terrified of refeeding that they not only refuse all oral feeds but may even repeatedly withdraw the nasogastric tube. A gastrostomy tube is much harder to withdraw, as it can be secured much more firmly. The management of gastrostomy feeds is similar to that of n-g feeds. A fuller description of their use is provided by Neiderman et al. (2000). The legal and ethical issues associated with enteral feeding are discussed in Chaper 17.

Refeeding safely (refeeding syndrome)

Refeeding syndrome (see Chapter 7) is a potential complication of refeeding and may be fatal. Patients most at risk are those with a low body weight (e.g. BMI 14 or less), prolonged malnutrition or rapid weight loss (Melchior, 1998). Other factors which may contribute include hypophosphatemia, thiamine deficiency and prolonged QT intervals on ECG (Melchior, 1998; Ornstein, Golden, Jacobson, and Shenker, 2003). Medical monitoring and routine observations during refeeding are essential in preventing and detecting refeeding syndrome. This should include food and fluid intake and output, vital signs, rapid weight gain (which may indicate fluid overload), electrolytes, oedema, gastrointestinal complications and congestive heart failure (American Psychiatric Association, 2000).

Standardised protocols for managing refeeding syndrome have not been established due to limited available data. A suggestion for managing those at risk of refeeding syndrome may involve the following:

1   Commence prophylactic phosphate, thiamine and multivitamin supplements prior to and during refeeding (Birmingham, Alothman, and Goldner, 1996; RANZCP, 2004).
2   Avoid consumption of high carbohydrate fluids (soft drinks, fruit juices and cordials) to minimise the risk of reducing serum phosphate levels.
3   Monitor biochemistry daily for the first week and second daily for the second week. Alterations in biochemistry and observations prior to and during refeeding must be addressed (Birmingham and Beumont, 2004; Kohn, Golden, and Shenker, 1998).
4   Feeding should be introduced slowly and gradually increased as tolerated (see section on nutritional requirements).
5   If symptoms of refeeding syndrome arise, nutrient intake should be reduced or suspended until further continuation is medically indicated (RANZCP, 2004).

Conclusion

Nutritional intervention is one of the central components of the treatment of any eating disorder. It does, however, have the potential to exacerbate disordered eating behaviour. Therefore careful and knowledgable consideration of the complexities involved and strategies required to refeed and to foster healthy eating behaviour are essential. Key components for successful intervention in nutrition include a therapeutic alliance, parental involvement, refeeding safely and facilitating normal, healthy eating behaviours.

References

American Psychiatric Association (APA, 2000). Practice guideline for the treatment of patients with eating disorders (revision). *American Journal of Psychiatry* (suppl.), *157*, 1.

Andersen, A.E., Bowers, W., and Evans, K. (1997) Inpatient treatment of anorexia nervosa. In D. M. Garner and P. E. Garfinkel (Eds.), *Handbook of treatment for eating disorders* (2nd ed.). New York: Guilford Press.

Beumont, P.J.V., Beumont, C.C., Touyz, S.W., and Williams, H. (1997) Nutritional counselling and supervised exercise. In D.M. Garner and P.E. Garfinkel (Eds.), *Handbook of treatment for eating disorders* (2nd ed.). New York: Guilford Press.

Birmingham, C.L., Alothman, A.F., and Goldner, E.M. (1996). Anorexia nervosa: Refeeding and hypophosphatemia. *International Journal of Eating Disorders, 20* (2), 211–213.

Birmingham, C.L., and Beumont, P. (2004). *Medical management of eating disorders.* Cambridge: Cambridge University Press.

Brooks, M., and Melink, G. (1995). The refeeding syndrome: An approach to understanding its complications and preventing its occurrence. *Pharmacotherapy, 15* (6), 713–726.

Kohn, M.R, Golden, N.H., and Shenker, I.R. (1998). Cardiac arrest and delerium: Presentations of the refeeding syndrome in severely malnourished adolescents with anorexia nervosa. *Journal of Adolescent Health, 22,* 239–243.

McVeagh, P., and Reed, E. (2001). *Kids food health, nutrition and your child's development, from school-age to teenage.* Sydney: Finch Publishing.

Melchior, J.C. (1998). From malnutrition to refeeding during anorexia nervosa. *Current Opinions in Clinical Nutrition and Metabolic Care, 1* (6), 481–485.

National Institute for Health and Clinical Excellence (NICE, 2004). *Eating disorders: Core interventions in the treatment and management of anorexia nervosa, bulimia nervosa and related eating disorders: A national clinical practice guideline.* London: NICE.

Neiderman, M., Richardson, J., Farley, A., and Lask, B. (2001). Naso-gastric feeding in early-onset eating disorders. *International Journal of Eating Disorders, 29,* 441–448.

Neiderman, M., Zardy, M., Tattersall, M., and Lask, B. (2000). Enteric feeding in early-onset anorexia nervosa. *International Journal of Eating Disorders, 28,* 470–475.

Ornstein, R.M., Golden, N.H., Jacobson, M.S., and Shenker, I.R. (2003). Hypophosphatemia during nutritional rehabilitation in anorexia nervosa: Implications for refeeding and monitoring. *Journal of Adolescent Health, 32* (1), 83–88.

Patchell, C. (2000). Feeding school-age children and adolescents. In C. Holden, A. Macdonald, and B. A. Wharton (Eds.), *Nutrition and child health.* Sydney: Baillière Tindall.

Royal Australian and New Zealand College of Psychiatrists (RANZCP, 2004). Clinical Practice Team for Anorexia Nervosa. Australian and New Zealand clinical practice guidelines for the treatment of anorexia nervosa. *Australian and New Zealand Journal of Psychiatry, 38,* 659–670.

Royal College of Psychiatrists (2005). *Nutritional guidelines for anorexia nervosa.* Council Report 130 (CR 130). London: Royal College of Psychiatrists.

Russell, J., Baur, L., Beumont, P., Byrnes, S., and Zipfel, S. (1998). Refeeding of anorexic: Wasteful not wilful. *The Lancet, 352* (9138), 1445–1446.

Windauer, U., Lennerts, W., Talbot, P., Touyz, S.W., and Beumont, P.J.V. (1993). How well are 'cured' anorexia nervosa patients? *British Journal of Psychiatry, 163,* 195–200.

12 Family approaches

Evidence-based and collaborative practice

Peter Honig

Introduction

Family approaches to the treatment of childhood and adolescent onset eating disorders mean that parents, siblings and any significant others with whom the patient is closely connected may be included in the assessment and treatment process. This involvement is necessary both as a means of gathering information about the problem and in order to establish how family members might be able to support the young person by constructing a home environment in which eating, and subsequent retention of food can become an ordinary activity. Eating disorders, whether life threateningly severe anorexia nervosa in teenagers or food faddiness in younger children, have the capacity to create highly aroused emotions in families.

Family approaches such as eating disorder focused family therapy (see below for detailed description), parental counselling or multifamily group therapy all emphasise the need for the family context to become focused on the primary goal of supporting the patient in the task of eating. 'Support' will look different at different stages – sometimes requiring a high level of parental responsibility in the preparation and delivery of food with very consistent rules at the table. At other times the task may be the opposite – learning how to hand back responsibility to their daughter and intrude less. Whatever the strategy, it is obvious that families need to be involved in a process of discussion and reflection on how these strategies might be created and put into practice. Where this proves problematic, attention may need to be paid to patterns of communication between family members that work against this. In addition, in order to achieve a context of support, family approaches should have an educational component in which all available knowledge about the particular disorder is shared (see Chapter 9).

There are competing perspectives on the family therapy of eating disorders. One is that it is the psychological intervention which produces the best outcome for children and adolescents diagnosed with anorexia nervosa (NICE, 2004) and that families should also be included for the treatment of bulimia nervosa (NICE, 2004). Another is that the evidence base for these claims is so meagre as to be almost meaningless (Fairburn, 2005) and in relation to other eating disorders there is no evidence at all. A third perspective is that current family therapy practices are resulting in the emergence of families that are resources both for recovery and for understanding and that their expertise should be a significant driver in the search for new knowledge and solutions (Honig, Dargie, and Davies, in press; Kingsley and Kingsley, 2005; Maisel, Epston, and Borden, 2004; Rhodes, Baillee, Brown, and Madden, 2005). There is probably some truth in all these perspectives and each is worthy of exploration.

The development of evidence

Researching the efficacy of family therapy for the treatment of anorexia nervosa began with the Philadelphia team (e.g. Minuchin, Rosman, and Baker, 1978). It was continued by the Maudsley Hospital group in London through the 1980s and 1990s (e.g. Dare, Eisler, Colahan, Crowther, Senior, and Asen, 1995) culminating with the production of a treatment manual of this approach (Lock, Le Grange, Agras, and Dare, 2001). Latterly, the development of multifamily group therapy has proved of considerable interest (Schmidt and Asen, 2005).

In the UK a comprehensive analysis of research evidence has recently been completed by the National Institute for Health and Clinical Excellence (NICE, 2004). This body is responsible for producing guidelines for evidence-based treatments in the National Health Service. Based on this analysis the guidelines recommend, as a first line of treatment, that 'family interventions that directly address the eating disorder should be offered to children and adolescents with anorexia nervosa'. This recommendation was based primarily on the finding from the first randomised control trial comparing family therapy with individual psychoanalytically oriented psychotherapy (Russell, Szmukler, Dare, and Eisler, 1987). The study found that patients receiving family therapy performed better on a variety of outcome measures at follow-up. Other research trials have both supported and refined clinical understanding of the benefits of family therapy in the treatment of anorexia nervosa (Eisler, Dare, Hodes, Russell, Dodge, and Le Grange, 2000; Geist, Heinmaa, Stephens, Davis, and Katzman, 2000). The relative benefits of conjoint (patients and parents seen together for therapy) and separated family therapy (patients seen on their own and parents seen without the patient – but with the same therapist) have been investigated by Robin, Siegel, Moye, Gilroy, Dennis, and Sikand (1999) who found that both forms of family therapy have equal efficacy.

The focus of any family intervention, at least in the early stages of treatment, should be on helping parents to take a high level of responsibility for managing their child's eating. This is most clearly described in Lock et al.'s manual (2001). While there is no evidence that shows a better outcome is achieved when siblings are involved in therapy, it is widely accepted and again recommended in UK guidelines (NICE, 2004), that siblings should be offered involvement in family therapy. Such involvement serves two purposes: the opportunity for siblings to be part of the solution to the problem and for siblings to communicate how the eating disorder is affecting them and the relationship to their sibling.

The model described in Lock et al.'s manual emphasises a number of different stages that make up the course of family treatment. (These stages are not connected to the three stages of recovery described in Chapter 9.) In Stage 1 there is an explicit focus on refeeding and the priority of returning the patient to physical health through achieving weight gain. Parent(s) are encouraged to mount a counter-attack on the illness in order to 'save their child's life' and despite the developmental inappropriateness of the task they become responsible for all aspects of the refeeding process. In practice this means that parents are supported to become somewhat tunnel visioned, putting aside differences that they may have or issues they wish to discuss which are not necessarily connected to the illness. Attention is paid to negotiations between parents (where there are two) regarding a consistent approach to food preparation and mealtimes. The details of this process are likely to differ from family to family, but the principle is invariant. As part of the treatment parents are encouraged to learn more about anorexia nervosa so that they can become more confident in their own abilities as parents and less guilt-laden that they may have caused the problem. Learning to 'separate' the illness from their child is likely to be a central part of this process. (For further discussion about the theory and technique of 'externalisation' see Chapter 9 and also Maisel et al., 2004.)

Stage 2 of manualised treatment occurs when the patient has entered a steady phase of weight gain and there is significantly less tension connected to mealtimes. This is likely to coincide with a gradual return to better physical health. At this point it may be helpful to explore other areas of discussion that have been held back by the urgency of Stage 1. These discussions may be about issues that are not obviously connected to the illness. It would be made explicit at this point by the therapist that such discussion is only recommended provided it does not result in a lack of focus on the main task of maintaining gradual weight gain. Stage 3 of the manualised treatment occurs once the patient is returned to physical health and weight is stable. Focus in this phase will be very much away from the illness. Instead it addresses underlying issues such as the development of healthy teenager–parent relationships, so that all transactions are no longer centred on the issue of eating.

The concept of stages implies some sort of discretion between stages and a smooth transition from one to the next. In reality it does not happen in this way. Stage 1, for instance, may take many years to complete – and sadly for some may never be achieved, as teenagers move into adulthood and parents become less influential.

Manualised treatments are often regarded with some scepticism by clinicians. There are usually concerns about how such treatments do not account for variations amongst patients and their families. They can be experienced as a 'one size fits all' approach. In addition, they offend the aesthetic quality of therapy as they can feel like constraints to creativity. However, the advantage of a manualised approach is that it attempts to distil the active ingredients which appear to be of value in adolescents with anorexia nervosa. It may therefore be of particular benefit to those clinicians with little experience and may serve as a guide to those with more, who will inevitably at times experience difficulties helping some families. In addition patients and parents are increasingly interested in knowing about treatment regimens for any illness. It is therefore on balance helpful to have a document in the public domain that describes family therapy for anorexia nervosa.

As the evidence grows, practices which reflect this evolve and develop. Possibly the most significant of these is the use of multifamily group therapy. Whilst this model of delivering family interventions has a history stretching back to the 1970s (Asen, Dawson, and McHugh, 2001), it is only perhaps in the last 10 to 15 years that it has been adapted significantly to the treatment of anorexia nervosa (Scholtz, Rix, Scholz, Krassimar, and Thomke, 2005).

There is less evidence for the value of family therapy for other eating disorders. There are no randomised control trials in this age group that compare psychological treatments for any eating disorder besides anorexia nervosa. One small study (Dodge, Hodes, Eisler, and Dare, 1995) investigated the outcome following family therapy for eight patients diagnosed with bulimia nervosa. They found a reduction in some bulimic behaviours with a continuation of some other symptoms. Whilst the evidence remains small it is nonetheless considered best practice and developmentally appropriate to involve parents, at the very least, in any treatment. However, another study (Perkins et al., 2005) has found that a high percentage of patients with bulimia nervosa do not wish their parents to be involved in treatment. This group of patients has a number of factors in common that are linked to the desire for parental exclusion: a longer duration of eating disorder symptoms, a history of obesity, higher levels of depression and comorbid and impulsive behaviours. In addition these patients rated their mothers as having higher expressed emotion than those who were willing to involve their parents. (Expressed emotion is a concept that refers to levels of criticism, hostility, emotional over-involvement and warmth that a relative shows towards a psychiatric patient.) These findings have clear implications for the family treatment of bulimia nervosa. They point very much in the direction of interventions that are known to lower expressed emotion (e.g. psycho-education).

All of these developments in family treatments have a common thread: that parents are potential sources of support and recovery. They are no longer presumed to be the 'cause'. While families have probably not changed that greatly since Minuchin et al. (1978) were tracking dysfunctional patterns of communication that they considered to be causing one member of the family to exhibit 'psychosomatic symptoms', the perspective of the clinical field has transformed. This transformation has been documented by

Eisler (2005) who states that families can play a significant part in maintaining or alleviating the illness without necessarily having contributed to the development of it. It is therefore now the case that families and therapists can participate in an increasingly collaborative and resource-focused approach to treatment.

However, the evidence base for the treatment of eating disorders in childhood and adolescence is sparse. Whilst the current trend points towards a better and more sustained outcome following eating disorder focused family interventions, Fairburn's (2005) critique of the validity of the clinical trials reported in the literature reminds us that the evidence may only be relevant to a specific group of sufferers – those who are under the age of 19 with a duration of illness of less than three years. Given that the prime age of onset is mid-teens, this is clearly a significant finding which has important clinical application. However, there remains a limited evidence base of randomised control studies that makes comparison with other forms of psychological treatment difficult to assess.

Multifamily groups

Multifamily group therapy usually consists of between three and eight families meeting together with several therapists for a number of sessions (usually between eight and 12). During these sessions the families will discuss issues related to anorexia nervosa and participate in a meal together. Whilst evidence for the effectiveness of multifamily groups is awaited (there are currently a number of multicentre randomised control studies being conducted), there is a growing belief that bringing families together for treatment is popular with both the families and clinicians involved. There are currently multifamily groups in existence in a number of different settings (inpatient and outpatient) and reports of these (Honig, 2005; Schmidt and Asen, 2005) suggest a key factor of their success may be the collective sharing of experience and expertise, rather than the necessity for clinicians to follow a prescribed, manualised version of a specific model. The following comment by a parent who attended a multifamily group prior to and during her daughter's admission is fairly typical:

> I know from the first group family therapy [that my daughter] felt enormous relief that she was not the only one who was going through this horrendous experience, and we as adults also got great comfort from the fact that other families were also suffering. Also, meeting other families who were similar to us and not dysfunctional as we had felt at times in the early days. Group family therapy was always a place where emotions ran high but a place where one could show emotions.

The format of these groups varies from place to place, but the common features are:

1 An opportunity for patients and those close to them to meet others in similar situations – strength in collective experience.
2 Shared involvement in eating a meal.
3 Discussions proceeding to solutions about eating-related issues (e.g. how to encourage/support a reluctant child to eat a meal).
4 Explorations of potentially linked non-eating disorder themes (e.g. developmental issues and transitions in family life).
5 A resource-focused, non-pathologising approach to family involvement.

Some groups meet for intensive full days over a relatively short space of time (one week, followed by several follow-up days during the months ahead), while other groups meet on a weekly basis for several hours at a time. Some groups are closed to new members, others are open with families joining and leaving periodically. From this mix of formats it would seem that the key feature is the collective experience of learning together about anorexia nervosa and the ways in which it influences individual and family behaviours. Additionally, most of these groups will in some way utilise the 'expertise' of those families that have experience of the illness stretching back over time. In some groups experienced families are invited to share their knowledge of the multifamily group with new families and to discuss ways in which it was helpful to them. This may help to alleviate anxiety felt by new participants and acts as a bridge between clinicians and patients. In other groups more experienced families may be involved in the same therapy group as patients with a very recent diagnosis. This overlap offers opportunities for sharing expertise by integrating the perspective of experienced patients and families, so that it becomes an equally valid component of the therapeutic discourse.

Collaborative practices with families

Collaboration and partnership have become major themes within mental health service provision in general and in the treatment of anorexia nervosa in particular. What is meant by these words may vary, but they imply a greater sharing of responsibility between patient and clinician. Patients and their families are no longer seen only as passive recipients of treatment regimens, or objects of medical research. They are increasingly seen as having responsibility for their own health (or lack thereof) and capable of participating more fully in the design of their own treatment, provided that they are given all the information they require to make informed choices. With a disorder as focused on issues of control as much as anorexia nervosa is, such a discourse is of particular importance. This section describes a variety of practices that are collaborative in design although it is not meant to be an exhaustive list. By its very nature the idea of collaborative practice is best left to those parties directly involved in any one particular case or service.

Partnership and collaboration are meaningless concepts if there is an imbalance of knowledge amongst the parties concerned (patients, clinicians and carers). It would therefore seem self-evident that a sharing of information is likely to produce the best outcome in terms of working relationship between parties and possibly in terms of health outcome. In the case of anorexia nervosa Eisler (2005) has emphasised how enhancing parental problem-solving capacities and empowering parents can point the way to better outcome for patients. Putting these principles into practice is a challenge which ideally requires the input of all the parties. An example of such practice would be the provision by clinicians of accessible psycho-educational information about anorexia nervosa. This would consist of information that is readily available to the professional community (e.g. diagnostic criteria, epidemiology, prognostic factors, evidence-based treatment approaches).

To ensure that the information provided is useful to families it is important to know what they want to know and both when and how they want to receive it. Parents often say that having information about the likely course of anorexia nervosa is helpful, but that being presented with it at too early a stage is not, either because it is too negative or because there is too much information to take in on diagnosis. Consequently, repeated and various opportunities can be provided to impart this information. These can include: written materials, formal teaching by medical staff, one-to-one discussion with clinicians, meeting experienced patients and parents who have been involved with the illness for longer, and the use of internet resources. This approach can be defined broadly as psycho-educational.

For parents to play a truly collaborative role in treatment they will need to be meaningfully involved in decisions about their child's care. This is particularly crucial when a young person is admitted to an inpatient ward where it is so easy for professionals to 'take over' and for parents to feel undermined. A philosophy of parental involvement should guide the treatment team. This can differ depending on the setting, but examples might include attendance at regular review meetings and decisions about treatment (e.g. whether or not their daughter should be admitted to a ward). There should be opportunities to learn skills that are usually seen as in the domain of professionally trained staff: for instance, supporting their child to complete meals (for a description of one approach to family meals see Jaffa, Honig, Farmer, and Dilley, 2002). Involving families in the design and redesign of treatment programmes is a process that is most likely to lead to collaboration.

If progress is tracked throughout the course of treatment at regular intervals with key parties (patients, parents, clinicians) this provides opportunities for monitoring all aspects of management. Patients and their parents are then more likely to form a joint understanding of the problems, rather than being in conflict with each other. The role of the clinician in this process can be to help the family seek out and build on common ground. This may occasionally feel like bridging the divide between warring factions, where diametrically opposed views exist. The clinical management of young people with anorexia nervosa may indeed be an ideal training ground for anybody interested in a career in international diplomacy and peacekeeping.

Family therapy approaches that emphasise a focus on eating disorder symptoms similar to the model described by Lock et al. (2001) are more likely to result in partnership between parents, patients and clinicians. There is preliminary evidence (Krautter and Lock, 2004) that this model is experienced positively by patients and parents alike. A clinical example may illustrate this point:

Sally, aged 14, had a four-month history of anorexia nervosa characterised by significant weight loss on admission to an inpatient eating disorders unit (she weighed 73 per cent of expected weight for height). She had lost weight through restriction of food intake and excessive exercise. She was fearful of weight gain and had a terror of fat. She struggled to communicate verbally her thoughts and feelings and showed very little sign of emotion. Sally's parents were separated but she had regular contact with both, and they were strongly committed to involvement in her treatment. Treatment included: psycho-education, individual therapy sessions based upon motivational enhancement therapy (see Chapter 10), family therapy, multifamily group therapy (weekly for seven weeks) and monthly review meetings,

The family treatment broadly followed the model described by Lock et al. (2001) with the parents being encouraged to gain confidence in intensively supporting their daughter with eating. Initially they would take a high level of responsibility by preparing and portioning out Sally's meals. Gradually she gained more confidence in this process and 'allowed' this support to occur without the need for 'negotiation'. Negotiation previously had resulted in Sally always eating less and unproductive conflict.

As Sally steadily gained weight, and the highly charged emotional atmosphere surrounding meals subsided, it became possible to explore other important areas of concern to her not directly connected to eating behaviours. These areas included: friendship difficulties, the importance of exercise to her (she was a first-rate athlete) and how this could be managed in a healthy way in the future. She also had concerns about her mother's health and her own relationship with her father. Encouraging her to find her voice in the family context was therefore essential and an approach was taken in which Sally was supported in identifying the above areas of concern and in considering a process for communicating these concerns with her parents.

It is in the area of process that a collaborative approach can be of most significance. Sally understood that her individual and family therapists communicated openly with each other about her therapy. (Clearly where one therapist undertakes both roles clarity is required as to the rules of confidentiality, but generally the young person should be encouraged to share concerns with parents.) In the circumstances of this case, Sally had some brief meetings with the family therapist and her primary nurse prior to a number of family therapy sessions in which she was encouraged to voice the concerns with her parents that she had been discussing with her individual therapist. The family therapist focused on how to help her achieve this in a way that would allow her to feel in control of the process. Subsequently she was able to talk openly with both parents and surprised herself by addressing a number of areas that were previously too sensitive for her to approach for fear of upsetting her mother or father.

Sally made significant advances during her hospitalisation and in order for the therapist to learn what the family considered as some key factors in the process of change a collaborative mechanism was employed in the final session of therapy in which the mother's and Sally's perspectives were elicited. They were questioned about the admission and encouraged to identify significant moments. Without hesitation both Sally and her mother cited a conversation between them that had occurred approximately six weeks into the admission, immediately following a conversation that the mother had with a member of the nursing team. During this conversation the mother felt encouraged by the nurse to communicate her feelings to her daughter rather than to continue 'walking on eggshells' attempting to avoid conflict for fear of exacerbating her daughter's illness. In the conversation between Sally and her mother, a direct challenge was made to Sally's apparent reluctance up to that point for engaging in therapeutic conversations in whichever context they occurred. Her mother stated boldly that she thought Sally needed to make a decision about what she was doing in treatment – a metaphor really for what she was doing in relation to the illness. Until that time she was going through the motions of treatment (eating all the food on her meal plan, but not committing herself in any other way to treatment). Following this conversation Sally believes that there was a significant change in her attitude to treatment (again, for treatment read anorexia nervosa).

It is through this experience of exploring explanations of change that are described by patients and their parents that clinicians can learn so much. In the process they are likely to provide treatments that are more sensitive to the needs of those that they treat – and they are likely to encourage those that are receiving treatment to recognise their own resources. In this way they can help parents and patients to become experts on recovery rather than victims of illness.

There is further evidence that collaborative and multifamily approaches are received well by participating families (Asen, 2002; Colahan and Robinson, 2002). Given that motivation is such a key factor in anorexia nervosa, treatments that involve parents and that seem to be acceptable to both parents and patients would seem to be a significant advance on previous models of family therapy that were often experienced as 'pathologising' and contributed to a sense of guilt, particularly for the parents. Feedback from families has also highlighted the development of networks that are independent of clinicians and clinical environments. For instance, a parent who commented on a draft of this chapter wrote:

> It [the chapter] could highlight the invaluable support and friendships that develop between families as a result of sharing or coping with such a horrible illness. I am still in contact with people I met at group family therapy today, as there is a genuine understanding which is invaluable and will I hope remain forever.

Family therapy that purports to be collaborative should provide plenty of opportunity for feedback and be designed by both the therapist and the family. An example of this would be whether or not to include siblings in meetings. Parents often assume family therapy implies that attendance of all family members is required. Clearly, therapists have a responsibility to inform patients and their families about what is known to be effective treatment. Currently, evidence-based guidelines for anorexia nervosa (NICE, 2004) suggest that involving siblings in treatment does not have a significant impact on outcome for the patient. It is not known whether sibling involvement in the treatment of any other eating disorders is of significance.

What is unclear is the impact, both positive and negative, that involvement may have on the siblings themselves. In these circumstances, where there is insufficient evidence to make firm recommendations, discussions between the parties are again the best way to proceed to a decision. Parents know their own children better than the therapist. The therapist may have some expertise to offer in terms of questioning the impact that illness is having on all family members and on the relationships between them. However, developmental issues should be held in mind as questions of competing need are explored. For instance, is it more important for a brother or sister to take time out of their school and peer activities in order to be part of treatment for their sister? Usually a pragmatic approach can be adopted. Specific sessions can be provided that will focus on the sibling relationship and on issues that siblings are struggling with, which either they, their parents or the patient may wish to raise.

Once again this type of approach will emphasise the future-oriented perspective of eating disorder focused family therapy. The issue of how all family members can contribute to supporting the patient in her struggle to manage adolescence with an illness that is likely to last for some time can be discussed. The creation of unique arrangements for each family is a task best undertaken in a spirit of shared knowledge and partnership in which no single view holds sway. Collaboration is by its very nature a process with an unpredictable and unprescribable outcome. It is in the process of discussion between various parties to a problem that an acceptable solution is most likely to be found.

Other arenas that can promote collaboration are support groups for relatives. Nicholls and Magagna (1997) have described one such group for the parents of teenagers with a diagnosis of anorexia nervosa. Such groups provide an opportunity for parents to express their own feelings of sadness, frustration and anxiety in the safety and privacy of a context separate from their own child. This 'space' is important since high levels of expressed emotion (e.g. critical comments, hostility) with the patient present seem to result in higher rates of drop-out from treatment (Le Grange, Eisler, Dare, and Hodes, 1992). In addition, such groups can contribute to a growing confidence amongst parents that they can find solutions to bemusing scenarios. It is most likely that other parents will have been through similar difficulties and the collective experience of a group may be invaluable. Parents of recovered patients can be particularly helpful in this process as they help to maintain hope tinged with reality. It is therefore worth maintaining links with willing volunteers who have previously received treatment.

The harnessing of parental and patient expertise and discovering how this might be used in the 'training' of other parents and professionals are further examples of a collaborative approach to treatment (Honig et al., in press). The validity of patient and carer experience has increasingly been recognised by health-care services and a number of 'expert patient' programmes have been instituted in the UK, driven by an initiative of the Department of Health (2001). Generally these programmes have been used in the management of chronic medical conditions. One of their stated aims is to encourage 'people with chronic diseases to contribute their skills and insights for the further improvement of services and as advocates of others'. In the case of anorexia nervosa there is another driving force that makes such expertise significant. As has previously been mentioned, family 'dysfunction' has been implicated in the aetiology of eating disorders. Transformation from an identity as parents who have become victims of their child's illness to one in which they are recognised as experts may well have a positive impact on the course of their child's illness (see case example of Sally above). Rhodes et al. (2005) have explored this possibility further by creating an instrument designed to measure the development of parental expertise and then to see whether such expertise is correlated with better patient outcome.

In line with these approaches collaboration can expand from the individual to the collective experience. If parents and patients are to be partners in treatment it would seem logical that they become partners in the development of services and research. An example of this would be for a mental health service to consult regularly with its patients and their parents about their experience of treatment and how it might be improved. They will often provide a perspective that is not accessible to mental health professionals and they are likely to highlight areas not usually considered as important. Similarly, in research the patient and parent perspectives may point the field in the direction of hitherto unchartered territory. Maisel et al. (2004) have produced a body of work over the past decade that has come to be known as 'insider knowledge'. This knowledge provides a very rich description of the experience of anorexia nervosa from the perspective of those affected by this illness and important clues for those professionals whose job it is to offer treatment.

Conclusion

A family approach to the treatment of eating disorders in children and adolescents is now considered a central requirement. There is growing evidence that emphasises the likelihood of better outcome, at least in the treatment of anorexia nervosa, provided that this approach emphasises the importance of focusing therapy on eating disordered behaviours rather than on searching for underlying family pathology. Whilst similar claims cannot currently be made about the other eating disorders, there is a clinical consensus that supports family involvement on the grounds of developmental appropriateness and the need to ensure that families become contexts in which symptoms are not inadvertently maintained. The emphasis now needs to be on working collaboratively with families and placing parents in a position of partnership with those treating their child. The foremost principle of a collaborative approach is the development of communication mechanisms that operate in both directions: from clinician to patient/family and from patient/family to clinician. In this model there should always be opportunities for mutual influence in the creation and refinement of treatment programmes.

References

Asen, E. (2002). Multiple family therapy: An overview. *Journal of Family Therapy, 24,* 3–16.

Asen, E., Dawson, N., and McHugh, B. (2001). *Multiple family therapy: The Marlborough model and its wider applications.* London: Karnac.

Colahan, M., and Robinson, P. (2002). Multi-family groups in the treatment of young adults with eating disorders. *Journal of Family Therapy, 24* (1), 17–30.

Dare, C., Eisler, I., Colahan, M., Crowther, C., Senior, R., and Asen, E. (1995). The listening heart and the chi square: Clinical and empirical perceptions in the family therapy of anorexia nervosa. *Journal of Family Therapy, 17* (1), 31–57.

Department of Health (2001). *The expert patient: A new approach to chronic disease management for the 21st century*. London: Department of Health.

Dodge, E., Hodes, M., Eisler, I., and Dare, C. (1995). Family therapy for bulimia nervosa in adolescents: An exploratory study. *Journal of Family Therapy*, *17* (1), 59–78.

Eisler, I. (2005). The empirical and theoretical base of family therapy and multiple family day therapy for adolescent anorexia nervosa. *Journal of Family Therapy*, *27* (2), 104–131.

Eisler, I., Dare, C., Hodes, M., Russell, G., Dodge, E., and Le Grange, D. (2000). Family therapy for anorexia nervosa: The results of a controlled comparison of two family interventions. *Journal of Child Psychology and Psychiatry*, *41*, 727–736.

Fairburn, C. (2005). Evidence-based treatment of anorexia nervosa. *International Journal of Eating Disorders*, *37*, 26–30.

Geist, R., Heinmaa, M., Stephens, D., Davis, R., and Katzman, D. (2000). Comparison of family therapy and family group psychoeducation in adolescents with anorexia nervosa. *Canadian Journal of Psychiatry*, *45*, 173–178.

Honig, P. (2005). A multi-family group programme as part of an in-patient service for adolescents with a diagnosis of anorexia nervosa. *Clinical Child Psychology and Psychiatry*, *10* (4), 465–475.

Honig, P., Dargie, L., and Davies, S. (in press). The impact on patients and parents of their involvement in the training of health care professionals. Report of an audit from an eating disorders service. *European Eating Disorders Review*.

Jaffa, A., Honig, P., Farmer, S., and Dilley, J. (2002). Family meals in the treatment of adolescent anorexia nervosa. *European Eating Disorders Review*, *10*, 199–207.

Kingsley, J., and Kingsley, A. (2005). *Alice in the looking glass: A mother and daughter's experience of anorexia*. London: Piatkus.

Krautter, T., and Lock, J. (2004). Is manualized family-based treatment for adolescent anorexia nervosa acceptable to patients? Patient satisfaction at the end of treatment. *Journal of Family Therapy*, *26* (1), 66–82.

Le Grange, D., Eisler, I., Dare, C., and Hodes, M. (1992). Family criticism and self-starvation: A study of expressed emotion. *Journal of Family Therapy*, *14*, 177–192.

Lock, J., Le Grange, D., Agras, W., and Dare, C. (2001). *Treatment manual for anorexia nervosa: A family-based approach*. New York: Guilford Press.

Maisel, R., Epston, D., and Borden, A. (2004). *Biting the hand that starves you: Inspiring resistance to anorexia/bulimia*. New York: W. W. Norton.

Minuchin, S., Rosman, B., and Baker, L. (1978). *Psychosomatic families: Anorexia nervosa in context*. Cambridge, MA: Harvard University Press.

National Institute for Health and Clinical Excellence (NICE, 2004). *Eating disorders. Core interventions in the treatment and management of anorexia nervosa, bulimia nervosa and related eating disorders: A national clinical practice guideline*. London: NICE.

Nicholls, D., and Magagna, J. (1997). A group for parents of children with eating disorders. *Clinical Child Psychology and Psychiatry*, *2* (4), 565–579.

Perkins, S., Schmidt, U., Eisler, I., Treasure, J., Yi, I., Winn, S., et al. (2005). Why do adolescents with bulimia nervosa choose not to involve their parents in treatment? *European Child and Adolescent Psychiatry*, *14* (7), 376–385.

Rhodes, P., Baillee, A., Brown, J., and Madden, S. (2005). Parental efficacy in the family-based treatment of anorexia: Preliminary development of the parents versus anorexia scale (PVA). *European Eating Disorders Review*, *13*, 1–7.

Robin, A., Siegel, P., Moye, A., Gilroy, M., Dennis, A., and Sikand, A. (1999). A controlled comparison of family versus individual therapy for adolescents with anorexia nervosa. *Journal of American Academy of Child and Adolescent Psychiatry*, *38* (12), 1482–1489.

Russell, G., Szmukler, G., Dare, C., and Eisler, I. (1987). An evaluation of family therapy in anorexia nervosa and bulimia nervosa. *Archives of General Psychiatry*, *44*, 1047–1056.

Schmidt, U., and Asen, E. (2005). Editorial: Does multi-family day treatment hit the spot that other treatments cannot reach? *Journal of Family Therapy*, *27* (2), 101–103.

Scholtz, M., Rix, M., Scholz, K., Krassimar, G., and Thomke, V. (2005). Multiple family therapy for anorexia nervosa: Concepts, experiences and results. *Journal of Family Therapy*, *27* (2), 132–141.

Treasure, J., and Ward, A. (1997). A practical guide to the use of motivational interviewing in anorexia nervosa. *European Eating Disorders Review*, *5* (2), 102–114.

13 Cognitive behavioural approaches

Deborah Christie

Introduction

The old adage 'it's not what you do it's the way that you do it' is an often repeated mantra with therapeutic principles of warmth, genuineness and empathy being as critical to successful outcome as much as slavish devotion to theoretically driven therapeutic techniques (Fonagy and Target, 1996). In the treatment of anorexia nervosa (AN) in children and adolescents the importance of the therapeutic relationship and empathic engagement has been emphasised in recent clinical guidelines (Ebeling et al., 2003; NICE, 2004). However, for adults there is evidence that cognitive behavioural therapy (CBT) is potentially the most effective in producing long-lasting change for adults with eating disorders (Roth and Fonagy, 1996). This is especially so for patients with bulimia nervosa (BN) (Fairburn, 1997). Ten years ago the lack of evidence on working with children and adolescents was reflected by the content of a special issue of a professional journal for clinical psychologists, dedicated to eating disorders, which contained no articles about working with children (Bell and Vetere, 1996). Ten years on and little has changed with very few well-controlled, methodologically sound treatment trials in children with AN (NICE, 2004) and no published controlled treatment trials for adolescents with BN or eating disorder not otherwise specified (EDNOS). The lack of evidence for what works best in children and adolescents is primarily due to methodological issues associated with diagnostic and developmental issues that make it difficult to evaluate 'properly' a single 'manualised' treatment approach (see Gowers and Bryant-Waugh, 2004).

There is evidence that CBT, appropriately modified for age and cognitive level, can be used effectively with children with depression, anxiety and somatising disorders (Grossman and Hughes, 1992; Harrington, Whittaker, Shoebridge, and Campbell, 1998). Therefore, the use of CBT for eating disorders in children and adolescents remains as one potential approach that can be helpful. For eating disorders, there is evidence to support the need to embed individual work within a wider systemic approach and engage families and siblings in the treatment plan (Le Grange, Eisler, Dare, and Russell, 1992; Lock et al., 2001; Robin, Siegel, Moye, Gilroy, Dennis, and Sikand, 1994).

Critics of CBT have argued that the approach can be reductionist and individualistic. However, practitioners have responded with developments in the use of CBT with children incorporating aspects of systemic therapies (for review see Christie and Wilson, 2005).

As a general principle individual therapy, regardless of style, should give the child a private and personal space (see Chapter 14). It is critical that the parents support the treatment and respect the privacy of the therapeutic session. This is more likely to occur if the therapist is open and willing to share successes with the parents via colleagues from a team who are offering direct support to the parents in a parents' group, parental counselling, or family therapy sessions (see Chapters 9 and 12). Therapy – whatever its label – ultimately has to help the child make sense of her world and how to cope with it.

The first part of this chapter briefly describes learning, cognitive and behavioural theories that have contributed to the development of techniques that can be used with children who have a range of eating disorders. Obviously, any 'how-to' chapter runs the risk of presenting a series of techniques driven by dogma rather than practice. It may also be so theoretically driven that the reader may be suspicious that the author has ever seen a patient. The ideas presented here are not part of a research-driven treatment manual. They are primarily driven by the unifying theoretical framework of cognitive behavioural theory. However, I have also included ideas that have been taken from other theories and therapies, including motivational interviewing and systemic therapies where they empirically 'fit' with the CBT goal. In the real world of clinical practice where no one is 'excluded' from treatment (unlike in a randomised controlled trial) there are times when it essential to follow the patient rather than to doggedly follow a model. The techniques described here have been developed from a belief that 'therapy' is a set of tools and techniques that can be used by innovative and skilled therapists (of any persuasion) to help children unlock their worries and unhappiness. These techniques should also help children and their families rebuild the way they behave, feel and think about their lives. It offers a selection of ideas that have helped silent children to talk and given silenced children an opportunity to articulate their needs to those adults charged with their care.

Learning theory

The most important principle of learning theory is the way in which animals (including humans) learn about the relationship between an experience (the stimulus) and their reaction to that experience (the response). Classical conditioning was formalised by Pavlov (1927). He observed that laboratory dogs anticipated the arrival of food by salivating when they heard a bell signalling the arrival of the food. This suggested that the dogs had linked the two events (bell and food) together. The biological response (salivation) to a stimulus (food) was designated the unconditioned response (UR). The food was the unconditioned stimulus (US). If any US (e.g. food) consistently occurs after a different event or stimulus (e.g. a bell), the animal becomes conditioned to respond to the preceding event. The salivation is now a conditioned response (CR), which will occur following presentation of the new event (the bell) that has become the conditioning stimulus (CS).

This simple and elegant representation of a chain of events was applied to other stimulus–response pairings. Emotional responses (like an increase in heart rate), which occurred following an aversive stimulus like an electric shock (US), could be triggered by a non-aversive conditioning stimulus (CS), like a red light. The conditions under which this stimulus–response pairing could occur were limited. In order for the response to become conditioned, both stimulus events must occur in the same order and be reasonably close together (contingency rule). After the response has become conditioned, if the second stimulus does not appear the conditioned response will eventually stop (extinguish).

The way a behaviour could influence (or operate on) the environment was described by Thorndike (1898). Operant conditioning described how behaviour that was followed closely by a reward would be reinforced and would be likely to occur more frequently. In contrast, behaviours that were closely followed by an unpleasant or aversive experience (negative reinforcement) would be less likely to occur. If the behaviour resulted in the *avoidance* of a punishment this would cause an increase in the behaviour's frequency, just as did gaining a reward. Interestingly, if the behaviour was performed to avoid a punishment, it was very unlikely to become reduced in frequency. In contrast, it may only take a few occasions where a reward is not given for an animal to learn that the relationship between the two events (behaviour–reward) is no longer present. If, however, the reward is offered unpredictably, the likelihood of the behaviour continuing is increased. Because the reward is unpredictable, the animal will keep on producing the behaviour in 'the hope' of ultimately getting a reward.

Behaviour management

The theoretical relationship between stimulus and response and behaviours and outcome were used by Mowrer (1960) to explain fear and avoidance behaviour in humans. If an unpleasant experience (e.g. vomiting) is associated with a behaviour (e.g. eating or swallowing), the child will reduce that behaviour, therefore avoiding the negative experience. The physiological symptoms associated with fear are unpleasant, therefore behaviour occurs that avoids the stimulus and therefore avoids the fear. The principles of stimulus association, and the contingent reinforcement of behaviour, provide a theoretical framework that helps to both explain and modify behaviours. Most parents will have been trained by their babies to pick them up to avoid the negative reinforcement of the baby crying.

In children, it is important to recognise that the nature of the reinforcement (i.e. positive or negative) is defined by the receiver, not by the giver. Getting angry and telling children off may be seen as punishment (negative reinforcement) by an adult, whereas in contrast the child may see the adult's behaviour as attention and therefore positive, regardless of the negative content (shouting and yelling). This will therefore result in an increase in behaviours that obtain the attention. Concrete or abstract rewards (money, sweets, praise, or star charts), if provided every time a particular behaviour occurs, will increase the frequency of the behaviour.

Consistency at the beginning of a management programme is critical. Every time a desired behaviour (completing homework, finishing dinner, eating a new food), occurs, it should be rewarded. As the desired behaviour becomes well established, the frequency of the rewards can be altered. For example, instead of giving an older child a concrete reward every night, acknowledging the behaviour with a small tick on a chart and then giving pocket money based on the number of ticks obtained at the end of the week can be just as effective.

To reduce an undesirable behaviour, ignoring (non-attending) and helping the child to find an alternative behaviour can be effective. The unwanted behaviour will decrease if it is not being reinforced through attention. However, if a previously learned (but unwanted) behaviour continues to receive sporadic reinforcement (e.g. child gets attention one night out of seven, or the parent gives in to a demand) the behaviour will continue, with the child 'hoping' that it will be eventually reinforced at some point in time.

Principles in practice

A systematic evaluation of behaviours, events and outcomes (functional analysis) can be used to help clearly describe factors that are involved in precipitating and maintaining specific behaviours. This analysis does not focus on what has first caused the behaviour to develop (predisposing factors). Carefully kept diaries allow the events that occur before a behaviour (antecedent stimuli or precipitating factors) to be clearly defined. The behaviours are described in detail and the consequences (reinforcement) of all components of the behaviour are described. This allows the behaviour therapist to formulate what events are triggering the behaviour, what events and behaviour of others are maintaining the behaviour, and what activities performed by the individual and those in their environment are providing positive and/or negative reinforcement.

Behaviour therapy and eating disorders

The principles of learning theory underpin techniques used by a behavioural therapist in the treatment of an eating disorder. As part of this model, measures of the severity of the condition for children with eating disorders (e.g. weight–height ratio, behaviour ratings, the child's rating of body image, shape and weight on linear scales) can be used to define clear and specific outcome measures incorporated into a treatment programme. Desired behavioural change associated with different aspects of the disorder (target weight, mood changes on rating scales) can also be considered as treatment goals. A behavioural formulation must include clearly stated goals that incorporate measurable behavioural change. This could include:

- when the child eats
- who is present at mealtimes
- what happens at mealtimes
- types of food the child will eat
- quantity of food eaten
- stimulus–response situations associated with eating that need altering.

This model works best with younger children with selective eating (SE) and other presentations characterised by a phobic avoidance of food, such as functional dysphagia. For many of these children there is a history of an unpleasant experience when very young. This may have been vomiting or choking associated with feeding at the time of a stomach bug or viral infection or in the presence of gastro-oesophageal reflux. Food and associated environmental stimuli therefore become the conditioning stimuli. The behaviour of avoiding food (or limiting intake to a few 'safe' stimuli) acts to avoid the conditioned fear.

For children with a marked avoidance of a large number of food types, exposure to non-preferred foods is often associated with retching or vomiting (negative reinforcement). A critical first step towards the development of treatment for this group of children is identifying these early precipitants and the current factors maintaining the avoidance behaviour.

> James, 14, had been a faddy eater after weaning and had only eaten chips, bread and butter, and crisps since the age of three. He thought he might be sick if he tried different foods and therefore avoided trying anything new. A programme of gradual introduction of new foods was used to help him learn that he would not be sick (desensitisation) and helped gradually increase the range and quantity of new foods he was able to eat.

The use of behaviour therapy in an eating disorder treatment programme means, for example, that the child is being asked to stop 'not eating' and stop 'losing weight'. The abnormal eating behaviour must be replaced with the alternative behaviour of normal eating and weight gain. A behavioural approach would therefore reward (positively reinforce) eating/weight gain with treats or exercise and punish (negatively reinforce) not-eating/weight loss, usually with bed rest – anathema to those with AN, or loss of 'privileges'. This was the mainstay of treatment for many years and persists in some units.

Comparisons of behavioural programmes focusing on reward versus punishment suggest limited success. Short-term success of strict punitive programmes is no greater compared to more humane approaches, whereas there is some evidence to suggest a greater risk of relapse. Management programmes that focus entirely on behavioural weight gain are punitive and inappropriate on both ethical and moral grounds when working with a deeply distressed child.

Behavioural techniques have a role to play in changing concrete, measurable aspects of behaviour but will result in very little change in the thoughts, beliefs, or feelings that form the basis of AN and related eating disorders.

Cognitive behavioural therapy and eating disorders

Beck (1967) has postulated that emotional responses are a result of how individuals structure their experience. Depression is a set of symptoms that arise from a pervasive triad of negative attitudes about the self (being unworthy and inadequate), the world (filled with insurmountable obstacles), and the future (unchangeable and pervasive hopelessness).

The combination of cognitive therapy with methods for behavioural change resulted in the formal development of CBT (Hawton, Salkovskis, Kirk, and Clark, 1989). The primary goal of CBT is to understand how an individual's thoughts and feelings are associated with the environment. It is important to make clear how these thoughts influence feelings during certain events (e.g. eating – 'I am a bad, weak person') and what thoughts and feelings are associated with the consequences of the behaviour (e.g. vomiting – 'I feel empty and happy'). CBT therefore initially focuses on the here and now. Its success in the treatment of adult eating disorders has been extensively documented, particularly for BN and increasingly for AN (Fairburn, 1997; Vitousek and Orimoto, 1993).

Creating a focus

Fairburn, Shafran, and Cooper (1998) have argued for the role of self-control as a core maintaining factor in development of eating disorders (see also Slade (1982)). They advocate the importance of focusing cognitive treatment on this core feature linking the need for control to starvation and the over-influence of shape and weight, low self-worth and self-esteem (Fairburn et al., 1998). This has implications for working with children and adolescents where the development of independence, self-identity and control over their environment are key developmental tasks (Christie and Viner 2005). It is important therefore that when working with young people the first goal should be to engage the young person in the therapeutic process by creating a shared focus. This can be done by asking them what they would want to talk about or think about if the session was going to be useful or helpful. This introduces the potential for the young person to have some control in the session over what to work on. It also enables the therapist working with the individual to invite the young person to think about what other people (e.g. parents, doctors and friends) might be wanting them to be thinking about.

Cognitive behavioural therapy and children

CBT works to help the person understand the links between negative thoughts (which are usually automatic), feelings and actions. Therefore, an initial step is to try to help the young person understand this relationship.

Therapist: What would you *think* might have happened if you were lying in
bed at night and heard a crash in the room next door?
Child: Maybe the cat has knocked something over.
Therapist: What would you *do*?
Child: Just turn over and go back to sleep.
Therapist: How do you *feel*?
Child: Don't know. maybe cross because I will have to tidy it up?

An alternative explanation is then discussed:

Therapist: What if you don't have a cat?
Child: Maybe someone has broken in.
Therapist: How would you feel now?
Child: I'd be scared . . . or worried.
Therapist: What would you do now?
Child: I'd hide under the covers.

This helps children to begin to see that they can think different things about an identical situation and that what they think will make them feel and behave differently.

Thinking things through: thought diaries

Keeping diaries of thoughts, behaviours and feelings is an important part of CBT with adults (Hawton et al., 1989; Kendall, 1991). For children, however, there are many reasons why this may be problematic. The first difficulty for many children is being able to keep the diary during the school day. Problems at school may be missed or altered by memory if they do not manage to remember what they wanted to write. Children can also forget to keep track of problem thoughts that are attached to difficult feelings. They may also feel unable to write down things that might be read by their parents. They may have learning difficulties and be unable to write sufficiently well to keep the diary. Another difficulty may be an inability to conceptualise the difference between thoughts and feelings.

> Felicity, 10, kept a diary for two weeks. Her thoughts were 'I'm sad' and her feelings were 'I'm sad' every day.

Young and Faneslow-Brown (1996) have described a more child-friendly thought diary using a cartoon format that is more easily completed by children. It allows them to choose the most important event of their day. The drawings also provide material that can be used in the therapy sessions. The cartoon attempts to distinguish between the thought bubble that is things you think inside your head ('I thought I'd get told off', 'I thought I'd be sick') and the speech bubble, which is the feeling you might say out loud ('I feel scared, worried, sad'). It is clear for many children that this is a difficult distinction to make. A slightly modified version of the diary sheet completed by a child with food avoidant emotional disorder is shown in Figure 13.1.

The thought diaries can be used as part of the initial assessment or continued throughout the treatment phase. Generally, however, children begin to get bored with having to remember to keep the diaries after two to three weeks. The diaries offer a starting point and can be reintroduced as a way to monitor changes in the child's thinking patterns during therapy.

Completing the diaries

CBT with an adult requires the patient to act in a collaborative manner with the therapist. Many children with eating disorders, particularly those with AN, are at best ambivalent about the need to change. The eating disorder can be thought of as their answer to their problem. As they have solved their problem, why should they want to change either their behaviour or the way they think about it? How will that change their experience of the world? Motivation and commitment to change also vary depending on the type of eating disorder:

- Children with AN generally do not want to carry on being unhappy, but neither do they want to change their calorie intake under any circumstances. They are unlikely to want to write down – with any honesty – what they have eaten on a daily basis.
- Although children with food avoidance emotional disorder (FAED) report that they would like to eat more, they often struggle to complete any behavioural tasks outside the therapy sessions. The nature of CBT allows this difference between what is said, what is done and what is felt to be examined and worked on in the therapy session.
- Children with selective eating often seem to want to increase the range of

Figure 13.1 Gail (FAED) was 80 per cent weight for height and would become very distressed when she talked about not being able to eat as much as her brother and sister. She insisted that she wanted to be bigger despite struggling to increase her weight. Gail is able to distinguish between her thoughts (not knowing what she is going to do) and her feelings of being nervous and scared. Gail's picture of 'what happened' (a family outing) shows that although objectively she is much thinner and smaller than her parents, she portrays herself as much bigger than them and places herself in the centre of the family (right in the middle of her parents). This gives the therapist another form of communication to ask questions about, as well as helping Gail make links between what is said, done, written, thought and felt.

foods they can eat. However, the entrenched nature of the disorder means there is often a pervasive hopelessness about the possibility of change, which reinforces their restricted food intake. Those selective eaters who are determined to change will keep diaries with immaculate precision, whereas those who are unable to do so may have more entrenched underlying emotional difficulties that have not emerged in the initial assessment.

Motivation and engagement

Poor motivation and lack of engagement will limit therapeutic effectiveness (NICE, 2004). Motivational interviewing (MI) is an approach that focuses on addressing an individual's resistance and/or ambivalence to change (Miller and Rollnick, 2002; and see further Chapter 10). MI was developed for conditions where clients were resistant to change and specifically emphasises the importance of 'rolling with resistance' rather than directly challenging the view of the client. A recent systematic review identified MI as having potential effectiveness in a range of physical health settings (Knight, McGowan, Dickens, and Bundy, 2006). Treasure and Ward (1997) have described the use of MI in adults with AN. The aim is to direct the client towards identification of what would make change important as well as how to make change a priority and enhance confidence in the ability to change. One way of beginning this process is to talk about the advantages and disadvantages of weight loss, not eating or vomiting, etc., then begin to help direct the client to identify for themselves what the advantages of change are, so they begin to outweigh the advantages of not eating, being ill, etc. The therapist takes the position of a coach encouraging and helping identify statements that indicate intention to change and moments of optimism. MI has recently been reported as an additional component to a CBT programme for adolescents with AN (Gowers and Smyth, 2004).

Working with silence and worry

Doing good: feeling bad

One of the unifying or core features of all eating disorders is low self-esteem. Children with eating disorders may be 'good' at home and 'doing well' at school but 'feeling bad'. Many children with AN present as 'perfect children'. They may be described as compliant, quiet, well behaved, top of their class. In contrast, they may feel bad, sad, hopeless and worthless to such a degree that they literally want to disappear.

> Jane, 15, described how when she was about 11 years old children always wanted to be her friend at school and would fight to sit next

to her. She found this distressing: 'I didn't deserve to have people like me so much.'

A response to this lack of self-worth is to try to become as small as possible as if in an effort to disappear. Many actively attempt to achieve this through starvation, whereas others are less consciously aware of their self-imposed progressive malnutrition. One of the aims of therapy, therefore, should be to help the child feel comfortable about who she is and who she wants to be. Children rarely need to learn to eat but they do need to learn to like themselves. For many children this may involve being given permission to not 'do good' all the time in order to 'feel good'. Beginning this process can take a long time. Many children with AN are furious with their parents for having brought them to therapy, and with therapists for forcing them to sit through what they see as pointless (and painful) discussions. In our experience anger, conflict, or assertion are often discouraged in families of children with AN. The only way such children can structure their experience (see Beck, 1967), i.e. impose some control over their environment, is to stop eating. To impose similar control over the therapeutic experience may require them to be silent. Sitting with a child in silence for an hour feels extremely persecutory and may 'replay' the angry silences that parents might have used to 'punish' their refusal to eat. Developmentally the young person may not have developed abstract thinking skills which when exacerbated by the effect of low weight may make it hard to articulate her problems and impair the ability to think about the impact of the condition in the future.

'All About Me'

'All About Me' is a board game with a numbered path through a jungle scene (Hemmings, 1991). A set of cards with questions or incomplete sentences is used to facilitate movement around the board. The way the game is played is limited only by the inventiveness of the therapist and the child's willingness to answer the questions honestly. The cards contain uncompleted sentences that can be preselected to focus on a specific aspect of the child's life:

- Family (a brother is . . .? a father is . . .?)
- Emotions (I feel happy when . . . I feel sad when . . .)
- Experiences (my favourite joke is . . .)
- Behaviour (I like to eat . . .).

The format of the game is non-threatening and can help test hypotheses generated in the initial formulation about underlying issues, e.g. which questions can the children answer and which do they say 'Don't know' to. The emotional content of the cards can be mixed and matched according to the needs of both the therapist and the child. It can also create a link between sessions. If nobody gets to the end of the path through the jungle, places can be marked for the following session. The cards can be saved and sorted into categories for discussion in other sessions. The therapist's participation in the game also provides a model that talking about feelings can be safe. The only rule is that there are no rules.

> Sarah, 14, had AN. She was so furious with her therapist that she played the game on her own, reading the cards to herself and refusing to allow the therapist to throw the dice.

> Karen, 14, had suffered from AN since the age of eight. She would ask to play the game whenever she became so anxious that she wanted to leave the room. Playing the game allowed her to defy the 'anorexia' by staying and talking.

> Pauline, 13, had AN and only ever spoke to her therapist when they played the game.

Post-it notes and puppets

Some children find it easier to use a 'surrogate' to speak on their behalf. Puppets can be used as a way of helping young people to find their voice (Fredman and Christie, in press).

> Jane (FAED), 13, found it impossible to speak in the individual sessions. She would often respond to questions about what she might be thinking about by screaming and climbing over the back of her chair so she could hide in the corner of the room. She had a small finger puppet that she brought into the sessions with her. I started to wonder what the puppet was thinking about our conversations and asked it if it would mind helping Jane and me work out what I could do to be helpful. As I didn't speak 'puppet', I asked if Jane could help me by writing down what the puppet thought on Post-it notes. Jane stuck the Post-it notes on her arm so that I could read them. We got the puppet to help us work out what Jane was thinking about and how she was feeling. The puppet gave us some good ideas about what Jane and I could talk about in order to help everyone stop worrying about her. Jane began to put her own answers on Post-it notes – which she stuck on to my arm.

Emotions wall

Children who are able to keep the thought diary for only a few days, or who struggle to write anything more than a few words, clearly indicate that they are unable or unwilling to identify and describe their feelings. If they are not 'upset' they are 'fine', with no in between. Such children present with two emotional conditions: 'okay/not okay'. They seem unable to differentiate or describe distressed, angry, sad, worried, happy, thrilled, etc. They may have very little contact with either their own emotional state or that of others and find it hard to differentiate and describe emotions in others, particularly their parents.

The first step towards finding a safe way to think about these things is to build a list of words that describe emotional states, e.g. happy, sad, angry, cross, lonely. These 'feelings' are things that are inside us. The child is encouraged to write these on a piece of paper. The therapist then gives the child a piece of paper that has a wall drawn on it. This is stuck over the emotions, blanking them out. The next task is to cover the wall with graffiti. The 'graffiti' represent the various ways that people can act and behave: crying, laughing, smiling, shouting, hitting, eating, not eating.

The aim of the exercise is to think how what is on the wall can be connected to one or more of the feelings behind the wall. The therapeutic task is to try to think about how to connect what we see on the wall and what lies behind it. Paradoxes can be explored: for example, crying with sadness or happiness; smiling when happy or angry but not wanting to hurt someone's feelings. The multiple links between feelings that are 'inside' and expressed emotions can be explored for both the child and those around her. How does she know what her mum is feeling about her not eating? What does she think when her parents are shouting at her? Moving the wall down (using an eraser or using two sides of paper) to show both the behaviours and feelings at the same time will allow the child to make connections, as the ideas are explored. This can be done using concrete examples by joining up words with felt pens or string.

Worry bag

Binnay and Wright (1997) have described a technique, used primarily for assessment, called 'the bag of feelings'. The child is given a drawn outline of a bag and encouraged to draw her worries inside it. Sometimes 'worry' seems such an overwhelmingly large concept that it feels as if it will consume the child. The idea that worry is normal is discussed, but also that some people have more than others. The aim is to help the child to externalise 'the worry' (White, 1985; also see Chapter 9). Defining the worries and making them seem more 'real' or concrete can help the child feel they are easier to manage. The therapist offers various pieces of paper to the child and suggests that these could be used to represent all the worries she has now.

Let's pretend that this sheet here is your biggest worry. Can you think how the big worry might be made up of worries about all sorts of different things? For example, can you colour in, or mark off, how much worry is about school?

This first part of this process gives the child explicit permission to have the worry. Each worry is subdivided into smaller and smaller sections until the paper is all used up. The paper can be cut up (like a jigsaw). All the pieces are then put into a big envelope, which has been decorated and labelled as 'My worry bag'. At different sessions, a worry can be taken out of the bag and discussed. Each worry can be further broken down into even smaller parts, both verbally and concretely, by cutting it in half again and again and again.

> Maya (FAED), 10, chose to subdivide her big worry about school into worries about finding her way around, not being able to carry her bags, not being able to make friends, not getting her homework done, no one speaking to her. Each worry was assigned an appropriate amount of space and then returned to the worry bag, except for the one piece (or worry) to be discussed.

Problem-solving strategies can then be used to think about how to resolve the worry, or tasks can be set to challenge negative thoughts about what might happen.

> Ali (BN), 13, made a list of all the people who spoke to her at school during the week and brought it with her to the next therapy session. She was then able to take 'people might not speak to me' out of the worry bag and throw it in the bin.

This symbolic way of disposing of problems is a powerful reinforcing technique, particularly for young children. The process can be repeated as sometimes resolving one problem makes other linked problems disappear. Children can also decide how much of their worries they want to face at any time.

> Lucy (FAED), 10, and Josh (SE), 6, always liked to empty out the worry bag to see how much was in there.

Children can also choose where they want to keep the worry bags. If they feel that their parents are unable to cope with their worries, they may decide to keep the worry bag in the therapist's room.

> After two weeks Josh (SE), 6, decided he would take the worry bag home with him so that he and his mum could get rid of the worries without having to wait for his therapy sessions.

The worry bag can be completed with silent children who are able to communicate by writing or drawing, although they may not wish to speak.

Focusing on the future: being a detective

For many children in the grip of an eating disorder it can be impossible to imagine how life could be if the eating disorder was not around to bully them and control their life. Behavioural experiments can encourage them to try out different behaviours and observe the impact of these on their thoughts and feelings. The impact of changing behaviour, how this affects thoughts or feelings and how it changes other people's responses, can then be explored in the therapy session. Younger children can use this technique too, although it requires careful explanation and practice. In the first part of the session the child is asked what she thinks would happen if she were to behave in a different way (i.e. eat more):

- How would *she* feel?

Then other people's reactions are discussed:

- Who would notice you were eating more?
- What would they say?
- Who in the family would be the most surprised?
- Would your friends at school notice?

The next step is to discuss the idea that coming to therapy is like being a detective, looking for clues to why there are worries and problems:

- What would happen if you were a detective all week, not just in this room?
- What would happen if you went home and ate more than normal (e.g. took a second piece of toast at breakfast)?

Children are asked to keep a secret diary and to try to record people's reactions and how they feel when, or if, they do things differently. Parents are not told that their child is going to try to do this. This technique produces several kinds of information that can be incorporated into the assessment and treatment. First, it is a way of establishing the child's engagement in the process of change. If she has not been able to complete this task, then focusing on self-directed change may not be helpful at this stage. If she has been able to eat a bit more, the parent's response (if any) can be discussed with the parents via the family therapist or parental counsellor as well as with the child.

> Lizzie, an 11 year old with FAED, was 80 per cent weight for height. The therapeutic team felt that her parents were not taking an active role in helping her eat more. Lizzie was able to ask for more breakfast on a few occasions but reported that only her older sister and brother noticed this and made any comment. There was no reaction from her parents at all. The week after this 'experiment', she lost 500 g. Work with the parents was intensified to encourage them to acknowledge their role in helping Lizzie to gain weight.

A similar approach is used in brief solution focused therapy (George, Iveson, and Ratner, 1999). The aim is to ask young people to describe how their preferred future looks and notice ways they have already found to challenge the 'problem' story. This is done by asking the 'miracle question':

> Martin (15, AN) was asked to imagine that he had gone to sleep and when he woke up the concerns and worries that had brought him to meet that team were no longer around. He was asked to talk about what this would look like and describe what he would notice about his life that gave him clues that this 'miracle' had happened. He talked about how he would wake up and be able to eat breakfast without his mother nagging him. He and his parents would talk about doing fun activities and he wouldn't have to come up to the hospital. He would be going to school and would be allowed to go out more with his friends as his mother wouldn't be worried about him missing meals.

The young person is asked to identify times in the past when they noticed that they had been as close as possible to this future position and talk about what had enabled these moments to occur. Focusing on these solutions enables the identification of strengths, abilities and resources that can be used to amplify change and reinforce future change.

The therapist can use the preferred future as a way to set homework tasks (Molnar and De Schazer, 1987). The homework tasks invite the young person to look out for signs that they and the people around them are moving towards their preferred future. One of these tasks is to pretend that the miracle has happened for 30 minutes each day when they wake up and report on what happened. Just as in the detective role play, the young person is not required to tell people specifically about the task.

Relaxation and guided imagery therapy

Relaxation is a well-documented technique used to counteract physiological symptoms of anxiety (Peveler and Johnston, 1986). It is often coupled with a list of anxiety-producing images of increasing intensity, where the relaxation is used to reduce the anxiety associated with each image. Involvement in fantasy or other thoughts is a normal process, especially in children, which has often been harnessed to bring about behavioural or somatic changes (Olness and Gardner, 1988). These techniques are variously referred to as 'guided imagery', 'relaxation with mental imagery', or 'cognitive reconstruction', and sometimes reference is made to 'hypnosis' or 'hypnotherapy'. The state of mind achieved can perhaps be best described as an intense imaginative involvement on the part of the subject, combined with belief in what is happening. After the session, subjects are often so relaxed that they may feel inclined to go to sleep. Even quite young children can be helped by hypnotherapy. Results on gender differences have suggested that there is a tendency for girls to respond better than boys (LeBaw, Holton, Tewell, and Eccles, 1975; Sokel, Christie, Kent, Lansdown, and Atherton, 1993).

Guided imagery or relaxation therapy can be used with a wide range of childhood problems. The most important component is a comprehensive assessment and formulation of the problem. The idea that being more relaxed and calm will help the child feel less worried is explained. The child is reassured that she will be in control at all times and must therefore work with the therapist to decide where she wants to be in her 'story'. Children can also be encouraged to choose someone to help them in the story. This can be a real person or a fantasy figure. The way the process is explained to children is also determined by their interests and age. The first stage is to explain that the therapist is going to show them how to use what goes on inside their head to help with their symptoms. For younger children (and some older ones) the term 'magical thinking' can help to engage them. Computer-literate children are attracted to the idea that they can use their mind like a computer to search through directories to find the programme that controls 'worry'. There is no standard text or perfect story. Each child writes her own script including where she wants to be, who will be there and what she wants to do when she gets there. The therapist uses this information to construct a story that involves images and ideas that help to reduce or control symptoms.

The following story was composed with a 10-year-old girl (Kate) with a lifelong history of faddiness and selective eating. She retched every time she tried to eat a new food and would only eat peanut butter sandwiches, cheese and tomato pizza, and apples. In the initial assessment she had talked about how much she enjoyed horse riding. She decided that she wanted to be on a horse in her story. She was asked to close her eyes if she could (although this was not essential). She was then asked to make herself comfortable and to concentrate on the therapist's voice. She was told she would have to remember the story so she could tell it to herself when she was at home.

Imagine you are standing at the top of a flight of stairs. As you go down the steps, take a big breath in through your nose and then blow out slowly.

The therapist models this while they are talking and then counts slowly from one to ten breathing with the child, using the tone of voice (low) and speed of delivery (slow) to regulate and slow down the respiratory rate.

At the bottom of the stairs, there is a large, heavy door in a wall. Slowly put out your hand and push the door. It slowly opens. Through the door, you can see a field. You start to walk through the door and feel the soft grass beneath your feet. The grass is a beautiful green and up above the sky is as blue as blue can be. Beside you there is a pretty little stream which is tinkling over the pebbles. You look around and feel the warm sunshine on the back of your neck. There is a gentle breeze blowing. You start to walk through the field following the stream and notice all the flowers. As you slowly breathe in you can smell the beautiful perfume of the flowers. The sun is as warm as can be and is beginning to make you feel a little sleepy. You hear the sound of a waterfall and start to walk towards it. As you walk into the clearing, you see a beautiful brown horse standing by the waterfall. He paws the ground as if he has been waiting for you. You slowly get up on to the horse and he starts to walk, slowly at first. The wind is blowing in your hair as the horse starts to canter, getting faster and faster as you ride across the meadow. You ride and ride feeling free as a bird. The wind blows away all the tension and worry in your shoulders and your arms.

As he returns to the stream, you slowly slide off his back and sit down beside the stream. You feel calm and relaxed and decide to sit in the warm sun listening to the sound of the water trickling through the rocks, just to sit and rest for a while. The horse stands beside you gently breathing in and out. It's as if you can understand him as he pushes your hand gently towards the water encouraging you to take a drink of the water from the stream. You slowly lean over and put your hand into the crystal clear water lifting out a handful of water. As you put it to your lips, the water runs down your throat. As it goes down your throat and into your tummy, it starts to make your stomach feel warm and relaxes your throat all the way from the top to the bottom. You know that if you were to eat anything new you would have no feelings of sickness. Your throat and stomach feel relaxed and able to try anything new. The horse helps you to understand that if you come here anytime before you have your meal you'll be able to try new foods without feeling sick. You put your hand round the horse's neck and let him help you up. You slowly walk away from the stream back through the meadow towards the gate. You can come here anytime you want, to this special place. When you reach the gate, you turn around and see the horse is waiting for you, guarding the stream for you. You push the gate and go through waving goodbye to the beautiful horse . . .

Slowly you begin to climb back up the stairs.

The therapist counts the child back up the stairs, explaining that when she gets to the top she can open her eyes if she needs to and come back into the room.

A simple linear scale can be used to help children indicate how nervous or anxious they felt before they began listening to the story and how they felt after it. Kate was asked to practise the story every night for ten minutes before her evening meal, and then try a small taste of new food from her mother's plate. Her parents were asked to make sure she was given privacy to complete the relaxation. They were not asked to monitor or encourage her to complete the relaxation. The children are completely in charge of doing or not doing the task. This is partly because there is nothing quite as unrelaxing as being told to relax, but also that failure to practise is a motivational issue which can be worked on in other sessions. For some children it may be helpful to record the story on tape so that they can listen to it on a personal stereo. The therapist can also stop as the story develops, to check on details, like the colour of the sky, who they have met, and what they want to do next in their adventure.

Despite being reportedly desperate to change her eating habits, Kate had been unable to stop feeling anxious and distressed when she thought about trying new foods because of the anticipatory retching. After the first session she was given food diaries to keep. She was asked to practise the technique every night for a fortnight. The next session she reported that she had been able to try a wide range of new foods with no retching, nausea, or discomfort. Once she had desensitised herself to 'new foods' she was able to stop the relaxation before mealtimes. Twelve months later, Kate was eating a wide and varied diet and had become increasingly confident and outgoing.

Token charts with a difference

As discussed in the earlier section on learning theory, behaviours are likely to increase when they are rewarded or reinforced. Rewarding successes with attention and tokens on charts are both well-documented reinforcement tools. Despite this, many parents report having tried – and failed – to use token charts with any success. This is usually because the goals that have been set are often too big to be achievable, e.g. asking a selective eater to eat a new meal every day to get a token. Another problem is that the token chart may be visually unrewarding, particularly for pre-teen children. The child may find it hard to link the behaviour with the chart or have beliefs and feelings about the behaviour that make the token insufficiently 'rewarding'. Images that can be incorporated into the therapeutic process can be used as the 'chart' with the picture built from components that are the reward 'tokens'. These images can have a meaning associated with the symptoms: flowers that grow as the child attaches petals, caterpillars that get longer and longer until they become a butterfly, and mountains that are difficult to climb alone.

Growing a flower

Anya (FAED) 9, was given the goal of eating a small teaspoon of something she hadn't tried before, from her mother's plate, before eating her regular meal. She was to sit and eat with the family, regardless of what she was having. She was asked to keep a diary of each new taste and say whether she did or didn't like it. She was told that it was possible that there would be things that she wouldn't like. The 'task' was to try things, with no expectation that she would like everything new. Her parents were encouraged to help her select one small teaspoonful but were not required to either encourage or argue with her. As before, Felicity was asked to take responsibility for completing the task.

The following session the list of tried foods was discussed. For each new food that was considered 'okay' the name of the food was written on a paper petal made from sticky paper (in lots of colours). Near she was given a large 'petal-less' flower which she then stuck the new petals on around the centre. This flower became her food menu. She used this to help her move on to the next stage, which was to choose one of the foods on the petal and have a small portion of it as part of her normal meal as well as continuing to try new teaspoonfuls. Larger outer petals were used to record the 'okay' foods eaten as part of a meal and small petals for new foods were added to the growing flower (Figure 13.2).

The hungry caterpillar

Young boys may find the idea of making a flower unappealing. A caterpillar can be used as a metaphor for growth and change with the sections of the body or feet used as the 'tokens'. The child can make the caterpillar as long and curvy as he wants to.

Enhancing self-esteem

Children with eating disorders have low self-esteem. Both the flower and caterpillar can be used to identify and positively reinforce successes and achievements. The child and therapist explore things that the child is good at. For a child preoccupied with shape and weight the positive and functional aspects of her body can be discussed instead of the reported negative physical aspects, e.g. 'my legs are *fast*' instead of 'my legs are *fat*'.

The process of thinking of what they are good at can be difficult for

Figure 13.2 Anya was able to add these petals to her food flower over a three-week period. The inner petals were small tastes and the outer petals were increasing portion sizes of different foods.

children who cannot think of anything good about themselves. Even this difficulty, however, can be incorporated into a homework task in which the child has to find out what each member of her family thinks are her 'good points'. The therapist can then discuss with the child what she agrees with and see if there is evidence to support the child's refusal to accept positive self-attributes.

Scaling the mountain: an incredible journey?

Measuring where people are and where they would like to be can be tricky, especially when several people in the system may have different goals. CBT therapists use scales to measure specific symptoms (anxiety or pain thermometer where 0 = no anxiety, 10 = extreme anxiety). Solution focused therapy uses scales to identify how close to the desired future an individual might be with 10 being the day after the miracle and 0 being the furthest away you have ever been (George et al., 1999). These scales help the child identify small steps that need to be taken to move up (or down) a scale and can be used to measure progress in therapeutic tasks. Imagining the journey from problem to solution as a mountain is a concrete representation of a scale (0 = when you first became ill, 10 = when you no longer need to come here) as well as a metaphor for the therapeutic relationship:

> Trying to get better sometimes feels like trying to climb a very, very high mountain, so high you don't feel you will ever get to the top. Being here is the beginning of a journey. The journey has a beginning – the bottom of the mountain (which is today), and an end (which is where you want to be when we don't need to see each other any more).

Children are encouraged to define their own preferred future (what they want to achieve or change). The child is not required to think about how she has got to the bottom of the mountain and often having come into a therapeutic programme there has been some movement towards the top. The therapist is someone who is coming with her on the journey but the child is going to have to do her own climbing. We can use this model to explain the need to make steady progress. The child is not expected, nor should she expect to run up all the way. Parents and children can also see that there may be times when they will need to stop and have a rest. The mountain can be represented in any medium the child wishes. It can be drawn as a homework task and then figures can be made to represent the child. These can then be stuck on to the mountain as the child progresses through the treatment programme. Older children may prefer the therapist to draw the mountain for them and just point to where they think they have reached. Other family members can be drawn, cut out and attached if they have contributed to the achievement of particular goals. Lack of progress or non-completion of a homework task can be formulated as stopping for a rest, rather than failure, which helps to maintain motivation and engagement. The mountain can be adapted to represent many different metaphors of change:

- For the silent and distressed child with AN the journey represents the therapeutic relationship. The child may want the therapist to stand in front and help pull her along, or may prefer the therapist to stay behind to 'catch her' in case she starts to slip backwards. The way the 'anorexia' is holding up the journey, setting traps or obstacles, can be discussed.
- For children with FAED, the thoughts and feelings can be considered as luggage, an enormous heavy bag that makes it difficult even to begin the journey. This then allows the therapist to introduce the idea of looking inside the bag and trying to sort out which thoughts are connected to which feelings, and those that might be discarded, instead of bringing them along on the journey to the top of the mountain. This can be combined with the worry bag technique.
- For children who eat a limited range of foods, the mountain becomes a three-dimensional token chart with their progress toward their targets clearly visible.

Melanie, 9, began treatment for functional dysphagia and engaged quickly in completing diaries and drawing her mountain. After a few sessions (both individual and parental), it became clear that rapid behavioural change had been easily achieved in the past but this was always followed by relapse. Changes in the treatment plan were explained to Melanie and her parents by saying that the difficulty wasn't climbing the mountain but the tendency to keep slipping back down. Rather than trying to achieve specific (behavioural) goals and climb the mountain, we were therefore going to work together to 'tunnel through' the problems and worries and get to the other side where food and eating were no longer bullies.

Conclusion

CBT involves the examination and re-evaluation of dysfunctional thoughts that are driving problem behaviours and emotional responses. This rather sophisticated and at times complicated task can be beyond even adults, and certainly for most children caught in the grip of a life-threatening eating disorder. It may also be difficult for the child who is overwhelmed by her own inability to eat more than a handful of food types, albeit in sufficient quantity not to be life threatening. Fitting therapy to the child rather than trying to fit the child to therapy has meant that traditional CBT approaches are being modified to incorporate ideas from systemic models in order to more explicitly include the family in the treatment of children and adolescents (for a review see Christie and Wilson, 2005).

The techniques presented in this chapter are offered as resources that allow therapists to make contact and engage with children even though they are being asked to think about their difficult and painful situations. For these children, many of their 'negative thoughts' may be based in reality (e.g. abusive families, poor living circumstances, difficulties at school). It is a difficult task to acknowledge reality without being drawn into the child's hopelessness. Certainly a therapist who fails to acknowledge what is real will lose credibility. However, it is the role of the therapist to keep hope alive and work with the child within their wider system

Unlike many adults, young children rarely have moments of intense 'insight'. They are unable to come up with 'rational reframing' of abusive experience and do not like to be told that the way they think is 'dysfunctional'. Very few are comfortable being asked to write a record of their misery. However, children do seem to think about what is talked about in sessions and make connections between their thoughts and feelings. The aim of therapy is to achieve changes in behaviour accompanied by changes in the way the child thinks. If the therapist acts to facilitate change using a model which is collaborative and empowering, then the child will be in a position to own that change and see it as something they have achieved rather than it having been imposed upon them. Therapy is a long, often tiring, and always incredible journey. The child cannot climb the mountain alone and needs the therapist to be there to hold her hand, catch her when she slips or falls and help her see that she can get to the top. At times there will be discoveries that may help the child, like a well cared for flower, grow and blossom. We must believe that eventually it is possible for all children, like the caterpillar, to emerge as beautiful butterflies.

Summary points

1 Cognitive behavioural techniques are part of a set of approaches used to help children unlock their worries and unhappiness.

2 Learning theory uses the principles of stimulus association and the reinforcement of behaviour to provide a theoretical framework which helps to both explain and modify behaviours. Behaviours *increase* when they are rewarded (or to avoid punishment). To *reduce* an undesirable behaviour, ignoring (non-attending) and helping the child to find an alternative behaviour can be effective.

3 Functional analysis allows the behaviour therapist to formulate events that are triggering, maintaining and providing reinforcement for the behaviour.

4 Measures of the severity of an eating disorder include:

   • weight–height ratio

- behaviour ratings
- descriptions of body image, shape, and weight.

5 Cognitive behavioural therapy is successful for the treatment of adult eating disorders by:

- making the relationship between thoughts and feelings explicit
- focusing on the here and now.

6 Cognitive behavioural therapy with children:

- helps them see the link between thoughts and feelings
- finds ways to help those who are silent
- makes worries concrete and manageable
- shows the impact of different behaviour on others.

7 Motivational interviewing and systemic therapies can be used in parallel with CBT techniques in order to enhance the therapeutic relationship and effectiveness.
8 Relaxation and guided imagery help reduce anxiety associated with eating.
9 Age-appropriate images and metaphors can be used to motivate children and adolescents' resolve to address eating difficulties and enhance self-esteem.

References

Beck, A.T. (1967). *Depression: Clinical, experimental and theoretical aspects*. New York: Harper and Row.

Bell, L., and Vetere, A. (Eds.). (1996). Eating disorders (special issue). *Clinical Psychology Forum, 92*.

Binnay, V., and Wright, J.C. (1997). The bag of feelings: An ideographic technique for the assessment and exploration of feelings in children and adolescents. *Clinical Child Psychology and Psychiatry, 2*, 449–462.

Christie, D., and Viner, R. (2005). Adolescent development. In R. Viner (Ed.), *ABC of adolescent health. British Medical Journal, 330*, 301–304.

Christie, D., and Wilson, C. (2005). CBT in paediatric and adolescent health settings: A review of practice based evidence. *Paediatric Rehabilitation, 8* (4), 241–247.

Ebeling, H., Tapanainen, P., Joutsenjoa, A., Koskinen, M., Morin-Papunen, L., Jarvi, L., et al. (2003) *Practice guidelines for treatment of eating disorders in children and adolescents*. Helsinki: Finnish Medical Association.

Fairburn, C.G. (1997). Eating disorders. In D.M. Clark and C.G. Fairburn (Eds.), *Science and practice of cognitive behaviour therapy* (pp. 209–241). Oxford: Oxford University Press.

Fairburn, C.G., Shafran, R., and Cooper, Z. (1998). A cognitive behavioural theory of anorexia nervosa. *Behaviour Research and Therapy, 37*, 1–13.

Fonagy, P., and Target, M. (1996). Should we allow psychotherapy research to determine clinical practice? *Clinical Psychology Science and Practice, 3*, 245–250.

Fredman, G., and Christie, D. (in press). Working with puppets and children. *Clinical Child Psychology and Psychiatry*.

George, E., Iveson, C., and Ratner, H. (1999). *Problem to solution: Brief therapy with individuals and families*. London: BT Press.

Gowers, S., and Bryant-Waugh, R. (2004). Management of child and adolescent eating disorders: The current evidence base and future directions. *Journal of Child Psychology and Psychiatry, 45* (1), 63–83.

Gowers, S., and Smyth, B. (2004). The impact of a motivational assessment interview on initial response to treatment in adolescent anorexia nervosa. *European Eating Disorders Review, 12,* 87–93.

Grossman, P.B., and Hughes, J.N. (1992). Self-control interventions with internalizing disorders: A review and analysis. *School Psychology Review, 21* (2), 229–245.

Harrington, R.C., Whittaker, J., Shoebridge, P., and Campbell, F. (1998). Systematic review of the efficacy of cognitive behaviour therapies in child and adolescent depressive disorder. *British Medical Journal, 316,* 1559–1563.

Hawton, K., Salkovskis, P.M., Kirk, J., and Clark, D.M. (1989). The development and principles of cognitive-behavioural treatments. In K. Hawton, P.M. Salkovskis, J. Kirk, and D.M. Clark (Eds.), *Cognitive behaviour therapy for psychiatric problems* (pp. 1–12). Oxford: Oxford Medical Publications.

Hemmings, P. (1991). *All about me*. London: Barnardo's.

Kendall, P.C. (Ed.). (1991). *Child and adolescent therapy: Cognitive behavioural procedures*. New York: Guilford Press.

Knight, K.M., McGowan, L., Dickens, C., and Bundy, C. (2006). A systematic review of motivational interviewing in physical health care settings. *British Journal of Health Psychology, 11* (2), 319–332.

LeBaw, W., Holton, C., Tewell, K., and Eccles, D. (1975). The use of self-hypnosis by children with cancer. *American Journal of Clinical Hypnosis, 17,* 233–238.

Le Grange, D., Eisler, I., Dare, C., and Russell, G.F.M. (1992). Evaluation of family therapy in anorexia nervosa: A pilot study. *International Journal of Eating Disorders, 12,* 347–357.

Lock, J., Le Grange, D., Agras, W., and Dare, C. (2001). *Treatment manual for anorexia nervosa: A family based approach*. New York: Guilford Press.

Miller, W., and Rollnick, S. (2002). *Motivational interviewing: Preparing people for change* (2nd ed.). New York: Guilford Press.

Molnar, A., and De Schazer, S. (1987). Solution-focused therapy: Toward the identification of therapeutics tasks. *Journal of Family and Marital Therapy, 13* (4), 349–358.

Mowrer, O.H. (1960). *Learning theory and behaviour*. New York: Wiley.

National Institute for Health and Clinical Excellence (NICE, 2004). *Eating disorders: Core interventions in the treatment and management of anorexia nervosa, bulimia nervosa and related eating disorders; a national clinical practice guideline*. London: NICE.

Olness, K., and Gardner, G.G. (1988). *Hypnosis and hypnotherapy with children*. New York: Grune and Stratton.

Pavlov, I. (1927). *Conditioned reflexes*. Oxford: Oxford University Press.

Peveler, R., and Johnston, D.W. (1986). Subjective and cognitive effects of relaxation. *Behaviour Research and Therapy, 24,* 413–420.

Robin, A.L., Siegel, P.T., Moye, A.W., Gilroy, M., Dennis, A.B., and Sikand, A. (1994). A controlled comparison of family versus individual therapy for adolescents with anorexia nervosa. *Journal of the American Academy of Child and Adolescent Psychiatry, 38,* 1482–1489.

Roth, A.D., and Fonagy, P. (1996). *What works for whom: A critical review of psychotherapy research*. New York: Guilford Press.

Slade, P.D. (1982). Towards a functional analysis of anorexia nervosa and bulimia nervosa. *British Journal of Clinical Psychology*, *21*, 167–179.

Sokel, B., Christie, D., Kent, A., Lansdown, R., and Atherton, D. (1993). A comparison of hypnotherapy and biofeedback in the treatment of childhood atopic eczema. *Contemporary Hypnosis*, *10*, 145–154.

Thorndike, E.L. (1898). Animal intelligence: An experimental study of the associative processes in animals. *Psychological Monographs*, *2* (8).

Treasure, J., and Ward, A. (1997). A practical guide to the use of motivational interviewing in anorexia nervosa. *European Eating Disorders Review*, *5*, 102–114.

Vitousek, K.B., and Orimoto, L. (1993). Cognitive-behavioural models of anorexia nervosa, bulimia nervosa and obesity. In K.S. Dobson and P.C. Kendall (Eds.), *Psychotherapy and cognition* (pp. 191–243). San Diego: Academic Press.

White, M. (1985). Fear busting and monster taming: An approach to the fears of young children. *Dulwich Centre Review*, 29–34.

Young, J., and Faneslow-Brown, P. (1996). Cognitive behaviour therapy for anxiety: Practical tips for using it with children. *Clinical Psychology Forum*, *91*, 19–21.

14 Individual psychotherapy

Jeanne Magagna

Introduction

Marie, a 12 year old with anorexia nervosa, was asked in her individual assessment why she felt no one liked her. She answered: 'Because I'm fat.'

'Would you like to draw a picture of yourself?' I asked. Marie hesitated for a moment and then drew the picture shown in Figure 14.1.

'Yes, you feel very fat indeed,' I said.

'I am very fat', she replied.

And now how do I respond? I thought.

Despite her experience of being fat, Marie is outwardly very thin and emaciated. No matter how often people tell her she is thin and not fat, her reality is that she is unlikeable because of 'fat'.

Figure 14.1 Marie's self-portrait.

The focus of psychodynamic understanding is to listen while constantly being attuned to everything that is happening. A sense of 'fatness' when actually emaciated is linked with a child's lack of an inner mental structure. Ordinarily, such structure gives meaning to emotional experiences and so puts them into some manageable psychological form. Instead of an inner mental structure, the child with anorexia nervosa (AN) 'holds herself together' through attachment to a 'pseudo-autonomous self' (a term which I use here to refer to the child's own protective measures rather than depending on her parents). With this pseudo-autonomy, she barricades herself against accepting nurture, both emotional and physical (Goodsitt, 1997).

Marie illustrates her dilemma through a drawing in which a locked door imprisons her and also barricades her against a relationship with her mother (Figure 14.2) (Rey, 1994). Marie's hands are used to control herself so she is also not allowed to eat food on her plate. Palazzoli (1974) suggested that the child with AN, through her symptom of starving, is trying to negotiate control and autonomy with her family. The 'pseudo-autonomy' of a child or adolescent with AN should not be confused with the desire for autonomy of a child who has internalised good experiences with understanding parents, and has thus matured sufficiently to struggle for more autonomy and control over her own life. The more mature child gradually enters relationships outside the family. The child with AN is basically unable to achieve dependency

Figure 14.2 Drawing of a girl barricaded in a prison cell.

in an intimate relationship. Her control is used as a defence against intimate relationships with people (Rosenfeld, 1987). It leaves an inner self starved of understanding and support. For example, suicidal impulses or even suicidal attempts can be hidden from the parents in alliance with this 'pseudo-autonomous' controlling self.

Gradually in psychotherapy, linking Marie's inner and outer reality creates a path towards understanding herself and the feelings which have accumulated inside her, becoming bigger and uglier with time. Consequently her sense of herself is developed. But while Marie's sense of self developed, her sense of her body being 'fat and ugly' was fully maintained. This was her reality which needed to be deeply understood (Farrell, 1995).

Much later in her therapy when I asked, 'What else about you besides your "fatness" makes you unlovable?' Marie was able to give a fuller answer. 'I'm shy, quiet, scared other girls won't like me. I lack confidence. I'm less clever than the others. I have different hobbies from them.' With the acceptance of her bodily 'ugliness' by me, Marie was gradually able to believe that I could tolerate disagreeable experiences. She writes:

> There is a sadness inside
> That is not able to go out.
> It makes me feel bad
> In my throat
> In my head
> There are tears in my eyes
> Crying in my voice
> Creating confusion in my heart.
> But slowly
> The cry inside me
> Becomes a scream which comes out.

Through providing regular, frequent and consistently timed therapy sessions as well as a listening and thinking place in my heart, which is the essence of empathic listening, Marie slowly found that the protective door to her inner experiences opened so that she could gradually share as much as she was capable of feeling at one time.

Marie arrived for treatment having suffered from AN for eight months, during which she had an unsuccessful hospital admission. She had a history of obsessional behaviour dating from around the age of five. This seemed linked to the arrival of a baby sister that promoted extreme jealousy and hatred, which was probably controlled by Marie's obsessional rituals. Marie retreated to her bedroom when distressed. At school she performed well academically and became excellent in gymnastics. The main problem as she perceived it was that she was superficially liked, but had no real friends. At 12 years of age, when she arrived for therapy with me, Marie complained that she was being teased at school. Her parents were also experiencing marital conflict accompanied by denying difficulties both for themselves and the children.

Marie primarily led the unfolding process in the therapy. As a psycho-dynamic therapist I could give depth of meaning to her words, thus holding her emotionally so she could tolerate some of the pain of knowing herself and her relationships with significant others. Primarily though, Marie's journey was one in which she was free to explore as much or as little of herself as she felt able and willing to get to know. Her 'protective door', which I call her 'pseudo-autonomous self', served as her method of preventing too much psychic pain. The 'pseudo-autonomous self' is felt to be superior to the adults, independent of human needs and in control. The child's healthy self is dominated by it. Marie was attached to her 'pseudo-autonomous self' rather than being able to depend on others. 'Anorexia is my best friend,' Marie says. 'I don't want to lose that!'

The development of a dependent, trusting relationship with the therapist and a sufficiently secure and containing external environment to allow Marie to 'open the door' to her suffering took time. She had to be physically nourished far sooner than her emotional self could be sufficiently healed.

What is complicated, though, is that the decision for the child to have therapy is a parental one, often precipitated because of the life-threatening aspects of the eating disorder. Coming into the therapy room, therefore, can initially feel like being force-fed. For this reason it was essential to point out that whereas Marie may not have had a choice about coming to therapy she did have a choice about whether she spoke or did any work in the therapy through thinking alongside me, even if she was silent.

Sensations, emotions and perceptions are often not encapsulated in words when a child with an eating disorder begins therapy. For this reason it is helpful to provide puppets, dolls, toy animals, drawing material, building blocks, cars and fences. It is striking how often an older adolescent may take an interest in these 'children's things' as a means of enacting some as yet unformed verbal thought. It may be simply the force or gentleness of a gesture in handling the toys that conveys a sense of persecution, hurt, or anger.

In one therapy session a 12-year-old boy with selective eating said, 'I'll never play with those toys. They are for younger children.' However, he frequently began sessions by rolling a train over several bodies of the dolls or knocking the dolls' heads together. As is often the case, his hands were able to 'speak' first and lead the way for me to explore how going to sleep was difficult for him because at night he was continually haunted by nightmarish creatures in his dreams, which he had kept private throughout much of his life.

Communication is always taking place in therapy. It is a luxury for the therapist to have communication through words from the child. Much of what needs to be understood is first put into words and given meaning through the therapist's physical and emotional experiences felt when anticipating the child's arrival for therapy, or sitting in the room with the child during the session, or pausing after the child has departed. This is the therapist's countertransference which is the primary fulcrum for making a timely interpretation, sensitively attuned to the child's current emotional experience and capacity to tolerate mental pain.

Transference and countertransference represent two components mutually giving life to each other and creating the relationship between the child and her therapist. Marie's therapy demonstrates this clearly and I shall be giving full illustrations later, but for the moment I would like to discuss these two concepts in a little more detail. The transference of the child refers to her behaviour toward the therapist and her work. The child transfers both positive and negative aspects of her parental figures – both internal and external – on to the personality of the therapist. The nature of this transference then determines how the child relates to the therapist at any moment in time. 'Gathering the transference' implies scanning all the stories the child brings about experiences outside the therapy as well as the child's dreams, while focusing on the emotions that are most immediate and pressing in the child at that moment. Psychoanalytic practice is still often misunderstood as focusing on reconstruction of historical events, rather than dealing with the child's experience in the here and now. However, the primary tenet of current psychoanalytic thinking is that internal change can best be facilitated through interpretations that meet anxiety at the moment at which it is being experienced. The material that Marie brought involved consideration not only of the content and mood of her communications but also precisely how this provided clues to what was happening between us in the session. Her remarks were also given meaning through their chronological sequence in the session. Often reading notes of a session from end to beginning enables one to more fully understand the transference anxieties the child has in relation to the therapist at the beginning of the session. I also attempted to ask myself: 'What does this story about the past or the future, this story about something outside the therapy room, unconsciously tell me about the nature of Marie's current preoccupations in relation to the therapeutic relationship with me?'

It is mainly through the countertransference that the therapist feels and can understand what the child feels and does in relation to the therapist. For this reason understanding the countertransference is the central focus of psychoanalytic psychotherapy (Hinshelwood, 1994). Often children with eating disorders cannot find or will not share words with their therapist. Marie was no different. At times in the silence I would feel frustrated and impotent. This was particularly true when I was having difficulty attuning to my countertransference. But what is the countertransference really? It consists of various levels of emotional experience. First, countertransference is based on a connection with the child's impulses and defences and also an identification with her currently present internal parental figures transferred on to the therapist.

As well as this, the child's transference to the therapist is a response to the therapist's real and fantasised countertransference (Racker, 1974: 131). For example, the child's unconscious is quite skilled in seeing and projecting into problematic aspects of the therapist's personality. The child can project into the therapist's wish to be all-knowing, or her wish to be a mother, or into the therapist's aggression and defences against it (Brenman-Pick, 1985). In particular, the child often projects into the therapist's guilt about not being a loving or adequate person in some way. If I, as a therapist, can be still and in the silence listen to what is going on deeply within myself in the presence of Marie, then there is no need for me to question her penetratingly in order to extract some words from her.

Problems in making progress in therapy are often viewed by therapists as the child's difficulties. But the child wouldn't be coming to therapy if she didn't have problems in facing psychic pain and putting her emotions into a symbolic form. Hence, however defended or hostile a child is in relation to therapy, I view the primary problem as being a problem of how I, the therapist, work on my countertransference in relation to the child. Having a capacity to dip into the riches of my own emotional experience is essential. Some people are natural therapists, but many require the rigour of personal psychotherapy or psychoanalysis to tap the reservoir of pent-up confused emotions. Left unrecognised, such emotions can distort communication between the child and the therapist. For example, a therapist lacking self-esteem may feel she deserves to be disliked by the child and fail to understand the child's fear of personal awareness and intimacy with others. Alternatively, needing reassurance that she is a 'successful and loved therapist', the therapist may be placatory and charming to the child and fail to acknowledge the child's latent hostility in the transference. This can often lead to a therapist's over-identification with the child and hostility to the parents for not being adequate in meeting the child's needs.

Working on the child's transference to the therapist and the therapist's countertransference responses is the essence of psychodynamic psycho-therapy (Money-Kyrle, 1978). In eclectic weekly psychotherapy seminars with colleagues, who have cognitive behavioural, cognitive analytic, Jungian, Freudian, Kleinian, as well as other individual and family therapy orienta-tions, we have found that it is essential to embody these concepts of transfer-ence and countertransference in each of our different kinds of therapy. What differs is the particular style with which we use our understanding of these concepts.

As the focus of this chapter is on working in individual psychodynamic psychotherapy such as Marie's, I shall briefly refer to a range of crucial therapeutic issues regarding this kind of work. In fact, throughout the chapter I shall be returning to Marie's story to illustrate many of the issues and concepts central to psychodynamic work with children and young people who have eating disorders. Some of the crucial therapeutic issues include:

- the treatment frame

- duration of treatment
- suitability for psychotherapy
- assessment for psychotherapy
- aims of psychotherapy and the therapeutic method
- using dreams for initial assessment and ongoing assessment of therapeutic progress.

The treatment frame

The context of individual assessment and therapy for children is crucial. Anyone treating a child with an eating disorder must be closely allied with a physician. A doctor should take medical responsibility for the ongoing evaluation of the patient's physical condition. The psychotherapist needs to have a clear set of guidelines for the minimum weight for the child's age and height and degree of physical ill health that warrants hospitalisation.

It is likely that during difficult moments in therapy and during the therapist's holidays the child with an eating disorder may wish to diet and discontinue therapy. This is part of her style of dealing with the psychological pain of separation. For this reason, it is irresponsible for a therapist to embark on individual therapy without ascertaining that there is an effective therapeutic link between the parents and a colleague who will assist the parents at difficult times. It is not uncommon for a child to stop therapy, engage in starving or bingeing, using laxatives and exercising while at the same time fostering the parents' denial that the child has a problem warranting therapy. Sometimes the child may also hide weights or overload on water to conceal her true weight from the parents. It is, of course, essential to accompany individual therapy with some ongoing work with the family or parents. The most effective therapeutic frame I have encountered has involved the following:

1   At least two family assessments to ascertain strengths, weaknesses and patterns of relating.
2   An individual assessment with the child to ascertain the individual pathology underlying the eating disorder, bearing in mind that both AN and bulimia nervosa (BN) have typical behavioural patterns that conceal a wide range of emotional difficulties.
3   A medical practitioner to monitor weight changes regularly and to liaise with the parents and child regarding the child's physical health.
4   Parental or family work accompanying the individual therapy. This provides support for the child and enables the parents or family to find a safe context in which they can explore the problematic aspects of their relationships and develop their capacities.
5   Consideration of possible hospital provision in case the child's health deteriorates. This is particularly important for those children with severe difficulties, when they are faced with the initial holiday separation from the therapist.

Duration of treatment

Accepting the need for an adequate duration of treatment is very important. More than one eating disordered child has expressed her fear: 'When I look all right on the outside, I am afraid no one will now notice how bad I feel inside.' In saying this, she expresses her fear that she must continually display her 'starvation' for fear that other people will do as she does, that is, deny inner emotional states and focus only on weight gain and pubertal development. The therapist needs to reassure the child that she will be able to receive therapy until it is no longer needed. A minimum of two years is generally required to assist a child to develop a stable psychic structure. However, this may not always be possible. Family therapy accompanied by a briefer period of individual counselling can also be useful to enable a child to experience feelings in a more mature way and remain emotionally linked to others.

Suitability for psychotherapy

Because of the limited resources for individual treatment and the efficacy of family therapy, individual therapy is often provided for children who cannot develop their capacities for owning and containing their emotions through family therapy alone. It is common for someone with an eating disorder to have disturbed psychic functioning involving the denial of painful emotions. This denial impedes taking care of the infantile parts of the self and thus prevents the development of emotional maturity. For this reason, individual therapy is potentially suitable for all children with an eating disorder, as long as the child is willing to come regularly to the sessions and the external network of professionals and parents can support the treatment. The more crucial questions are:

1   Is the therapist suitably qualified to work with this child's particular difficulties as well as having a compatible personality willing to tolerate the full brunt of the child's projections of mental pain (Meltzer, 1967)?
2   Does the therapist have the willingness and capacity to work on the countertransference experiences to meet the needs of a child who has not yet transformed bodily experiences into emotions suitable for language – for example, the silent, negative, or borderline psychotic child?
3   What help can be provided for a child who 'closes her mind and mouth' to psychotherapy, as she transfers her starving and bingeing impulses for food to a rejection of the therapist or to a very demanding wish to be with the therapist all the time?
4   Is inpatient treatment initially necessary to support the child in undertaking the burden of working through her difficulties?

Assessment for psychotherapy

As I approach an assessment interview, I bear in mind three patients. One is an adolescent with AN who told me that she had never told the doctors who had treated her for several years prior to seeing me, or me in two years of therapy, about repeated experiences of sexual abuse in her early childhood. When asked why not she said, 'No one has ever asked about sexual abuse. I felt awkward in bringing it up myself.' She said she feared both her parents and I would blame her for the abuse taking place. The second patient told me she had never told anyone about 'her voices'. When asked why this was, she said she was afraid people would think she was 'crazy' and anyway she liked her voices because they kept her 'company'. She said she was 'afraid of losing them'. The third patient, when asked about different suicidal impulses said she had none. However, when I asked her to describe a dream, it conveyed such a picture of hopelessness and despair that I pressed her further. She then did say that she had secretly recently taken an overdose but didn't want her mother to know.

Beware of the 'mask' of the child with AN or BN. An eating difficulty, whether it is bulimia or anorexia, involves the use of 'pseudo-autonomy' and projection of feelings. The pattern of eating difficulties may appear similar in many children while masking a variety of psychiatric symptoms. A child with an eating disorder may be experiencing vivid auditory or visual hallucinations or ever-present 'imaginary friends'. Because of the anorectic child's use of 'pseudo-autonomy' to feel and appear 'normal', such pathological phenomena are frequently concealed. For this reason, it is important to provide an individual assessment of approximately an hour for each child with an eating disorder. It is helpful to have at least one free-flowing assessment interview, in which the child is encouraged to use the opportunity to think about herself rather than supply information. Factual information can be gained in a subsequent interview and in other therapeutic settings. Fortunately, through her drawing, Marie was able to vividly portray the isolation of her inner self behind the protective cover of the locked door (Figure 14.2). Even if family therapy is the treatment of choice, each child with severe problems also deserves the right to a private space apart from the family to think about her life and those issues that initially may be difficult to share with the family.

In individual assessments I have found it helpful to ask the child to draw a picture of a person. Then I ask the child to tell me about the person and create a story for that person. Subsequently, with the assistance of the child, I try to find similarities and differences between the person in the story and the child I am meeting. The rest of the session is used as a space for the child to explore issues of her choice. Spontaneous play and drawings are used for the assessment of a younger child. When the child has difficulty in speaking about herself, I discuss her difficulty in meeting a stranger, her fear of my criticism and of me. I find it helpful to give her a family set of small cloth dolls and ask her to speak from the perspective of various family members, as I interview the doll family regarding 'their picture' of the child's life in her family. I also encourage the child to tell me a dream, any recurring dreams and dreams from her past. In this way I gain access to the child's psychic structure.

Figure 14.3 illustrates how I consider the child's psychic structure. The key components are a maternal figure, a paternal figure, sibling figures and the infantile self. These paternal and maternal figures are typically used by children to represent the nurturing, procreating and regulating roles of each parent. An examination of the maternal figure reveals the quality of nurturing and physical comfort and security provided, the capacity to receive distressed aspects of the infantile self and the ability to modify pain. Evaluation of the paternal figure includes noting the capacity to regulate emotion so that feelings are neither too intense nor too restricted, to differentiate good from bad, to provide limits and also an ethical code out of concern for the self and others. An assessment of the nature of the relationship with siblings and peers includes looking at the way in which conflicts between love, jealousy and anger are expressed in these relationships, and also noting the capacity to

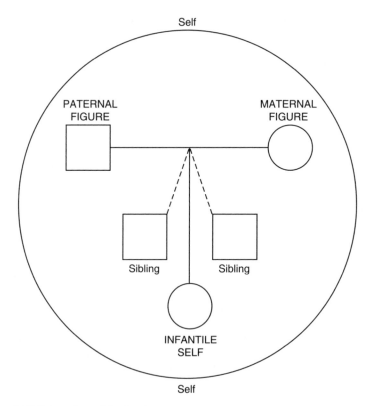

Figure 14.3 Internal psychic structure.

acknowledge the existence and needs of siblings. I find that often hostility of the child with an eating disorder towards the parents is displaced on to the siblings.

My primary question during an assessment is: What capacity does the child have, in identification with internal figures, to look after her own infantile self? In empathetically listening to a child, I hear the child's stories and tone of voice, as well as noting my emotional responses to the child's predominant attitudes to her experiences. I then develop a picture of the current relationships between the parental figures and infantile self in the child's internal world. Evaluation of the child's relationship to the parents involves the place of emotional and intellectual nurture in the child's life and her attitude to discipline by school figures. I also consider the child's capacity to allow the internal parental figures to be together in various creative ways, including procreation and the care of the siblings. This can be shown through scenes in dreams in which a couple are co-operatively doing something worthwhile.

The nature of the internal parental figures will be influenced by the qualities of real parents and by the child's own feelings towards them. A stable sexual identity is based upon acknowledgement of one's gender, as well as identifying with both internalised parental figures performing their task of looking after the infantile self and joining together in creative ways. The child's experience of her own body is influenced by these identifications and reflected in her sense of physical security and physical movement, as well as in the themes of her play, dreams, and stories. Here are some remarks of Marie which illustrate her internal configurations:

> My mother isn't able to understand me. There is no point in talking to her, she just gets upset.

> My father is angry with me all the time, not with anyone else.

> My sister is a 'greedy pig'. She gets everything she wants.

> If I had to depend on my parents, I'd commit suicide.

Marie was explicit in showing that at that moment in time she was dominated by internal parental figures who could not be depended upon, who did not understand. She projected her own feelings into her 'angry' father, 'greedy' sister, and 'non-understanding', fragile mother. The parental figure takes little responsibility for potentially overwhelming feelings such as greed, jealousy, anger and the incapacity to understand feelings in herself. The child-part of the personality feels so antagonistic to the parental figures that she would prefer to manage without them rather than face the frustrations of depending on them. Perhaps most striking was the inability of Marie to face the problems of relying on her parents.

Marie was reliant on her own 'pseudo-autonomous' methods of taking care of herself. By this I mean she was reliant on controlling activities involving concrete activity such as dieting, counting calories and exercising, rather than relying on either her parents or an inner capacity to have empathy and tolerance for her own emotional experiences.

The psychotherapist needs to assess the severity of the self-protective structure represented by the child's belief: 'I can take care of myself through physical and emotional dieting or through bingeing.' The stronger this defence, the more likely that in the initial part of therapy there will be problems during separations and holidays. I have earlier highlighted how vital it is to have a supportive therapeutic team of parents and professionals.

Aims of psychotherapy and therapeutic method

A psychotherapist's task is in many ways similar to that of parents. For this reason, psychotherapy is not a mode of treatment in which children must have good verbal capacity or intelligence. Equivalents of the parent–child relationship include a focus on the child's inner and outer experiences, consistency of care, specific and defined boundaries, and acceptance of the child even when she is destructive or rejecting. Also, a reliable and regular framework of meetings allows the child to develop trust in the therapist.

In these meetings, the therapist needs to be attuned to the emotional experience of the child, to give meaning to her communications. This is similar to a mother using her own emotional experience, coupled with her thinking, to make sense of the baby's expressions of physical and emotional states. This is particularly important to remember for a child with an eating disorder who often lacks integration of her physical and psychological experiences (Winnicott, 1958). Because such lack of integration may be linked to a mismatch in communication in her primary experiences with her parents, a child with an eating disorder needs the therapist to consider her very early infantile experiences expressed in the child's demeanour, including sensations and movements of the body. The therapist must do this before the child can put her experiences into a symbolic form for communication. Only then can an integration of the physical and psychological self occur (Farrell, 1995).

Particularly at the beginning of therapy, the child often projects unbearable emotion and physical experiences on to the therapist before being able to feel, let alone verbalise, the experience. For example, hunger, nausea, tiredness, physical discomfort, anger and sadness may often be first experienced by the therapist. The therapist then uses her own physical and emotional experiences felt in the presence of a child to understand these projections. The essential therapeutic task is to share the entire experience of the child, empathising with as much of the child's inner feelings as she will allow. Rather than intruding with questions or comments to the child, it is often appropriate for the therapist to speak 'with the child's voice', suggesting that the child's non-verbal communication has been understood. For example:

> Marie was silent, face turned sideways with her hair hiding her eyes. She briefly glanced at me before retreating to look at the picture on my desk. I described the debate inside her: a debate about whether she talks with me or stays quietly alone. I also discussed how it seemed as if I were expecting something from her and that she had told me she didn't want to talk with me. 'Yes,' Marie said in a dismissive way. I said she spoke as though I really was a nuisance. I added, using a loud and angry intonation, as though I was speaking with Marie's voice, 'Things are all right. Let them be. Don't upset me by talking about something. It just causes problems.'
>
> Then Marie began talking about how the maths teacher always shouted at the children. Only later was she able to admit being angry with me. I described how Marie wished that I would simply listen to what she was saying and think about it. Then I commented on how she had experiences that she felt unable to put into words, and that she wished I could experience her depth of feeling without her having to put it all into words for me. Marie nodded affirmatively in response.

Healthy psychological development can be ensured only through the presence of an effective inner psychic structure, functioning as parents' understanding the emotions of a child and inspiring hope for the future. Through the therapist's work of bearing feelings and giving them meaning, the child can begin to experience being understood and accepted. This experience and further experiences of being helped in this way can then be internalised into the inner world of the child to form a resilient mental structure for transforming unbearable sensations into feelings suitable for thoughts. The structure is designed to 'hold in mind' these intense and/or unbearable loving, hating and conflictual feelings until thoughts about them can emerge.

Using dreams for initial and ongoing assessment

Regardless of their underlying difficulties, children with eating disorders tend to progress through similar phases of emotional development in the course of therapy. This is well illustrated by the dream life of the child, which functions as a kind of internal theatre with internal family figures entering into emotional relationships and conflicts with one another (Meltzer, 1987).

Stable developments and growth of inner strengths in the personality structure of the child are most reliably traced through assessing her dream structure and her emotional relationship to her dream experiences. At present, the study of psychic development as observed through the dream process is a poorly researched area, yet the dream and the child's relation to it potentially present one of the clearest pictures of the child's developing emotional capacities.

In the examples provided it will be clear that in an effective therapy there will be changes in both the child's attitude to her dreams and in the dream's content and structure. If the therapy is progressing well, the child will show a developing sense of responsibility for the feelings expressed in the dreams. One can view the dreams as unconscious thinking, equivalent to the action and play of young children. As the child discusses her dream, the therapist can focus on how the mind copes with emotional experiences and how it deals with the distortions formed by the conscious self during the day (Meltzer, 1983). The focus of the therapist's interpretative work is to help the child look once again at her relationship with the parental figures as re-enacted in the relationship with the therapist. There is a gradual demarcation between the infantile feelings of the child and more mature parts of the child's personality. Maturity is characterised by having responsibility for thinking about emotional experiences and a growing, loving concern and sense of responsibility for destructive feelings and actions. The phases of the eating disordered child's dream life reflecting psychic development seem to follow this sequence:

1   There is difficulty in remembering dreams and/or difficulty accepting they are meaningful. There is a sense of a rigid barrier between rational thoughts and the spontaneous expression of feelings. This should change during the course of a successful therapy of any theoretical orientation.

2   Dreams are described in which the child is overwhelmed with feelings that take over her sense of self. Examples might be:

> The child dreams that she is a Porsche. She has completely lost her own physical identity as she becomes an expensive racing car.
>
> Or
>
> The child awakens from dreaming that she is disintegrating while falling off a cliff.

3   Dreams are described in which the child uses 'pseudo-autonomy' as a means of caring for her distressed self. For example:

> When the therapist is ill, the child dreams that she is in a hospital with the therapist's face appearing and then disappearing. The child is then left in a room in which big, fat cats and rats, as well as black, furry monstrous creatures, are coming out from cages. She is terrified. She then pets a black creature and says: 'Isn't it nice!' She has turned to a part of herself which gives her protection, but this is a

false sense of safety, used to deny difficulties with separation from the nurturing therapist.

4   Dreams have more human figures in them and unwanted feelings of the child are projected into these figures so that they, rather than the child, become the owner of these feelings. Meanwhile, the self is experiencing a sense of hating, disowning, and/or being frightened of these feelings in others. The child, in describing the dream, has not yet begun to acknowledge these disowned parts of herself. For example:

> She dreams there is a teacher scolding all the other children in the class for being noisy and wanting too much attention.

5   Dreams are described in which the child projects her vulnerable feelings into others and, identifying with a parental figure, she takes care of her feelings located in others. At this point, the parental figure has developed the capacity for understanding and concern, but the child has not yet fully owned her dependent, vulnerable feelings located in 'the others needing care'. For example:

> She dreams that a baby is falling off a cliff, but she has adequate lifesaving equipment and is able to rescue the baby. She had previously reported the dream of falling off the cliff.

6   The dreams suggest a more open acknowledgement of feelings in the self, but they are still uncontained and often seem to be on the verge of being enacted in the child's external life. For example:

> She dreams of getting into her parents' bed with a boy and then having a huge feast prepared by her aunt. Here she is confused between the wishes for physical comfort, sexual intimacy and food. However, she has been able to dream rather than act out these confusions as she had in the past.

7   The dreams suggest that not only is the child more openly able to acknowledge her own feelings and locate them in herself, but also she is able to accept responsibility for her destructive feelings and show inklings of maternal concern both for herself and for her siblings. The feelings seem more contained, as though there is the possibility of thinking before acting on the feeling. For example:

> She dreams she is shouting at her mother while her mother is talking to one of the younger children in the family. Then she decides she can join in the conversation too. She doesn't need to interrupt it by shouting. Later she is playing on the beach with her baby sister.

8   In the dreams there is a fluctuation between dependence on parental functions in herself and the therapist (representing understanding parental figures) and the use of 'pseudo-autonomy'. For example:

> She dreams she is in a snowdrift. She is cold and being pushed down by the weight of the snow. She keeps going, but then she sees a light and she struggles to reach it. In this dream there is a hint that turning towards insight, in herself and in her therapist, might help her with the depression she feels as she acknowledges her loneliness.

9   In the dreams there is more frequent evidence of a developing capacity to acknowledge feelings, think about them and take responsibility for what they imply. There is a sense that the internal capacity to parent oneself, in identification with good parental figures, is being established. For example:

> She cries in the dream, feeling sad when she quarrelled fiercely with her mother. In speaking to the therapist about the dream, she realises that she has been feeling more kindly towards her mother and treating her with more consideration. As she talks about this dream she is able to show responsibility for the punitive way she handles arguments with her mother. She describes how she is trying to reach some resolution of the conflicts.

By the termination phase of therapy the child is able to move from the egocentric position of thinking only of her needs to a position of concern for her 'baby self' as well as her internal and external siblings and parental figures. In this stage of therapy there is a continual struggle between loving feelings and angry, jealous feelings. However, the loving feelings tend to dominate the child's relationships with others as well as her relationship with her 'baby self'. She no longer regularly treats her body or her feelings in a 'pseudo-autonomous' way, but rather she attempts to take seriously her emotional and physical needs. She is able to truly 'parent herself'.

The initial phase of therapy: the total transference

Although it is essential for the psychotherapist to continually evaluate not only internal psychic development but also ongoing external relationships with family, school and peers, the scope of this chapter is limited to describing psychotherapeutic progress and impediments to growth present in either therapist or child. These developments or impediments emerge and are understood through transference and countertransference communications present in dreams, drawings, verbal, and nonverbal communication during the various phases of therapy.

Although as a therapist I am filled with willingness to offer hope and understanding to Marie, she arrives being cajoled by her parents into coming to the eating disorder clinic. She feels 'too fat'. Her parents haven't told her she is too fat, but she is aware that there are girls thinner than her in the gymnastics class. She outwardly appears angry that she has been brought to the clinic, but I am aware that this anger conceals fear of intrusion by the entire inpatient and outpatient eating disorders team.

Psychodynamic psychotherapy is characterised by a focus upon the total transference of the child to the entire institution, rather than solely to the individual therapist. By this I mean that the whole of the child's current emotional response to the setting, staff, and institution procedures – such as physical examinations, weighing, and dietary advice – are gathered into the transference relationship to the therapist. In this context 'gathering into the transference relationship' (discussed earlier) implies that the psychotherapist holds herself as representative of all clinical activity in relation to the child and her family (Janssen, 1994). In gathering the transference with Marie it was also essential to look at her previous relationship with the paediatric unit where she had had an unsuccessful admission. While there she had been isolated from friends and the team attempted to offer social contact as rewards for eating, a task that she didn't accomplish and perhaps found impossible. This led to an increase of resentment towards both her parents and the hospital. 'The problem is that I am fat and my parents and the nurses want to make me fat,' said Marie.

Understanding her total transference to the institution meant understanding that Marie felt threatened by the whole pattern of treatment – the intrusions through physical examination, family therapy and refeeding in the inpatient unit, as well as the threat of intimacy and understanding provided by individual psychotherapy (Magagna, 1998). Marie desperately needed me to understand that her 'delusion of fatness' was a bodily experience, which felt terrible. She had 'fat', which she knew spoiled herself and needed to be controlled and eliminated. Marie also equated thinness with the possibility of feeling beautiful and being liked by friends rather than isolated at school.

Like many children with eating disorders, Marie did not fear getting tall. In fact, she wanted to be taller. I felt Marie equated tallness with an inner bone structure holding flesh. She also did not mind having hard bulging muscle because her flesh would be structured by the muscle. It was the 'fat' without any inner structure that bothered her and she feared we were all trying to make her 'fatter'.

Dreams in the initial phase of therapy

Marie brought several nightmares, typical of this first phase of therapy. These included the following:

> Marie awakens at night because of a nightmare consisting of a horde of people banging on a wall to come in. She sees a crack in the wall appearing as though they may be successful.

and

> In her nightmare, the shadow of a huge man is falling on the wall and she can hear footsteps as though he is about to enter her bedroom. Marie awakens and cannot get back to sleep.

These dreams suggest that Marie has a physical sensation of occupying a space that is being intruded upon by sinister, destructive forces or people. She depicts herself as being vulnerable and weak, while being devoid of any hostile emotions. There is a sense that she sees herself as good and the horde as a malevolent intrusion.

Countertransference issues and making an interpretation in relation to the total transference of the child

Marie is fixedly holding on to 'I am fat. The only problem is that the hospital wants to make me fatter and that makes me feel terrible.' As a therapist, I am wanting to share understanding of how I think the problem is much more complicated than simply 'feeling fat'. I believe that her repressed rage and anger at people closest to her for not being exactly as she wants them to be in relation to her creates a sense of being filled with internal parents who are damaged by her rage and anger. Her body, a woman's body, is identified with that of her mother's. Hence, she occupies a body that is damaged, not able to hold feelings or sensations in a manageable form and is therefore fat and lacking a solid internal structure. I also think that in her dream she has projected her destructive feelings on to the sinister invaders. I wonder if she has also been sexually or physically abused, since a significant number of children with eating difficulties have also experienced physical violence or sexual abuse. This needs to be addressed as soon as some trust emerges in relation to some member of the team. However, Marie is saying: 'The hospital wants to make me fatter.' My countertransference is that she needs help and I wish to help by lending further insight into the symbolic meaning of her dilemmas. But this would simply lead Marie to feel I am making her 'fatter', with more unmanageable feelings. At this point in the therapy I needed to step into Marie's position and see her through her own eyes. I realised stepping into her position and seeing myself and the hospital through Marie's eyes would involve inhibiting my countertransference wish to rescue or nurture Marie through providing insight beyond that which she had already shared with me. So I simply said to her, 'You feel you need to be in control. This control of fatness makes you feel safe. You feel you need to be in control of the situation here.'

'Yes,' said Marie. 'I write down every calorie that I eat.'

In this initial phase of therapy Marie could only bear to hear descriptions of the ways in which she tried to protect herself from feeling anxious. Originally, when I offered what I felt were more insightful interpretations, I felt that when they were rejected they were simply incorrect. However, when I see with Marie's eyes, I realise that in my therapeutic zeal I provided too much understanding that was simply threatening her 'pseudo-autonomy', which she needed to hold herself together. She needed to barricade her 'crying self', for she felt I was a threat to her safety. I am reminded that in the picture Marie drew (Figure 14.2) there is a big lock closing the door to her mother, as though her mother was a threat.

The main problem in the countertransference at this stage is that the therapist often feels rejected and constricted by the child's barricades against intimacy with her feelings and a dependent relationship on the therapist. Anger and frustration are often present as one gets rejected and imprisoned by the slowness of pace required to enable the child to develop trust in the dependability and thoughtful sensitivity of the therapist.

If a therapist needs to be liked by the patient and cannot tolerate the experience of being a bad persecutory figure, there is a tendency to 'split the transference'. This can lead to terrible acting out by the patient in relation to the inpatient staff and parents. This problem is more fully explored elsewhere (Magagna and Segal, 1990). Gathering the positive transference and allowing the negative transference to remain split off can occur for a variety of reasons. These include the following:

1   The therapist has too great a need to feel liked by the patient or vice versa.
2   Either due to a transference of a weak, damaged parental figure on to the therapist or because the therapist is not sufficiently strong, the patient feels the need to protect the therapist from her destructive feelings.
3   The patient is afraid of the therapist and afraid of what will happen if she is destructive to the therapist.
4   The therapist has not sufficiently integrated her own latent destructiveness and thus is blinded to the hostile, destructive aspects of the patient in the session.

Assessment of the patient for borderline psychotic features is particularly important before treatment emerges, for it is particularly with this kind of patient that split transferences can lead to severe treatment difficulties with even the most experienced psychotherapist, regardless of her theoretical approach.

When I hear stories of the patient giving presents to the therapist early in the treatment while giving hell to the inpatient staff or parents I become alarmed that the patient is latching on to the therapist in a very primitive 'skin-to-skin' way. This means that separation from the therapist leaves the patient feeling torn away, thrown away by the therapist. Many eating disorders can be rooted in early infantile rage about separations from the primary parental figure. A mother may be weaning the baby from the breast, having another baby, separating in order to have time for sleep, work, or another person, like the father. Rage about unmet needs, but also a possessive rage and panic about separation, are often some of the fundamental issues to be addressed in working with a child with an eating disorder.

In therapy the issue can be acted out by the patient who feels she has a good experience in the session with an idealised therapist but then goes out of the sessions with an internal image of a therapist who cruelly abandons her. During the interim between sessions, all inpatient staff or parents are then seen as representatives of the cruel therapist and are treated miserably by the patient. It is for this reason that any kind of regular therapy requires the therapist to fully prepare the child for separations and gather in the transference the variety of feelings about ends of sessions, holidays and the ending of the therapeutic work.

Gathering the transference in this way is necessary throughout therapy, not only in relation to crucial issues of separation, but also in relation to all the other themes the child brings in her stories. The therapist's task is to ask how the theme of the story may be relevant to the therapeutic relationship at that immediate moment in the session. For example, when Marie described how her mother always made her wait for 10 to 30 minutes to be collected after her gymnastic class, I became aware that I was being invited to identify with Marie and criticise her busy but thoughtless mother. (How much easier it is to identify with a child's grievance towards her mother, rather than oneself!) However, gathering the transference meant that I noted I was two minutes late for that day's session and she had had to wait three days since the previous session. I said, 'I seem a therapist who does not think of you, your waiting, when I arrive several minutes late, and walk by you in the unit, not offering you a session, but talking to the nurses instead.'

The transference interpretation is a primary method of psychodynamic work, but by no means the only one. I also wondered with Marie how she might talk more directly to her mother and also me. I tried to explore her anxieties about talking directly about a conflict she was experiencing. I noticed that repetitive discussions regarding food intake and weight control, needing to lose or gain weight, often occurred at the very moment Marie and I were talking about conflictual issues which really mattered to her. I silently noted that when you depend on another person and need them to be available, one of the worst things is that you cannot control them. That is the problem with depending on another person. On the other hand, food intake and weight gain can be controlled. Obsessional control of the body often occurred when Marie was most frustrated and hopeless about working out conflicts with an important person upon whom she depended.

Boredom in the countertransference often occurs when food issues are being examined yet again. I discovered that at times Marie existed only in the world of food and dieting with the recurring 'pseudo-autonomous' fantasy of being in control of 'a body'. This was how she emptied her mind of intense emotions and conflicts in relation to me, whom she could not completely control during the session. Gradually we jointly developed some way of describing how Marie safely went back to her attachment to 'food talk' as a method of moving away from something difficult. For example, on one occasion when we tried to explore together why the 'food talk' had emerged, Marie said, 'I tell you something insignificant and you make a mountain out of a molehill. You make my problems bigger than they were in the first place.'

Middle phase of therapy: complications in the integration of split-off personality aspects

... Let us pause from thinking and empty our mind. Let us stop the noise. In the silence let us listen to our heart. The heart which is buried alive. Let us be still and wait and listen carefully. A sound from the depth from below. A faint cry. A weak tapping. Distant muffled feelings from within. The cry for help. We shall rescue the entombed heart. We shall bring it to the surface, to the light and the air. We shall nurse it and listen respectfully to its story. The heart's story of pain and suffocation, of darkness and yearning. We shall help our feelings to live in the sun. Together again we shall find relief and joy.

Leunig (1990: 31–32)

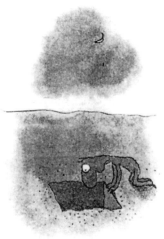

Figure 14.4 'Let us listen to our heart' (Leunig, 1990). Copyright © Michael Leunig, 1990. Reprinted with permission.

The middle phase of therapy is characterised by the child developing some trust in the capacity of the therapist to understand and accept her emotional experiences. The therapist's ability to do this is greatly influenced by her own willingness to remain emotionally alive to her own feelings and bear the psychic pain of accepting intuitive insights that the child consciously and unconsciously highlights in the therapist's personality. For example, Marie said, 'I have defeated a famous consultant and I will defeat you.' Here she was aware of how her exploration of her own motivation was interfered with by my anxious wish to facilitate a successful therapy.

A psychoanalytic psychotherapist is required to have an extensive personal therapy herself, to develop access, through dreaming and free associating, to both loving and destructive aspects of her personality and the capacity to integrate such parts of herself that may previously have been projected. Yet, however much psychotherapy a therapist has, there remain deeper conflicts and buried hurt (Figure 14.4), which can easily be projected into the child or simply split off from the central core of the therapist's personality. I believe that the need to repair this buried part of the personality and become what one truly can be is part of the unconscious motivation for people choosing to work psychotherapeutically with children having eating disorders.

The child's unconscious messages to the therapist provide the most penetratingly honest and helpful supervision to the therapist in facilitating repair of internal damage both in the child and in the therapist herself. The best psychotherapy is a 'duet for two' in which buried and undeveloped parts of both the child and the therapist's personality are resurrected through neurotic and psychotic transferences of the child. Healing becomes possible through the way in which the therapist with considerable patience listens carefully, works on her countertransference to the story of the child's story of pain and yearning (Leunig, 1990), and lends insight on the basis of understanding the countertransference. If the therapist does not develop in the course of being with a child in therapy it seems likely that the child will reach some kind of impasse in the therapy.

It is a fallacy to assume that I can truly change another human being. In any case, my primary psychotherapeutic aim is to modify my countertransference responses which ultimately inform all that I am and do with Marie. I shall now delineate some recurring experiences in the transference and countertransference that have initially created an impasse but, through work in the countertransference, have facilitated development of Marie's internal psychic structure.

Six recurring problems

I have already mentioned that the underlying nature of various eating disorders varies and reveals a multiplicity of pathological states of mind. Despite this, there are some common challenges in the middle phase of therapy with a child with an eating disorder. They are often present at different phases of the therapy, but it is in the middle phase of therapy, when the child has become more fully known to the therapist, that the underlying pattern can be seen more clearly. I shall illustrate these six challenges to therapeutic progress with clinical vignettes. The challenges include:

- silence
- hostility, fear and revenge
- rivalry
- obsessionality and intellectualisation
- eating difficulties forming part of the transference
- placatory external progress masking inner difficulties.

Silence

I have only twice had the experience of treating a child with an eating disorder without moments or hours of silence. There is always communication taking place between the child and the therapist, but when the child is silent the therapist is particularly impelled to understand the prevailing mood derived from the child's attitude to the therapist and the therapist's conscious and unconscious responses to the child (Magagna, 1996). If I, as a therapist, can be still and in the silence listen to what is going on deeply within myself in the presence of Marie, then there is no need for me to penetratingly question her (Leunig, 1990).

During Marie's silences I have always felt that she required some silent space, lasting three or four minutes. I have never felt that I should be quiet for longer than that. She needed to feel that I was able to continue to reflect on the relationship between us and wasn't completely controlled by her silences. If Marie arrived and was silent, I often reviewed our previous meeting aloud, trying to focus on ways in which she may have felt understood or not understood by me. I also looked at her experience of the ending of the previous session as well as how it may have affected the space between the sessions. Most importantly, I have needed to decide carefully whether or not I spoke directly to Marie, or whether she required that I spoke in the third person, wondering aloud, not looking at her directly, creating a stage to the side of her where I could explore the meaning of her emotions through a story or discussion with myself, with her choosing to listen or not listen. She needed to feel that therapy was not a recreation of being 'force-fed' by a controlling figure.

Because my countertransference responses to Marie's silence could seriously impede Marie's progress, it was essential to probe the depth of my own emotional response before venturing to speak. Outside the session, I would review the day in case my own issues or issues within the team were dominating and interfering with countertransference work of the therapy. If I did not monitor my own countertransference experience, I was unwittingly scripted into a counter-therapeutic role.

With Marie, it was useful during the silence to ask myself: Who is Marie being? What am I feeling? What am I supposed to be feeling in the role in which Marie has cast me? What is the meaning of Marie's drama into which I am being invited to participate? By using my countertransference responses, involving understanding Marie's feelings projected into me in the silence, I was able to give her the experience that unbearable feelings could be contained and thought about. Gradually she was able to give her own experiences a symbolic form, sometimes first in a drawing and then giving them a name. Only later was she able to consider them. There were three main problems in my countertransference responses when Marie was silent, as follows.

1   I could feel too hurt and despairing about my ineffectiveness as a therapist, forgetting that I needed to use that sense of ineffectiveness to understand Marie's inner experiences.

2   I could become overprotective, worrying that she wouldn't even come to the session if I didn't find some way of becoming just exactly the way she wanted me to be. This often stemmed from not sufficiently owning my hostile feelings and elaborating on them as part of what she was trying to communicate to me.

3   I could get angry that she was not speaking and making my work easier for me, thus allowing me to feel I was in a helpful therapeutic situation with her. My wish to be 'a good therapist' was dominating the need simply to try to help her understand her emotions and integrate them within her personality.

These countertransference experiences created an impasse in Marie's therapy until I could transform them through understanding. To expand on and illustrate these points, here are some vignettes of repeated countertransference and transference problems occurring between therapist and child in the silences. They include:

- overprotectiveness
- fear
- uselessness, rejection and despair
- need for primitive communication – heart-to-heart without words
- allowing separateness.

OVERPROTECTIVENESS

Marie arrived and was silent. She had missed the previous session without calling to let me know she was not coming. I decided to ask her delicately why she had not come to the session. Marie responded that sometimes she did not come because she had other engagements, while at other times she simply did not feel like coming. I didn't say any more. It seemed to me she didn't want to discuss the matter further. Her head was bent as though she was on the point of falling asleep and she did sleep momentarily. I remained quiet.

In this instance, I became too gentle and ineffective, overanxious about hurting Marie's feelings in the course of therapy. Further examination of the countertransference made me realise that my gentleness was a counterreaction to my anger that Marie never bothered to phone and cancel the session or phone after the session to explain why she hadn't come.

FEAR

The child's need for the protective armour of 'pseudo-autonomy' must be respected. For Marie, too much deep insight put too forcefully, or too 'emotionally intimate' interpretations, would often lead me to become frightening. Overcome and threatened by powerful feelings Marie would stop speaking as a way of protecting herself. She was holding herself together through silence. She didn't trust me. When I talked about her feeling that she had to have the protection of silence and I respected this silence, Marie would sometimes spontaneously speak: 'You are always acting as though you know what I feel', or 'I feel miserable.' But when I attempted to speak with too much comprehension of underlying feelings, Marie would say, 'I don't want to know about my feelings! I am sick of them!'

USELESSNESS, REJECTION AND DESPAIR

I have to admit that at times I am simply useless when I keep on saying the same old interpretation using the same imagery. It inspires neither curiosity nor interest in the child and certainly does not foster progress. But the child's silence is a real test of whether or not the therapist will accept projections of helplessness, inadequacy and rejection. I had to differentiate between Marie's powerful 'pseudo-autonomous self' actively attempting to reduce me to impotence by silent, supercilious contempt and another process when by rejecting me she was actually trying to communicate an unbearable experience of being rejected herself. How can one tell? Bodily language gives a partial clue, but it is only through the emotional tone in the silence, heard in the countertransference, that one can really tell. A different relationship, coloured by more loving, trusting feelings, needs to exist before there will be a projection of a painful sense of being rejected.

> After one silence lasting for over five minutes (during which I spoke part of the time), Marie told me that she really thought that I wouldn't have gone on a mid-term holiday just when she was worried about returning to school. She thought that was a clear indication that really I just cared about myself.

Here, the quality of Marie's silence made it obvious that she felt rejected by me.

NEED FOR PRIMITIVE COMMUNICATION – HEART-TO-HEART WITHOUT WORDS

> Marie was sitting in the waiting room with her mother. She had her back turned to her mother and her eyes brimmed with tears. When she came in she was silent. She sat with her legs dangling over the chair, in a slightly sideways position in relation to me. It seemed that

she was alive with painful emotions, not suggesting that I should keep out. In this situation I waited in silence.

Marie needed a safe quiet space before tears fell from her eyes. It was important for me to be there experiencing the depth of her feeling. I did not assume that crying meant sadness because it could hide a multiplicity of feelings. In fact, later when I described how tears could have so many meanings, Marie said she was sad because she was always angrily pushing her mother away even when she wanted her mother near her. She didn't understand why that was. I realised that this was also a common feature of our therapeutic relationship and later I mentioned this.

ALLOWING SEPARATENESS

Because of the seriousness of Marie's underlying emotional disturbance, sleeping difficulties and serious eating disorder, her mother and father had become more and more overprotective. At the time of her referral she was often either sleeping in her parents' bedroom or having one of the parents sleep near her bed in her room. Because of her own anxiety, mother watched her 'like a hawk' and when Marie was on the ward there were times that she required close supervision. Her enmeshed relationship with Marie had prompted mother to search her diary and drawers.

It was important for Marie, therefore, that therapy not be a re-creation of an intrusive relationship. She needed to know that I could be different from her and tolerate not knowing what she felt. Plying her with too many questions would also encourage her to be passive, waiting for me to take responsibility for the sessions. She might need to answer questions to please me, to allay my anxiety about her. I found that allowing some silence for a few minutes and exploring what I was wondering about, without a question-mark ending my sentence, was often a more helpful way to be working in the session. This allowed me to think about Marie's experiences without pressuring her to feed me her thoughts at that very moment.

Hostility, fear and revenge

Minuchin's aim of helping staff and parents to work together (Minuchin, Rosman, and Baker, 1978) to provide firm boundaries and rules for the child is suitable for many children with eating difficulties if compassion and sensitivity to the child's terror is present in the parents. However, I have discussed how the more vulnerable, helpless, chronically starved, or emotionally disturbed child may feel almost addicted to a 'pseudo-autonomous self' as a protection against an intense fear of losing a sense of herself. Without the firm psychic boundary provided by psychic manoeuvres of behaviours such as starving, dieting, exercising, vomiting and the use of laxatives, the child could feel as if she is exploding into fatness or 'falling into bits'.

When behavioural procedures, including staff supervision of exercising and vomiting, were prescribed for Marie, she responded by cutting her stomach at night, hurling abuse and hitting the staff. She also made an attempt to run away from the ward. It was easy to notice Marie's violence, but much more complicated for staff to maintain a containing emotional stance, experiencing not only her anger but also her extreme terror. Marie was terrified because her entire protective armour was being broken into. As a result she felt her sense of self was being destroyed by the regime that said she must eat and not vomit. In other words, Marie's feeling was that her 'pseudo-autonomous self', struggling like a soldier in a combat field, was being destroyed by external authoritarian controls and that nothing would be left of her. Death, or superficially cutting herself, seemed to be the last weapons to which she could resort to win the battle of who was in control. Her attempts to die or harm herself not only symbolised her sense of her self being destroyed, but also portrayed her view that death was a wonderful relief from the terror of psychic fragmentation.

When Marie hit out, it was easier to be in touch with her aggression rather than her terror. There was an enormous need for the team and her parents to unite and bear anger, despair, fear and other uncomfortable countertransference feelings. When we were not successful in doing this, our rage with Marie for making us virtually impotent to help her was redirected to other staff members and the parents.

In the therapy the focus was on Marie's collusion with her 'pseudo-autonomous self' – the self that was fighting us to stay alive as her 'bodyguard', but was actually cruelly taking away her life along with any hope in the staff and me. When I said this to Marie she responded, 'At last – it took long enough for somebody to see this.'

The 'pseudo-autonomous' self was felt by Marie to be her only protection until she developed an inner psychic structure that was more helpful to her. At the same time she was terrified that it was forcing her to lose a helpful rapport with me and the adults who were trying to help her. Aggressive encounters provoking the danger of revengeful responses from the staff and me were an exciting camouflage for this primitive terror of the death of her physical and emotional connectedness to life.

Rivalry

As the child settles into the group life of a ward, or develops a more dependent relationship with the therapist seen on an outpatient basis, rivalry with 'the other children' being treated by the therapist may propel her towards being 'the illest child'. Unlike school, where the teacher notices achievement, the child may feel that the therapist is only interested in problems and therefore the aim of being singled out by the therapist may consciously or unconsciously involve trying to cause the most worry and concern. This pathological need to be 'the illest' in competition with the other patients can lead to chronic difficulties, particularly when the child is an inpatient.

As the relationship with Marie developed, I became increasingly aware that, although I perceived her to be less depressed and to be experiencing more intimate relationships with friends and her family, she continually complained, 'Things are as bad as ever . . . I'm always a loner at school because no one likes me. I didn't do as well as the others on my school project . . . I am not ever able to talk to my mother as long as I would like because she is always busy.'

As I began to review the sessions in this context, I became aware that each time Marie noticed a child more ill than her, the intensity of her complaints about 'things being as bad as ever' tended to increase. One day, she laughed with embarrassment as she told me that while at the entrance to the newspaper shop she had 'accidentally' knocked over a younger, iller child whom she had previously seen with me. Marie then told me, 'It's your job . . . from morning till night. You have patients, one after the other . . . until you are fed up . . . I wonder what I should tell you to get you involved . . . so as not to bore you . . .'

I realised then that Marie had to be 'a very ill child' to keep me as worried about her as an outpatient as I had been when she was the newest and illest child admitted to the inpatient ward. She was continually consciously or unconsciously in competition with 'the others'. No matter how much better and livelier she felt, I was to know she was 'miserable'. This was done to maintain the position of 'the most important child', gaining most of my concern for her difficulties. She described it as her need 'stick to me like ivy'.

Obsessionality and intellectualisation

Obsessionality and intellectualising are used in lieu of having the capacity to regulate emotions and actions through thinking about one's emotional experiences. Control through dieting is used to stop eating impulsively, in an out-of-control way. Phobias of certain foods may be present along with excessive dieting. Accompanying these symptomatic behaviours are underlying fantasies which, when understood, lend meaning to problematic eating or vomiting patterns and the use of laxatives. The child's mind functions in a way similar to that of the child's eating style. When there is no adequate mental structure for 'digesting' intense emotions through lending thought to them and integrating them within the psyche, the child seems to be on a 'mental diet' in which she avoids getting emotionally near certain crucial issues. An instance of this is the fact of Marie's sexual abuse. It was clear that unless Marie had brought a particular dream, I might never have begun to talk about the sexual abuse by her older neighbour occurring over a two-year period. Marie said she felt too guilty to discuss that situation.

I also became aware that, in order 'to please me', Marie brought issues about her relationships with family members and dreams in which she knew I was interested because of the light they shed on her inner psychological situation. However, the reality was that once her feelings were more obvious to her, she resorted to being emotionally distant from what she was describing. Alternatively, she blunted the emotional relevance of what she was saying by running through a variety of topics without wanting to stop and think about what she was saying.

Cold intellectual control was used to protect her from a torch of burning emotions which threatened her equanimity. So, for example, she reported with great calmness how she had been in an argument with her father in which he had lost his temper, pushed his fist right near her face and said that he would bash it into pieces and throw her out of the house if she didn't start being more obedient to her mother. I was to imagine the scene and experience the feeling of terror and horror she regularly experienced at home.

Covering the heart through intellectualisation or obsessional control can be a necessary protection for a child to retain her sanity when she is overwhelmed by emotions which she cannot psychically contain. When I prematurely tried to look at Marie's emotional responses to her father, she simply spoke in a flat, detached way to me saying, 'I love him. This is the way he is and I have to accept that.' I learned from this that the child's fear of some internal catastrophe leads to a distancing of emotions by projection and 'intellectual control'. Until the inner structure of the child is ready to hold intense emotions, she can only gradually allow herself to be freed from the cover of cold intellectualisation. Meanwhile, the therapist must hold and explore the intensity of emotions within herself (Kennedy and Magagna, 1994).

Eating difficulties forming part of the transference

> If you spit in the air, it will fall on your face.
>
> (Midrash Rabbah, Ecclesiastes 7: 9)

I have already outlined 'the treatment frame' for psychotherapy and highlighted the role of parents who are usually asked to work together to help their child to eat. But it can often be easy for the therapist to forget that, in the course of treatment, changes in the child's eating difficulties are linked to the transference consisting of the developing relationship with the therapist, who is now representative of the child's internalised parents. My primary task as a therapist was to gather Marie's infantile feelings into the transference relationship with me and free her from some of the unmanageable intensity of feeling that interfered with her eating and psychological functioning. This was extremely important because Marie's mother would simply have felt too attacked and shattered if she had been on the receiving end of all Marie's feelings that had become liberated during her therapy.

A consequence of 'gathering feelings into the transference' is that the therapist has to accept the child's growing dependence on her as well as the brunt of the child's hostility. At times this involves the therapist feeling guilty at letting the child down. It is often difficult for therapists who have not had psychotherapy themselves to realise just how vulnerable the child is once she appreciates her relationship to the therapist.

In the first phase of her therapy, although Marie began eating with slightly less difficulty, she had days when she approached me as though the moment I opened my mouth I was going to scold her or make her feel terrible. Occasionally I had the sensation at times that my face was being transformed from Little Red Riding Hood's grandmother into the devouring wolf. There were days when the inpatient staff and later Marie's parents had to work strenuously to assist her to come to her therapy sessions. I had prepared them for the fact that 'terrible food' often gets transferred on to 'the terrible therapist' and that persecutory anxieties about food, now directed towards the therapist, could be understood in the therapy. But it was very uncomfortable to accept being transformed into a monster – very easy to believe that I was being viewed as bad because I was an intrusive, inadequate, unloving therapist.

I realise now how important it is for me, and new therapists in particular, to accept that although we do make therapeutic errors by not understanding or being too intrusive, part of the child's negativity invariably stems from the situation itself. The point made earlier that children with eating disorders tend not to choose therapy but are required to have it by their parents is significant here. In addition to this, some of the negative feelings once projected into the food are transferred into particularly the eyes, mouth and words of the therapist. Such words are equated with 'fattening food', making the child feel worse. The therapist's eyes are often felt to be sending rays of hate or depression into the child to shatter her. Understanding is felt to be like 'dieting' which becomes addictive, controlling the child's mind and taking it over, so understanding also becomes dangerous.

The thought that if you spit in the air it will fall on your face was helpful in describing Marie's transference relationship to me during the middle phase of therapy. Having made significant progress during the first term of therapy, I was shocked that during my first three-week holiday Marie lost several kilos. Later I realised that this is typical in the middle phase of therapy. When the child has developed a good therapeutic alliance with the therapist, however much the therapist discusses a change in the rhythm of sessions, the child's response to separation from the therapist is either consciously or unconsciously generally one of feeling unsupported and unloved. Marie said, 'You just don't care about me. I always try to make my best efforts to please you, but then with you, like with everyone else, things always end like this . . . in being rejected.' Her 'spitting on me' for leaving her created an image of my being a bad, uncaring therapist. This bad therapist was relocated in the food, which then became more noxious to her during the holiday, 'the spit falling on her face'. Hence she lost weight.

But it was not only a therapeutic holiday that could create a significant fluctuation in Marie's acceptance of food. When she was cross with me for saying 'the wrong thing' she would say, 'Right, I'm not going to eat now.' She would leave the session keeping her mouth closed to food for hours and sometimes longer. Just as mother's food is equated with mother, so too does emotional food eaten during the course of therapy become associated with the therapist representing the child's relationship to her internalised mother. I gradually became confident that if Marie felt adequately supported by me internally, she would attempt to eat food no matter how difficult her experiences were. In doing this, I felt she would be identifying with 'a good mother' who felt her child needed to eat, no matter how unhappy or lacking in hunger the child was. Certainly Marie's experience was that when she was filled up with anger or jealousy or unhappiness she both felt 'full up' and also that the food was 'horrible, tasting like cardboard'.

Gradually Marie and I developed 'a common metaphorical language' in which it was understood that her relationship with food was linked to her relationship with me, her therapist, representative of the 'parents-in-her-mind', the internalised parents. As we did this, I gradually stopped silently criticising the parents for not adequately helping her to eat when there were 'blips' and instead began understanding the meaning of her not eating. I now realise that Marie starved for many reasons including when she was angry with me. She starved to be in control of uncontrollable feelings experienced when outside the session, starved in identification with me starving her of therapy, starved instead of mourning the loss of different earlier developmental stages of our therapeutic relationship, starved because that was her routine way of facing a problem when I or a parent wasn't around to help her with an emotional conflict.

Placatory external progress masking inner difficulties

Attending the child's inner reality is so important for the child. I have seen many children who have eaten to get out of hospital as quickly as possible and free themselves from the eyes of the nurses. Their aim in getting out was to lose weight again. The book *Anorexics on Anorexia* gives many accounts of feeding programmes without psychotherapy, which leave the patients feeling like this: 'What really surprised and shocked me was the fact that the focus was on feeding me up to produce a change in my body, but never once did they take my mind into consideration. The way I was feeling did not seem important to them. I received very little in the way of counselling' (Shelley, 1997: 3). Although this may be partly a projection of the child's state of mind on to hospital staff, a treatment programme that does not have stated therapeutic aims beyond that of weight gain promotes a distorted picture of psychological development both to the children and their parents. Likewise, children can quickly work out what they feel is 'the right attitude' to get discharged from hospital. For those of us, parents or clinicians, who are prone to rely on the child's comment that 'My weight is right now, everything is fine, now I should stop therapy', it is essential to remember that this is but the surface. Before making a decision to end Marie's therapy I needed to understand her inner reality through listening 'with my heart' to her mood in describing her feelings. It was through the countertransference, accompanied by looking at her dreaming process, that I was able to ascertain both Marie's capacity to struggle with and ultimately integrate the destructive aspects of her personality, motivated by her love for others and for herself and also her capacity to bear rather than deny frustrations in the achievement of her personal goals.

When beginning work with Marie, I found myself unwittingly involved in the content of what she was saying about not wanting to eat, feeling everyone was controlling her, making her eat high calorie food, and so on. At that time it felt essential for me to have the support of a supervision group. The emotional support of this group facilitated listening with 'a third ear' to the emotional tone – a kind of accompanying music – in Marie's communication. This kind of listening then allowed me to begin to describe:

- how she was speaking
- how I felt before, during and after she was speaking
- what my feelings revealed about her current inner state, often projected into me.

Recognising a placatory tone and discussing it openly can often bring great relief to children in therapy. One creative way of exploring a countertransference sense of 'placatory pretence' on the part of the child has been shared with me by a supervisee (Neil, personal communication):

> I try to simply discuss the feeling of pretence directly with the child. On one occasion when I tried to explore this, the child said that the feeling was almost always there and that it spoiled everything for her. I suggested to her that the feeling of pretence might be linked to the angry feelings she tried to keep at bay. Using the image of a theatre set, I suggested to her that, every time 'Anger' sees 'enter stage right' in the script, the director (her) pushes 'Anger' stage left and buries it in a box behind the set. Other feelings come and go, but without 'Anger' the play is lacking. 'Upset' and 'Tearful' try hard to understudy but they are just not good enough. Not only that but 'Pretence' (who is really 'Anger' in disguise) insists on rubbishing everything else that goes on so the director, no matter how hard she tries, is left feeling awful inside. The child laughed at this, but I felt that she understood what I was getting at. She joked at the end of the session that she would think of ways of letting 'Anger' have a few lines now and then.

No matter how many years of experience as a therapist I have, it is necessary for me to continually notice a child's immediate response to my comment or interpretation, as did the therapist in the example. I say this because Marie's responses provided a means of ongoing supervision of my work with her. I could use her response to my words to answer questions as to whether my interpretation enabled her to feel:

- accepted rather than criticised?
- understood rather than penetrated with insight?
- interested in further exploration of her emotional life rather than in control, which prompts retreat to superficial intellectual levels or attack on my interpretations?

Working well together as a clinic team creates an emotional climate fostering a shift from intellectual exercises with the child to a mutual exploration of crucial issues. When the team is experiencing too much conflict, I find that either I or other team members can get stuck as therapists because our attempts to understand the child change to criticising the child and parents for various reasons, including 'not working' or 'not co-operating'. At these moments I realise that, just as parents sometimes direct unexpressed frustration on to the child, so too does the clinic team. Therapeutic impasses are quite likely to occur just at this time. When I or another therapist decide to discuss a session with a child in our small supervision group, we are frequently surprised by how just the thought of working together with colleagues in this helpful and supportive way promotes a shift in our relationship with the child so that strangely the next therapy session is 'not as stuck' as the previous one.

The ending phase of therapy

Termination of Marie's treatment reawakened old issues she had in relation to her parents. She had become dependent on the understanding provided in the twice-weekly therapy sessions. At the end of therapy there was the problem of her rage with me for not being 'an everlasting therapist', like her 'everlasting food machine', which she drew earlier in the therapy (Figure 14.5). In contrast to the therapist, the everlasting food machine can be a possession under Marie's control. She could choose when to take or reject food. But Marie's future stability was dependent on how she internalised the therapeutic relationship, a relationship never totally under her control. It would depend on how she continued the process of discovering and thinking about aspects of herself that emerged in her relationships by day and were portrayed in her relationships with internal figures in her dreams at night. I suggested to Marie that she continue an ongoing structured inner dialogue by self-analysis done through a journal written at intervals similar to her therapy sessions. This process assisted her mourning for the therapy space, which ultimately she had been able to use. Two follow-up sessions, at a time of her choice in the following several years, were part of the termination plan.

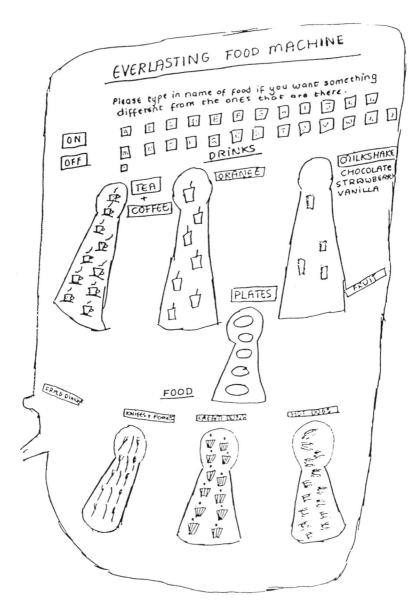

Figure 14.5 Picture of everlasting food machine.

Marie returned for a follow-up appointment some years later. She had maintained a healthy weight and was eating normally. Finding pleasure in her studies as well as her friendships, she was able to communicate much more openly both with her parents and her boyfriend. However, Marie said she was always aware of the pressure on women 'to be thin and beautiful'. I felt that Marie's therapy had been helpful to her.

Successful therapy involves the child taking responsibility for looking after herself while remaining intimately connected to others upon whom she depends. It involves the development of concern for the feelings of others. There is a frequency of dreams in which supportive figures are able to meet distress in others. For example, Marie had a dream that she was looking after a little girl who was crying. She also described the dreams discussed earlier. Most particularly though, a successful outcome in therapy involves forgiving the parents for not being 'perfect' but rather being human with frailties and problems of their own. However, it may also involve separating, at least temporarily, from parents whose problems grossly interfere with the child's psychological development.

Conclusion

Individual psychodynamic psychotherapy is costly in the short term because with a child with a severe eating disorder it is not something that can be successfully completed in six months. However, if the therapist and child are able to sustain a good therapeutic alliance to work through some of the child's central conflicts, psychotherapy provides a substantial base of security for the psychological well-being of the next generation of children. When a child leaves therapy I regularly ask myself: 'What kind of a parent will this child be?'

My therapeutic endeavours with Marie were to enable her to own rather than project parts of her personality and unresolved emotional conflicts on to her child. Without therapeutic help it would certainly be very difficult for Marie to bear the intensity of her own possessiveness, hostility and intense love in years to come. Left untreated, mothers who have suffered from AN of necessity can predominantly resort to denial of conflict and 'pseudo-autonomous' methods rather than containment of anxiety when raising their own children. So we then see another generation of difficult lives (Stein, 1994).

A good outcome for Marie, or any other boy or girl having psycho-dynamic psychotherapy, would be a realised capacity to become an adult able to deal both with her own love and hate and that of her children. Most important, though, is the development of a capacity for concern both for oneself and for others as well as forgiveness of the parents for not being 'perfect'. Through identifying with more healthy internal parents by the end of therapy the child is beginning to develop a good sense of self and self-esteem.

Summary points

The key issues addressed in this chapter are:

1   Recognising the inner world reality of children with eating disorders, which leads to acute emotional conflict and fierce protective defences against too much psychological pain.
2   Assessment and treatment of children within a psychodynamic psychotherapeutic framework.
3   The therapeutic use of the concepts of 'transference' and 'countertransference', both in their wide application to institutions and in their personal application to the working life of the individual therapist.
4   The role of dreams in understanding the development of the inner world of the child towards psychological health.
5   Some specific complications and impediments to growth during the beginning, middle and ending phases of psychotherapeutic treatment.

Acknowledgements

This is written with gratitude to the eating disordered children who have shared their dreams, drawings and feelings with me and to other colleagues who have shared their work for use in this chapter.

References

Brenman-Pick, I. (1985). Working through in the counter-transference. *International Journal of Psychoanalysis*, 66, 157–166.
Farrell, E. (1995). *Lost for words: The psychoanalysis of anorexia and bulimia*. London: Process Press.
Goodsitt, A. (1997). Eating disorders: A self-psychological perspective. In D. Garner and P. Garfinkel (Eds.), *Handbook of treatment for eating disorders* (2nd ed.). New York: Guilford Press.
Hinshelwood, R. (1994). *Clinical Klein*. London: Free Association Books.
Janssen, P. (1994). *Psychoanalytic therapy in the hospital setting*. London: Routledge.
Kennedy, R., and Magagna, J. (1994). The aftermath of murder. In S. Box, R. Copley, J. Magagna, and E. Moustaki Smilansky (Eds.), *Crisis at adolescence* (pp. 203–221). London: Jason Aronson.
Leunig, M. (1990). *A common prayer*. North Blackburn, Victoria, Australia: Collins Dove.
Magagna, J. (1996). Understanding the unspoken: Psychotherapy with children having severe eating disorders. In *Psychosomatic problems in children* (ACPP Occasional Paper No. 12). London.
Magagna, J. (1998). Psychodynamic psychotherapy in an in-patient setting. In J. Green and B. Jacobs (Eds.), *The child psychiatry inpatient unit* (pp. 124–143). London: Routledge.
Magagna, J., and Segal, B. (1990). L'attachement and les processus psychotiques chez un adolescente anorexique. In R. Broca (Ed.), *Psychoses and creation* (pp. 121–137). Seuil: Diffusion Navarin.

Meltzer, D. (1967). *The psychoanalytic process*. London: Heinemann.

Meltzer, D. (1983). *Dreamlife*. Strathclyde: Clunie Press.

Meltzer, D. (1987). *Studies in extended metapsychology*. Reading: Radavion Press.

Minuchin, S., Rosman, B., and Baker, L. (1978). *Psychosomatic families*. Cambridge, MA: Harvard University Press.

Money-Kyrle, R. (1978). Normal counter-transference and some of its deviations. In D. Meltzer and E. O'Shaughnessy (Eds.), *The collected papers of Roger Money-Kyrle* (pp. 330–342). Perth: Clunie (original work published 1956).

Palazzoli, M. (1974). *Self-starvation*. London: Jason Aronson.

Racker, H. (1974). *Transference and countertransference*. London: Hogarth Press.

Rey, H. (1994). Anorexia nervosa. In J. Magagna (Ed.), *Universals of psychoanalysis* (pp. 47–75). London: Free Association Books.

Rosenfeld, H. (1987). *Impasse and interpretation*. London: Tavistock Publications.

Shelley, R. (1997). *Anorexics on anorexia*. London: Jessica Kingsley.

Stein, A. (Producer). (1994). *Formerly anorectic mothers and their young children* (videotapes). London: Tavistock Clinic.

Winnicott, D. (1958). *Collected papers: Through paediatrics to psycho-analysis* (pp. 243–254). London: Tavistock Publications.

15 Physiotherapy and exercise

Morag Close

Introduction

Anorexia nervosa, bulimia nervosa and related eating disorders are complex illnesses involving physical, social and psychological factors. In no other disorder is the complicated interplay between biological and psychological as well as sociocultural factors expressed so conspicuously as in the genesis and maintenance of anorexia nervosa (Vandereycken, Depreitre, and Probst, 1987). In an attempt to resolve as many as possible of the problems associated with eating disorders, it is now widely accepted that treatment plans need to involve several different types of therapy. These therapies may include individual psychodynamic psychotherapy, cognitive therapy and family therapy. However, one therapy that is often ignored is physiotherapy. This chapter is written by a physiotherapist based in a specialist eating disorder service for adolescents. It is recognised, however, that the material covered will not only be relevant to other physiotherapists, but also to occupational therapists, nurses and anyone else working with eating disorder patients.

Anorexia nervosa, bulimia nervosa and related eating disorders are so body focused, with distorted body image, fear of fatness, preoccupation with body weight and shape and often excessive exercising that it is difficult to understand why it has taken so long for physiotherapy to be included in treatment plans. Physiotherapists are accustomed to using a holistic approach to treatment and include in their range of treatment skills, exercise and movement, relaxation, massage and breathing exercises. In childhood and early adolescence, eating disorders can pose particular problems for treatment as the child concerned may not have learned to use the language for describing emotions. Indeed, many of the features of anorexia nervosa can be seen as a manifestation of the difficulty in appropriate expressions of emotion. Yet most of the treatment available within an eating disorder service is verbally based. The nonverbal techniques of physiotherapy can successfully facilitate and reinforce the work being done by other members of the team.

The importance of dealing with the body experience (the thoughts and feelings a person has about being in their own body) and not just the mind is well recognised. For example, Vandereyken et al. (1987) have written about the need to focus explicitly (and not just verbally) upon the body experience of patients with anorexia nervosa. Beumont, Arthur, Russell, and Touyz (1994) have reported positive results for including an exercise component in the treatment plan for patients with eating disorders, which includes both progressive therapeutic movement and educational elements. Others have produced an activity protocol handbook (Thomas, and Markin, 1996/97). It is of note that therapists working independently in different parts of the world have felt it relevant and appropriate to develop essentially similar exercise programmes.

In an inpatient setting, the support from members of the multidisciplinary team and from the other patients plays an important part in making these treatment plans both acceptable and workable. Some of the ideas in this chapter, however, can be successfully adapted for use on an outpatient pro-gramme, but will in most cases require family support. Early involvement of a physiotherapist or exercise therapist might help to reduce the need for hospital admission in some individuals as a greater understanding of the actual needs and function of the body can be reached. Regardless of the setting, body-focused techniques can be of value in many of the eating disorders that affect children and adolescents.

Exercise

Excessive exercise and overactivity are common features of anorexia nervosa, especially the purging subtype, and may affect as many as 50 per cent or more of patients (Shroff et al., 2006). Those who do exercise excessively tend to maintain a lower weight, have been ill for longer and appear to stay ill for longer (Solenberger, 2001). Adolescents with AN tend to engage in excessive exercise in the year before the onset of their illness (Davis, Blackmore, Katzman, and Fox, 2005). By the time a child or adolescent is admitted to hospital these symptoms may have reached alarming proportions. Energy that should be channelled into linear growth, physical maturation and sustaining vital functions is lost in over-exercising. Many hours a day may be spent in the pursuit of thinness and much of this exercise may be done in secret. Children often set alarm clocks to get up early enough to complete exercise routines before anyone else is awake to notice what they are doing. This compulsion to exercise may have started as an attempt to lose weight but has spiralled out of control to become excessive. Any interruption to this covert routine will result in the child feeling the need to recommence the whole obsessive cycle. When prevented from exercising, anxiety levels rise alarmingly and all thoughts are concentrated on how to catch up and complete what is believed to be an essential routine.

Excessive exercising is less common in bulimia nervosa, in which there is more likely to be a history of chaotic exercising. They may over-exercise for days and then do nothing for weeks, resulting in feelings of guilt and failure. The other early onset eating disorders are not characterised by exercising.

Young people with eating disorders may have begun exercising in the pursuit of fitness and a healthy body, or for recreation or pleasure. This type of exercise often takes place with peers in a group situation, as in team sports, but as exercise becomes more demanding and compulsive it becomes concentrated into solitary activities, e.g. running or swimming, leading to social isolation. For some young people, exercising excessively may not only be aimed at losing weight but also acts as a defence against having to think about worries and fears. If the body is always on the move there is no time to think and uncomfortable and worrying thoughts can then be ignored. It may also be an attempt to try and leave something bad or distressing behind.

> Belinda, 13, was in the school running team. She found that when she was actually running she no longer worried about her home problems. As her difficulties there increased, so her running increased, until much of her day was spent either in running or planning on how she could run. If she was prevented from running she became increasingly agitated and distressed, not only because it gave her time to think, but also because she developed feelings of guilt about not being able to run.

Over-activity presents itself as restlessness, inability to sit still, aimless wandering and a constant need to maintain movement. If asked to sit, the patient will start rocking, or leg swinging, or constantly jiggling one part of the body. This seems to be most pronounced in the severely emaciated and a common pattern is that the activity level increases as the weight decreases (Beumont et al., 1994).

Physical problems that may develop with excessive exercise

There are many physical problems related to eating disorders, with many children and adolescents who are seen by eating disorder teams having serious medical complications. Any exercise additional to such normal activities of daily living as walking to the bathroom or climbing the stairs may be contra-indicated until the child is medically stable.

Local joint problems are common in those patients who exercise excessively. The weight-bearing joints, particularly the knees, are most often affected. Restricted range of movement, pain and swelling and occasionally hypermobility may occur. Untreated these can result in permanently damaged joints and early onset of osteoarthritis. The wasting of the muscles that support these joints results in a loss of the protective element of muscle control and can leave a joint more liable to serious ligamentous damage.

> Belinda, prior to admission to the eating disorder unit, had been

running for several hours each day, trying to run harder and faster each time. Both knees were swollen and tender to touch. They had restricted range of movement, with flexion deformities at rest, and both patellae were tethered.

Young people who include hundreds or, in some cases, thousands of sit-ups in daily routines may damage the skin over the spine. This type of damage, which can occur anywhere in the emaciated body that is subject to friction, e.g. toes or feet in running shoes, can develop into sores and ulceration. There is then a real danger of infection, not only locally but also systemically, as the weakened body struggles to cope with additional demands.

Options for treatment

The problems of excessive exercise and over-activity, with resultant body damage, need to be resolved and the body allowed to repair itself. Various suggestions may be considered:

- rest
- full activity, provided weight is gained steadily
- a prescribed exercise plan allowing an agreed amount of safe exercise.

As a method of restricting exercise, prescribed rest has many disadvantages. Total bed rest is only advocated for those patients with cardiovascular problems or other acute life-threatening symptoms. It is very difficult and time-consuming to enforce and may need 24-hour supervision as the patient still experiences an overwhelming need to exercise, despite her poor physical health.

Nursing staff are put in a particularly difficult position. On the one hand they are responsible for ensuring the child remains in bed, effectively policing activity, with the resultant battle of wills that this entails. On the other hand, they are trying to build up a supportive relationship and help the child overcome feelings of loss of control and dependence. For patients, it can be a time of acute anxiety as they worry about weight increase. Exercise may have been such an important part of their lives that its loss can be very traumatic. Exercise stimulates the release of endorphins and a subsequent 'feel-good factor'. This is similar to the 'high' produced by drugs and alcohol and to be totally deprived of it produces the same cravings and feelings of loss.

Osteoporosis is a real danger for patients with anorexia nervosa because of the loss of bone density. Bed-rest is followed by an efflux of calcium from the skeleton, which would further reduce bone mass (Rigotti, Nussbaum, Herzog, and Neer, 1984). Therefore, an early return to partial and then full weight-bearing exercise is advocated. The option of bed-rest should only be used if absolutely essential to stabilise a patient medically, and for as short a period as possible.

There are several disadvantages to the second choice of treatment – full activity. Until muscle bulk and strength have been increased to a satisfactory level, weight-bearing joints are unprotected. Excessive exercising can lead to damage to these joints with resultant osteoarthritic changes. Overload on bones with low mineral density can lead to stress fractures. Strain on the cardiovascular system may lead to serious medical complications. The energy being produced by increased food intake is being dispersed by excessive activity and not channelled towards repair and growth. Therefore, it takes much longer to regain a healthy weight. Too early a return to full activity can in this way prolong the time required to restore physical health.

The third option of a prescribed exercise plan is probably the most suitable in many cases. This is a plan of exercise, drawn up by the physiotherapist and patient together, and is aimed at strengthening and toning muscles as weight is regained, maintaining flexibility of joints and improving circulation. Muscles that have wasted because their bulk has been converted into energy will only be restored to normal size by exercise as well as food. People with eating disorders often seem to have an inaccurate understanding of how their bodies work and have become absorbed in common misconceptions about exercise, e.g. the need to do several hundred sit-ups each day to strengthen the abdominal muscles. It is by challenging these false beliefs and providing accurate information that intellectual ammunition can be reinforced to overcome irrational and illogical fears. Physiological changes that take place during the illness need to be explained and the patient requires help to accept the need for balance between energy input and output.

A prescribed exercise plan can of course be used with outpatients, provided parents or carers are willing and able to give sufficient support and supervision to make the plan workable.

Prescribed exercise plan

Each patient should have individual time with the physiotherapist on a regular basis, if possible about once a week. The exercise plan should be agreed and time arranged when a daily routine can be supervised. If the concept of working together is developed rather than that of being told what to do, a relationship built on trust can be established gradually, i.e. therapeutic alliance (see Chapter 9). The agreed exercise plan will depend on the weight and physical condition of the patient. Any joint problems should be assessed and suitable treatments applied, e.g. ice, support, ultra-sound, etc.

In many cases the exercise plan will start with non-weight-bearing exercises while lying or sitting. Static contractions of various muscle groups can help develop a better understanding of how a muscle works. This is done by actively tightening a muscle group without producing joint movement. The muscle is seen to change its form from soft to hard and back to soft again. Often a young person is confused and convinced that a muscle that is soft and relaxed is not muscle at all but fat. This is particularly true for the muscles of the back of the leg (the hamstrings), and the muscles on the inside of the thighs (the adductors). When sitting, the patient will avoid sitting back on the chair as this causes the hamstring muscles to spread out and the adductor muscles are loose and relaxed. This is interpreted by a young person with an eating disorder as having fat and flabby thighs. By being shown how a muscle can change from soft to hard and being helped to understand why this happens, patients can learn to accept their bodies more readily.

It is important to treat each person as an individual and allow a certain amount of controlled flexibility in the development of the exercise plan. This allows the patient to feel involved and means that particular personal concerns can be addressed. It is usual to start with the larger muscle groups – the thigh, hip, gluteal and abdominal muscles – as these are often the most wasted and are those that cause the most concern to the patient as bulk is being restored. These are the muscle groups that support the body in the upright position and relieve the stresses on the weight-bearing joints, so it is important that their strength is improved as soon as possible.

As physical improvements take place and strength is gradually restored, muscle control is regained and the non-weight-bearing exercises, e.g. straight-leg raises, knee rolls, etc., can be progressed to partial weight-bearing exercises. These can be performed sitting with the hands supporting some of the body weight, kneeling on all fours, or standing using a chair or wall for support. Such exercises involve gradual weight-bearing to the bones of the wrist, the hip and the spine, which are the areas that seem to suffer the most from low bone mineral density (BMD). Selective use of a static bicycle can be useful to strengthen thigh muscles and improve cardiovascular fitness. It is also a partial weight-bearing activity, but it needs to be well controlled lest it be misused.

Full weight-bearing exercises should be introduced when the patient is no longer in the wasting phase of the disorder. These should include strengthening, flexibility and aerobic exercises. Examples of these are:

- strengthening exercises – using resistance of gravity, body weight, or apparatus
- flexibility exercises – stretches in standing positions
- aerobic exercise – dance or similar low-impact activity.

Graded partial and full weight-bearing exercises are important to prevent bone loss and reduce the risk of osteoporosis. The prescribed exercise plan is useful, as it fulfils the patient's need to exercise in a safe and controlled manner and allows the body to repair and develop healthily.

Group activities

As well as individual time spent with the physiotherapist, group activity sessions can also be helpful. Young people with eating disorders are often self-absorbed and isolated. They tend to lose the ability to move freely and expressively and instead hold themselves in a tight, controlled way. Movement to music, including dance, is popular and can be used to encourage freedom of movement. Working with partners or in small groups can reintroduce communication by touch, a skill that has often been lost.

Team games allow the naturally competitive spirit to be expressed. Ball games help to improve co-ordination skills that may have been affected by muscle weakness. Childhood games such as Grandmother's Footsteps, Dead Lions, and Musical Statues need an element of control (positions have to be held in a 'frozen' mode), and are an enjoyable way of helping to develop a correct feeling for and interpretation of muscle state. 'Rhythmic Stabilisations' is a popular exercise for rebuilding trust and allowing proximity. Children work in pairs and one person puts her hands on the other's shoulders and tries to push or pull her out of position, while the other person resists the movement. It can be done with the eyes open and then closed. It helps to redevelop the proprioceptors of the joints (the sensory nerve endings which recognise position). This allows patients to know where their bodies are in space and to have a more accurate knowledge of their body shape. Most important of all is relearning how to have fun and enjoy physical sensations.

As freedom of movement returns and the understanding of how the body works increases, the need for periods of calm and stillness become more acceptable. Patients should be helped to realise that 'doing nothing' is not a negative state. It is a positive state in allowing the body to rest, repair if necessary and prepare for activity. When a healthy nutritional state is regained it is time to move away from 'exercise' towards more normal physical activities. Children and adolescents with eating disorders would normally be participating in sports at school or college and need to return to these. However, there is also a need to understand that when energy is expended it must be replaced. They can start learning how to achieve this balance during the recovery stages. Once they approach a healthy weight they can be encouraged to participate in such sports as swimming or playing badminton. This helps social interaction and overcomes the hurdle of doing things again in front of other people and of revealing their new shape to the world.

Young people often find it difficult to realise that ordinary activities like shopping, walking and dancing all demand energy. It is by gradually increasing activities and learning to adjust the diet accordingly that it is possible to understand the balance that must be achieved for a healthy weight to be maintained. When plans to resume other activities are being made, advice should be given to join group activities such as badminton, swimming with friends, hockey, football, or yoga, as these are less likely to become compulsive, rather than participating in solitary activities like running or working out in a gym. It may also be necessary to suggest that patients do not restart activities that have previously taken over their lives.

Body awareness

Low self-esteem is common in young people with eating disorders and is often accompanied by poor posture. Typically the shoulders are held hunched up and pulled forward. The head is often dropped down and the arms are held across the body, even when walking. This position often causes aching muscles, headaches, poor breathing patterns and constricted circulation. It also influences the way other people see the individual and, perhaps more importantly, how patients see themselves. It can reinforce the feelings of hopelessness and helplessness, and in some cases heighten the feelings of being a victim and unable to change anything. Improving a patient's presentation can be a positive step towards boosting self-esteem, but it does need to be handled sensitively or it might make matters worse by further eroding confidence. Giving support to a young person who is trying to make changes will produce better results than just demanding change.

The first approach can deal with the side effects of the slumped, hunched posture – the aches and pains. Once the problem areas have been identified, the patient can be shown how to change posture to relieve the symptoms and encouraged to do this regularly. The physiotherapist can indicate the changes that need to be made, using a mirror if she agrees. Exercises to strengthen the back and neck muscles can be included in the general exercise plan. Once confidence is returning, group sessions can be used to reinforce the individual work. It is important to remind patients that the way they carry themselves may well reflect the way they feel about themselves, but continuing with old habits may perpetuate the feelings of misery once they have moved on in other ways. By making simple changes, distressing symptoms can be relieved, confidence gradually restored and self-esteem improved.

> Hilary, 16, had a long history of anorexia nervosa. On admission to hospital she presented a picture of total despondency. When sitting, her head was held down so that her hair fell across her face, her shoulders were hunched and her arms held tightly across her body. During her physiotherapy sessions she learned upper body stretches and loosening exercises. Gradually, inch by inch, she was able to lift her head and put her hair back away from her face. Initially this was only possible for short periods and in the privacy of the physiotherapy room. As her mood improved and she regained some self-confidence, she was able to transfer these changes to the unit where she continued to improve with the support of the nursing staff and other patients.

Discussion on posture and body awareness often leads quite naturally to the changes that occur to the body during puberty. Many patients complain that they have 'never been this weight before' and that, as their clothes do not fit any more, this must mean that they are fat. Helping them to understand pubertal changes can ease the transition from emaciation to health.

Relaxation

Relaxation is more than a cessation of effort; rather, it is a positive change and refinement of activity (Keable, 1985). It is also a switch from an active to a rest mode of coping with stress (Stoyva and Anderson, 1982). Patients with eating disorders can find this concept difficult to grasp. For weeks, months or years they may have been coping with feelings of insecurity or fear by refusing to release their control over their bodies. The primitive fight and flight instinct is awakened as the body reacts to a perceived threat and this is reflected in the classic posture of tension with the head held down and forward, the shoulders hunched, the arms held flexed and close to the body and the fists clenched.

Under normal circumstances, once anxiety has passed, the muscles holding the tense posture relax and body tension is released. When anxiety is prolonged there is no release, tension mounts and the tense mode becomes 'normal'. Many patients with eating disorders have no concept or memory of how it feels to be relaxed. At stressful times they will curl up tightly. Even when sitting they will perch precariously on the edge of the chair unable to sit back and relax. Relaxation training assists by teaching how to recognise tension, helping to understand how tension can escalate and showing how to release tension as it develops.

There are two progressive physical relaxation techniques that focus on changing the body's response to stress. The Jacobson method (Jacobson, 1938) teaches systematic contraction and relaxation of those groups of muscles particularly affected by tension. Attention is then paid to the changes that occur with these actions, so that the difference between a muscle that is tight due to stress and one that is relaxed can be distinguished. This method seems to be more suited to those patients with bulimia nervosa. This is probably because they do not continuously hold their whole bodies in a rigid, controlled manner and can therefore recognise and feel muscle contraction followed by relaxation.

The Mitchell method of relaxation involves contracting those muscles acting as antagonists to muscles held tense by stress. This action results in reciprocal inhibition and decreases tension in tight muscle groups (Mitchell, 1977). For example, when the shoulder depressors are contracted, the shoulder elevators are released. Using this method to work through different joints, the body gradually changes from a position of stress – tight and closed – to a position of relaxation – loose and open. It is this method that seems to be most successful when working with patients with anorexia nervosa. Such patients often hold their bodies so rigid and 'closed' that it is impossible to elicit any further contraction in the muscle groups that are tense, but by contracting the opposite muscle groups reciprocal inhibition occurs and relaxation takes place.

Whichever method is used, the aim is to help the young person become aware of physical tension and develop some self-control in reducing it. These practical physical methods of relaxation can be easily explained and understood. They allow the patient to feel more in touch with the body and the changes that occur as tension rises. It is important, however, to start slowly and be sensitive to the difficulties in making changes. The old, seemingly comfortable and comforting ways are being put aside, but the new ways do not feel immediately safe. It may be some time before major change can be made.

Initially, it is probably better to teach relaxation in an individual session. The patient may find the 'letting go' quite frightening and needs to be able to stop if the feelings of loss of control become too great. Allowing her to choose a starting position that feels comfortable, e.g. curling up in a ball and covering with a blanket to reduce the feelings of vulnerability, may help to overcome some of the early resistance. At first, it may only be possible to work at reducing tension in one limb, e.g. the arm, or a part of a limb, e.g. the hand, but as trust is established and confidence returns it is usually possible to incorporate the whole body. It is important for the patient to understand that it is a skill that is being learned and that practice will be needed to improve, in the same way that it is necessary to practise riding a bicycle or playing a musical instrument.

Once the fear has abated, relaxation can be incorporated into group sessions. Slow, gentle, stretching exercises with appropriate music can start a relaxation session and may help to encourage those who are reluctant to participate. It is also helpful to try the relaxation techniques in different positions, e.g. lying and sitting. Once comfortable with their new skills, they can be encouraged to adapt the methods they have learned to use in particularly difficult situations. This can be done by focusing on relaxing those muscle groups that react most to tension, e.g. the shoulder elevators, the finger flexors and the muscles that clench the teeth. Releasing the tension in these muscles can significantly alter tension levels. It can also be seen as good training for the future, for school or college examinations, or a driving test.

Massage and touch

Touch, a very simple form of communication, is used in many ways in everyday life, e.g. shaking hands, putting an arm around someone, holding hands, or stroking. Patients with eating disorders have often become isolated within their families and the normal expressive touching between the family members may have been lost. Caring, reassuring touch for someone who is confused can make that person feel wanted and valued (Montague, 1971). Touch can be used as a form of communication to reach those who feel alienated or disturbed in order to help them understand their world (Pratt and Mason, 1981). Those who are confused and bewildered by what is happening to them and those who no longer understand the meaning of words have to rely on tactile and other forms of nonverbal communication (Poon, 1995). For some patients, however, particularly those who have been physically or sexually abused, touch has unpleasant connotations and may revive painful memories. It is particularly important, therefore, that therapeutic touch is presented in a sensitive way. It should be introduced in a calm, unhurried manner with respect for personal boundaries.

Tactile experiences can provide feelings of safety and assurance (Mason, 1985). Physiotherapists are privileged in being authorised to touch, not only in the form of treatment for specific ailments, but as a means of communication. For patients with eating disorders, massage can help to re-establish pathways of communication, release some of the tension they find so difficult to release themselves and help them become more positively aware of their bodies.

Before starting massage, a clear explanation of the planned treatment should be given, permission obtained to proceed and an understanding reached that it should stop whenever the patient so requests. Starting by working with a hand or a foot can be a way of introducing massage to a child or adolescent who is apprehensive or unsure about the treatment. As trust is developed, it is usually possible to include massage to the neck and shoulders to release the tension that is so often present there. Experience has shown that for those patients suffering from tension headaches, massage to the neck and shoulders followed by a forehead massage can bring great relief.

Some patients are reluctant to remove their clothes for massage and this problem can be overcome by covering the area to be treated with a towel and massaging over this. Hopefully, as they become more comfortable with the treatment, they can be encouraged to dispense with the towel and when they become confident enough to remove their clothing from the area to be massaged. Some enjoy massage with oils and taking part in the selection of those which are suitable for treatment.

During the massage, the therapist should be constantly alert to feedback, whether visual or verbal. Emotions may be suppressed and one of the mechanisms of suppression is muscle tension (Thornquist and Bunkan, 1991). Massage and relaxation can enable the patient to get in touch with deep feelings in the subconscious that need to be aired (Davison, 1995). The physiotherapist may not have the counselling skills necessary to deal with this, but by involving the other team members a way of working together can be evolved to the benefit of the patient.

Those patients who are initially the most withdrawn and hesitant in expressing themselves verbally often become the most responsive to the therapies of massage and touch. They have come to understand that touch can be pleasurable and that it can be used to communicate when words are difficult or impossible. Young patients have often been seen giving massage to anxious or distressed friends when together in an eating disorder unit.

Breathing exercises

Patients with eating disorders are usually very anxious, with high levels of body tension. They may have experienced panic attacks in the past or currently be experiencing them as a result of the additional stress of being in treatment for an eating disorder. Panic attacks are very frightening and distressing, both for the patient and for family and friends. The physiotherapist can explain the mechanics of a panic attack and then work with the patient to help her learn techniques to control it. A concise explanation of how tension and anxiety can affect the body should be given, with simple diagrams illustrating breathing patterns, if necessary. It is the breathing pattern that changes most as tension levels rise. Many patients have breathing rates that are two or three times faster than normal. The normal respiratory rate of 10 to 15 respirations a minute may increase to 25 to 35 per minute. This change has probably taken place over a period of weeks or months and because breathing is an automatic activity may not have been noticed.

Overbreathing, by eliminating too much carbon dioxide, results in respiratory alkalosis. This can produce many symptoms including palpitations, chest pain, dizziness, faintness, headache, numbness, pins and needles, excessive sighing, tremors, depersonalisation, sleep disturbance, sweating and lack of concentration. Many of these symptoms are familiar to patients with anorexia nervosa or related eating disorders. Once they understand that these symptoms are normal physical responses to an abnormal level of anxiety they can be helped to learn how to control them. There need to be both short- and long-term aims of treatment, and the patient needs to understand that it will take time and effort to make the necessary changes. The short-term aim, until a new breathing pattern is established, is to help patients recognise the situations that trigger the onset of symptoms and to teach them how to control their breathing at those times. The long-term aim is to decrease the breathing rate so allowing the carbon dioxide levels to rise and reduce respiratory alkalosis. This reduction in respiratory rate may take weeks or even months to achieve.

The patient should be seen alone and encouraged to listen to herself breathing. This can prove quite difficult and may result in breath-holding or the breathing of excessive volumes of air. With gentle encouragement, however, most people are able to do this. They then try to listen to the rhythm of their breathing. There are various ways of making this easier. Young children seem to like the idea of picturing the pendulum of a clock and identifying whether their breathing is like a cuckoo clock – very fast – or a grandfather clock – very slow – or somewhere between the two. Older children can use the idea of music rhythms to pick up their own breathing pattern and to feel comfortable with listening to it. Once they can do this they are asked to 'listen in' several times a day and to notice what causes change. As well as noticing the speed of their breathing, they are also asked to be aware of where they are breathing. They do this by putting one hand on the upper chest and the other hand on the abdomen, just below the ribs at the front. They can then feel the actual movement that is taking place. Once the habitual pattern of breathing has been established, it is possible to work towards change.

When learning to control breathing the patient is encouraged to recognise that the inspiratory phase of breathing is the active part of breathing. In this stage the young person learns to contract the diaphragm and to keep the work of the chest muscles to a minimum. This gives the feeling of the 'tummy' filling up with air and, if the hands are in place, pushing the lower hand up. In patients with eating disorders this needs to be carefully explained or they become distressed by seeing their 'tummies' becoming 'fat'. The expiratory phase of breathing is passive, with the diaphragm relaxing and the natural recoil in the lung tissue allowing the lungs to collapse down. It is this phase that seems to be the cause of most of the problems for patients. They may have been forcing the air out or not allowing complete relaxation of the lungs to take place, resulting in rapid expiration and a consequential excessive loss of carbon dioxide.

Susie was acutely anxious with a respiratory rate of 35 per minute. She was constantly pacing and when persuaded to sit was unable to keep still. Diaphragmatic breathing was started to help to reduce her anxiety levels. At first she found this difficult as she worried about her tummy looking fatter when she was breathing. Gradually, however, she was reassured and started to find the breathing control exercises helpful. She was able to slow her respiratory rate and as her anxiety levels started to fall she became less agitated and her need for constant activity reduced.

It may take some time before the change in breathing pattern feels comfortable and encouragement should be given to practise for short periods throughout the day until it becomes easier. Coloured stickers can be given to children to put in their rooms, or on their pencil cases or books to help them to remember to do this. New breathing patterns are easier to learn when lying down with the knees bent as this allows the most freedom for the diaphragm. However, it is often when sitting that the most stressful situations occur, e.g. mealtimes or in school, so the new breathing skills should also be practised sitting.

Once a smooth pattern of diaphragmatic inspiration, followed by a relaxed phase of expiration, is established, it is possible to slow further the breathing rate. A short pause, during which the patient consciously relaxes, follows the expiratory phase of breathing. The pause may be very short initially, but gradually lengthens as the patient becomes more confident. Some patients are eventually able to insert a further pause after the inspiratory phase and consequently lower even further their breathing rate. Regular practice is encouraged as this is the only way that permanent change will occur. Many patients find that these breathing control exercises, combined with the relaxation techniques, are very helpful if they are having trouble getting to sleep.

In the short term, the patients have to be reminded that they may still experience some of the symptoms brought on by hyperventilating. Until their new skills are established it may be difficult to control their breathing when anxious. At these times they should be encouraged to think about breathing 'slower and lower' until they regain control. Breathing exercises can be introduced into group relaxation sessions and it is often useful for young people to monitor each other's breathing patterns. This can lead to interesting discoveries about their own breathing and can be used in a positive way as they learn how to help each other when distressed. As patients with eating disorders become more sensitive to change in their bodies, they learn to recognise tension as it is developing. They can deal with it earlier and take control of it before it takes control of them.

Help at home

The family or carer of a young person with an eating disorder has a vital part to play in her continuing recovery. The work with the physiotherapist can be done on an outpatient or inpatient basis, but the family should be involved early, so that the techniques can be learned by parents. Support can then be given to the patient, both in practising new skills and in overcoming problems as they arise. Returning to school after a period of ill health can be a troublesome time; friendships have moved on and the feeling of being left out is quite common. Difficulty in concentrating and pressure to catch up can raise tension levels.

Time should be set aside on a daily basis to practise relaxation techniques and charts or diaries can help this to be organised. Avoiding activities that have previously become compulsive is advisable and new activities that might replace them should be carefully planned. Families that are very involved in sport and exercise may need help to understand how other less demanding activities can be beneficial, or how more of a balance can be maintained. Solitary activities should be avoided and family and friends encouraged to be supportive of this. A family trip to the swimming pool, rather than a solitary visit, is less likely to turn into compulsive length swimming.

Dancers present particular problems when looking for change. Many ballet schools require their dancers to be thin and some will only accept children with a weight–height ratio that is known to cause unwelcome and damaging changes to the body. The adult dance world is beginning to realise that low weight can produce more problems than advantages, and more attention is being focused on the importance of a healthy diet and a healthy body for dancers. This message should be conveyed to ballet and dance schools. Meanwhile, parents should be encouraged to consider a school's attitude on these matters when making decisions with their children about which school to attend.

Case studies

As a means of illustrating the use of the techniques described in this chapter, two case illustrations follow.

Case 1

Victoria, 14, was admitted to hospital following sudden rapid weight loss. She was unhappy at boarding school and admitted to worrying a lot. She loved sport including horse riding, skiing and all school team sports, but had also been exercising secretly and confessed to doing 2000 sit-ups each day. An exercise plan was drawn up with her and within a day or two of starting this she managed to stop doing her sit-ups. Massage was given to release the tension in her shoulder and neck muscles and the Mitchell method of relaxation taught to give her the skill to release the tension herself.

On admission, her breathing rate had been 24 per minute, so diaphragmatic breathing exercises were started. Three weeks later, as she started talking about some of her problems with her psychotherapist, her breathing rate escalated to 30 per minute and she felt increasingly restless and agitated. Massage was increased to twice a week, and she was helped to control and slow her breathing rate by using the diaphragmatic breathing she had been learning. Relaxation practice was agreed for a set time each day. Over the next two weeks she regained control of her breathing and was able to release tension before it overwhelmed her.

Once a healthy weight had been regained, physical activities were gradually reintroduced, and Victoria started horse riding for an hour each weekend. Through trial and error and lots of discussion about the need to balance energy output and input, Victoria realised and came to accept the need to increase her diet as she increased her level of activity. Prior to discharge from hospital she planned ways to do this when she returned to school and decided on times each day she could continue to practise her relaxation and breathing control exercises.

Case 2

Eileen, 14, was admitted to hospital with an 18-month history of anorexia nervosa. She had been exercising frantically in her bedroom and had become isolated from her peers. She admitted to being a worrier and suffered from tension headaches. Her posture indicated her inner tensions with her shoulders held up, her head held down and her arms wrapped tightly around her body. An exercise plan was agreed and, apart from some secret exercising soon after admission, Eileen was able to follow her plan. She was very quiet and rather isolated on the unit, often curling up and sucking her fingers. She was an inpatient for some months and always attended her physiotherapy sessions. She asked for and enjoyed massage to her neck, shoulders and head, and reported great relief from her tension headaches.

Eileen struggled with talking about her problems and was often withdrawn from the other young people on the unit. However, she appeared to draw strength from the nonverbal treatment of massage and therapeutic touch. She gradually became more involved in the movement sessions and at the end of these she could be seen to be less tense as she moved more freely and her posture improved. By the end of her stay she was joining in the football sessions with great enthusiasm.

Conclusion

Physiotherapy and controlled exercise can play an important part in the treatment of anorexia nervosa and related eating disorders. Together they aim at developing an awareness of the link between mind and body. Without this knowledge, it is difficult to see how a full understanding of an eating disorder can be achieved. Physiotherapy reinforces and complements in practical terms the work being done by other members of the team and can be both educational and supportive. To be successful, however, it needs to be presented as a positive aid to recovery, rather than a negative restriction on activity. The emphasis is on working with patients to help them recognise and interpret correctly their body experiences. With this knowledge, it is possible to work with them to solve some of the problems presented by their illness. As a greater awareness develops, they are able to work constructively to make the changes necessary to break out of the self-destructive cycle that has developed. This allows them to move on towards improving both physical and mental health.

Summary points

1 Physiotherapy, relaxation and exercise programmes play an important part in the management of early onset eating disorders.
2 The focus is on the body experience.
3 Communication can be both verbal and by touch.
4 The parents (and other family members) should be involved.

References

Beumont, P.J.V., Arthur, B., Russell, J.D., and Touyz, S.W. (1994). Excessive physical activity in dieting disorder patients: Proposals for a supervised exercise programme. *International Journal of Eating Disorders, 15*, 21–36.

Davis, C., Blackmore, E., Katzman, D., and Fox, J. (2005). Female adolescents with anorexia nervosa and their parents: A case control study of exercise attitudes and behaviours. *Psychological Medicine, 35*, 377–386.

Davison, K. (1995). Eating disorders. In T. Everitt, M. Dennis, and E. Ricketts (Eds.), *Physiotherapy in mental health* (p. 309). Oxford: Butterworth-Heinemann.

Jacobson, E. (1938). *Progressive relaxation: A physiological and clinical investigation of muscle states and their significance in psychology and medical practice* (2nd ed.). Chicago: University of Chicago Press.

Keable, D. (1985). Relaxation training techniques – a review – Part 1: What is relaxation? *British Journal of Occupational Therapy, 48* (4), 99–102.

Mason, A. (1985). Something to do with touch. *Physiotherapy, 71*, 167–169.

Mitchell, L. (1977). *Simple relaxation.* London: John Murray.

Montague, A.M. (1971). *Touching: The human significance of the skin.* London: Harper and Row.

Poon, K. (1995). Touch and handling. In T. Everitt, M. Dennis, and E. Ricketts (Eds.), *Physiotherapy in mental health* (p. 94). Oxford: Butterworth-Heinemann.

Pratt, J.W., and Mason, A. (1981). *The caring touch.* London: Heydon Press.

Rigotti, N.A., Nussbaum, S.R., Herzog, D.B., and Neer, R.M. (1984). Osteoporosis in women with anorexia nervosa. *New England Journal of Medicine, 265*, 601–660.

Shroff, H., Reba, L., Thornton, L., Tozzi, F., Klump, K., Berrettini, W., et al. (2006). Features associated with excessive exercising in women with eating disorders. *International Journal of Eating Disorders, 39*, 4.

Solenberger, S. (2001). Exercise and eating disorders: A 3 year inpatient hospital record analysis. *Eating Behaviours, 2*, 151–168.

Stoyva, J.M., and Anderson, C.D. (1982). A coping-rest model of relaxation and stress management. In L. Goldberger and S. Breznitz (Eds.), *The handbook of stress – theoretical and clinical aspects.* New York: Free Press.

Thomas, A.B., and Markin, D. (1996/97). *A proposed activity protocol for individuals recovering from eating disorders.* St Pauls Hospital, Vancouver. Unpublished manuscript.

Thornquist, E., and Bunkan, B.H. (1991). *What is psychomotor therapy?* Oslo: Norwegian University Press.

Vandereyken, W., Depreitre, L., and Probst, M. (1987). Body oriented therapy for anorexia nervosa patients. *American Journal of Psychotherapy, 41* (2), 252–259.

16 Schooling

Anna Tate

Introduction

Education and the school environment play an important part in the lives of all children, including those with eating disorders. Children and adolescents with anorexia nervosa tend to be particularly enthusiastic and conscientious about their schoolwork, whilst at the same time frequently suffering from unrecognised cognitive deficits (see Chapter 8) which means that they may have to work even harder than others to achieve at the same level. This makes the role of schooling of considerable relevance.

There is no stereotypical presentation in school for a child suffering from an eating disorder. Childhood onset eating disorders affect boys and girls from all socioeconomic groups and the full spectrum of intellectual ability including those with learning difficulties. School attainment varies according to personal circumstances and individual academic potential:

> Cameron, 15, with anorexia nervosa (AN), was not a high academic achiever but he was a good artist, a talented footballer and he enjoyed playing guitar in a rock band. Like his dad, he planned to pursue a career in the building trade.

> Michelle, 12, had specific learning difficulties in mathematics, spelling and reading, resulting from poor abstract reasoning and poor ability in the rapid processing, long-term storage and recall of visual information. These difficulties had been identified and were being well managed by her teachers until the onset of AN, when they were compounded by Michelle's low self-esteem, negative mood and sense of ineffectiveness. She began to compare herself unfavourably with peers even when producing good work, saying, for example, 'I can never be as good as other kids' and 'I do badly in subjects I used to be good in.'

In general children suffering from AN have good school attendance and continue to attend even after significant weight loss. They tend to be polite, compliant pupils who present no overt behavioural difficulties at school. They are often described by teachers and parents as being perfectionists and solitary children who have difficulty in relating to peers, working in groups and contributing in class discussions or as having become isolated from their peer group. They may also find it difficult to ask for and use help and support from teachers. Sometimes teachers describe them as vulnerable, shy and in need of being looked after.

In contrast to this, children suffering from bulimia nervosa (BN) tend to be less predictable, may be more challenging and may present with antisocial and risk-taking behaviours either in or out of school. Some may find the regularity of school attendance and the demands of school-work difficult to manage consistently and may take time off school and fall behind with their work. Others may be unable to regulate the amount of work they do in the same way that they are unable to regulate calorie intake:

> Geraldine, 16, was suffering from BN. Neither of her parents could care for her and she was entirely dependent on her own resource-fulness. She saw academic success as a means to gain control over her life but was unable to moderate the amount of time she spent on schoolwork, rising in the early hours to study when she had worked solidly throughout the previous evening. At the same time her sexually promiscuous behaviour jeopardised her chances of academic success.

Children suffering from BN may consume a great deal of teacher time and support, but if they are unable to be consistent they may be rejected by teachers as too needy, irresponsible and unreliable, or because they are considered to be an adverse influence on peers.

Children suffering from food avoidance emotional disorder (FAED) and some of those with other eating difficulties (see Chapter 4) may manifest school-phobic and refusal behaviours and may be selective about what they will or will not do in school:

> Stephen, 12, had poor school attendance because he was always tired due to extremely restricted food intake. He was actively avoid-ing both social contact with boys who frightened him because they were physically bigger and stronger than he was, and the maths lessons, which he found difficult and hated.

Some common features of eating disorders are not connected with food, weight or shape: alexithymia (an inability to put feelings into words); sensitivity; obsessionality; low self-esteem or self-hatred; perfectionism;

competitiveness and a denial of sexuality, are often present in children with eating disorders. Some children suffering from eating disorders are adept at concealing difficulties and the teacher may be unaware of any problem until it has become severe.

The struggle with control involved in any eating disorder, coupled with a lack of assertiveness and/or an inadequate sense of self-worth, can result in the child becoming increasingly secretive. She may be unable to sustain social interactions and become isolated at school. The denial of sexuality, both for those children who are sexually active as well as those who are not, may further separate the child from others, as children tend naturally to discuss, support one another and share developmental stages in the process of physical and psychological maturation.

Adolescent inpatients suffering from eating disorders may demonstrate an incapacity to mentalise (the ability to think about one's own and others' affective states and thereby separate one's own thoughts and feelings from those of others), a capacity necessary to function successfully in the social world (Allen, 2003; Wood and Lewer, 2004). Alexithymia and a poor capacity to mentalise tend to heighten and reinforce the child's sensitivity to personal criticism: the child may be unable to distinguish self-criticism from the opinions and feelings of peers and teaching staff.

This presentation can be very confusing to teachers, especially with respect to a competent, high-achieving pupil. Nunn's notion of emotional dysphasia (2001) provides a useful way of conceptualising the child's difficulty as a problem of processing and regulating emotional experience: of receiving accurately the feelings of others; of expressing personal feelings clearly; and of processing and regulating personal experience. The child may be unable to process accurately the emotional component of communications that take place as part of normal everyday school life and interactions including those inevitably embedded within the judgement of schoolwork. During the process of marking and feedback from the teacher, the pupil with an eating disorder may incorrectly receive praise as criticism.

An inability properly to process emotional communication, in the form of both verbal and nonverbal cues, can intensify an existing poor sense of self-worth into self-loathing and result in a powerful sense of shame. Shame is quite distinct from poor self-esteem and the pupil may feel utterly unworthy of support, comfort, attention and help from a teacher, acceptance by peers, or any form of recognition in terms of being competent or possessing skills, insight or knowledge.

In the pupil suffering from AN, an existing submissiveness can magnify to become a pronounced passivity. The pupil may frequently apologise unnecessarily. The teacher's view of the child as a polite, competent pupil may be at odds with the child's own view and neither might understand that the other has a different view:

> Claire, 16, apologised every time she was able to answer a question in class, when she asked to use a computer and when reporting back on having completed a set task. She would not enter a doorway before anyone else and sat separately from the group on an uncomfortable seat in a cold and draughty position.

In the pupil suffering from BN, this lack of self-worth can lead to a flight from reality into exciting and reckless behaviours. Teachers may confuse this avoidance and denial with carelessness and irresponsibility and may respond in a critical manner that confirms the child's poor self-worth. Clinical experience suggests that the pupil who experiences acute self-loathing may be craving for attention and recognition from others, which brings a further sense of shame for being needy and lacking in self-sufficiency. The pupil feels guilty for and unworthy of the attention that is craved.

Sometimes school grades are the only measure by which the pupil suffering from an eating disorder can quantify or gauge success and approval: a scenario of 'I am only as good as the grades I achieve'. However, it is important that children have more than one source of self-esteem and teachers can help achieve this by validating the child rather than simply validating the work the child produces; by noticing effort, encouraging and facilitating the expression of opinions as well as noticing and valuing the child's personal qualities and individual strengths.

Many children suffering from eating disorders put pressure on themselves to achieve the highest grades, even though they may have difficulty in believing that their work has merited the grade and, having done so, feel it is imperative to be awarded the same grade for all work. Thus children suffering from an eating disorder may experience school as more stressful than other children of a similar age and ability.

Self-pressure is a component of perfectionism and is also associated with obsessionality. Sometimes the seemingly mechanical and mindless copying out of work may provide for the pupil a means of blocking out intrusive thoughts including those concerned with eating. Sometimes it may indicate that the child is unable to tolerate mistakes. Feelings of envy, rivalry and competitiveness can also be components of perfectionism. The child may be unable to name, control or explain such feelings but may unconsciously act upon them: envy can be provoked by an overwhelming desire to be noticed, worthy and to be the best:

> On transferring to a school with a reputation for the highest academic achievement and social status, Cherry, 14, was anxious to be accepted. She single-mindedly tackled every aspect of school life with equal determination, academic work, sport and competitions. Cherry's driven desire for acknowledgement and success left her isolated and feeling rejected by peers.

It is important for teachers to understand that, whatever others may think, the child's subjective perception of her own performance may be very poor, and the experience of persistent hard work may carry no intrinsic rewards for the child. Indeed, the desire to be perfect can create an unobtainable goal. It may be in the pupil's best interests for the teacher to acknowledge the pupil's own poor judgement of her work and to differentiate this view from that of the teacher.

School provides a high degree of structure in a child's day. Some children suffering from BN may find it difficult to consistently sustain the routine and expectations of school. Those presenting with refusal behaviours may find school a threat as they will have less control over their environment:

> Judith, 14, would only eat two specific foods and had been consistently underweight prior to inpatient treatment. At school she had refused to participate in certain subjects and would not engage in any educational task that involved the word 'chocolate', including, for example, in the title of a novel.

However, schoolwork can represent what is known and what is dependable. It can be used as a prop by some children suffering from eating disorders to provide a sense of purpose in an otherwise confusing and chaotic life. The child may find comfort in using schoolwork as a distraction from painful feelings:

> Nell, 15, lived at home with her mother and brother. As a young, single parent, Nell's mother was busy with a full-time job and an active social life. During a period of inpatient treatment it was noted that Nell's mother was unreliable. She frequently cancelled appointments, changed agreed arrangements and arrived late when collecting Nell or returning her to the treatment setting. It was noted that when Nell's mother was late, she isolated herself from peers and got out her schoolwork. She could rely on the order that her school day provided through its timetable and on her teachers' commitment to the cycle of setting, marking and returning work.

The normality and distraction of schoolwork can also provide a sense of purpose in the life of a pupil who feels hopeless and suicidal. The irony of a child working towards examinations at the same time as expressing a wish to die indicates a fragment of hope in the face of total despair:

> Howard, 16, was admitted to hospital at 63 per cent weight for height suffering from AN. He needed to be nasogastrically fed and

he had no wish to live. However, he attended school voluntarily and insisted that the hospital teacher liased with his school so that he did not fall behind with his examination work.

Professional roles and boundaries

Frequently the concerns of teachers regarding a child suffering from an eating disorder appear minor, for example, poor eye contact, and go unreported. Consequently, it may be difficult to formulate a comprehensive picture of how the child is managing at school. It is usually helpful, once the child has come in contact with a clinical team, for a clear channel of communication to be established with the child's school via a designated member of school staff. The clinical team will need information about the child's cognitive ability, attainment, general health, attendance, friendships, experience of bullying, relationships with staff and behaviour in school. The school will require guidance regarding whether the child is at a safe weight to attend school and participate in the full range of school activities and also advice regarding how the school can best meet the holistic needs of the child. This degree of liaison is desirable for children receiving outpatient treatment as well as those returning to school following a period of inpatient care.

The clinical team will need to continue to liaise with the school representative, who will be responsible for disseminating relevant information and recommendations from school to the clinical team and vice versa. Good communication will establish a supportive framework in which the child works towards recovery. As stated previously, in school the child may be experiencing intense feelings of rivalry, guilt, anger, envy, anxiety, fear, greed, shame and hopelessness, but may be unable to put these feelings into words or distinguish personal feelings from the feelings of others. Consequently, the child may be unable to form appropriate attachments with others. She may inadvertently attempt to get her emotional needs met through a relationship with a teacher. Frequently, interactions with the child challenge the teacher's self-image and confidence:

> Sophie, 12, a high achiever, masked her inner feelings of worthlessness and presented as self-assured and haughty. Those around her, including teachers, often felt foolishly incompetent in her presence and wary of her because she appeared to be so superior. She was teased by peers for being a snob.

The child's feeling of worthlessness may thus be evoked in the teacher, without the teacher being aware that this is happening. Additionally, similar feelings of worthlessness may be evoked in the teacher, when relating to the child's parents. Sometimes this process can result in the teacher acting unprofessionally. The teacher may begin to feel an overwhelming sense of inadequacy in relating to and dealing with the child: feeling incompetent or unintelligent, as if not in charge of the subject matter being taught; or socially inept, gauche, unattractive, fat or unfashionable. Such feelings are likely to distance the teacher from the child and make it more difficult to communicate with her. The teacher may reduce contact with the child, giving less attention and appropriate support. In order to feel competent the teacher may try to impress the child with her own knowledge and expertise or unconsciously assume responsibilities for the child which are outside the professional role.

Alternatively, the teacher may develop a special, exclusive relationship with the child, perhaps believing that other staff are unable to relate to the child because they have less experience, insight or understanding. Having established the trust of the child, and possibly the parents, the teacher may feel in a more knowing and powerful position than other staff. Such feelings are likely to bring the teacher closer to the child. The teacher may begin to see the child as a victim, feel sorry for her and begin to act in an overprotective or inappropriately familiar manner. The hypersensitive child will notice any change in dynamics with the teacher, however subtle this may be. Reduced teacher contact is likely to confirm a child's sense of unworthiness and shame. Increased teacher interest may satisfy a desire to be special but may also intensify guilty feelings.

As a rule of thumb the teacher should avoid intimacy with the child, limiting physical comfort if the child is upset and not engaging in conversations about eating and weight. Teachers do not have the authority to insist that a child eats, or to supervise the child in the lavatory to check for purging or vomiting. Within professional role boundaries, teachers can support the child by providing clear expectations, limits, consistency and appropriate firmness, and by validating the child's strengths and capacity to cope. In this way the teacher will help the child to develop social skills and sources of self-esteem that are not entirely dependent on academic attainment. Furthermore the teacher can provide valuable feedback to parents and the treatment team.

The member of staff nominated by the school to liase around the treatment can help to ensure that professional boundaries are respected and that the roles and responsibilities in school are clearly defined and agreed between the school, the clinical team and the parents. Teachers who have had or who are suffering from an eating disorder may not be in the best position to accept responsibility for supporting a child with similar difficulties.

Education as part of a multidisciplinary assessment

The following questions can form part of an educational assessment in the clinical team both for children receiving inpatient and outpatient treatment:

1   Is the child anxious about work and/or relationships at school?
2   Does the child spend unnecessarily long periods of time on schoolwork at the expense of other age-appropriate and more sociable activities?
3   Does the child have regular work habits and patterns of attendance?
4   Does the child avoid any activities at school?
5   Is there undue pressure on the child to achieve and, if so, from whom?
6   Are any difficulties the child experiences understood by the parents and the school?
7   Is the school suitable to meet the child's educational and emotional needs?
8   What can the school do to meet the child's educational and emotional needs?

The team will need to compare the child's level of ability with the child's level of attainment to elicit whether the child is underachieving or striving to achieve, each a signal for concern. This information should be available from classroom-based assessments and previous test results. Psychometric assessment is in most cases not essential, but can be helpful in complex and puzzling situations:

> Samantha, 13, was underweight and failing to grow. Her attendance at school had dropped from 70 per cent to 52 per cent and many of these absences were unauthorised. Teachers thought that poor attendance was adversely affecting Samantha's general progress. Samantha's mother thought that she had learning difficulties and that the school was failing to meet Samantha's needs. Teachers from the treatment team felt unable to clarify Samantha's actual potential because she presented in class as immature and depressed.
>
> Psychometric tests indicated that Samantha's ability was in the average range although her depressed mood may have resulted in an underrepresentation of her actual capabilities. Her scores on literary tests were four to five years below her chronological age. This discrepancy was accounted for by a lack of consistent educational and environmental stimulation rather than by a specific learning difficulty.

In addition to information about attainment, attendance and social interactions, it is helpful to try to understand the quality and nature of the child's experiences at school in all the educational settings the child has known, including preschool settings, as well as the parents' hopes, expectations and concerns regarding their child's education. This can be obtained in a semi-structured interview with the parents and written up in the form of a report that is circulated to members of the clinical team and the parents.

A history of the child's educational experiences will help to reveal patterns of attachment and coping skills and will differentiate new behaviours from existing, well-established ones:

> It was discovered that Constance tried unsuccessfully to form intense, exclusive friendships with popular girls who preferred to be part of a wider friendship group. Her mother said that, prior to onset of her eating disorder at 13, Constance had been 'broken-hearted' when her desired friend had rejected her. Feeling 'special' following her parents' separation subsequently became an important theme in Constance's treatment.

A further issue that might emerge from a thorough assessment is the tendency for some children suffering from an eating disorder to become attached on the periphery of a group with whom the child appears to have little in common. This may be especially the case when group members possess attributes which the child finds attractive and desirable:

> April, 13, attached herself to a high-achieving group of confident and stylish girls, although she herself was completely unassertive and could only aspire to their fashionable dress and academic attainments.

Many children suffering from eating disorders have been the victims of bullying at school. Such experiences may predate onset, act as a trigger in onset or occur once pupils become aware that a peer is losing weight.

A child suffering from an eating disorder may be more vulnerable to risk-taking behaviours than other children of a similar age, ability and social background, including smoking, drug taking, sexual experience and rule breaking.

> Nora, 12, attached herself to an antisocial group who flouted conventional expectations and openly challenged authority at school. This group may have appeared particularly attractive to Nora, who could only turn her anger in against herself. Alternatively, the group may have confirmed Nora's sense of worthlessness and of being an outsider. Whatever the attraction, Nora began to take risks along with other members of this group.

Information elicited through the assessment process sometimes reveals that the parents have not tuned in sufficiently to such difficulties at school in time to offer support, or they have been worried about their child but not acted upon their concerns:

Lindsay identified with a group of 'boffins' who polarised themselves from other students because they wanted 'to get on'. Lindsay,
15, was not a high achiever but strove to achieve the same standard. Her father said that the boffins rejected Lindsay with withering
looks and under-the-breath remarks. Lindsay was particularly self-
conscious as she wore an orthodontic brace which caused her to
lisp. Tuning in to Lindsay's needs became an important focus for
work with her parents.

Parents often say how helpful it has been to piece together the whole story
of their child's education, especially as this process can increase understanding of the child's difficulties or identify a specific need that has previously
been missed in the anxiety of trying to manage:

Joe, 12, was 'a loner' throughout his early education and had not
contributed to oral work in class. He was slow to complete his work
and his parents said that on some days it was an achievement just
to get him into school. His parents were dreading Joe's transfer to
secondary school but Joe preferred his new school especially as,
for the first time, he had male teachers. He made friends but was
bullied for being small.

Information obtained during the initial educational assessment
interview indicated that Joe had a speech and language difficulty
and subsequent assessment for this resulted in specific strategies
that could be used in school. He began to make more significant
progress when given simple, concrete instructions and educational
tasks that were scaffolded, broken down into tasks with each
leading logically on to the next stage (Vygotsky, 1978).

The clinical team can use all the assessment information available to decide
whether the child is appropriately placed in a school setting. This would
ideally be one in which teachers work with the parents and the clinical team in
order to prioritise:

- enhancing the child's self-esteem
- facilitating and encouraging the child's interaction with peers and adults
  at school
- targeting ways in which the child can demonstrate strengths at school
- meeting the child's individual educational and emotional needs.

A school that has inflexible, rigid expectations, values academic achievements
over and above individual endeavour, actively encourages competition
between peers, requires pupils to be extremely independent of adult support

and does not prioritise the child's individual educational and emotional needs may hinder the child's recovery.

To avoid making unrealistic expectations and unmanageable plans it is helpful to be clear just what a school can reasonably offer a child suffering from an eating disorder. A school that cannot help is not necessarily a bad school but may be unsuitable for this particular child. In some circumstances a child may have to change schools; other children may be able to benefit from treatment interventions without any support from school.

How much school?

Retaining a link with school can be beneficial for the child even after having become quite seriously ill from an eating disorder. The child will have to cope with the demands of school life on recovery and the treatment plan can address the issues that will facilitate this while at the same time monitoring the child's capacity to cope at school during the crucial period of regaining and maintaining a healthy weight.

The main concern is often how to balance the child's physical safety with some normal, age-appropriate expectations. It may be necessary for the child receiving outpatient care to attend school on a part-time basis or to study at home on work set and marked by teachers. Limiting a child's attendance at school can be used positively to help the child, family and school staff accept the severe consequences of the eating disorder and the extent to which this may disrupt normal, everyday life. The clinical team will need to evaluate:

- the child's physical state to determine a safe level of activity
- the availability of adult supervision at home during the day
- the school's flexibility in supporting arrangements that meet the child's needs.

Clinicians, parents and teachers can then attempt to agree a school programme that meets the child's needs; the same plan would not work for all children. This plan should consider the family's capacity to cope at home as well as assessing the contribution the school can make.

Part-time school programmes can sometimes be designed to suit both the needs of the child and the availability of parents to provide supervision at home, for example:

- Attending only morning or afternoon school may provide a good opportunity for the child to eat lunch at home with proper parental supervision.
- Attending school only to pursue certain subjects may be relevant for adolescents preparing for examinations.

- If a parent works part time, attending school when the parent is at work may be more convenient for family life.

However, there will be occasions when parents are not able to supervise the child at home during the day or the school is unable to accommodate the particular needs of an individual child and at such times it will be necessary to compromise to produce the best arrangements possible.

Reintegration into school

For the child who has been too frail to attend school while receiving out-patient treatment and for the child preparing for discharge from inpatient care the prospect of a return to school may be daunting. The child may require help to think about how to explain a lengthy absence and support to cope with relationships and the workload. The teacher may need to consider how best to prepare the class for the return of its absent member and agree with the child and parents about what is said.

The pace of reintegration into school should be matched to the child's capacity to cope. Sometimes it is helpful for a member of the clinical team to visit the school as this can produce information not contained in reports, including insight into the child's daily physical environment, the size and layout of the school site and the number of stairs inside the building. For the child, a preliminary 'ice-breaking' visit is useful to re-establish a presence at school.

The child who wants to attend school may be sufficiently motivated to gain some weight in order to do so. Linking school attendance with healthy eating enables the child to justify weight gain by saying 'I had to put weight on so that I could go to school'. A pre-arranged reintegration plan linked with targeted weight gain involves the child in accepting some responsibility for weight gain and working steadily towards recovery. However, the same management may not work for those children who are anxious about losing support from the clinical team or for those who feel unworthy of having pleasurable experiences and who may find ways to sabotage these. For such children, the target may be to work towards connecting them with relevant peers and adults in the school community without linking school attendance to weight gain. Fluctuations in weight may need to be tolerated within a safe range.

Assigning a buddy who can act as a friend and support the child during the school day may help the integration process. The well-being of the buddy will need to be considered in addition to that of the child with the eating disorder. Many children have been drawn into hiding food and keeping secrets about the eating habits of those suffering from eating disorders. The buddy should have a teacher to turn to if the role becomes difficult, with the teacher monitoring the relationship in the best interests of both parties involved. The advantages of allocating a buddy usually outweigh any disadvantages. Basically, the buddy takes an interest in, gives support to and provides company for the child with an eating disorder. The buddy is likely to create social inter-actions that the child enjoys but may not initiate independently and the com-pany of a buddy can distract the child from drifting into an internal world dominated by thoughts about food.

The child will in most cases also require support in the form of regular, individual meetings with a teacher nominated for this purpose. Initially these should be scheduled meetings as the child may be unable to ask for attention or initiate contact. The predictability of regular meetings will help the child to feel connected to the teacher and more able to use the meeting. Once a relationship has been established, the meetings can take place less frequently and more spontaneously.

As a general rule, the greater the concern there is about the child at school, the more frequently the meetings should be held. The agenda may vary according to the needs of the child, but the teacher can encourage the child to talk about positive experiences at school in order to acknowledge and valid-ate strengths and the ability to cope, and can use ideas and support from colleagues within the school and treatment team to help the child develop strategies for dealing with difficulties.

The volume and content of schoolwork

It is surprising how many school subjects involve topics about body image, weight, food and eating. A modern foreign language usually contains a whole module about meals, eating out and buying food. Food technology, biology, anatomy, psychology and sport education involve units relating to calories, food intake, fitness and body image. This is the very subject matter that morbidly preoccupies the child suffering from an eating disorder. If school-work is to provide distraction and normalisation, then the content of the child's curriculum may require some monitoring.

The child may not be well enough to continue studying the entire curric-ulum even when attending school full time. Some children of low weight will experience concentration difficulties and may become anxious and less able to think and achieve. Others, fearful of falling behind, will increase the amount of time spent on schoolwork to the exclusion of other age-appropriate activities. It is most helpful when the responsible adults, parents, teachers and clinicians agree a manageable workload with the child and quantify this in terms of time and curriculum content. Some children will be motivated to gain weight by the harsh reality of a reduced curriculum. Others will be unable to think so coherently. Close adult supervision may be required to ensure that the child complies with agreed time limits and puts work aside or leaves it unfinished.

The child working temporarily at home will be completing work without supervision or support from a teacher. In these circumstances, teachers can help by avoiding repetitive, routine work and setting tasks involving creativ-ity, research, analysis and communication skills that require the child to think and express opinions. Targeting the child's strengths will help her gain confidence and increased self-esteem.

Examinations can act as a trigger in the onset of an eating disorder or can impose an additional stress that may hinder recovery. However, parents may be concerned about reducing the extent of their child's examination course work, fearing that she will fall behind and be in danger of having future life chances jeopardised. Withdrawing a child from examinations or restricting the number of subjects studied warrants careful consideration and each case will need to be decided individually. However, clinical experience suggests that reducing the number of subjects studied brings a corresponding increase in the child's ability to cope and succeed and may therefore be beneficial in the long term.

Parents' anxieties about school issues are sometimes easier for them to vocalise than concerns about the eating disorder. However, it is imperative that the child's healthy physical and psychological development is given priority over academic attainments, even when the child is studying for examinations. Clinicians will need to ensure that this is understood and respected by all concerned. What happens to the child in the future can be decided once the child's eating and weight have become more stable and of less concern.

How the school curriculum can help

Creative activities can provide the child with a positive outlet for self-expression. They can act as a counterbalance to the powerful destructiveness of self-starvation, initiate social interaction with others and facilitate communication without the necessity of speech. For example, dance can help the child to develop a more positive body image and provides a method of moderate exercise (Elliott, 1998). Yet the child suffering from an eating disorder may avoid creative subjects at school, opting for more academic studies, or may use creativity as another means to achieve, focusing on knowledge and technique rather than ideas and expression:

> Susan, 12, was very studious. She was an accomplished pianist but had only ever played classical music. When she played a popular hit song, she received spontaneous appreciation and the acceptance of her peers. The brief musical performance had conveyed the sense of fun Susan had been unable to show through verbal communication. She began to develop a new image and subsequently played electric guitar in a rock band.

Children suffering from eating disorders are often accomplished artists or good at drama or dance. They are perceptive observers of others and often extremely good mimics or cartoonists, with the ability to portray critically or humorously the mannerisms and characteristics of those around them. All these creative attributes attract the attention of peers and usually stimulate praise and admiration. The child suffering from an eating disorder may derive a real source of enjoyment and pride from such skills and may be able to accept the praise and acknowledgement for these apparently frivolous activities that they are unable to accept for more serious school tasks. Creative activities should not be confused with creative therapies such as art or music therapy, but such activities are therapeutic in their own right because they provide an outlet for self-expression and a method of communication. It is helpful when they are incorporated in class work or the community life of the school, for example, in the production of posters or a magazine, or in concerts, plays and performances.

Children suffering from eating disorders often sit in class working throughout the lesson without talking or being spoken to by anyone:

> Gareth, 12, suffering from FAED, was of very low weight but attended school regularly because he was under pressure from his father to achieve. He never spoke to anyone while he was there and would not ask for help from teachers even though he had considerable difficulty in coping with the work.

It is important for teachers to talk to children like Gareth in order to interrupt a self-enforced ostracism. This simple strategy might not occur to a busy teacher. Yet the teacher's lack of direct, individual attention and communication may reinforce the child's feeling of worthlessness. The task is to help the child find a voice: to offer an opinion and feel heard in order to make a contribution to the group. Talking directly to the child, for example once every 15 minutes, during the lesson will over time result in the child making spontaneous remarks. Moreover, actively seeking the opinion of the child and using the child's knowledge and expertise will gradually facilitate her assimilation into class discussions and eventually into the peer group.

Collaborative work with peers is beneficial to the child suffering from an eating disorder because it requires the ability to compromise as well as assertiveness and communication skills. These attributes are usually the very weaknesses of children suffering from eating disorders who therefore find it difficult to work co-operatively with other children and tend to take up a solitary role or work alone. The success of collaborative work in helping a child suffering from an eating disorder is dictated by the skill with which the teacher organises pairs and groups. This task has to be carefully considered in each individual case:

> Julia, 11, was intelligent but withdrawn and completed work without a flicker of emotion or interest. She was matched with Bridget,

also 11, a lively and sociable girl who found concentration difficult to sustain. She was interested in the work but not always able to understand it. This was a successful match. Bridget made Julia laugh and demonstrated a lot of care and concern for her feelings. Julia explained the work to Bridget, which increased her enthusiasm and energy for it. When the work was completed Bridget acted as a communication bridge between Julia and the class, which drew in Julia and made her part of the peer group.

An unsuccessful match was that of Isabel and Peter, both 14. Isabel made good contributions to class discussions but always chose to work alone. Her work was perfectly presented but the content did not correspond with the scholarly profile she assumed in class. Peter was unassertive but understood the work and needed to be allied with a confident partner. When working together, Isabel took control, completing the task without including Peter. It was as if she were a demonstrator and Peter a spectator. The teacher had to intervene to facilitate and supervise a more co-operative working relationship, challenging Isabel to seek Peter's opinion and share decision making with him, while challenging Peter to be assertive and demand a more active role in the shared tasks.

Talking to the 'silent' child and managing collaborative work in class are teaching strategies that complement treatment interventions because they will help counteract alexithymia and support the child in the process of developing the capacity to put feelings into words.

Self-evaluation involves the child in reflecting on personal performance as well as setting targets in school. Evaluation by peers involves classmates appraising the performance of a peer. These forms of evaluation are recognised as integral to good teaching because they have a positive influence on pupil self-esteem, social skills and pupil autonomy (Gipps, 1994). Self-evaluation is particularly helpful to the child suffering from an eating disorder because it requires the child to see herself as an object of her own thoughts and to verbalise perceptions of her own performance in relation to the requirements of the task, her own personal best and the performance of others, thereby facilitating the capacity to mentalise.

Personal target setting creates a cycle in which the pupil's success fosters increased motivation and can result in intrinsic satisfaction and a sense of personal achievement leading to a new target. The teacher may need to supervise the pupil's own target setting to ensure that the goals are appropriate, realistic and achievable, but the process of self-evaluation can enable the child to shift from a harshly self-critical position to one of beginning to acknowledge and enjoy success and progress.

Peer evaluation requires the child to hear the opinions and judgements of peers. This is particularly difficult for those with a poor capacity to mentalise but can be efficacious in facilitating the development of this capacity because it requires the child to see herself as others do. Furthermore, the child is involved in a process of giving feedback to others and communicating with them about a standard. Peers can successfully challenge the perfectionist's self-criticism and give work its due praise and admiration. The teacher should encourage the child with an eating disorder to listen to praise as well as criticism. If the child heeds the latter, she should also pay attention to the former.

Managing the child's feelings

Essentially the school is of greatest help to a child suffering from an eating disorder when the ethos is consistent with that of a therapeutic milieu (Hersov, 1994: 985):

> A structured environment that provides a variety of human relationships, satisfactory emotional interactions, opportunities for new learning and experiences, mastering of new situations and the development of personal and social competence. It should aim to meet the child's need for respect, appreciation, approval and praise, to reduce anxiety, guilt and psychological conflict. To strengthen existing competencies and develop new coping skills where possible.

School can be identified as a place where the child can 'take a break' from worries. The teacher can encourage and remind the child to set aside worries during the school day and 'take a break'. The aim is to help the child to contain worries but not bottle them up. The teacher might say 'You look a bit worried, I thought you were going to take a break from worrying during school time', acknowledging the child's feelings but implying that they can be managed.

It may help the child to have a worry book in school (Sharman, 1997). The worries are recorded either at a prescribed time or as the need arises and read later in the day with either a parent or designated professional, enabling teachers to focus on the child's coping strategies and strengths during the school day.

Teachers will sometimes unwittingly encourage perfectionist tendencies and praise pupils for meticulous, unblemished work. However, it is a painful irony that this praise does not appear to help the child suffering from an eating disorder to have a better self-image, but actually appears to reinforce the child's sense of inadequacy and/or the desire to produce perfect work. Challenging the child's criticism of the work can help her to tolerate mistakes, develop a more realistic attitude and accept both praise and criticism from the teacher. In order to give appropriate feedback, the teacher should listen to the child's self-criticism and aspirations and then engage in discussion about them. Instead of responding to the child's dissatisfaction by saying 'Don't be silly, this is excellent', the teacher can say 'What is it about your work that you don't like?', or 'What would you change to improve it? The teacher might openly disagree with the child, saying, for example, 'We have a different opinion about this, don't we?' Or the teacher might state the view that the pupil is not yet ready to give in work that contains mistakes. If there is a trusting relationship between them and the child seems strong enough, the teacher might begin to take in work as finished even when the pupil would like to do more to it. Some children can only learn to tolerate the idea that work is not perfect by the teacher taking control over when the work is finished.

These kinds of interaction separate the child as an individual, with feelings, standards and wishes, from the work, which is a product of knowledge, skill and effort. The child with a poor self-image may only find self-worth in academic achievements and may constantly strive for perfection in order to satisfy a need for approval from others. The child may see the schoolwork as significant whereas she, as a person, remains insignificant and worthless, or she may believe that adults are only interested in the work produced rather than the person who produced it. Challenging these misperceptions will enable the child to begin to verbalise feelings and develop a capacity to mentalise.

The child who has a history of severely low weight may seem locked in a hopeless cycle of disappointment and failure and it may be difficult for the teacher to establish a good relationship with such a child. The child may sabotage any progress by denigrating or destroying work or compare it unfavourably with that of peers. The teacher may not be able to remain positive in the face of such powerfully negative behaviour. In such circumstances, it will be imperative for the teacher to find a strength which that child possesses so that the child can use it to make a contribution to the class group:

> Kimberley, 13, had a five-year history of inpatient treatment for AN. She was too unwell to concentrate on age-appropriate academic work but rejected other work as babyish and, at the same time, was fiercely self-critical of her own inability to cope. Two interests gave her expertise in the peer group: her knowledge of pop music and her skill with make-up and nail varnish. These interests, and her talent for acting, were used to engage Kimberley and give her a role in the group. Insufficient in themselves to reverse her entrenched, poor self-image, they provided moments of fun and distraction, relief from the ordeal of her illness.

Any strategy aimed at managing the needs of a child suffering from an eating disorder will take time to be successful and will require faith, consistency and persistence from the teacher. Teachers should not be put off by apparent failure and should persevere with a positive belief that they will be successful and that the child will eventually respond. Nonetheless, at times, teachers are likely to feel powerless, frustrated and hopeless. When this happens, they should seek the support of colleagues in the school or clinical team to discuss, understand and control feelings which may otherwise interfere with the capacity to make objective decisions about the child's needs.

Working with inpatients

Children suffering from eating disorders who are admitted for inpatient treatment are likely to present with a wide variety of educational needs. At one end of the spectrum may be a child admitted to interrupt and reverse a pattern of weight loss. At the other end there may be children suffering from intractable conditions, those who have suicidal ideas or those suffering from pervasive refusal syndrome (PRS; see Chapter 4). Nonetheless the educational task is largely consistent with that for outpatients but the inpatient unit teaching team will have the benefit of easy access to the clinical team.

The education programme should be designed to be relevant and complementary to the treatment programme and is likely to vary in different treatment settings. At best it will provide opportunities for both individual learning and learning in groups and a balance between creative and academic educational activities. For planned short admissions and for children studying for examinations, the aim may be to provide as much continuity of education as circumstances allow. For longer, more open-ended admissions, the curriculum may need to support children through times when they are unable to function at a level commensurate with age and ability and keep them purposefully and constructively occupied until they are ready for more age-appropriate educational demands.

When children are discharged from hospital following a lengthy admission, their personal achievements are often negated or minimised by references to what they have missed. This is especially true of schoolwork. It may not be helpful if a child is expected to catch up and may be more appropriate to make a plan for the child that gives them a fresh start. Furthermore, the child's schoolwork completed during a hospital admission should be valued and celebrated as a part of their scholastic achievements and included in the child's portfolio of work or record of achievement.

Pervasive refusal syndrome: special considerations

Finally, a word about some special considerations relating to pervasive refusal syndrome (PRS). The child suffering from PRS is uniquely dependent on adults and requires particular consideration and management. She is most likely to require inpatient treatment. The teacher should have some expectations, however small, while at the same time carefully nurturing and protecting the child so that she feels safe and secure in the classroom. Recovery from PRS is very gradual.

Children suffering from PRS tend to be intelligent and observant. They continue to be aware of what is going on around them even when giving no indication that they are alert or interested. They should attend school but as they make no effort to look after themselves teachers must work cooperatively with nursing staff to ensure they receive proper physical care in the classroom. They should be placed in whatever position is most comfortable for them. Astrid, 13, lay on three beanbags because she could not sit in a chair. Their clothing should be properly adjusted so that it is not twisted or uncomfortable and does not leave them exposed and they should be neither too hot nor too cold.

Children with PRS require a programme in which they have some individual teacher attention, some attention from peers, some time working alone and some time when they are required to be a member of the group. The individual attention should be uninterrupted time when teachers can focus their undivided attention on the child, reading a story or doing an activity on behalf of the child, for example, making a bracelet with beads. At other times, peers can be encouraged to give attention, for example, by commentating on classroom activities or by describing and showing completed work.

It is important for children suffering from PRS to have time alone in the classroom without attention from teachers or peers. They can be given a choice either to have a break from the demands of individual or group work, or to listen to what is going on around them. Reports from children who have recovered from PRS suggest that they make good use of this time. Listening to what is going on around them has stimulated their interest in what is happening as well as in relating to particular children. Children suffering from PRS can be helped to feel part of the group by the way they are positioned in the classroom, being asked rhetorical questions, and when they are recovering being given a small task:

> Astrid loved dance. First she listened to the musical accompaniment, then watched with interest, then took part passively; she did not have to move but others danced around her. A breakthrough came in a session where dances were being made using the theme of fire. Astrid was lying on three beanbags, everyone was still, dramatically she flicked up her thumb, the flame that started the fire, and the group dance began.

Children suffering from PRS need face-savers. Their complete refusal is so dramatic that the smallest improvement is noticeable and likely to arouse a reaction from adults and children:

The first known, independent classroom activity, undertaken by Stephanie, 10, was when she made a house from Lego, but no one saw her do it. At the time, her teachers were placing a different activity in front of her at different times of the day. On this particular occasion it was a tray of Lego. Stephanie acknowledged that she had made the house and her teachers realised that she needed some privacy in which to begin to experiment with other activities. They ensured that everyday objects such as a bookstand and pencil pots were placed on the table to provide a shield behind which Stephanie could begin to work.

Conclusions

When assessing how the child with an eating disorder is coping in school, it should not just be learning that is taken into consideration. If school management complements treatment aims, school can play a role in enhancing the child's self-esteem, facilitating relationships with peers and encouraging contributions to group activities. The child with an eating disorder needs to 'find a voice' and a place in the school community. The experience of illness may create change: the child may make new friends and take up new interests. Teachers should work with parents and the clinical team so that school can make a positive contribution towards recovery and the future well-being of the child.

Summary points

1 School issues should be part of a multidisciplinary assessment and treatment programme.
2 The child's physical and psychological well-being should take precedence over academic success.
3 Effective communication systems need to be established between teachers and clinicians.
4 The school can play a positive role in the child's recovery when it aims to improve the child's self-esteem and encourages interaction between peers.
5 The child's curriculum may need to be modified, limiting the time spent on academic subjects in favour of creative activities.
6 Teachers may need support from clinicians in order to understand the best ways of helping children with eating disorders.

References

Allen, J.G. (2003). Mentalizing. *Bulletin of the Menninger Clinic*, *67* (2), 91–112.
Elliott, R. (1998). Creative dance and movement in child pyschiatry. *Clinical Child Psychology and Psychiatry*, *3* (2), 251–265.

Gipps, C. (1994). *Beyond testing: Towards a theory of educational assessment*. London: Falmer Press.

Hersov, L. (1994). Inpatient and day hospitals. In M. Rutter, E. Taylor, and L. Hersov (Eds.), *Child and adolescent psychiatry: Modern approaches* (3rd ed.). Oxford: Blackwell.

Nunn, K. (2001). In search of new wineskins: The phenomenology of anorexia nervosa not covered in DSM or ICD. *Clinical Child Psychology and Psychiatry, 6* (4), 489–503.

Sharman, W. (1997). *Children and adolescents with mental health problems*. London: Baillière Tindall.

Wood, D., and Lewer, L. (2004). *Affect regulation, mentalisation and the therapeutic milieu*. Paper presented at the Annual Meeting, Child and Adolescent Faculty, Royal College of Psychiatrists, Edinburgh, UK.

Vygotsky, L. S. (1978). *Mind in society. The development of higher psychological processes*. Cambridge, MA: Harvard University Press.

17 Ethical and legal issues

Anne Stewart and Jacinta Tan

Introduction

Management of eating disorders in children and adolescents is frequently complex, difficult and demanding. The physical, social and psychological consequences of the disorder can be serious, yet at the same time the young person may not acknowledge either the disorder or the need to have treatment. This poses difficult clinical and ethical dilemmas for both clinicians and parents. Initiating and maintaining a therapeutic alliance is clearly a key aspect to treatment. However, clinicians can feel overwhelmed by the difficulties they face in treating young people with eating disorders and may be unsure how best to proceed. The aim of this chapter is to clarify the dilemmas facing clinicians and families, and to provide a framework for an ethical approach to treatment that takes into account legal boundaries, clinical effectiveness and service issues.

The chapter begins with a summary of the UK National Institute for Health and Clinical Excellence (NICE) guidelines relevant to this area and the broad principles for treatment. Two case vignettes are then presented, illustrating a range of different dilemmas. A framework for understanding and resolving ethical dilemmas is put forward, making reference to relevant research. This includes a discussion of how to facilitate competence and healthy treatment decision making within service limitations. Finally, recommendations are made to enhance ethical practice within teams and develop effective collaboration with young people and families.

Summary of NICE guidelines regarding broad principles for good practice, compulsory treatment and confidentiality

A number of countries have now developed guidelines for management of eating disorders (e.g. American Psychiatric Association, 2006; NICE, 2004). The NICE guidelines[1] for eating disorders were developed in the United Kingdom following extensive review of the literature and appraisal of the best evidence available. They are intended to provide evidence-based guidance regarding the management of anorexia nervosa (AN), bulimia nervosa

(BN) and related presentations in individuals aged 8 years and over. The guidelines highlight a number of broad principles for good practice. These include the need to provide information to young people and families on aspects of eating disorders and their treatment, and the need to work collaboratively as far as possible. Building up a treatment alliance is emphasised as a cornerstone of treatment.

The guidelines also make specific reference to the issues of compulsory treatment and confidentiality. They state that where a young person is refusing treatment, consideration should be given to the use of mental health legislation or parental consent to enable treatment to take place. The guidelines state that parental consent should not be used indefinitely because this does not confer protection of the child's rights that are found in the use of formal legislation. Also, the legal basis under which treatment is given should be carefully recorded in the notes. If children or adolescents are refusing essential treatment, it is recommended that a second opinion is sought from an eating disorder specialist. Finally, if both a young person with anorexia and her parents are refusing treatment when this is clearly in her best interests, consideration should be given to the use of childcare legislation to override the parental decisions in the light of their difficulties in exercising their parental responsibilities. The NICE guidelines also state that young people's confidentiality should be respected wherever possible. Adopting these broad guidelines can enhance effective management of young people with eating disorders.

Case vignettes

Lucy, age 17

Lucy is a 17 year old with a two-year history of AN. She lives at home with her parents and younger siblings and developed eating problems following an increase of weight in puberty. At the time she was also experiencing bullying at school and the loss of a close friend who moved away. There is a family history of an eating disorder in her mother and severe depression in an aunt. She was referred to the outpatient department with her family and attended reluctantly, having to be brought by her parents.

On assessment, Lucy was found to be very low in weight, lacking in energy and suffering dizzy spells. Outpatient treatment was commenced, involving family therapy focusing on the eating problem, as well as supportive individual sessions. The initial focus was on building up a therapeutic alliance. Her parents were encouraged to help Lucy establish a regular meal plan and begin to put on weight. During an individual session, Lucy disclosed that she occasionally cut herself to relieve stress, but asked the therapist not to tell her parents.

Weight gain was slow. After three months of treatment Lucy's weight was much the same as when first seen. Her parents were encouraged to take a firmer approach at mealtimes. However, they found this very difficult and could not manage the conflict that arose. They asked if she could be admitted to hospital for further treatment. Lucy was adamant that she did not want to be admitted; she said that she would stop eating altogether if she was admitted to hospital. She said that she felt fine at the weight she was and that she just needed to be left alone to get on with her life. Her parents reported separately to the therapist that she was very unhappy at school, had not made any new friends and rarely went out.

The weeks went by and Lucy managed to stabilise her weight, however she failed to gain any weight. Meanwhile a bone scan showed very low bone density. Her parents were at a loss to know how they could help, and asked again if Lucy could be admitted to hospital. The therapist called a case conference involving Lucy, her parents, her schoolteacher and a member of the inpatient unit. The treatment team found it hard to agree on the way forward. On the one hand, her individual therapist felt that the main focus should be to continue to engage and motivate Lucy, whilst helping the family to continue taking care of her. The therapist felt that admission might damage the alliance that they were beginning to make. On the other hand, the inpatient team and family therapist were concerned about her deteriorating physical state and lack of progress and believed that she should be admitted for more intensive treatment.

Anna, age 13

Anna is a 13 year old who has had difficulties with eating since the age of 7. She was referred to Child and Adolescent Mental Health Service at the age of 11 and shortly after was admitted to an inpatient eating disorder unit where she required nasogastric feeding. She was discharged at her target weight and initially maintained her weight. However, over the next few months she gradually lost weight again and, despite intensive work by the outpatient team, her eating problems became entrenched once more.

She is an only child and much loved by both her parents. Early development milestones were normal but she had a history of selective eating as a child and there was some concern about her growth. There is no family history of eating disorders.

Anna's weight continued to decline and her physical state deteriorated. Her weight was now 70 per cent weight for height and she had a very low blood pressure and pulse rate. She was admitted voluntarily to another inpatient unit. There, she gained weight steadily. However, she was ambivalent about getting better and insisted that she should opt out of treatment and go home. At this stage she was no longer at a life-threatening stage, although staff felt that she would be likely to deteriorate again if she left hospital prematurely.

Anna's parents were very anxious not to lose her affection and were concerned about her long-term outcome and their ability to help her progress in their care. At the same time Anna did not want her parents involved in the treatment as she believed that family sessions were causing a deterioration in her relationship with them.

Ethical dilemmas arising from the vignettes

A range of ethical dilemmas arises in the treatment of young people with eating disorders, as illustrated by the cases of Lucy and Anna. Both Lucy and Anna are ambivalent about treatment, in common with many young people with eating disorders. As with most adolescents, they are struggling with issues of control and are reluctant to subject themselves to a treatment which they perceive takes away their control. In addition they are at a developmental stage when the impulse of the present moment, such as the drive to lose weight, is more important than a distant goal, such as the prospect of recovery. Although having an eating disorder may initially increase self-esteem, over time the young person may increasingly feel bad about herself and fail to develop a positive sense of identity. Giving up an eating disorder will be hard if there is no clear sense of an identity without the eating disorder.

Clinicians treating Lucy and Anna may experience a dilemma between allowing them to make their own decisions on the one hand or alternatively taking away their choice due to a desire to protect and treat. Their parents also may experience similar dilemmas. For Lucy and Anna to recover and remain in a healthy state, they need to be actively involved in their own treatment. But before that can happen they may need to be supported in a way that feels intrusive or controlling to them (Tan, Hope, Stewart, and Fitzpatrick, 2003c). It can be hard to know to what extent and how early in treatment the young person should be able to make treatment choices. It may be difficult to assess how competent the young person is to make choices, particularly when they appear intellectually able to rationalise, yet are making decisions that are clearly not in their interest. With Lucy, who is nearly 18, there may be pressure to allow her to make what she perceives as a lifestyle choice, as evinced by the 'pro-anorexic' movement (Charland, 2004; Udovitch, 2002). There have been debates about whether adult patients with AN should be allowed to refuse treatment even if death is the likely result, or offered palliative care as opposed to treatment aiming for recovery (Draper, 2000; Russon and Alison, 1998; Williams, Pieri, and Sims, 1998). Using compulsory treatment or more informal coercion raises ethical dilemmas regarding the rights of adolescents to choose. Moreover, compulsory admission can be carried out using different legal means and the clinician is faced with a difficult choice concerning which route to go down. Differences of opinion within the team may impair the treatment decision-making process. Finally, issues relating to confidentiality frequently emerge in treatment. Adolescents may wish to keep aspects of their treatment confidential, which raises a dilemma for clinicians who have to balance this wish with the need to keep parents adequately informed, particularly with younger patients. The issues affecting Anna and Lucy will be discussed in detail using the Four-Framework Grid, a theoretical tool that will now be described.

The Four-Framework Grid: a theoretical tool for considering ethical and legal issues in eating disorders

The authors have developed a theoretical tool for considering ethical and legal issues alongside the clinical context and resource issues called the 'Four-Framework Grid' (Tan, 2004; Tan and Stewart, 2003), shown in Figure 17.1. This tool provides an overview of the relevant issues to be

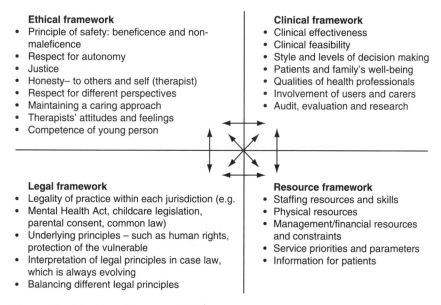

Ethical framework
- Principle of safety: beneficence and non-maleficence
- Respect for autonomy
- Justice
- Honesty– to others and self (therapist)
- Respect for different perspectives
- Maintaining a caring approach
- Therapists' attitudes and feelings
- Competence of young person

Clinical framework
- Clinical effectiveness
- Clinical feasibility
- Style and levels of decision making
- Patients and family's well-being
- Qualities of health professionals
- Involvement of users and carers
- Audit, evaluation and research

Legal framework
- Legality of practice within each jurisdiction (e.g.
- Mental Health Act, childcare legislation, parental consent, common law)
- Underlying principles – such as human rights, protection of the vulnerable
- Interpretation of legal principles in case law, which is always evolving
- Balancing different legal principles

Resource framework
- Staffing resources and skills
- Physical resources
- Management/financial resources and constraints
- Service priorities and parameters
- Information for patients

Figure 17.1 The Four-Framework Grid.

considered in working with any patient in the health-care setting, but is particularly applicable to young people with eating disorders. The four key areas in the grid concern the frameworks for the arenas of ethical, legal, clinical and resource issues. The content of each framework can be modified to suit each particular clinical context. The grid provides a structured way to consider each arena in turn while acknowledging the interaction between all the arenas. Each framework is discussed in turn.

Ethical framework

Central to this ethical framework is the consideration of Beauchamp and Childress' Four Principles (Beauchamp and Childress, 2001), namely: beneficence, non-maleficence, respect for autonomy and justice. Other relevant ethical principles include:

- being honest with the family, young person and oneself
- respecting the different perspectives of the patient and other family members
- maintaining a caring approach
- cultivating an awareness of one's own feelings and attitudes and working ethically within teams.

Finally, assessment and promotion of competence is also discussed within this framework.

Beneficence

Beneficence, the doing of good to the patient, involves ensuring the safety of the patient and prevention of adverse consequences of the illness. It is important, therefore, to determine the potential risk of the eating disorder. Physical assessment and investigation should be carried out to determine whether there is any immediate physical risk (indicated by rapid weight loss, collapse, bradycardia, exercise-induced chest pain, diminishing exercise tolerance, muscle weakness or low urine output) as well as the longer term risks, for example, reduced bone density. As well as consideration of physical risks, there needs to be assessment of psychiatric morbidity, including risk of suicide, as well as possible social and educational risks.

Alongside determination of risk and need for treatment, the beneficial effect of the proposed treatment needs to be ascertained. Unfortunately, there is to date relatively little published treatment outcome research in adolescent eating disorders (Wilson and Fairburn, 1993). However, the evidence basis there is should guide the clinician in formulating a treatment proposal that includes strategies with known beneficial effects, for example, involvement of the family within treatment (Eisler, Dare, Russell, Szmukler, Le Grange, and Dodge, 1997; Lock, Couturier, and Agras, 2006).

The relative lack of efficacy of current treatments means that it can be difficult to help a sizeable minority of patients to achieve good functioning, let alone full recovery. This raises the ethical issue of whether there is true benefit in engaging in strenuous attempts to deliver treatment where patients have longstanding illness with a long history of treatment attempts and a wish to refuse further treatment. Yet the research suggests that improvement and recovery can still occur after long periods of illness, which implies that it may be problematic to conceptualise AN as a permanent or terminal disorder for which the clinician should offer no further treatment. For children and adolescents, who in any case may have a better prognosis for recovery associated with early onset (Strober, Freeman, and Morrell, 1997), this suggests that there is always a potential benefit for treatment and an associated potential for recovery.

Non-maleficence

Non-maleficence is the avoidance of doing harm to the patient. Having assessed the risks of the eating disorder and determined the need for treatment, it is important to discuss with the young person and the family the potential harm of treatment as well as the benefits. As previously stated, there is limited research on treatment outcome. Moreover, research concerning the benefits or otherwise of inpatient treatment is almost non-existent. It has been suggested that there may be adverse consequences following this form of treatment (Gowers, Weetman, Shore, Hossain, and Elvins, 2000). These include individual aversive aspects of admission, lack of social contact, disruption of schooling and family life, as well as the experience of being controlled and reduced autonomy for the young person. These potential effects have to be taken into consideration before deciding whether to admit Anna or Lucy. The short-term benefits of improved physical state will have to be balanced against the possible harm of inpatient treatment. In addition, the long-term outcome of compulsory treatment is not really known, although short-term effects are generally good. Indeed, weight restoration can be lifesaving.

The lack of clear outcome research means that other factors, such as patient preference and clinical feasibility, need to be more prominent in the decision making. This especially applies when it is difficult to demonstrate benefit to the interventions, which may actually be harmful. Some clinicians believe that apart from issues of the deprivation of liberty, the use of compulsory treatment is harmful both to patients and to the therapeutic alliance (Rathner, 1998).

Autonomy

In the treatment of eating disorders a common dilemma is how to balance up respect for autonomy with the need to take care of the young person. We would argue that as well as autonomy being respected, it needs to be promoted and developed. Young people become autonomous if they grow up in a context of appropriate protection, opportunity to develop and explore choice and an experience of nurturing (Stewart, 2000). In the same way, the context of treatment for the young person with an eating disorder should ideally contain all these elements in order to promote the development of autonomy. In other words, the professional will need, wherever possible, to provide a combination of caring and boundaries, constantly being aware of the need for the young person to make choices. Thus the dilemma between care taking and autonomy can be reframed as the need for appropriate care taking and respect for autonomy. The skill for clinicians is working out where the balance needs to lie at any particular time. Making these dilemmas overt to the young person and family can be enormously helpful in steering a course away from the battleground of having to care for and protect versus respect for autonomy.

The autonomy of the family is another issue to be considered, particularly for younger adolescents, which is also framed as the right to family life as upheld in the Human Rights Act 1998.[2] Families often make decisions in groups and it is important that the integrity of the family unit should be respected where possible and appropriate, which also helps to support the young person while promoting his or her development of autonomy (Stewart, 2000; Tan, 2005).

Even if compulsory admission is being contemplated, with potential loss of autonomy, it is possible to relate to the young person in a way that promotes her autonomy. This can be done by taking time to listen to her views, to give information, and to carefully go through the risks and benefits of each option. The desire for confidentiality also raises important issues of autonomy. During the process of therapy Lucy disclosed issues regarding self-cutting that she wished to keep secret from her parents. This posed a dilemma for the therapist as to whether to override her wishes and inform her parents, or respect her desire for confidentiality. The NICE guidelines emphasise the important principle of confidentiality. However, this has to be balanced with the responsibility of parents and the need for them to be kept informed. In a situation where the young person is self-harming, the clinician needs to weigh up the respect for confidentiality with the safety of the young person and the adverse impact of maintaining secrets within the family. Thus the right to confidentiality, which is part of respecting autonomy, has to be balanced against considerations of non-maleficence, beneficence and protection.

Justice

Beauchamp and Childress (2001) suggest that justice has different aspects: distributive justice; respecting rights; respecting the rules of law; and reparative justice. In the current treatment environment of managed care or limited resources, there are dilemmas of how to engage in ethical practice with respect to meeting the needs of all patients, while working within constraints imposed by the relative scarcity of funding, scarcity of skills and time, and differential funding for different services or individuals. The consideration of compulsory treatment should also be done while bearing in mind issues of justice with respect to human rights, patient dignity and the rights of access for the patient, as well as those around her, to the appropriate treatment and support.

Honesty

It is important to be open with the patient and family about the limitations of the treatment proposed and the dilemmas concerning treatment. Being truthful can sometimes be painful for the young person and family, particularly if there is bad news about the consequences of the illness. Giving the information in manageable chunks, dealing with one's own fear of telling bad news, providing the right setting and supporting the young person and family can all be helpful. It is important to be aware that the manner in which we convey information may have a major impact on how the young person and family interpret this information.

Respect for different perspectives

It is important to listen to the perspectives of the young person, her parents, siblings, the general practitioner and others involved. Refusal of admission by the young person or parents may in fact be reasonable. The parents may be aware how difficult separation from home will be for their daughter and may prefer to continue with the treatment programme at home. Alternatively, the parents may be reluctant to agree to admission because of the difficulty in taking a decision that is counter to their daughter's wishes. If this is the case, they may need support to take this difficult decision.

Maintaining a caring approach

Throughout the process of treatment decision making, the relationship which the professional has with the young person is essential. A caring approach that respects the individual's views is important to patients and is likely to promote collaboration with treatment (Stewart and Tan, 2005).

Taking account of therapists' feelings/attitudes

Therapists may experience a wide range of emotional responses within the therapeutic context. These feelings may arise from previous experience or background or may be linked to their own confidence in dealing with eating disorders. Being faced with a stubborn young person who is refusing to eat and with a distraught family may evoke anger, distress, irritation and/or intense empathy in therapy. Indeed, patients with AN generate more anger, distress and feelings of helplessness in health professionals than other patients (Brotman, Stern, and Herzog, 1984). It is important for therapists to acknowledge the feelings that arise when treating eating disorders and be open about the impact of their own background and personality.

Being aware and taking account of therapist reactions and attitudes, rather than ignoring them, can illuminate the therapeutic process and also help the therapist to understand some of the feelings expressed by the parent, and to avoid punitive attitudes towards patients. Most patients with eating disorders are female and reflection on how gender of both the patient and the therapist might affect the treatment process is also important.

Treatment is often long term and some therapists are at risk from burnout or overinvolvement with families. Therapists need to be aware of powerful countertransference feelings that may arise and ensure that they have regular supervision in order to remain effective in therapy, tailoring their involvement to what is helpful to the young person and family.

Developing ethical practice within teams

Treatment of eating disorders should involve teamwork. Relationships within and between treatment teams can become difficult, particularly if the young person poses a high risk (Jarman, Smith, and Walsh, 1997) and differences of opinion can exacerbate splits within the family. Developing an ethical way of working within teams can facilitate effective and efficient clinical work. There are a number of ways in which teams can do this (see Figure 17.2). Developing a shared reflectiveness about the work, including an awareness of one's own motivation and values, is important, as is being up to date on the evidence for the different treatment approaches and being aware of the relevant legal boundaries. It is important for team members to respect each other's views and engage in a collaborative approach regarding decision making with each other as well as with the family and young person. Being open about the dilemmas within the team in balancing competing principles and frameworks can also be very helpful for the family.

Competence of the young person to make a choice

Whether or not a young person is competent to make her own choice about treatment has to be considered. Confusingly, there are two different terms

- Being reflective about the work.
- Awareness of team members' motivation and values.
- Knowledge of recent literature on effectiveness.
- Awareness of relevant legal boundaries.
- Respect for each other's views.
- Collaborative approach regarding decision making.
- Openness about the dilemmas in weighing up competing principles and frameworks.

Figure 17.2 Ethical practice within teams.

that are frequently used interchangeably – 'capacity', and 'competence' – usage also varies between countries (Tan and Jones, 2001). In the UK, 'capacity' tends to refer to the legal concept of the ability to make treatment decisions, the criteria of which are laid down in case law and statute law. 'Competence' tends to refer to a looser clinical notion of this ability. This is the usage that we will employ here. 'Capacity' has various definitions in the law of different countries, but generally encompasses the ability to understand treatment information, process this information to arrive at a choice, and to communicate the choice. 'Competence', in contrast, is poorly defined, but many clinicians would consider additional factors such as consistency of a decision over time, the impact of mental disorders such as depression, the basis of relevant beliefs (for instance, whether they are grounded in delusions), and the ability to apply information to the self (Grisso and Appelbaum, 1998).

Weithorn and Campbell (1982) found that the criteria for capacity, which are largely intellectual in nature, were fully satisfied to adult standards by the age of 14 and with simplified information by the age of 9 years. Young people with eating disorders should be encouraged to make their own decisions where possible. The key components of competence are: understanding the relevant information; appreciating the situation as it relates to them; being able to weigh up the information; coming to a rational decision; and communicating choice (Grisso and Appelbaum, 1998). Competence in young people with eating disorders may be hard to assess. The young person may be intellectually able to make a choice. However, the eating disorder may be affecting their value system or identity in a way that compromises their ability to make informed choices (Tan, Hope, and Stewart, 2003a, 2003b). This needs to be taken into account in assessing whether a young person is able to make her own treatment decisions.

There are a number of factors that facilitate competence and healthy treatment decision-making in young people (see Figure 17.3). First, building up a trusting relationship with the young person is a crucial part of this

- Provision of information.
- Carefully go through risks and benefits of each option.
- Having adequate time for full explanations and answers to questions.
- A setting free of distractions or interruptions.
- Assess consent for different things separately, allowing the opportunity to choose wherever possible.
- Respect of young person's views.
- Building up a trusting relationship with the young person and their family.
- Absence of coercion.
- Motivational approach with young person/family.
- Make overt the decision-making dilemmas.
- Conceptualise treatment refusal as an evolving process.
- Allow sufficient time to make decision.
- Reassurance of their choice and right to withdraw (although making it clear what the bottom line is).

Figure 17.3 Strategies to facilitate competence in young people.

process. It is important that the young person feels respected rather than coerced (Stewart and Tan, 2005). Second, it is important to provide information and carefully go through the risks and benefits of each option within a setting that is free of distractions. Having adequate time is essential in order to provide full explanations and answer any questions. Third, taking a motivational approach can facilitate the decision-making process (see Chapter 14). This includes encouraging the young person to weigh up the disadvantages and advantages of change or no change, identify areas of concern and clarify future goals and ways of achieving them. Finally, sufficient time needs to be allowed for the young person and family to make the decision. It is helpful to consider decision making as an evolving process as the young person develops a stronger relationship with the treatment team.

Legal framework

In this framework, clinicians need to be aware of the legality of practice within the specific jurisdiction, and the underlying principles such as human rights and protection of the vulnerable. Different legal principles need to be balanced against each other. The potential use of mental health legislation, parental consent, common law and childcare law all need to be considered carefully. The legal framework described in this chapter is for England and Wales (different statutes apply in other countries). Readers from other jurisdictions are encouraged to apply the principles in this framework to the legislation relevant to their own particular settings.

Balancing different legal principles – the legal framework with minors

In England and Wales, the legal framework around which decisions regarding children and young people are made are based on the Children Act 1989, the Family Law Reform Act 1969, the Mental Health Act 1983 and common law derived from case rulings. Figure 17.4 provides a summary of the law relating to consent in young people in England and Wales, which will not be discussed in detail in this chapter. Interested readers can read Hope, Savulescu, and Hendrick (2003) for an account of the relevant legal aspects. This account will instead focus on the principles of the legal basis for treatment without consent.

In the area of psychiatric treatment for children and in particular adolescents, there is a convergence of several disparate statutes which differ in spirit but are equally applicable to the treatment of children: first, childcare law with its emphasis on welfare of the child and parental responsibility; second, case law and legislation that emphasises capacity and autonomy of individuals who possess capacity, and treatment in best interests of those who do not; third, mental health legislation with its emphasis on protection of the mentally disordered. Mental health professionals treating young patients with eating disorders must navigate this complex legal landscape by balancing

Those under 16
- Presumed not to have capacity to consent unless they satisfy health professionals that they do have capacity (also known as 'Gillick competence').
- If they are 'Gillick competent', they can give valid consent to medical treatment although parental involvement is recommended.
- If the patient refuses consent, those with parental responsibility or the courts can give consent to treatment in the child's best interest (Children Act 1989).

Those age 16 and 17
- Presumed to have capacity to give valid consent to medical treatment unless the contrary is shown (Family Law Reform Act 1969).
- Parental consent is needed if they do not have capacity.
- If the patient refuses consent, then those with parental responsibility, or those with proxy powers to consent under the Mental Capacity Act 2005 (due to come into force 2007), or the courts can give consent in the young person's best interest .

Those over 18
- At present no one but the patient can consent over the age of 18 in England and Wales, even if the patient lacks capacity.
- From 2007 patients lacking capacity can have decisions made on their behalf by proxy decision-makers under the Mental Capacity Act 2005.

For all ages
- The Mental Health Act 1983 can be used to treat patients without their consent in the presence of mental illness if they are at risk of serious harm.

Figure 17.4 Summary of the law relating to consent in young people in England and Wales.

the different legal principles contained in all the different statutes, even though they can often only use one statute at a time.

The law in most countries, in addition to allowing treatment without consent for children and adolescents in certain circumstances, also allows parents the right to provide consent on behalf of their offspring. It is often appropriate for children and adolescents with eating disorders to have treatment under their parents' consent. It may indeed be a relief for young people to sense clear boundaries laid down by their parents. Parents may need help to develop the confidence to be clear with their daughter about what is needed. Patients report that the notion of informal compulsory treatment is acceptable to them (Tan, 2006). Usually, when a child is admitted to hospital under parental consent, they comply with the treatment. However, for those that continue to resist, the relatively informal process of parental consent may become inappropriate because there is no right of appeal, and in such cases clinicians may need to consider the use of more formal legal means to impose treatment, such as mental health legislation, guardianship orders or treatment orders.

Alternatives to compulsory treatment

Before deciding that compulsory treatment is necessary it is important to explore systematically all the possible alternatives. These include: engaging the patient and family; listening to the patient and being empathic; understanding the difficulties but at the same time taking an encouraging and firm approach. A greater intensity of outpatient involvement including home treatment or day-patient programmes may be preferable (if resources allow). However, despite these alternatives, compulsory treatment may sometimes be essential.

Interpretation of legal principles in case law

Case law tends to consist of extreme or unusual cases which have caused sufficient controversy or conflict to be brought to court. At the same time, the precedents set by case law are often applied to medical practice as general principles. It is important that there should be careful distinction between the (unusual) facts of the particular cases taken to court and the aspects of the judgments which relate to the specific circumstances, and the more general principles laid out or confirmed by the judges. There is a possibility for clinicians to be conservative in their interpretations of the scope or application of case rulings because of a wish to avoid litigation over failure to observe the law. These factors work together to make the awareness, careful interpretation and application of case rulings to everyday clinical practice an important issue.

Factors influencing the route of compulsory treatment chosen

There are a number of factors that may influence which route to compulsory treatment is chosen, including the age of the young person, the degree of behavioural disturbance or resistance, whether there is support from parents, the context in which the disturbance occurs, whether there is time to facilitate consent and whether the adolescent is competent to make a decision. The potential advantages and disadvantages of the various routes, as just described, will need to be taken into account. Finally, the competence of the professional team and availability of a range of treatments may also impact on the route chosen.

With younger adolescents or children it may be appropriate to encourage parental consent. With older adolescents, particularly if there is a high degree of resistance, mental health act legislation may need to be used. Where there is lack of support or neglect in the parents, a care order obtained from the courts may need to be used. Where there is support from parents but a difficulty in enabling the child to have treatment an inherent jurisdiction of the High Court may be supportive to parents and provide a helpful legal structure to enable the child to receive treatment. In case of emergencies, common law may need to be used in the first instance.

The therapeutic alliance and compulsory treatment

Where compulsory treatment is used, it is essential to maintain the therapeutic alliance with young people and their parents. Providing information, listening to the young person and their family and respecting their views and concerns will help with this process. Tan (2006) found that young people may view compulsory treatment as either supportive or coercive depending on how it is carried out and the nature of the relationship with the professionals.

Clinical framework

Clinical effectiveness

In working with eating disorders there needs to be a consideration of the evidence base for the treatment. Despite many advances in the understanding of AN, the disorder remains difficult to treat. Many different forms of treatment have been tried over the years but it is still not known what are the most effective approaches (Wilson and Fairburn, 1993). There is, however, accumulating evidence for the efficacy of family therapy (Eisler et al., 1997; Robin, Siegel, Moye, Gilroy, Dennis, and Sikand, 1999; Russell et al., 1987). The recent NICE guidelines as well as the APA guidelines recommend this. With regard to inpatient treatment, operant behavioural techniques gained popularity in the 1960s and 1970s but these approaches were later challenged and considered to be unnecessarily harsh (Steinhausen, 1994). Young people gained weight in hospital but tended to lose it after discharge. Inpatients who gain weight under the pressure of persuasion and within a context of fear very often relapse after discharge. There is some evidence that less coercive programmes with less emphasis on rapid weight gain can be more productive (Touyz, Beumont, and Dunn, 1987). The challenge for inpatient units is to be able to operate a structured programme that respects the individual and promotes autonomy rather than enforces compliance. A number of studies report that patients themselves report that programmes including bed rest and a firm approach can be helpful, although when applied too rigidly or harshly can be unhelpful (Griffiths et al., 1997; Tan, 2006).

Clinical experience suggests that inpatient admission may be essential in terms of providing an immediate safe environment for weight restoration. The short-term outcome and needs have to be balanced against the possible longer term outcome. This has to taken into consideration before deciding to undertake a programme of intensive treatment in hospital. In terms of balancing the advantages and disadvantages of admission, the short-term difficulties may be necessary to save life or overcome an impasse in order to promote a long-term healthy outcome.

In summary, the evidence basis for inpatient care and the evidence for the effectiveness of different forms of outpatient treatment needs to be carefully considered. In all cases, there should be discussion with the young person and family on the advantages and disadvantages of the various options and respect for their views.

Clinical feasibility

As well as being aware of the evidence base, it is important to assess whether a treatment is clinically feasible; for example, whether there are appropriate clinicians available to carry out the work, or whether there is an inpatient unit easily accessible.

Levels and style of decision making

It is helpful to be aware of the style of decision making with which the patient is comfortable. Tan (2005) found that young people may prefer either a largely individual decision-making style or a group decision-making style. In relation to treatment decisions in eating disorders, some young people prefer to make the decision themselves, whilst others prefer to make a decision along with parents and professionals. Age, personality characteristics and severity of illness may all influence this preference.

In addition, the level of the decision to be made needs to be clarified. The young person and family may have agreed to admission and treatment for the eating disorder. However, when it comes to mealtimes the strong 'anorexic urge' can take over and make it difficult for the patient to choose to eat. Predicting this makes it easier for her to be given support and encouragement at this time. Knowing that overall the patient wants to get better can make it easier for parents and professionals to cope with the inevitable distress that she may express at being 'made' to eat.

Well-being of patient and family

Lucy and Anna were reluctant for their parents to participate in the therapy. Research indicates the importance of involving the family in treatment that directly relates to the eating disorder (Eisler et al., 1997). The NICE guidelines also indicate the importance of involving the family in treatment that directly relates to the eating disorder. Clearly, it is important to involve the parents wherever possible. Nevertheless, the young person may still insist that their parents are not involved and very occasionally may even ask for help without their parents' knowledge (more commonly in BN rather than AN). With younger adolescents it is very clear that parents do need to be involved wherever possible, even if the young person is reluctant. However, for those aged 16 and 17 the situation is less clear. The clinician may face a dilemma of having to balance the right of the adolescent to have individual treatment with the duty of the parent to take parental responsibility (enshrined in the Children Act 1989).

Another important consideration is whether the treatment is acceptable to patients and their families. Adequate time is needed to listen to the wishes and concerns of the family and the young person. Families who have a daughter with an eating disorder often feel helpless and guilty, blaming themselves for the eating disorder. Working with such families can be very challenging. Many issues come to the surface that are mirrored in society as a whole, including power imbalances, the role of women, the role of parents and the importance of body weight and shape (Orbach, 1978; Russell, 1995). Being aware of these issues and having regular supervision can make it easier to deal with them.

Qualities of health professionals

The qualities of the health professional may significantly affect clinical decision making. Tan (2006) and Stewart and Tan (2005) have indicated the qualities in the health professionals that are likely to be important in helping patients to progress clinically. Those qualities which patients themselves had found helpful are shown in Figure 17.5. These include: being kind and approachable; being able to empathise with and understand the painful experience that is being endured; being respectful of the individual and able to discern a person's real personality and wishes in the middle of difficult situations; being able to stand firm and not be hoodwinked by the protestations that AN may cause a person to have, for example: lying or refusing treatment, even if he or she might want treatment; able to understand and respect a person's individual needs and tailor treatment accordingly: for example, the level of restriction or freedom needed and the pace of treatment; able to decisively take control and protect the person from herself if she is out of control and not able to help herself; being fair to all patients and not favouring one over another, particularly in an inpatient setting where patients compare treatment; and being able to offer patients confidentiality in their therapy but at the same time willing to offer parents support, advice and help.

Involvement of patients and carers

Ideally, patients and carers within a service should be involved in all aspects of management, including contributing to staff interviews, development of audits and service development. They may have useful ideas to contribute and the process of involving them enables them to take some ownership for

- Kind and approachable.
- Able to empathise.
- Able to respect the young person and see the individual behind the eating disorder.
- Able to stand firm.
- Able to understand and respect the young person's needs.
- Able to take control where necessary.
- Fair to all patients.
- Able to offer confidentiality.
- Able to manage anxiety in themselves and in the young person/family.

Figure 17.5 Qualities in professionals that assist recovery (Tan, 2006).

the service that is being offered. Once involved in developing services and programmes, the treatment decisions may be easier to negotiate.

Need for audit, evaluation and contribution to research

It is important to set up structures for evaluation and audit of the service. Professionals need to be aware of the outcome of treatment in order to extend their learning and adapt the service accordingly. Given the sparseness of knowledge about effective treatments for child and adolescent eating disorders, services have a responsibility to encourage the development of evaluative research and to contribute wherever possible.

Resource framework

Health professionals as gatekeepers and providers of services

There are potentially conflicting ethical issues of justice, resource allocation and duty of care when health professionals are responsible for all three. It is important to consider what resources are actually available, as providing the most effective treatment can depend on the availability of resources. The clinician may be in the difficult position of deciding between the need for intensive treatment of one individual and the need to provide treatment for others who are seriously ill and still on the waiting list. For Lucy and Anna, the decision to move towards inpatient treatment may be partly affected by what resources are available in the community.

As well as staffing resources, it is important to pay attention to the physical resources. Within inpatient units, the environmental setting needs to be conducive to recovering from an eating disorder, with attention paid to comfort as well as ease of access to school and other facilities. Care should be taken to provide meals that are attractive and tailored to the individual's needs.

Service parameters and priorities

Political and economic pressures can have a profound effect on the development of treatment programmes. Clinicians and managers have to work within a financially restricted and target-driven climate that can hamper long-term work with eating disorders. The goals of managers may differ from those of clinicians. Separation of management and clinical work can lead to decision making at a level which is divorced from the reality of clinical treatment. This may reduce innovation and lead to more rigid structures and systems. Ethical values needs to be at the cornerstone of service delivery. However, a service that is significantly financially restricted may make it more difficult for the patient to gain trust. This can result in difficulties with engagement or formal complaints. Maintaining a close partnership between managers and clinicians is essential and can aid development of services.

The development of specialist eating disorder services can lead to fragmentation of local care. Inpatient admissions generate income and have therefore flourished, even though the need for intensive community care is well known. Indeed, the lack of resources for community treatment may increase the need for inpatient admission. Time devoted to service development, including provision of services across a whole community, may lead to a more efficient and cost-effective service in the long term.

Information for patients

There is a need to provide accessible written material for patients, their parents and siblings, and teachers. There are new opportunities but also threats to be found in the new technologies for communication and information which are becoming increasingly accessible to a majority of the population. Many professional and eating disorder organisations have produced materials for patients and their families to read, including material specially produced for adolescents (Eating Disorders Association, 2005; Royal College of Psychiatrists, 2004, 2006). Internet-based resources for treatment delivery and self-help strategies have also been growing (Eating Disorders Association, 2006; Murphy, Frost, Webster, and Schmidt, 2004). However, this free access to information has its dangers, as exemplified by the 'pro-anorexia' movement. Websites produced by individuals ascribing to this philosophy have varying stances about whether AN is desirable, but generally agree that AN is a lifestyle choice. In some of these sites, people suffering from AN exchange tips and suggestions that, along with media images of excessively thin role models, can be particularly hazardous to impressionable young people (Fox, Ward, and O'Rourke, 2005; Morrison, 2003).

Using the Four-Framework Grid

Managing refusal of treatment by an adolescent with an eating disorder

Children and adolescents with eating disorders may be seriously ill and require intensive outpatient treatment or inpatient admission, yet may refuse this treatment. There are a number of factors to be taken into account when deciding whether a young person can refuse treatment, which involve all four arenas contained in the Four-Framework Grid.

In the consideration of clinical factors, the potential risk of the illness needs to be ascertained. This requires a careful assessment of the physical and psychological consequences of the eating disorder and consideration of all the possible treatment options, the evidence basis for these options, and the best fit of options to the situation, as well as acceptability to the particular patient and family. The likely benefit and harm of the treatment need to be considered. A compulsory admission may be lifesaving in the short term, but the longer term effects are less certain. There may be specific individual difficulties relating to the young person's dislike of being in a unit away from home as well as reduced contact with local friends, family and school. She will have less autonomy and responsibility and may feel overcontrolled. The benefits and harms relating to outpatient treatment need consideration in the same way.

It is important to check what the young person knows about the proposed treatment, including the process of admission, if inpatient treatment is recommended, and what their fears are about this. The clinician should take time to ascertain the wishes of the adolescent and her parents. The patient's understanding of inpatient admission and their reasons for refusing it need to be discussed. If the parent also refuses consent, are the reasons sensible? It is important to clarify whether the young person is willing to engage in other treatment options. If admission is not to occur, it is important to consider whether the parent will be able to keep her safe and promote recovery at home.

All clinical issues should be considered with respect to which option provides the greatest long- and short-term benefit as opposed to the least long- and short-term harm. The physical or psychiatric risks may indicate the need for admission. If the young person is unwilling to be admitted, it is important first to try alternatives to compulsory admission. Identifying the reasons for refusal and providing careful explanations within the context of a motivational approach can be helpful. It is important to avoid getting into battles with a young person and scare tactics are generally not helpful. The aim throughout is to promote healthy autonomy and competence.

An assessment of the competence of the young person to make a decision is important. The eating disorder and any comorbid conditions such as depression may be affecting her ability to decide for herself (Tan et al., 2003a, 2003b, 2003c). The treatment team needs to ensure that it is fair both to the patient and family but also fulfilling its duties of care, including providing adequate respect of autonomy while protecting vulnerable patients.

With regard to resources the options need to be considered against the constraints of the resources available. At the same time, ethical issues such as balancing issues of distributive justice and duties to the individual patient will need to be discussed in collaboration with management.

Finally, in consideration of the legal factors, along with the importance of understanding the legal rulings and statutes applicable to the issue of treatment of eating disorders in young people, the principles and spirit of the law should always been borne in mind. These usually appeal to ethical principles and should be considered in deciding which legal routes to use.

A treatment decision-making algorithm for inpatient admission

Figure 17.6 shows an algorithm for deciding whether to admit a young person and, if the admission needs to be compulsory which route to pursue. The first step is to engage the young person and her parents and to seek

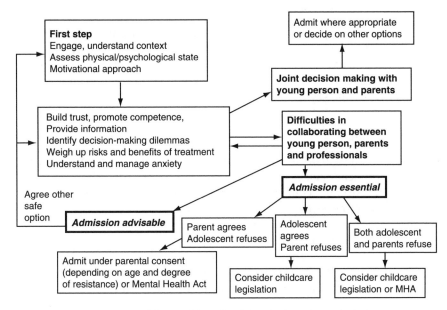

Figure 17.6 Treatment decision-making algorithm for inpatient admission.

to understand the context. A comprehensive assessment of physical and psychological state is essential. The second step is to provide information on the disorder and options for treatment, to build trust and promote healthy decision making. The risks and benefits of treatment need to be discussed with the patient and her parents and the decision-making dilemmas identified. Anxiety about the process in patients, carers and professionals needs to be understood and managed. Hopefully, this will lead to a process of joint decision making. Other relevant adults, for example, schoolteachers or other family members, may also contribute to this process.

In cases where it is not possible to agree, an assessment needs to be made as to whether the treatment, for example, hospital admission, is advisable or essential. If it is advisable but not essential, another safe option can be agreed and further work done to engage the patient and build up trust and motivation. Regular assessments need to be carried out. If at some point, admission is considered to be essential, then the decision to undertake compulsory admission may need to be taken. If the parents agree to the admission despite refusal of the adolescent, the young person can be admitted under parental consent, although if there is a high degree of resistance and the adolescent is older, there needs to be consideration of the use of the Mental Health Act. In contrast, should the adolescent agree to admission but the parents disagree despite the risks of not being treated, there may need to be consideration of compulsory treatment under childcare or guardianship legislation. Where both adolescent and parents refuse treatment, a care order, the Mental Health Act or intervention by the courts may be needed.

Conclusions and practical recommendations

The treatment of children and adolescents who suffer from eating disorders can be difficult because of the range of clinical, ethical and legal issues involved. We suggest that having a systematic way of considering these can be helpful, particularly as issues in one arena usually affect issues in another. We have outlined some key recommendations in Figure 17.7.

Summary points

1   Ethical and legal dilemmas are common in treatment of eating disorders.
2   The treatment alliance is the cornerstone of treatment.
3   Ethical working requires consideration of clinical, ethical, legal and resource frameworks.
4   An important aim is to promote competence and healthy decision making in the young person and family.
5   Collaborative decision making is crucial.
6   Respect is needed for the different views of young people and parents.
7   Openness about the dilemmas can facilitate collaboration.

- **Treatment alliance**
  A firm treatment alliance with the young person and the family is the cornerstone of treatment. Time needs to be spent building up this alliance.
- **Information about the eating disorder and treatment**
  It is important to make sure that the young person and their family are aware of the symptoms and consequences of an eating disorder and what the treatment involves.
- **Collaborative decision making**
  Wherever possible, it is important to work collaboratively, identifying the options with the young person and family and weighing up with them the benefits and risks of the different options. Making decisions in advance can be helpful.
- **Least invasive treatment**
  Bearing in mind the principle of no harm, the treatment chosen should be the least invasive whilst at the same time being potentially beneficial for the patient.
- **Ethical team working**
  A reflective working practice within teams can enhance the clinical work.
- **Openness about dilemmas**
  Being open about the dilemmas with the young person and the family can improve the treatment alliance and collaborative working.
- **Promote autonomy and competence**
  Keeping the goal of promotion of autonomy and competence in mind can enhance treatment decision making.
- **Listen to and respect the young person**
  It is important to be aware of the young person's views and their reasons for treatment refusal.
- **Take time**
  Unless there is serious risk it is possible to take time to make decisions, allowing the chance to build up a relationship and collaborative way of working.

Figure 17.7 Practical recommendations.

Acknowledgements

The authors would like to thank Professor Tony Hope for his comments on the draft for this chapter. We would also like to thank Professor. Walter Vandereycken for his helpful comments on the algorithm (Figure 17.6). Much of the recent research by Tan et al. cited in this chapter has been conducted with funding from the Wellcome Trust.

Notes

1 The National Institute for Health and Clinical Excellence (NICE) is the independent organisation responsible for providing national guidance for the United Kingdom on the promotion of good health and the prevention and treatment of ill health. Although not accorded the status of strict policy, NICE guidance is usually adopted by the National Health Service as the standard for best practice, and is thus highly significant to clinicians working within the National Health Service in the United Kingdom, who would have to justify any deviation of clinical practice from the guidelines.
2 The Human Rights Act 1998 Article 8: Right to respect for private and family life: 1. Everyone has the right to respect for his private and family life, his home and his correspondence; 2. There shall be no interference by a public authority with the exercise of this right except such as is in accordance with the law and is necessary in a democratic society in the interests of national security, public safety or the economic well-being of the country, for the prevention of disorder or crime, for the protection of health or morals, or for the protection of the rights and freedoms of others.

References

American Psychiatric Association (2006, May). *Practice guidelines for the treatment of eating disorders*. Retrieved July 4, 2006, from http://www.psych.org/psych_pract/treatg/pg/prac_guide.cfm

Beauchamp, T.L., and Childress, J.F. (2001). *Principles of biomedical ethics* (5th ed.). Oxford: Oxford University Press.

Brotman, A.W., Stern, T.A., and Herzog, D.B. (1984). Emotional reactions of house officers to patients with anorexia nervosa, diabetes and obesity. *International Journal of Eating Disorders, 3*, 71–77.

Charland, L.C. (2004) A madness for identity: Psychiatric labels, user autonomy, and the perils of the internet. *Philosophy, Psychology and Psychiatry, 11* (4), 335–349.

Draper, H. (2000) Anorexia nervosa and respecting a refusal of life-prolonging therapy: A limited justification. *Bioethics, 14* (2), 120–133.

Eating Disorders Association (2005). *Information about eating disorders: Information for young people*. Retrieved March 6, 2006, from http://www.edauk.com/info_guide_1.htm

Eating Disorders Association. (2006) *Self help network*. Retrieved March 6, 2006, from http://www.edauk.com/shn/index.htm

Eisler, I., Dare, C., Russell, G., Szmukler, G., Le Grange, D., and Dodge, E. (1997). Family and individual therapy in anorexia nervosa – a five year follow-up. *Archives of General Psychiatry, 54*, 1025–1030.

Fox, N., Ward, K., and O'Rourke, A. (2005). Pro-anorexia, weight-loss drugs and the internet: an 'anti-recovery' explanatory model of anorexia. *Sociology of Health and Illness, 27* (7), 944–971.

Gowers, S.G., Weetman, J., Shore, A., Hossain, F., and Elvins, R. (2000). Impact of hospitalisation on the outcome of adolescent anorexia nervosa. *British Journal of Psychiatry, 176*, 138–141.

Griffiths, R., Gross, G., Russell, J., Thornton, C., Beumont, P.J.V., Schotte, D., et al. (1997). Perceptions of bed rest by anorexia nervosa patients. *International Journal of Eating Disorders, 23* (4), 443–447.

Grisso, T., and Appelbaum, P.S. (1998). Abilities related to competence. In: T. Grisso and P. S. Appelbaum (Eds.), *Assessing competence to consent to treatment: A Guide for physicians and other health professionals* (pp. 31–60). Oxford: Oxford University Press.

Hope, T., Savulescu, J., and Hendrick, J. (2003). *Medical ethics and law: The core curriculum.* Edinburgh: Churchill Livingstone.

Jarman, M., Smith, J.A., and Walsh, S. (1997). The psychological battle for control: A qualitative study of health-care professionals' understandings of the treatment of anorexia nervosa. *Journal of Community and Applied Social Psychology, 7*, 137–152.

Lock, J., Couturier, J., and Agras, W.S. (2006). Comparison of long term outcomes in adolescents with anorexia nervosa treated with family therapy. *Journal of the American Academy of Child and Adolescent Psychiatry, 45*, 666–672.

Mental Health Act Commission (1997). *Guidance note 3: Guidance on the treatment of anorexia nervosa under the Mental Health Act 1983.* London: The Stationery Office.

Morrison, G. (2003). *Fatal trend: pro-anorexia nervosa websites.* Retrieved May 6, 2005, from http://preteenagerstoday.com/resources/articles/fataltrend.htm.

Murphy, R., Frost, S., Webster, P., and Schmidt, U. (2004). An evaluation of web-based information. *International Journal of Eating Disorders, 35* (2), 145–154.

National Institute for Health and Clinical Excellence (NICE, 2004) *Eating disorders: Core interventions in the treatment and management of anorexia nervosa, bulimia nervosa and related eating disorders. Clinical guideline 9.* Retrieved July 25, 2005, from http://www.nice.org.uk/pdf/cg009niceguidance.pdf

Orbach, S. (1978). *Fat is a feminist issue.* London: Arrow Books.

Rathner, G. (1998). A plea against compulsory treatment of anorexia nervosa. In W. Vandereycken and P. J. Beumont (Eds.), *Treating eating disorders: Ethical, legal and personal issues* (pp. 179–215). London: Athlone Press.

Robin, A.L., Siegel, P.T., Moye, A.W., Gilroy, M., Dennis, A.B., and Sikand, A. (1999). A controlled comparison of family versus individual therapy for adolescents with anorexia nervosa. *Journal of the American Academy of Child and Adolescent Psychiatry, 38*, 1482–1489.

Royal College of Psychiatrists (2004). *Leaflet 24, for parents and teachers. Eating disorders in young people.* Retrieved April 6, 2006, from http://www.rcpsych.ac.uk/info/mhgu/newmhgu24.htm

Royal College of Psychiatrists (2006). *Eating disorders – New and improved leaflet.* Retrieved April 6, 2006 from http://www.rcpsych.ac.uk/info/help/anor/index.asp

Russell, D. (1995). *Women, madness and medicine.* Oxford: Blackwell.

Russell, G.F.M., Szmukler, G.I., Dare, C., and Eisler, I. (1987). An evaluation of family therapy in anorexia nervosa and bulimia nervosa. *Archives of General Psychiatry, 44*, 1047–1056.

Russon, L., and Alison, D. (1998). Does palliative care have a role in treatment of anorexia nervosa? Palliative care does not mean giving up. *British Medical Journal,* *317* (7152), 196–197.

Steinhausen, H.C. (1994). Anorexia and bulimia nervosa. In M. Rutter and E. Taylor (Eds.), *Child and adolescent psychiatry* (3rd ed., pp. 425–440). Oxford: Blackwell.

Stewart, A. (2000, August). *What is adolescent autonomy and how can clinicians promote it?* Paper presented at the Fourth International Conference on Philosophy and Psychiatry: Madness, Science and Society, Florence, Italy.

Stewart, A., and Tan, J. (2005). *The views of patients regarding the treatment decision making process in anorexia nervosa – practical implications of the findings from an empirical medical ethics project.* Workshop at the 7th International Conference on Eating Disorders, London, 4–6 April.

Strober, M., Freeman, R., and Morrell, W. (1997). The long-term course of severe anorexia nervosa in adolescents: Survival analysis of recovery, relapse, and outcome predictors over 10–15 years in a prospective study. *International Journal of Eating Disorders, 22,* 339–360.

Tan, J. (2004). *Medical ethics as a tool in treatment dilemmas in eating disorders.* Paper presented at the Royal College of Psychiatrists Eating Disorders Special Interest Group Meeting, London, 19 March.

Tan, J. (2005). *Can she REALLY decide? An ethical approach to choice and compulsion in anorexia nervosa.* Presentation in plenary session Coercion, Collaboration and Choice (Chair, Stephen Touyz), at the 7th International Conference on Eating Disorders, Imperial College, London, 4–6 April.

Tan, J. (2006). *Competence and treatment decision-making in anorexia nervosa.* Unpublished DPhil thesis, University of Oxford.

Tan, J., Hope, T., and Stewart, A. (2003a). Anorexia and personal identity: The accounts of patients and their parents. *International Journal of Law and Psychiatry, 26,* 533–548.

Tan, J., Hope, T., and Stewart, A. (2003b). Competence to refuse treatment in anorexia nervosa. *International Journal of Law and Psychiatry, 26,* 697–707.

Tan, J., Hope, T., Stewart, A., and Fitzpatrick, R. (2003c). Control and compulsory treatment in anorexia nervosa: The views of patients and parents. *International Journal of Law and Psychiatry, 26* (6), 627–645.

Tan, J., and Jones, D.P.H. (2001). Children's consent. *Current Opinion in Psychiatry, 14,* 303–307.

Tan, J., and Stewart, A. (2003). *Ethical issues in the treatment of eating disorders.* Workshop at the International Conference on Eating Disorders, Imperial College, 1–3 April.

Touyz, S.W., Beumont, P.J.V., and Dunn, S.M. (1987). Behaviour therapy in the management of patients with anorexia nervosa. A lenient, flexible approach *Psychotherapy and Psychosomatics, 48,* 151–156.

Udovitch, M. (2002) A secret society of the starving. *New York Times,* 8 September.

Weithorn, L.A., and Campbell, S.B. (1982). The competency of children and adolescents to make informed treatment decisions. *Child Development, 53* (6), 1589–1598.

Williams, C.J., Pieri, L., and Sims, A. (1998). Does palliative care have a role in treatment of anorexia nervosa? We should strive to keep patients alive. *British Medical Journal, 317* (7152), 195–196.

Wilson, G.T., and Fairburn, C.G. (1993). Cognitive treatments for eating disorders. *Journal of Consulting and Clinical Psychology, 61* (2), 261–269.

Appendix: Assessment instruments and interviews

Beth Watkins

Standardised methods are in common use to help describe and diagnose eating disorders. Within the adult population there is a wide choice of standardised methods for specifically assessing eating disorders. These fall broadly into two categories – self-report questionnaires and structured or semi-structured interviews. Most general psychopathology measures also have an eating disorders section. In contrast, there are very few similar measures for the child and adolescent populations. The general psychopathology measures may have eating disorder sections, e.g. the Diagnostic Interview for Children and Adolescents (DICA: Reich, Herjanic, Welner, and Gandhy, 1982), but it is often preferable to use a more detailed specific eating disorder psychopathology measure. This applies particularly when a more detailed profile of the child's eating pathology is required. Many of the specific eating disorder adult measures have been used with adolescents, but may lack data for adolescent norms. Few measures have been formally adapted for use with children, with one self-report measure specifically designed for children.

This Appendix includes some of the eating disorder instruments and interviews that have been used within the younger population and those instruments and interviews specifically designed for the younger population. Reliability and validity data are provided, for it is particularly important to ensure that adult-oriented assessment techniques are appropriate for use with younger patients. In general, they should be used only with considerable caution.

Adult questionnaires used within the child and adolescent populations, general eating disorder pathology

Eating Attitudes Test

The Eating Attitudes Test (EAT: Garner and Garfinkel, 1979) is a self-report 40-item measure that employs a 6-point Likert rating scale. It was designed to measure attitudes and behaviours associated with anorexia nervosa and, although not diagnostic, can be used to measure symptoms. Following factor analysis, a shorter 26-item version (EAT-26: Garner, Olmsted, Bohr, and

Garfinkel, 1982) was developed and found to be highly correlated with the original version ($r = 0.98$). The EAT is easy to administer and takes less than ten minutes to complete. This measure has seven factors: food preoccupation, body image for thinness, vomiting, and laxative abuse, dieting, slow eating, clandestine eating and perceived social pressure to gain weight. The measure proved to have high internal consistency for both an anorexia nervosa group (coefficient alpha = 0.79), and for a mixed group of anorexia nervosa and normal controls (coefficient alpha = 0.94; Garner et al., 1982). The EAT also proved to have high test–retest reliability ($n = 56$, $r = 0.84$; Carter and Moss, 1984).

The EAT has been found to differentiate between binge eaters and those with anorexia nervosa or bulimia nervosa (Prather and Williamson, 1988), and between normal controls and eating disorder groups (Garner and Garfinkel, 1979). However, the measure does not discriminate between those with anorexia nervosa and those with bulimia nervosa (Williamson, Cubic, and Gleaves, 1993). The EAT has also been found to be sensitive to therapeutic changes (Williamson, Prather, Bennett, Davis, Watkins, and Grenier, 1989) and has been shown to be moderately correlated with the Bulimia Test (BULIT: $r = 0.67$; Smith and Thelen, 1984) and the Bulimic Investigatory Test (BITE: $r = 0.70$; Henderson and Freeman, 1987). This is the only questionnaire that has been specifically adapted for use with children (ChEAT: Maloney, McGuire, and Daniels, 1988, see later).

Eating Disorder Examination Questionnaire

The Eating Disorder Examination Questionnaire (EDE-Q: Fairburn and Beglin, 1994) is derived directly from the Eating Disorder Examination interview (EDE: Fairburn and Cooper, 1993; see in detail below). It consists of 38 items which assess both behavioural and cognitive symptoms of eating disorders. The EDE-Q generates four subscales which represent restraint, eating concern, weight concern and shape concern. Reliability and validity of this measure have been shown to be acceptable in the adult population (Black and Wilson, 1996; Fairburn and Beglin, 1994). Normative data have been established for the Eating Disorder Examination Questionnaire (EDE-Q) in girls aged 12–14 years (Carter, Stewart, and Fairburn, 2001).

Eating Disorder Inventory

The Eating Disorder Inventory (EDI: Garner, Olmsted, and Polivy, 1983) is a 64-item measure, consisting of eight subscales: three to assess attitudes and behaviours towards weight, body shape and eating (Drive for Thinness, Bulimia, and Body Dissatisfaction) and five to assess psychological characteristics common to anorexia and bulimia nervosa (Ineffectiveness, Perfection, Interpersonal Distrust, Interoceptive Awareness, and Maturity Fears). Adolescent norms are available for this measure (Rosen, Silberg, and Gross, 1988;

Shore and Porter, 1990). The measure has been revised, to create the Eating Disorder Inventory-2 (EDI-2: Garner, 1991), with the addition of 27 additional items, forming three extra subscales – Asceticism, Impulse Regulation, and Social Insecurity. The measure has been used in groups with an age range of 11–18 years. More recently, the Eating Disorder Inventory-3 (EDI-3; Garner, 2004) has been developed. The inventory consists of 91 items organised on to 12 primary scales that yield six composite scores: Eating Disorder, Risk Ineffectiveness, Interpersonal Problems, Affective Problems, Overcontrol, and General Psychological Maladjustment. The EDI-3 includes a symptom checklist for binge–purge behaviours, which facilitates diagnosis of eating disorder. Normative data is available for women and girls with eating disorders aged 13–53 years. The measure has been shown to have good reliability across all eating disorder diagnosis, with test–retest coefficients ranging from 0.93 to 0.98 across scales and composite scores (Garner, 2004). Further reliability and validity data is reported in the EDI-3 professional manual (Garner, 2004).

The EDI and EDI-2 are widely used as screening measures and as measures of treatment outcome. It is also possible to detect subtypes of anorexia nervosa or bulimia nervosa, as well as symptom severity, using this measure. Garner et al. (1983) found that 88–93 per cent of subjects were correctly classified using the EDI, and also found that 85 per cent of subjects were correctly classified into bulimic and restrictor subtypes of anorexia nervosa, using discriminant analysis and comparing the self-report EDI with clinicians' ratings of the subscales. The concurrent validity between the EDI and the EAT is good, as scores on all of the EDI subscales have been found to be positively correlated with scores on the Eating Attitudes Test (EAT: Garner et al., 1982). Norring (1990) found that the Bulimia scale of the EDI is a stable predictor of binge eating at both one-year and two-year follow-ups, thus having high predictor validity. In a sample of 11–18 year olds good reliability was found for both the EDI and EDI-2 (Garner, 1991). In addition, Leung, Wang, and Tang (2004) found that the EDI had good transcultural validity in a sample of 2256 female Chinese high-school students aged 12–18 years, although highlighted the need for age-specific norms. A child version of the EDI and EDI-2 has been under development for several years, but only recently have studies investigating their psychometric properties been published (see below).

Questionnaire for Eating Disorder Diagnoses

The Questionnaire for Eating Disorder Diagnoses (Q-EDD: Mintz, O'Halloran, Mulholland, and Schneider, 1997) is a self-report questionnaire that takes approximately ten minutes to complete. It comprises 50 questions that are answered either yes or no, or using a Likert-type rating scale. Each question is linked directly to a *DSM-IV* (American Psychiatric Association, 1994) criterion for eating disorders diagnoses, and each question has a decision rule to facilitate the scoring of the questionnaire. The Q-EDD was designed to operationalise the *DSM-IV* criteria for eating disorders. It is a revision of the Weight Management Questionnaire (WMQ: Mintz and Betz, 1988), based on *DSM-III-R* criteria for eating disorders (APA, 1987), which was revised from Ousley's (1986) *DSM-III* questionnaire.

The measure differentiates between those who meet diagnostic criteria for an eating disorder and those who do not. Within the group who meet diagnostic criteria for eating disorders, it differentiates between individuals who meet the diagnostic criteria for anorexia nervosa and those who meet the diagnostic criteria for bulimia nervosa. Within the group that does not meet the diagnostic criteria for eating disorders, the measure differentiates between those who have some eating disorder symptomatology and those who are asymptomatic.

In a clinical sample that included some adolescents ($n = 37$, age range 15–44 years old, mean age 24.68 years, SD = 7.59), in which clinicians had independently diagnosed all participants as eating disordered, the Q-EDD and clinicians' independent diagnoses of anorexia nervosa and bulimia nervosa were 100 per cent in agreement. Calculations of false-negative rates were used to examine criterion validity, and it was found that there was 78 per cent accuracy between clinicians and the Q-EDD when differentiating eating disordered and non-eating disordered individuals. Of the 22 per cent of cases that were not deemed to reach diagnostic levels by the Q-EDD, 75 per cent were rated as non-eating disorder but symptomatic, with only 25 per cent (two cases) being rated as non-eating disordered and asymptomatic, using the Q-EDD. It is interesting that neither of the cases deemed to be non-eating disordered and asymptomatic by the Q-EDD were near normal weight (one severely underweight and one severely overweight), which may suggest a clinical diagnosis based predominantly around body weight (Mintz et al., 1997).

The measure has been used with a non-clinical sample of older adolescents. It has high test–retest reliability between eating disordered and non-eating disordered groups, and between eating disordered, non-eating disordered (symptomatic), and non-eating disordered (asymptomatic) groups, respectively. Inter-rater reliability on 50 randomly selected Q-EDDs produced 100 per cent agreement (Mintz et al., 1997).

Setting Conditions for Anorexia Nervosa Scale

The Setting Conditions for Anorexia Nervosa Scale (SCANS: Slade and Dewey, 1986) is a 40-item questionnaire that employs a five-point, Likert-type rating scale, and comprises five scales – dissatisfaction and loss of control (D), social and personal anxiety (S), perfectionism (P), adolescent problems (A), and need for weight control (WC). It was designed to identify those at risk of developing anorexia nervosa and bulimia nervosa (Slade, 1982) and has been used for this purpose in a large sample of adolescents (219 boys and

174 girls aged 14–18 years old) in a study examining the relationship of gender and family environment to eating disorder risk (Felker and Stivers, 1994). The SCANS exists both as a pencil and paper questionnaire and also in a computerised version (Butler, Newton, and Slade, 1988). The measure is quick and easy and can be used with younger adolescents as the reading level of the questionnaire is aimed at this age group. The measure takes between ten and 20 minutes to complete, and ten minutes to score. The SCANS has been used in a large sample of children and adolescents aged 11–16 years to assess two specific risk factors thought to be associated with eating disorder, namely perfectionism and general dissatisfaction.

Slade and Dewey (1986) found that the scales of the SCANS have a high internal consistency, with similar alpha coefficients being found on all scales in two separate non-clinical samples (coefficient alphas for sample 1 and sample 2, respectively, for each scale: D = 0.84, 0.89; S = 0.76, 0.81; P = 0.66, 0.66; A = 0.81, 0.83; WC = 0.81, 0.90). The SCANS adequately differentiates between non-clinical controls and eating disordered subjects, but does not discriminate between anorexia nervosa subjects and those with bulimia nervosa. Whilst this measure has been used in adolescent samples, no formal investigation of its psychometric properties in children and adolescents has been conducted.

Stirling Eating Disorders Scales

The Stirling Eating Disorders Scales (SEDS: Williams et al., 1994) is an 80-item, eight-scale measure designed to be used with eating disordered patients. The eight scales can be broadly split into two groups – four dietary scales: anorexic dietary behaviour, anorexic dietary cognitions, bulimic dietary behaviour, bulimic dietary cognitions; and four non-dietary scales: high perceived external control, low assertiveness, low self-esteem, and self-directed hostility. The measure was devised to produce a comprehensive assessment schedule that addressed not only the cognitive and behavioural aspects of both anorexia nervosa and bulimia nervosa, but also the cognitive/emotional features that have been shown to be important characteristics of both of the disorders, with the use of the four non-dietary scales.

For a sample group consisting of three comparison groups – anorexia nervosa (mean age 24.7 years, SD = 5.3), bulimia nervosa (mean age 25.0 years, SD = 4.9), and normal controls (mean age 23.8, SD = 4.9) – the three-week test–retest correlations for all eight of the Stirling Eating Disorders Scales produced highly significant correlations ($P < 0.001$) and the scale consistency for each of the eight scales is also high (Cronbach's alpha > 0.8; Williams et al., 1994).

All eight scales discriminate between eating disordered subjects and normal controls, whereas the four dietary scales discriminate between the anorexia nervosa group and the bulimia nervosa group. On the four non-dietary scales, there is no differentiation between the two eating disordered groups

(Williams et al., 1994). The concurrent validity between the SEDS and the Eating Attitudes Test-40 (EAT: Garner and Garfinkel, 1979) and the Bulimia Investigatory Test – Edinburgh (BITE: Henderson and Freeman, 1987), produced highly significant correlations, $P < 0.001$ (Williams et al., 1994). The reading age of the SEDS items have been calculated to be 9 years and 3 months. However, a recent study investigating the reliability and validity of the measure in a sample of eating disorder (n = 53) and control (n = 61) adolescents (mean age 15.6 years and 15.4 years respectively) found that many participants had difficulty with comprehension of particular items (Campbell, Lawrence, Serpell, Lask, and Neiderman, 2002). Nonetheless, the authors found the measure to have good criterion and discriminant validity, as well as high internal consistency in this age group, and suggested that the SEDS proved to be a good screening instrument for eating disorders in adolescents.

Body Shape Questionnaire

The Body Shape Questionnaire (BSQ: Cooper, Taylor, Cooper, and Fairburn, 1987) is a 34-item questionnaire with a six-point Likert-style rating scale, and was developed to measure body weight and shape concern in those with eating disorders or other body image related problems. The measure takes appproximately ten minutes to complete and may be useful for screening those at risk of developing eating disorders. However, as body weight and shape concern are only one of the criterion items in the diagnosis of eating disorders, this measure may be better suited for assessment of body weight and shape concern in community samples, or to assess any changes in body image disturbance of eating disordered patients in treatment over time. The BSQ has proved to be a significantly reliable measure overall, $P < 0.001$, with significantly high reliability for each of the 34 items, $P < 0.01$, for test–retest reliability (Rosen, Jones, Ramirez, and Waxman, 1996).

The BSQ correlates with other body image measures, such as the Body Dysmorphic Disorder Examination (BDDE: Rosen, Reiter, and Orosan, 1995) and has good concurrent validity, for both clinical and non-clinical samples, in that negative body image attitudes reported on the BSQ are correlated with other negative body image symptoms, such as concerns about appearance features that are non-weight related.

The BSQ has been widely used to examine body weight and shape dissatisfaction in adolescents from 12 years old upwards, usually in large school samples (e.g. Le Grange, Tibbs, and Selibowitz, 1995; Mumford, Whitehouse, and Choudry, 1992). It has also been used to examine sociocultural differences in body weight and shape dissatisfaction in adolescents (e.g. Mumford, Whitehouse, and Platts, 1991). In addition, the BSQ has been used with children as young as 7 years old without any reported difficulties (Evans and Le Grange, 1995).

Body Satisfaction Scale

The Body Satisfaction Scale (BSS: Slade, Dewey, Newton, Brodie, and Kiemle, 1990), is a 16-item, self-report questionnaire that measures body dissatis-faction. Each of 16 body parts is rated on a seven-point Likert-type scale, ranging from 'very satisfied' to 'very dissatisfied'. This questionnaire has two subscales, assessing dissatisfaction with the head and dissatisfaction with the body. It is useful in making a quick assessment of body satisfaction and has reasonably high internal consistency (coefficient alpha range = 0.79–0.89). The measure is well validated against other body satisfaction scales and is highly correlated with the BSQ. The BSS only takes about five minutes to complete and five minutes to score, but does not measure the nature of the dissatisfaction.

Cok (1990) used the BSS in a large sample of children and adolescents aged 11–18 years old, with no reported difficulties in the administration of this measure with the younger participants in the study. Similarly, Brodie, Bagley, and Slade (1994) did not report any difficulties with administering this measure to children in their study comparing pre- and post-adolescent girls.

Measures for children and young adolescents

Few self-report questionnaires have been adapted for use with children aged 12 and under – the Children's Eating Attitudes Test (ChEAT: Maloney et al., 1988), and the Kids' Eating Disorder Survey (KEDS: Childress, Jarrell, and Brewerton, 1992). Both the ChEAT and the KEDS were designed as screening tools for the general population and therefore have limited utility in a clinical setting. In addition, a child version of the EDI has been developed. However, psychometric data pertaining to this measure appears to differ somewhat between European and North American samples.

Children's Eating Attitudes Test

The Children's Eating Attitudes Test (ChEAT: Maloney et al., 1988) is a modified version of the Eating Attitudes Test (EAT: Garner et al., 1982; see earlier). It asks about perceived body image, obsessions/preoccupation with food and dieting practices. There are 26 questions and the rating of each question is via a six-point Likert-type scale. The wording of items on the EAT was modified in order to make the questions more comprehensible to children as young as 8 years old. The norms for this questionnaire were gathered from a sample of 318 children aged 8–13 years (mean age 9.7yrs), 92 per cent of whom were white, and all of whom came from middle to upper socioeconomic backgrounds. Instructions on how to complete the questionnaire are delivered orally to the child. In the case of children at the younger end of the spectrum, each item is also read to them. The measure is easy to administer and takes approximately 30 minutes to complete, including time taken to read the instructions to the child.

The questionnaire is especially easy to administer to children who have reached the reading level required to complete the questionnaire without help from the administrator, and thus can be administered to a large group. However, if administering orally to a younger child, this negates the benefits of it being a questionnaire measure, as staff resources are needed to read the questions to the child. Another problem with it is that it does not assess eating disorders per se, but rather attitudes toward eating and dietary behaviour. The ChEAT is not therefore diagnostic, but can be useful as a screening tool to assess children potentially at risk of developing an eating disorder. Both internal consistency and test–retest reliability are reasonably high, coefficient alpha of 0.76 and 0.81 respectively (Maloney et al., 1988). Smolak and Levine (1994) also found the ChEAT to have high internal consistency, coefficient alpha = 0.87. Concurrent validity test showed the ChEAT to be significantly correlated with weight management behaviour, $r = 0.36$, $P < 0.001$, and with body dissatisfaction, $r = 0.39$, $P < 0.001$ (Smolak and Levine, 1994).

Kids' Eating Disorders Survey

The Kids' Eating Disorders Survey (KEDS: Childress, Brewerton, Hodges, and Jarrell, 1993) was developed from the Eating Symptoms Inventory (ESI: Whittaker et al., 1989), which is based on *DSM-III* criteria, and was used in a high school survey of eating disorders in adolescents. Childress et al. (1993) developed the KEDS to address the marked differences in cognitive development between children and adolescents, by producing a simpler and shorter questionnaire, in which 'yes', 'no', and 'don't know' responses are all that are required. There are 14 items on the questionnaire, which include a set of eight drawings of boys and eight drawings of girls (body image silhouettes), which range from very underweight to very overweight. The child is asked to circle the drawing that looks most like them, in order to assess weight and body dissatisfaction. The measure was designed to be used within the general population as a screening device. The KEDS has been found to have highly significant test–retest reliability (0.83, $P < 0.01$) when readministered to 230 children within four months of the original survey (Childress et al., 1993). A study investigating the psychometric properties of the body image silhouettes section of this measure found that test–retest reliabilities were adequate to good (Candy and Fee, 1998). However, the results of extensive external validity studies are not yet available.

Eating Disorder Inventory for Children (EDI-C: Garner, 1991, 2004; Garner et al., 1983)

A preliminary version of an adaptation of the EDI for use with children has been developed in consultation with Garner, one of the original authors of the EDI (Franko et al., 2004). Sixteen items remain identical to the original 64-item, self-report EDI, whilst 29 items have been slightly reworded and 19 items have been changed significantly. A study to investigate the factor structure of this measure using non-clinical samples of 1073 white and 1155 black girls, aged 11–12 years, found that only three factors (bulimia, interpersonal distrust and maturity fears) corresponded to the original EDI subscales for both black and white girls (Franko et al., 2004). This suggests that an alternative factor structure for adolescents of this age may exist, or that clinical and non-clinical samples may differ. In this study, overall, the EDI-C showed significant overlap on five of the eight factors for the two different ethnic groups.

In addition, an adaptation of the EDI-2 for use with children is used widely in Europe. This version retains around two-thirds of the original EDI-2 questions, with the remaining questions using modified wording to better suit younger respondents (Eklund, Paavonen, and Almqvist, 2005). A recent Swedish study of 201 adolescent girls aged 13–17 years with a *DSM-IV* diagnosis of eating disorder and 2073 female non-eating disordered controls (mean age = 15.7, SD = 1.6) measures internal consistency, factor structure and ability to discriminate between eating disorder and non-eating disorder cases (Thurfjell, Edlund, Arinell, Hägglöf, and Engstrom, 2003). The authors found that the measure had good internal consistency in both the ED group (Cronbach's alphas for the subscales ranged from 0.70 to 0.91) and the control group (Cronbach's alphas for the subscales ranged from 0.52 to 0.92), with alpha coefficients for the total EDI-C score being 0.94 for the eating disorder group and 0.93 for the control group. This study also found that following factor analysis all EDI-2 subscales could be identified, indicating that the 11 EDI-2 constructs contribute to the EDI-C, although the authors suggest that the homogeneity and demarcation of these constructs in an adolescent population is not as clear as it is in the adult population.

In terms of discriminant validity, this measure performed well, correctly classifying 85.6 per cent of the subjects (86.9 per cent of the control group and 72.6 per cent of the eating disorder group), suggesting that the EDI-C may be a good screening measure for adolescents (Thurfjell et al., 2003). However, when this measure was used in a non-clinical sample of 898 children (481 girls and 417 boys) aged 9–16 years, the reliability of the original 11 factors was found to be low (Eklund et al., 2005). In this study, 27 items had such low commonality that they were removed from further analysis. The authors found a five-factor structure (when only the 64 remaining items were entered into the analysis), which had significant qualitative differences to the EDI-2 subscales, but had high reliability. They suggest that a modified structure comprising five subscales could be extracted to provide a meaningful measure for use in children aged 9–16 years (Eklund et al., 2005).

Thurfjell, Edlund, Arinell, Hägglöf, Garner, and Engstrom (2004) investigated the use of the EDI-C in a large mixed gender, non-clinical sample and concluded that the EDI-C could be a useful measure for both boys as well as girls, although separate norms were recommended for pre-adolescents and adolescents as well as for boys and girls.

Interview measures

There are at least four stand-alone interview measures in existence for the assessment of eating disorders in adults. Three of these are structured interviews – the Clinical Eating Disorder Rating Instrument (CEDRI: Palmer, Christie, Cordle, Davis, and Kendrick, 1987), the Interview for the Diagnosis of Eating Disorders (IDED: Williamson, 1990), and the Structured Interview for Anorexia and Bulimia Nervosa (SIAB: Fichter, Elton, Engel, Meyer, Mall, and Poustka, 1991). The fourth is a semi-structured interview developed by Cooper and Fairburn (1987) – the Eating Disorder Examination (EDE). This interview is the only instrument that has been adapted for use with children (Bryant-Waugh, Cooper, Taylor, and Lask, 1996). Here is a brief overview of the EDE and a detailed description of the child version of the EDE.

Eating Disorder Examination

The Eating Disorder Examination (EDE: Fairburn and Cooper, 1993) is an instrument designed to assess specific eating disorder psychopathology and is currently viewed as the 'gold standard' in eating disorders assessment (Wilson, 1993). It is a semi-structured, investigator-based interview, which means that the interviewer asks key questions but can then ask additional questions in order to clarify the concept that is being investigated. It is very important that all interviewers are trained to administer this instrument, to ensure that the key concepts being assessed by the EDE are clearly understood.

The EDE provides either frequency or severity ratings for key behavioural and attitudinal aspects of eating disorders and comprises four subscales: Restraint, Eating Concern, Shape Concern, and Weight Concern. The instrument also produces operationally defined eating disorder diagnoses for both anorexia nervosa and bulimia nervosa, based on *DSM-IV* criteria. The EDE is a present state interview, which produces information pertaining to the four weeks preceding the interview. However, on some key diagnostic questions the instrument is designed to enable the interviewer to question the subject about the previous three months, thus allowing sufficient information to be gathered to satisfy *DSM-IV* criteria for certain aspects of eating disorder diagnoses. The EDE has been used both as an assessment/diagnostic tool and as a means of monitoring progress within therapy (Beumont, Kopec-Schrader, Talbot, and Touyz, 1993). There are adult female norms available for both of these disorders as well as for other groups, namely restrained eaters, overweight individuals, dieters and normal controls.

The EDE has good reliability data, with coefficient alpha of the subscales ranging from 0.67 to 0.90 for internal consistency of the measure (Cooper,

Cooper, and Fairburn, 1989). These reliability data were gathered using a previous version of the EDE, when it included a bulimia subscale, which was subsequently dropped for the twelfth edition of the interview. There are no reported test–retest reliability studies for the EDE. Cooper et al. (1989) also demonstrated good discriminant validity for this measure, using a sample of 100 eating disordered patients and 42 normal controls. Rosen, Vara, Wendt, and Leitenberg (1990) found that the weight concern and shape concern subscales discriminated between patients with bulimia nervosa and a group of restrained eaters. The EDE has also been adapted for use in questionnaire format (see above). Although Carter et al. (2001) point out that self-report questionnaires such as the EDE-Q are briefer and cheaper to administer, it has been argued that some aspects of the specific psychopathology of eating disorders cannot be specifically assessed through the use of questionnaires (Fairburn and Beglin, 1994). In addition, the utility of questionnaires can be further diminished in children with low reading ability.

Child EDE

The child adaptation of the EDE (ChEDE: Bryant-Waugh et al., 1996) includes four main modifications. First, the language of the measure has been changed slightly to make the interview more comprehensible for children. Second, the introduction to the interview has been altered. The parents are asked to complete a diary, which is given to the child at the beginning of the interview and used as a memory cue.

Finally, two key items, namely importance of weight and importance of shape, are administered as a card sort task on the child adaptation of the instrument. Rather than being asked direct questions about the extent to which weight and shape are important in terms of self-evaluation, children are asked a more general 'What things are important to you in your judgement of yourself?' The child is given examples to help clarify the concept of self-evaluation, such as performance at school, popularity, looks, family harmony, talents, etc. The child is then asked what things are personally important and these are written on separate cards. The child is then asked to arrange them in order of importance (Bryant-Waugh et al., 1996).

Bryant-Waugh et al. (1996) piloted the children's version of the EDE with a group of 16 children aged between 7 and 14 in a child eating disorders clinic. They found that the interview was well-tolerated and on the whole the children co-operated well throughout. Most of the responses to individual items were found to be consistent with clinical observation, thus suggesting the potential validity of this measure. A further study was undertaken by Frampton (1996), who interviewed 30 clinical subjects and 30 normal controls between the ages of 8 and 14 years. He found that children given a clinical diagnosis of anorexia nervosa virtually mirrored the subscale scores of the adult anorexia nervosa standardised sample (Cooper and Fairburn, 1987). He also found that children given a clinical diagnosis of either selective eating (Chapter 4) or Food Avoidance Emotional Disorder (Chapter 4) scored similarly on the EDE subscales to the normal controls. This would suggest that this measure has a degree of discriminant validity, in that it can discriminate between those children with and without a clinical diagnosis of anorexia nervosa. More recently, a preliminary investigation of the psychometric properties of the ChEDE in a sample of 8–14 year olds found that alpha coefficients for each of the subscales indicated a high degree of internal consistency. In addition, interrater reliability was found to be high (r = 0.91 to r = 1.00) (Watkins, Frampton, Lask, and Bryant-Waugh, 2005). The child adaptation of the EDE has been translated into Dutch, German, Italian and Norwegian, with other translations in progress.

References

American Psychiatric Association (APA, 1987). *Diagnostic and statistical manual of mental disorders* (3rd ed., Rev.). Washington, DC: APA.

American Psychiatric Association (APA, 1994). *Diagnostic and statistical manual of mental disorders* (4th ed.). Washington, DC: APA.

Beumont, P., Kopec-Schrader, E., Talbot, P., and Touyz, S. (1993). Measuring the specific psychopathology of eating disorder patients. *Australian and New Zealand Journal of Psychiatry*, *27* (3), 506–511.

Black, C., and Wilson, G. (1996). Assessment of eating disorders: Interview versus questionnaire. *International Journal of Eating Disorders*, *20*, 43–50.

Brodie, D., Bagley, K., and Slade, P. (1994). Body image perception in pre- and post-adolescent females. *Perceptual and Motor Skills*, *78* (1), 147–154.

Bryant-Waugh, R., Cooper, P., Taylor, C., and Lask, B. (1996). The use of the eating disorder examination with children: A pilot study. *International Journal of Eating Disorders*, *19*, 391–398.

Butler, N., Newton, T., and Slade, P. (1988). Validation of a computerized version of the SCANS questionnaire. *International Journal of Eating Disorders*, *8*, 239–241.

Campbell, M., Lawrence, B., Serpell, L., Lask, B., and Neiderman, M. (2002). Validating the Stirling Eating Disorders Scales (SEDS) in an adolescent population. *Eating Behaviors*, *3*, 285–293.

Candy, C., and Fee, V. (1998). Reliability and concurrent validity of the Kids' Eating Disorders Survey (KEDS) body image silhouettes with preadolescent girls. *Eating Disorders: The Journal of Treatment and Prevention*, *6* (4), 297–308.

Carter, P., and Moss, R. (1984). Screening for anorexia and bulimia nervosa in a college population: Problems and limitations. *Addictive Behaviors*, *9*, 417–419.

Carter, J. C., Stewart, D. A., and Fairburn C. G. (2001). Eating disorder examination questionnaire: Norms for young adolescent girls. *Behaviour Research and Therapy*, *39*, 625–632.

Childress, A., Brewerton, T., Hodges, E., and Jarrell, M. (1993). The kids' eating disorders survey (KEDS): A study of middle school students. *Journal of the American Academy of Child and Adolescent Psychiatry*, *32*, 843–850.

Childress, A., Jarrell, M., and Brewerton, T. (1992). *The kids' eating disorders survey (KEDS): Internal consistency, component analysis, and test–retest reliability*. Paper presented at the 5th International Conference on Eating Disorders, New York.

Cok, F. (1990). Body image dissatisfaction in Turkish adolescents. *Adolescence, 25,* 409–413.

Cooper, P., Taylor, M., Cooper, Z., and Fairburn, C. (1987). The development and validation of the body shape questionnaire. *International Journal of Eating Disorders, 6,* 485–494.

Cooper, Z., Cooper, P., and Fairburn, C. (1989). The validity of the eating disorder examination and its subscales. *British Journal of Psychiatry, 154,* 807–812.

Cooper, Z., and Fairburn, C. (1987). The eating disorder examination: A semi-structured interview for the assessment of the specific psychopathology of eating disorders. *International Journal of Eating Disorders, 6,* 1–8.

Eklund, K., Paavonen, E.J., and Almqvist, F. (2005). Factor structure of the Eating Disorder Inventory-C. *International Journal of Eating Disorders, 37* (4), 330–341.

Evans, J., and Le Grange, D. (1995). Body size and parenting in eating disorders: A comparative study of the attitudes of mothers toward their children. *International Journal of Eating Disorders, 18* (1), 39–48.

Fairburn, C., and Beglin, S. (1994). Assessment of eating disorders: Interview or self-report questionnaire? *International Journal of Eating Disorders, 16* (4), 363–370.

Fairburn, C., and Cooper, Z. (1993). The eating disorder examination (12th ed.). In C.G. Fairburn and G.T. Wilson (Eds.), *Binge eating: Nature, assessment and treatment* (pp. 317–360). New York: Guilford Press.

Felker, K., and Stivers, C. (1994). The relationship of gender and family environment to eating disorder risk in adolescents. *Adolescence, 29,* 821–834.

Fichter, M., Elton, M., Engel, K., Meyer, A., Mall, H., and Poustka, F. (1991). Structured interview for anorexia and bulimia nervosa (SIAB): Development of a new instrument for the assessment of eating disorders. *International Journal of Eating Disorders, 10,* 571–592.

Frampton, I. (1996). *Are overvalued ideas about weight and shape overvalued ideas in the diagnosis of eating disorders? Evidence from early onset anorexia nervosa.* Unpublished research dissertation, University of Exeter.

Franko, D., Striegel-Moore, R., Barton, B., Schumann, B., Garner, D., Daniels, S., et al. (2004). Measuring eating concerns in black and white adolescent girls. *International Journal of Eating Disorders, 35,* 179–189.

Garner, D. (1991). *Eating disorders inventory 2: Professional manual.* Odessa, FL: Psychological Assessment Resources.

Garner, D.M. (2004). EDI-3 *Eating Disorder Inventory 3: Professional manual.* Odessa, FL: Psychological Assessment Resources.

Garner, D., and Garfinkel, P. (1979). The eating attitudes test: An index of the symptoms of anorexia nervosa. *Psychological Medicine, 9,* 273–279.

Garner, D., Olmsted, M., Bohr, Y., and Garfinkel, P. (1982). The eating attitudes test: Psychometric features and clinical correlates. *Psychological Medicine, 12,* 871–878.

Garner, D., Olmsted, M., and Polivy, J. (1983). Development and validation of a multi-dimensional eating disorder inventory for anorexia nervosa and bulimia. *International Journal of Eating Disorders, 2,* 15–34.

Henderson, M., and Freeman, C. (1987). A self-rating scale for bulimia: The 'BITE'. *British Journal of Psychiatry, 150,* 18–24.

Le Grange, D., Tibbs, J., and Selibowitz, J. (1995). Eating attitudes, body shape, and self-disclosure in a community sample of adolescent girls and boys. *Eating Disorders: The Journal of Treatment and Prevention, 3,* 253–264.

Leung, F., Wang, J., and Tang, C. (2004). Psychometric properties and normative data of the eating disorder inventory among 12 to 18 year old Chinese girls in Hong Kong. *Journal of Psychosomatic Research, 57*, 59–66.

Maloney, M., McGuire, J., and Daniels, S. (1988). Reliability testing of a children's version of the eating attitude test. *Journal of the American Academy of Child and Adolescent Psychiatry, 28*, 541–543.

Mintz, L., and Betz, N. (1988). Prevalence and correlates of eating disordered behaviour among undergraduate women. *Journal of Counselling Psychology, 35*, 463–471.

Mintz, L., O' Halloran, M., Mulholland, A., and Schneider, P. (1997). Questionnaire for eating disorder diagnoses: Reliability and validity of operationalizing DSM-IV criteria into a self-report format. *Journal of Counselling Psychology, 44*, 63–71.

Mumford, D., Whitehouse, A., and Choudry, I. (1992). Survey of eating disorders in English medium schools in Lahore, Pakistan. *International Journal of Eating Disorders, 11*, 173–184.

Mumford, D., Whitehouse, A., and Platts, M. (1991). Sociocultural correlates of eating disorders among Asian schoolgirls in Bradford. *British Journal of Psychiatry, 158*, 222–228.

Norring, C. (1990). The eating disorder inventory: Its relation to diagnostic dimensions and follow-up status. *International Journal of Eating Disorders, 9*, 685–694.

Ousley, L. (1986). *Differences among bulimic subgroups, binge-eaters, and normal dieters in a female college population.* Unpublished doctoral dissertation, University of Florida, Gainsville.

Palmer, R., Christie, M., Cordle, C., Davis, D., and Kendrick, J. (1987). The clinical eating disorder rating instrument (CEDRI): A preliminary description. *International Journal of Eating Disorders, 6*, 9–16.

Prather, R., and Williamson, D. (1988). Psychopathology associated with bulimia, binge eating and obesity. *International Journal of Eating Disorders, 7*, 177–184.

Reich, W., Herjanic, B., Welner, Z., and Gandhy, P.R. (1982). Development of a structured psychiatric interview for children: Agreement on diagnosis comparing child and parent interviews. *Journal of Abnormal Child Psychology, 10*, 325–336.

Rosen, J., Jones, A., Ramirez, E., and Waxman, S. (1996). Body shape questionnaire: Studies of validity and reliability. *International Journal of Eating Disorders, 20*, 315–319.

Rosen, J., Reiter, J., and Orosan, P. (1995). Assessment of body image in eating disorders with the body dysmorphic disorder examination. *Behaviour Research and Therapy, 33*, 77–84.

Rosen, J., Silberg, N., and Gross, J. (1988). Eating attitudes test and eating disorder inventory: Norms for adolescent girls and boys. *Journal of Consulting and Clinical Psychology, 56*, 305–308.

Rosen, J., Vara, L., Wendt, B., and Leitenberg, H. (1990). Validity studies of the eating disorder examination. *International Journal of Eating Disorders, 9*, 519–528.

Shore, R., and Porter, J. (1990). Normative and reliability data for 11–18 year olds in the eating disorder inventory. *International Journal of Eating Disorders, 9*, 201–207.

Slade, P. (1982). Towards a functional analysis of anorexia nervosa and bulimia nervosa. *British Journal of Clinical Psychology, 21*, 67–79.

Slade, P., and Dewey, M. (1986). Development and preliminary validation of SCANS: A screening instrument for identifying individuals at risk of developing anorexia and bulimia nervosa. *International Journal of Eating Disorders, 5*, 517–538.

Slade, P., Dewey, M., Newton, T., Brodie, D., and Kiemle, G. (1990). Development and preliminary validation of the body satisfaction scale (BSS). *Psychology and Health, 4,* 213–220.

Smith, M., and Thelen, M. (1984). Development and validation for a test for bulimia. *Journal of Consulting and Clinical Psychology, 52,* 863–872.

Smolak, L., and Levine, M. (1994). Psychometric properties of the children's eating attitudes test. *International Journal of Eating Disorders, 16,* 275–282.

Thurfjell, B., Edlund, B., Arinell, H., Hägglöf, B., Garner, D., and Engstrom, I. (2004). Eating Disorder Inventory for Children (EDI-C): Effects of age and gender in a Swedish sample. *European Eating Disorders Review, 12,* 256–264.

Thurfjell, B., Edlund, B., Arinell, H., Hägglöf, B., and Engstrom, I. (2003). Psychometric properties of Eating Disorder Inventory for Children (EDI-C) in Swedish girls with and without a known eating disorder. *Eating and Weight Disorders, 8,* 296–303.

Watkins, B., Frampton, I., Bryant-Waugh, R., and Lask, B. (2005). Reliability and validity of the child version of the eating disorder examination: A preliminary investigation, *International Journal of Eating Disorders, 38* (2), 183–187.

Whittaker, A., Davies, M., Shaffer, D., Johnson, J., Abrams, S., Walsh, B., et al. (1989). The struggle to be thin: A survey of anorexic and bulimic symptoms in a non-referred adolescent population. *Psychological Medicine, 19,* 143–163.

Williams, G., Power, K., Miller, H., Freeman, C., Yellowlees, A., Dowds, T., et al. (1994). Development and validation of the Stirling Eating Disorder Scales. *International Journal of Eating Disorders, 16,* 35–43.

Williamson, D. (1990). *Assessment of eating disorders: Obesity, anorexia and bulimia nervosa.* Elmsford, NY: Pergamon.

Williamson, D., Cubic, B., and Gleaves, D. (1993). Equivalent body image disturbances in anorexia and bulimia nervosa. *Journal of Abnormal Psychology, 102,* 1–4.

Williamson, D., Prather, R., Bennett, S., Davis, C., Watkins, P., and Grenier, C. (1989). An uncontrolled evaluation of inpatient and outpatient cognitive behaviour therapy for bulimia nervosa. *Behaviour Modification, 13,* 340–360.

Wilson, G. (1993). Assessment of binge eating. In C.G. Fairburn and G.T. Wilson (Eds.), *Binge eating: Nature, assessment and treatment* (pp. 227–249). New York: Guilford Press.

Author index

Subject index

Note: Page numbers in **bold** refer to figures and tables.